ENVIRONMENT, ETHICS, AND BEHAVIOR

The Psychology of Environmental Valuation and Degradation

Max H. Bazerman

David M. Messick

Ann E. Tenbrunsel

Kimberly A. Wade-Benzoni

Editors

The New Lexington Press
San Francisco

The New Lexington Press is an imprint of Jossey-Bass Inc., Publishers.

For sales outside the United States, please contact your local Simon & Schuster International Office.

TCF Manufactured in the United States of America on Lyons Falls Turin Book. This paper is acid-free and 100 percent totally chlorine-free.

Library of Congress Cataloging-in-Publication Data

Environment, ehtics, and behavior: the psychology of environmental valuation and degradation / Max H. Bazerman . . . [et al.].
p. cm. — (The New Lexington Press management series) (The New Lexington Press social and behavioral science series)
Includes bibliographical references and indexes.
ISBN 0-7879-0809-6 (hc : alk: paper).—ISBN 0-7879-0818-5 (pb : alk. paper)
1. Environmental management—Evaluation—Psychology. 2. Environmental degradation—Psychology. 3. Environmental ethics. I. Bazerman, Max H. II. Series. III. Series: The New Lexington Press social and behavioral science series.
GE300E56 1997
363.7—dc21 96-50093

FIRST EDITION

HB Printing 10 9 8 7 6 5 4 3 2 1

PB Printing 10 9 8 7 6 5 4 3 2 1

A JOINT PUBLICATION IN

The New Lexington Press Management Series

and

The New Lexington Press Social and Behavioral Science Series

CONTENTS

PART THREE
Mental Models of the Environment

PART FOUR
Assessment of Risk and the Environment

PREFACE

BETWEEN 1992 AND 1995, the four coeditors were all members of the Organization Behavior Department of the Kellogg Graduate School of Management of Northwestern University. The background support and inspiration for this project developed out of the supportive environment of the Kellogg School. Specifically, Dean Donald Jacobs and the Kellogg School provided the infrastructure for the creation of the Center for the Study of Ethical Issues in Business and the Kellogg Environmental Research Center. These two centers were the cosponsors of this project.

Specific funding for the conference on which this volume is based was provided by National Science Foundation Grant #SBR9511957, "Psychological Perspectives to Environmental and Ethical Issues in Management." The management of the conference, the administration of this volume, and the editing of the work that follows was provided by Claire Buisseret. Claire is an excellent project manager and editor, and the quality of the materials that follow have been enhanced by her contributions.

Evanston, Illinois
February 1997

MAX H. BAZERMAN
DAVID M. MESSICK
ANN E. TENBRUNSEL
KIMBERLY A. WADE-BENZONI

THE AUTHORS

HAL R. ARKES is a professor in the Department of Psychology at Ohio University. He received his bachelor's degree from Carleton College and his doctorate from the University of Michigan. His primary research interests are in the areas of medical and economic decision making. He has served as the 1993–1995 codirector of the Program in Decision, Risk, and Management Science at the National Science Foundation and the 1996–1997 president of the Judgment/Decision Making Society.

SCOTT ATRAN is chargé de recherche at Centre National de la Recherche Scientifique, CREA-École Polytechnique, in Paris, research scientist at the Institute for Social Research, and adjunct professor of psychology and anthropology at the University of Michigan, Ann Arbor. He holds a Ph.D. degree in anthropology from Columbia University. He has been assistant to Margaret Mead, curator of ethnology, American Museum of Natural History, coordinator of the Animal and Human Communication Program (Royaumont Center for a Science of Man, Paris), and organizer of the Chomsky-Piaget conference Language and Learning. Since 1981, he has held numerous research and teaching positions in France, Israel, and the United States. His research focus is on the cognitive foundations of biological classification, learning, and reasoning. He has published broadly on these topics, including the book *Cognitive Foundations of Natural History: Toward an Anthropology of Science* (1990). He is currently involved in joint research with Douglas L. Medin on ethnoecological knowledge and reasoning among Maya and Mestizo populations.

MAX H. BAZERMAN is the J. Jay Gerber Distinguished Professor of Dispute Resolution and Organizations at the Kellogg Graduate School of Management at Northwestern University. He is the author or coauthor of over one hundred research articles and the author of *Judgment in Managerial Decision Making* (3rd ed., 1994), the coauthor of *Cognition and Rationality in Negotiation* (1991, with M. A. Neale) and *Negotiating Rationally* (1992, with M. A. Neale), and the coeditor of four books on negotiation published with JAI Press and Sage. He is a member of the editorial boards of the *Journal of Behavioral Decision Making, Group Decisions and Negotiations, International Journal of Conflict Management, American Behavioral Scientist,* and the *Administrative Science Quarterly,* and is a member of the international advisory board of the *Negotiation Journal.*

ALICE H. EAGLY is a professor of psychology at Northwestern University. She received her bachelor's degree from Radcliffe College of Harvard University and her master's and doctoral degrees from the University of Michigan. She served on the faculties of Michigan State University, the University of Massachusetts-Amherst, and Purdue University before joining the faculty at Northwestern. Her research interests in the attitudes area concern attitude structure, persuasion, and the effect of attitudes on information processing. She also investigates a variety of gender issues including gender stereotyping and sex-related differences in social behavior and gender stereotyping. She is the author of *Sex Differences in Social Behavior: A Social Role Analysis* and *The Psychology of Attitudes* (1987, with Shelly Chaiken). She has also written numerous journal articles and chapters in edited books.

BARUCH FISCHHOFF is a professor of social and decision sciences and of engineering and public policy at Carnegie-Mellon University. He holds a bachelor's degree in mathematics from Wayne State University and master's and doctoral degrees in psychology from the Hebrew University of Jerusalem. He is a member of the Institute of Medicine of the National Academy of Sciences. He has served on the National Research Council Committees on Criteria for Allocating Federal R&D, Human Dimensions of Global Change, Risk Perception and Communication, and Environmental Justice. His current research includes risk communication, risk management, adolescent decision making, evaluation of environmental damages, and protective behavior.

SHANE FREDERICK is a doctoral student in the Department of Social and Decision Sciences at Carnegie-Mellon University. He completed an undergraduate degree in zoology at the University of Wisconsin-Madison and a master's degree in resource management at Simon Fraser University. His research interests include judgmental processes and biases in magnitude estimation, as related to contingent valuation, and psychological adaptation—particularly the acquisition, dissolution, and relative salience of different reference points.

DEDRE GENTNER is a professor of psychology and education at Northwestern University. Her research centers on processes of analogy and similarity in learning and reasoning. She received her bachelor's degree from University of California-Berkeley and her doctorate from UC-San Diego. She is a fellow of the American Psychological Association and the American Psychological Society and a past president of the Cognitive Science Society.

THOMAS N. GLADWIN is a professor of management and international business in the Stern School of Business of New York University, where he also directs the school's Global Environment Program. He has received numerous awards for research on environmental management and has authored over one hundred articles and eight books on the topic, including *Business, Nature and Society: Towards Sustainable Enterprise* (forthcoming). He received his bachelor's degree in business administration from the University of Delaware, and his master of business administration and doctoral degrees in business and natural resource policy from the University of Michigan.

RICHARD GONZALEZ is an associate professor of psychology at the University of Washington. He received his bachelor's degree in psychology from the University of California-Los Angeles and his doctorate in psychology from Stanford University. His research interests include decision making, statistics, and mathematical modeling.

LAURA HUTZEL is a graduate student in the Experimental Psychology Program at Ohio University. Her research interests are in the areas of judgment and decision making. She received her bachelor of philosophy degree in interdisciplinary studies with a minor in women's studies from Miami University.

DANIEL KAHNEMAN is the Eugene Higgins Professor of Psychology and professor of public affairs at Princeton University. He taught at Hebrew University, the University of British Columbia, and the University of California-Berkeley before moving to Princeton in 1993. His awards include the Distinguished Scientific Contribution Award from the American Psychological Association, the Distinguished Scientific Contribution Award from the Society for Consumer Psychology, and the Hilgard Prize for Career Contribution to General Psychology. His memberships include the Society for Experimental Psychology, the American Academy of Arts and Sciences, and the Econometric Society.

JACK L. KNETSCH is a professor of economics and of resource and environmental management at Simon Fraser University. He holds a doctorate in economics from Harvard University and received earlier degrees in soil science, agricultural economics, and public administration. His research has focused mainly on resource and environmental issues including property and legal institutions, policy design, and assessments of environmental values. This has increasingly included behavioral economics research. He has worked in government agencies in the United States and Malaysia, participated in various training, research, and advisory projects in a dozen countries, and has accepted visiting appointments at universities in Europe, Asia, Australia, and North America.

PATRICK KULESA is a graduate student in social psychology at Northwestern University. He received his bachelor's degree from Mount St. Mary's College in Emmitsburg, Maryland, and his master's degree from Purdue University. His research interests concern persuasion, attitudinal ambivalence, the impact of attitudes on information processing, and the link between attitudes, values, and political ideologies. He is also interested in the application of psychological theory and research methods to contemporary social issues, including the environment, welfare policy, and political participation.

GEORGE LOEWENSTEIN is a professor of economics in the Department of Social and Decision Sciences at Carnegie-Mellon University. He received his doctorate from Yale University and has taught or conducted research at the Institute for Advanced Study in Princeton, the University of Chicago, the Russell Sage Foundation, Carnegie-Mellon University, and the Institute for Advanced Study in Berlin. His research focuses on applications of psychology to economics, and his specific interests include decision making over time, bargaining and negotiations, law and economics, the psychology of adaptation, the psychology of curiosity, and "out-of-control" behaviors such as impulsive violent crime and drug addiction.

DOUGLAS L. MEDIN is a professor of psychology at Northwestern University. He is both chair of the psychology department and director of the Cognitive Science Program. He came to Northwestern University in 1992 after having been a faculty member at Rockefeller University, the University of Illinois, and the University of Michigan. He currently edits the Psychology of Learning and Motivation series published by Academic Press.

DAVID M. MESSICK is the Morris and Alice Kaplan Professor of Ethics and Decision in Management in the Kellogg Graduate School of Management of Northwestern University. He received his bachelor's degree in psychology from the University of Delaware and his master's and doctoral degrees in psychology from the University of North Carolina-Chapel Hill. He served on the faculty of the University of California-Santa Barbara (UCSB) for more than twenty-five years before joining the Northwestern faculty in 1992. At UCSB, he served as chair of the Department of Psychology (1982–1985) and was elected chair of the Academic Senate (1981–1982). His current research and teaching involves the application of psychological theory and methods to the study of ethical aspects of business decision making.

WILLIAM E. NEWBURRY is a doctoral candidate at New York University (NYU), where he is majoring in International Business and Management. He is also currently an associate researcher with the Global Environment Program. Prior to attending NYU, he worked for six years as a contracts administrator at McDonnell Douglas Corporation in St. Louis. He received his bachelor's degree in business administration from Northeast Missouri State University and his master's degree in international affairs from Washington University. He also attended the University of Tasmania, Australia, in 1988 as a Rotary Scholar.

EDWARD D. REISKIN is an associate researcher with the Global Environment Program, where he is working on the development of a sustainability impact assessment system. Prior to joining the program, he worked for seven years as an engineer and field manager for United Technologies Corporation in Connecticut and New York. He received his bachelor's degree in mechanical engineering from the Massachusetts Institute of Technology and his master of business administration degree, concentrating on management, economics, and international business, from New York University's Stern School of Business.

ILANA RITOV received her doctorate from the Hebrew University. She spent two years doing postdoctoral work at the University of Pennsylvania before returning to Israel to take a position at Ben-Gurion University.

PAUL SLOVIC is president of Decision Research and a professor of psychology at the University of Oregon. He studies human judgment, decision making, and risk analysis. He and his colleagues worldwide have developed methods to describe risk perceptions and measure their effects on individuals, industry, and society. They created a taxonomic system that enables people to understand and predict perceived risk, attitudes toward regulation, and the effects of accidents or failures. Slovic publishes extensively and serves as a consultant to many companies and government agencies. He is past president of the Society for Risk Analysis and in 1991 received its Distinguished Contribution Award. He also serves on the board of directors for the National Council on Radiation Protection and Measurements. In 1993, he received the Distinguished Scientific Contribution Award from the American Psychological Association, and in 1995, he received the Outstanding Contribution to Science Award from the Oregon Academy of Science.

ANN E. TENBRUNSEL is an assistant professor in the College of Business Administration at the University of Notre Dame. She received her bachelor of science degree in industrial and operations engineering from the University of Michigan and her master of business administration (MBA) and doctoral degrees from Northwestern University. She teaches management and negotiation courses at the undergraduate and MBA level and was the recipient of a teaching award for MBA negotiations at Northwestern University. Her research interests focus on decision making and negotiations, with a specific emphasis on ethics. Tenbrunsel has published in these areas in several refereed journals and is the coeditor of two books published in 1996.

LEIGH L. THOMPSON is the J. L. and Helen Kellogg Distinguished Professor of Organization Behavior at the Kellogg Graduate School of Management at Northwestern University. Her current research funded by the National Science Foundation examines social judgment processes in negotiation, social relationships in group decision making, and expertise. She received her doctorate from Northwestern. In 1991, she received a multiyear Presidential Young Investigator award from the National Science Foundation for her research on negotiation and group decision making. In 1995, she was a fellow at the Center for Advanced Study in the Behavioral Sciences. She has published her research in *Psychological Bulletin, Journal of Personality and Social Psychology,* and *Organizational Behavior and Human Decision Processes.* She is a member of the editorial boards of *Organizational Behavior and Human Decision Processes* and *Journal of Experimental Social Psychology.*

KIMBERLY A. WADE-BENZONI is a visiting assistant professor of organization behavior at the Kellogg Graduate School of Management at Northwestern University. She received a bachelor's in electrical engineering from Cornell University and master's and doctoral degrees in organization behavior from Northwestern University. Her current research interests in the general area of conflict management and decision making include intergenerational resource allocations, egocentric interpretations of fairness, self-enhancement biases, dysfunctional aspects of standards, and relationships. She has coauthored several book chapters, articles, and research papers.

ELKE U. WEBER received her doctorate from Harvard University. Her work is at the intersection of psychology and economics and examines the influence of individual and cross-cultural differences in information processing on utility assessment and risky decision making. She has been a professor in both psychology departments (University of Illinois at Urbana-Champaign, 1985–1988, and Ohio State University at present) and business schools (University of Chicago, 1988–1995; Otto Beisheim School of Corporate Management, Koblenz, Germany, 1995) and spent a year at the Center for Advanced Studies in the Behavioral Sciences at Stanford University. She currently serves on the editorial boards of four major journals and on a National Science Foundation grant review panel and has consulting experience with government agencies and private business. In 1988, she was awarded a Young Psychologist Award by the American Psychological Association, and in 1994, the Outstanding Young Investigator Award by the Society for Medical Decision Making.

ERIC W. WHITLEY is a student of cognitive science at Northwestern University and a partner in the Kiwi InterNet Group, which specializes in the design of network software and productivity tools.

ENVIRONMENT, ETHICS, AND BEHAVIOR

1

INTRODUCTION

Ann E. Tenbrunsel, Kimberly A. Wade-Benzoni, David M. Messick, and Max H. Bazerman

ENVIRONMENTAL PROBLEMS COME in myriad forms and plague members of all societies. They "have sprung full-blown in the past several decades to challenge, in the most severe cases, the very likelihood of human survival as a species (not to mention [survival of] other species) and, in less dramatic terms, basic levels of human health and well-being" (Orts, 1995, p. 137). Air pollution from population growth and unbridled consumption continues to be a major problem in many cities and countries. Global warming remains a threat and there has been a significant percentage of ozone depletion. Resources are rapidly diminishing and a large number of species face extinction.

These environmental problems are the result of the actions of individuals and organizations. Individual societal members and businesses make decisions that affect the environment, including whether to pollute, consume scarce resources, create and market dysfunctional by-products, and expose workers to hazardous substances. The pattern of past decisions made by individuals and businesses has already devastated many of the earth's systems. The resulting degradation, destruction, and wastefulness demonstrate the need to consider all factors—including social, psychological, economic, historical, and spiritual—that influence our decisions. This volume focuses on the psychological determinants, an aspect that, we argue, has not been given adequate attention in the past.

Overpopulation, pollution, and overconsumption are created by the decisions of the earth's human inhabitants. Changing these decisions is the key to saving the earth for future generations. Yet the vast majority of past research on global change has minimized the role of these decisions. Although the past decade has seen a dramatic growth in publications that focus on environmental issues, this literature has been dominated by the hard sciences and by policy statements and manuscripts aimed at the interested layperson. Most of this research focuses on obtaining more accurate information about the environment with the assumption that this information will be well used by the world's inhabitants. However, this book argues that the decisions of individuals and organizations are affected by more than just information and that psychological mechanisms are one of the neglected determinants. For example, a key discrepancy exists between our decisions (which have been so destructive to the earth) and the findings that people care a great deal about the environment and believe that the earth should not be degraded. Bazerman, Wade-Benzoni, and Benzoni (1996) have argued that an "attitude/behavior gap" exists in regard to environmental issues; most people have pro-environmental attitudes and yet engage in environmentally destructive behaviors. Knowledge about the physical state of the environment will not solve this puzzle. Rather, we need to better understand the psychology behind this inconsistency and to begin the search for pro-environmental reconciliation.

The chapters in this book address psychological factors that influence environmental decisions. These chapters were contributions to the conference Psychological Perspectives to Environmental and Ethical Issues, held at the Kellogg Graduate School of Management at Northwestern University in December 1995. The conference was a joint activity of the two new research centers at Northwestern: the Center for the Study of Ethical Issues in Business and the Kellogg Environmental Research Center. These new centers focus on the development of psychological and behavioral research on ethical and environmental issues relevant to the business world. This conference and book focus on the overlap of interests between these two centers.

The strategy used in creating this book was to invite leading psychologists to develop a chapter on the relevance of their psychological research to a better understanding of environmental and ethical issues. The reason for this strategy was the belief that important information exists in the psychological literature that has not yet informed the environmental domain. To flesh out our understanding of the psychological mechanisms that affect environmental decisions, this book brings together many of the leading social, cognitive, and decision psychologists who are interested in the interaction between psychological theory and contemporary environmental and ethical issues. Although a number of notable psychologists have made important contributions to our understanding of environmental issues, psychologists have not been a well-organized force in the most important ongoing debates on the environment. This book attempts both to consolidate existing knowledge and to stimulate discussion on future research topics. Thus, rather than just review existing psychological work on the environment, the editors encouraged leading psychologists to think to the future to identify research that is relevant to the environment and outlines future environmental research.

Environmental issues are affected by the actions of individuals. Yet we know fairly little about the psychology of individual action in environmental domains. Many argue that we need to change our behaviors in fundamental ways if we are going to save our environment. Changing behavior requires that we have a thorough understanding of the psychology of environmental behaviors. This book seeks to provide some of that understanding. It is organized into four content areas: Part One, "The Psychology and Economics of Environmental Valuation"; Part Two, "Barriers to Environmentally Friendly Behavior"; Part Three, "Mental Models of the Environment"; and Part Four, "Assessment of Risk and the Environment." Following is an overview of the contributions in each of these areas.

The Psychology and Economics of Environmental Valuation

The first section of the book offers chapters by Jack Knetsch, by Ilana Ritov and Daniel Kahneman, and by George Loewenstein and Shane Frederick. These chapters all provide useful insight into the problems of assessing the values that people place on environmental outcomes. All three chapters are supportive of the economic notion that it would be useful to be able to place a concrete value on environmental goods. Such valuation would allow society to better allocate limited resources. However, this group of scholars is also quite skeptical of the ability of humans to make these assessments in valid ways. Collectively, these chapters advance our understanding of the psychological difficulties in determining the economic value of environmental goods and outcomes and thus raise questions about society's ability to efficiently allocate these resources.

Knetsch's chapter carefully examines how society goes about the task of placing monetary values on environmental harms. He notes that standard practice has been to describe scenarios to respondents and to ask how much they would pay to prevent future occurrences ("willingness to pay").

He argues that economists have generally discussed this measure as if it would produce values equal to those of a "compensation-demanded" measure. Empirically, the amount of money demanded for compensation has proven to be far larger than the amount individuals are willing to pay for the same environmental good. Knetsch suggests that society's focus on the willingness-to-pay measure for environmental losses leads to a valuation that is far lower than individuals would demand for the environmental loss. Knetsch concludes by stating that society's lack of attention to the huge difference between these two measures, which economists often assume to be equal, can in turn result in suboptimal and anti-environmental behavior.

Ritov and Kahneman argue that the contingent valuation method for environmental assets and other public goods, which relies on the surveys of stated willingness to pay discussed by Knetsch, offers a reliable measure of attitude toward that environmental asset but does not provide a sound basis for actually valuing environmental assets. Ritov and Kahneman support their argument with evidence from a series of studies that shows inconsistencies in evaluation of alternative public goods but consistency with other measures of attitudes. One interpretation of these findings is that people view payments for the preservation of environmental assets as contributions, which express intensity of attitude, rather than as purchases within a standard economic model.

Loewenstein and Frederick attack the very difficult problem of inaccuracies in the prediction of future preferences (Kahneman and Snell, 1992).Loewenstein and Frederick note that environmental policy decisions require people to assess not only the consequences of future actions but also their preferences for those outcomes. They argue that there is good reason to expect systematic deviations from accuracy in predicted expected utility (PEU), and that if predictions systematically overestimate or underestimate the impact of environmental problems on experience utility, funds for the environment may be misallocated. The empirical study provided in this chapter suggests that people overestimate the effect of an environmental change on their quality of life, and underestimate their ability to adapt to change. Loewenstein and Frederick provide convincing arguments to shift environmental research to focus not only on the effects of environmental changes but also on how people will experience those changes.

Barriers to Environmentally Friendly Behavior

The second section of the book offers chapters by Leigh Thompson and Richard Gonzalez, by Ann Tenbrunsel, Kimberly Wade-Benzoni, David

Messick, and Max Bazerman, by Alice Eagly and Patrick Kulesa, and by Hal Arkes and Laura Hutzel. These chapters all offer insights into the psychological processes that create barriers to environmentally friendly behaviors. Behaviors that are detrimental to the environment are often not the direct result of people's indifference to environmental quality. On the contrary, people often harm the environment *despite* holding attitudes that are environmentally friendly. The chapters in this section probe some of the processes and mechanisms that create and maintain this seeming contradiction.

Thompson and Gonzalez address barriers to resolving environmental disputes. Their chapter builds on a behavioral decision theory perspective on dispute resolution by focusing on the uniqueness of environmental disputes. They provide a useful bridge from the negotiation literature to the area of environmental disputes. More importantly, they point out that although most of the negotiation literature focuses on differences in interests, many environmental disputes are complicated by differences in values. They note a variety of perceptions specific to the environment context, such as the perception of the "sacredness" of issues. Thompson and Gonzalez conclude by highlighting useful prescriptions for the negotiation of environmental disputes, ones that take into account the uniqueness of the environmental domain.

Tenbrunsel, Wade-Benzoni, Messick, and Bazerman note that a common solution to environmentally destructive behavior is to develop an environmental standard to which individuals are required or expected to adhere. Although appropriate in some situations, it is believed that standards can actually promote environmentally destructive behavior. This chapter investigates the various mechanisms by which standards promote undesirable actions. The authors first discuss the preference reversal that exists between assessments of single versus multiple policies, providing evidence that in single-policy but not multiple-policy assessments, meeting the standard takes priority over achieving the goal behind the standard. This chapter also discusses the motivational aspects of standards and regulations. It is argued that a standard may change one's motivation from intrinsically based to extrinsically based, resulting in a "no law against it" mentality. It is also suggested that the implementation of a standard-based system may actually result in the motivation to "beat the system," resulting in noncompliance and thus a very costly and ineffective solution. Finally, they discuss the uncertainty of standards as one factor that contributes to the inefficiencies of standard-based systems. The discussion concludes with an examination of the impact of standards on policy development.

Eagly and Kulesa argue that confronting people with well-reasoned persuasive messages often has little impact on their attitudes, especially if their attitudes are strong. People's attitudes have a tripartite structure that involves affective, cognitive, and behavioral components that are not always in perfect concordance. Thus one may abstractly like environmental quality (affective), believe that recycling improves environmental quality (cognitive), and yet not recycle (behavioral), possibly because of some perceived cost. Measuring attitudes toward specific activities, like recycling, rather than abstract concepts, like environmental quality, leads to greater consistency between attitudes and actions. Furthermore, pre-existing attitude structures are asserted to increase resistance to change through both active mechanisms (such as counterarguing the message) and passive mechanisms (such as ignoring or summarily rejecting the message). Attitude change is also made difficult because attitudes are interconnected: when one attitude is changed, there are psychological reverberations for others.

Arkes and Hutzel focus on the robust finding that people will try to avoid the appearance of wastefulness. For example, people will escalate their commitment to a previous purchase because they believe that so doing lessens the appearance of wastefulness. A second finding is that identifiable beneficiaries of an action are given more emphasis than anonymous beneficiaries. For example, money that will be used to save a few identifiable potential victims is of more value than money that will be used to save a large number of anonymous ones. Both of these findings have implications for motivating recycling behaviors. Through a thorough series of laboratory experiments, Arkes and Hutzel demonstrate that engineering a second use for an item—even a very nominal use—causes people to refrain from discarding an item after the first use. This finding is explained by the concept of wastefulness; individuals feel that forsaking the second use will seem wasteful. In addition, identifying a specific second use is shown to be a more effective means of promoting recycling than providing a generic second use.

Mental Models of the Environment

The third section of the book offers chapters by Scott Atran and Douglas Medin, by Dedre Gentner and Eric Whitley, and by Thomas Gladwin, William Newburry, and Edward Reiskin. All of these chapters focus on the mental models of people and how these models affect the environment. Mental models are cognitive representations of the world that people use to understand, predict, and solve problems. This section offers three different perspectives on how individuals understand the environment. Atran and Medin base their analysis on anthropological fieldwork with indigenous populations. Gentner and Whitley develop a unique experimental methodology that solicits responses of E-mail users to queries about overpopulation. Gladwin, Newburry, and Reiskin offer a conceptual critique of the unsustainability of the typical mental models of the "northern elite." Collectively, these chapters argue that if we are to change the behavior of individuals, we need to better understand the mental models that people have of the environment.

Atran and Medin report work associated with an interdisciplinary project that has as its focus the study of folkbiological knowledge in two distinct cultures. Folkbiology includes both the categorization of plants and animals and reasoning about them. Folkbiology is a core domain of human thought and, although knowledge possessed by members of different cultures may vary, a tendency to construct taxonomies of plants and animals and to use those taxonomies in reasoning may be universal. For technologically oriented Western cultures, it is asserted that folkbiological knowledge may be undergoing devolution, including a loss of ecological understandings. Atran and Medin trace the implications of differences in ecological knowledge (and associated mental models) for reasoning and for environmentally relevant behaviors (preservation or destruction of the rain forest).

Gentner and Whitley argue that faulty mental models are responsible for environmentally destructive behavior and, more specifically, for the overpopulation of the earth. These authors provide a fascinating methodology to tap into people's mental models. They obtain data from sending out electronic mail prompts to elicit mental models about (over)population. They suggest that mental models are characterized by inconsistencies and that these inconsistencies may lead to environmental problems. The chapter concludes with a discussion concerning how to change mental models and belief systems.

Gladwin, Newburry, and Reiskin argue that the steady deterioration of the earth's physical condition and our quality of life is the result of the deficient mental models of the "northern elite." Their chapter identifies four clusters of hypotheses that define the "unsustainable mind": (1) biases stemming from the cognitive limitations of our biologically inherited brain, which is maladapted to the modern challenges of systemic complexity; (2) biases due to overreliance on obsolete assumptions about the way the world works; (3) biases promulgated by a powerful programming of the contemporary mind according to modern myths and ideological doctrines that appear to serve the interests of a powerful elite; and (4) biases arising from the excessive deployment of ego-defense mechanisms that ward off realistic concerns posed by ecological and social deterioration. This fairly pessimistic contribution concludes with a series of prescriptions for changing the unsustainable mind.

Assessment of Risk and the Environment

The final section of the book offers chapters by Paul Slovic, by Elke Weber, and by Baruch Fischhoff. This set of chapters examines the complications inherently involved in dealing with risk. Environmental risks are many and varied. When the natural environment itself is at risk, we in turn are put at risk as its ability to provide its benefits to us is imperiled. Appropriate response to environmental problems is influenced by perceptions of risk associated with environmental changes. The authors discuss the risk assessment process and the difficulties humans face in responding to risk.

Slovic argues that danger is real, but risk is socially constructed. Risk assessment represents a fusion of science and judgment with psychological, social, cultural, and political factors. Thus, Slovic explains, risk assessment is inherently subjective. He reviews how our social and democratic institutions breed distrust in the risk arena. In addition, he contends that defining risk is an exercise in power and that whoever controls the definition of risk controls the rational solution to the problem at hand. His discussion points to the need for introducing more public participation into risk assessment and decision making in order to increase the legitimacy and public acceptance of resulting decisions.

Weber argues that perceptions of environmental changes are a critical factor in human adaptation to those changes. She empirically examines a sample of farmers to assess their expectations about global warming and their current and anticipated behavioral adjustments to this environmental concern. Her data indicate a positive relationship between belief in global warming and farm success. She further suggests that individuals do not automatically employ a full range of adaptive responses, even if they believe in the need for adaptation and change. Instead, individual differences seem to predispose them toward a certain class of responses. Additionally, engagement in one class of adaptation and risk reduction seems to limit awareness of other, potentially complementary, risk-reduction mechanisms. This result exemplifies a shortcoming in the human problem-solving process. People tend to stop the search process once a solution to a problem has been identified and, as a result, may fail to generate alternative or additional solutions. One policy implication is that it may be helpful to provide people with external guidance about the full range of adaptive risk-reduction responses available to them.

Fischhoff stresses the need to evaluate risks relative to one another. Individuals as well as governments are limited in the resources that they have to address risks. To reduce risks intelligently, it is necessary to understand the risks and how they may be ameliorated, but it is also necessary to decide which risks are the ones on which to focus. Having to allocate resources to different categories of risk requires that risks be compared or ranked, a process that evokes many complex and challenging problems. These problems are neither insoluble nor off-limits for psychologists and other behavioral scientists, and Fischhoff sketches out how each of the chapters in this volume could contribute to the understanding, comparison, and reduction of environmental risk.

Although we have categorized these chapters into sections that made sense to us, readers will notice that there are common themes that cross section boundaries. Regardless of their placement in this book, all of the chapters share a common purpose of bringing a psychological perspective to the study of environmental issues. We begin this book with a rather bleak portrayal of current environmental problems, but we believe that the chapters provide new insights that help to brighten the picture by the end of the book.

REFERENCES

Bazerman, M. H., Wade-Benzoni, K. A., and Benzoni, F. "A Behavioral Decision Theory Perspective to Environmental Decision Making." In D. M. Messick and A. Tenbrunsel (eds.), *Ethical Issues in Managerial Decision Making.* New York: Russell Sage Foundation, 1996.

Kahneman, D., and Snell, J. "Predicting a Changing Taste: Do People Know What They Will Like?" *Journal of Behavioral Decision Making,* 1992, *5,* 187—200.

Orts, E. W. "Reflexive Environmental Law." *Northwestern University Law Review,* Summer 1995, *89,* 1–139.

PART ONE

THE PSYCHOLOGY AND ECONOMICS OF ENVIRONMENTAL VALUATION

2

REFERENCE STATES, FAIRNESS, AND CHOICE OF MEASURE TO VALUE ENVIRONMENTAL CHANGES

Jack L. Knetsch

ESTIMATES OF ENVIRONMENTAL damages or costs are commonly used to set standards of care, stipulate compensation for injuries, and weigh the economic justification for a wide range of remedial actions. The intent of such evaluations is to assess losses or gains in terms of changes in the economic well-being or economic welfare of individuals affected by an action or activity—to determine, for example, if the welfare gains to those benefiting from a change outweigh the losses in welfare of those adversely affected.

The economic value of gains and losses in well-being is measured by individuals' willingness to sacrifice, what they are willing to give up to acquire something or willing to give up to keep it. "Benefits are measured by the total number of dollars which prospective gainers would be willing to pay to secure adoption, and losses are measured by the total number of dollars which prospective losers would insist on as the price of agreeing to adoption" (Michaelman, 1967, p. 1214). Because the compensation measure, the minimum sum people are willing to accept (WTA), will normally

This research was supported in part by the Social Sciences and Humanities Research Council of Canada and has benefited from the comments of Wiktor Adamowicz, Thomas Brown, Robin Gregory, James Konow, Seth Roberts, Clifford Russell, and the editors.

be far larger than the maximum sum they are willing to pay (WTP)—on the basis of recent evidence, from two to five or more times larger—the choice of which measure is used in a particular assessment has very significant practical importance. The issue to be addressed here is the criteria for choosing between the WTP and WTA measures in cases of environmental changes.

Current practice routinely assesses environmental losses and reductions in losses as well as environmental gains in terms of the much smaller sums of how much people are willing to pay (WTP) to avoid such impacts. In assessing monetary damages for environmental harms, for example, "virtually all previous [contingent valuation] studies have described scenarios in which respondents are asked to pay to prevent future occurrences of similar accidents" (U.S. NOAA, 1993, p. 4603). Given the large difference between the WTP and WTA measures of a loss, this usual choice of the WTP measure to evaluate losses will almost certainly seriously compromise the intent of such assessments.

The continued use of the WTP measure to assess losses as well as gains is in part due to the inability to elicit meaningful answers to WTA questions in the frequently used contingent valuation method of damage estimation. Typical of such justifications to use WTP rather than the more appropriate WTA in studies using such methods are these: "Many environmentalists have difficulty in envisaging the minimum compensation they would require to compensate them for the loss of a habitat. . . . To avoid these problems welfare change was measured in terms of WTP" (Willis and Garrod, 1993, pp. 6–7). "Respondents will be far less familiar with the notion of receiving compensation for losing something. . . . This is likely to cause far greater uncertainty and variability in answers to WTA questions than occurs with WTP questions. Therefore, the former are to be avoided in favour of the latter" (Turner, Pearce, and Bateman, 1993, p. 123).

This choice of using WTP to value losses and gains in contingent valuation studies, and in nearly all discussions of environmental changes, is commonly justified, or rationalized, by two widely held assumptions: (1) that there is, as economists have long asserted, no practical difference between the WTP and WTA measures, and use of either will result in equivalent assessments; and (2) the appropriate measure to use in particular circumstances is prescribed by existing legal entitlements.

Neither assumption appears to be correct. Instead of indicating equivalence, the empirical evidence shows large disparities between the measures. And rather than serving as a useful guide, appeals to extant rights will often dictate improper choices that will distort deterrence incentives, inadequately compensate injured parties, and lead to inefficient allocations of resources.

Rather than legal rights, the choice of measure that best reflects people's real changes in well-being seems more appropriately based on the reference state from which individuals judge positive changes to be either gains or reductions of losses, and negative changes as either losses or forgone gains. The position of people's reference state, on which these distinctions are based, seems to turn largely on expectations of normalcy and what people regard as fair.

The Measures and Disparities Between Them

The conventional assumption that for most evaluations the WTA and WTP measures lead to equivalent values except for a trivial difference due to income or wealth effects is one of long standing: "We shall normally expect the results to be so close together that it would not matter which we choose" (Henderson, 1941, p. 121). This remains the presumption of choice, as confirmed, for example, in the recent widely discussed review of damage assessment methods: "This is the conservative choice because willingness to accept compensation should exceed willingness to pay, *if only trivially*" (U.S. NOAA, 1993, p. 4603, emphasis added). The equivalence assertion provides a working justification for using the WTP measure to value losses as well as gains, as the choice of the more appropriate measure would presumably result in only a trivial difference in any actual estimate of value.

Although the equivalence assertion continues to be used to justify present valuation practice, it has little empirical support. Instead, the empirical evidence shows that losses matter much more to people, and consequently are far more valuable, than commensurate gains; and reductions in losses are worth far more than forgone gains.

The now widely reported results of survey studies and more persuasive real exchange experiments show large and systematic valuation disparities that are independent of transactions costs, repetition of trade offers,[1] income effects, or wealth constraints (for example, Knetsch and Sinden, 1984; Kahneman, Knetsch, and Thaler, 1990; Boyce and others, 1992). In one example, participants were willing to pay an average of $5.43 to acquire a prospect offering them a 50 percent chance to win $20; but these *same individuals* demanded an average of $10.50 to give up exactly the same entitlement of a 50 percent chance to win $20 (Kachelmeier and Shehata, 1992).

Similar larger valuations of losses relative to gains in people's actual behavior in making ordinary real choices have been documented (Kahneman, Knetsch, and Thaler, 1991). Frey and Pommerehne (1987), for instance, note that collective endowment effects clearly motivate the asymmetric treatment accorded the acquisition and retention of national art treasures. The valuation disparity, and the consequent reluctance to sell at a loss, has also been evident in the greater volume of house sales when prices are rising than when they are falling, and in the similar smaller volume of sales of securities that have declined in price relative to those for which prices have increased (Shefrin and Statman, 1985). Consistent with these findings, the greater sensitivity of investors to losses than to gains has been found to be associated with the historical premium they give up to invest in bonds rather than more volatile equities (Benarzi and Thaler, 1995). The strong reluctance to give up a default automobile insurance option when an otherwise more attractive choice is readily available (Johnson, Hershey, Meszaros, and Kunreuther, 1993), the typically greater demands for regulation of new environmental and other risks than of equivalent old risks (Sunstein, 1993), and the greater legal protection accorded losses over forgone gains in judicial choices (Cohen and Knetsch, 1992) are further examples of the difference in valuations of gains and losses.

The evidence strongly suggests that over a wide range of circumstances people weigh changes in entitlement levels in terms of an initial reference point and a kinked value function that is much steeper in the domain of losses than in the domain of gains, as illustrated in Figure 2.1.
A good commonly has one value to a person in terms of how much this individual is willing to sacrifice in order to obtain it; the identical entitlement has a different value in terms of how much this same person would sacrifice not to accept its loss. In instances where the same individual is observed to be willing to pay a relatively low price for an entitlement and then almost immediately demands a high price to give it up—or to display the same behavior in reverse order—(Kachelmeier and Shehata, 1992; Borges, 1995), it is very unlikely that the individual is not aware of the real worth of the entitlement. It is instead simply that the entitlement is worth one value when acquiring it and a greater value when giving it up. Consequently, a given change will have a greater or lesser impact on the welfare of an individual depending on whether it is viewed by the individual as being in the losses or in the gains: an increase in quality will be worth more if seen to reduce a loss than to provide a gain, a decrease more if perceived to impose a loss than to forgo a benefit.

Figure 2.1. Value Function Distinguishing Loss from Forgone Gain, and Reduction of Loss from Gain, in Terms of Reference Position on Quantity Axis.

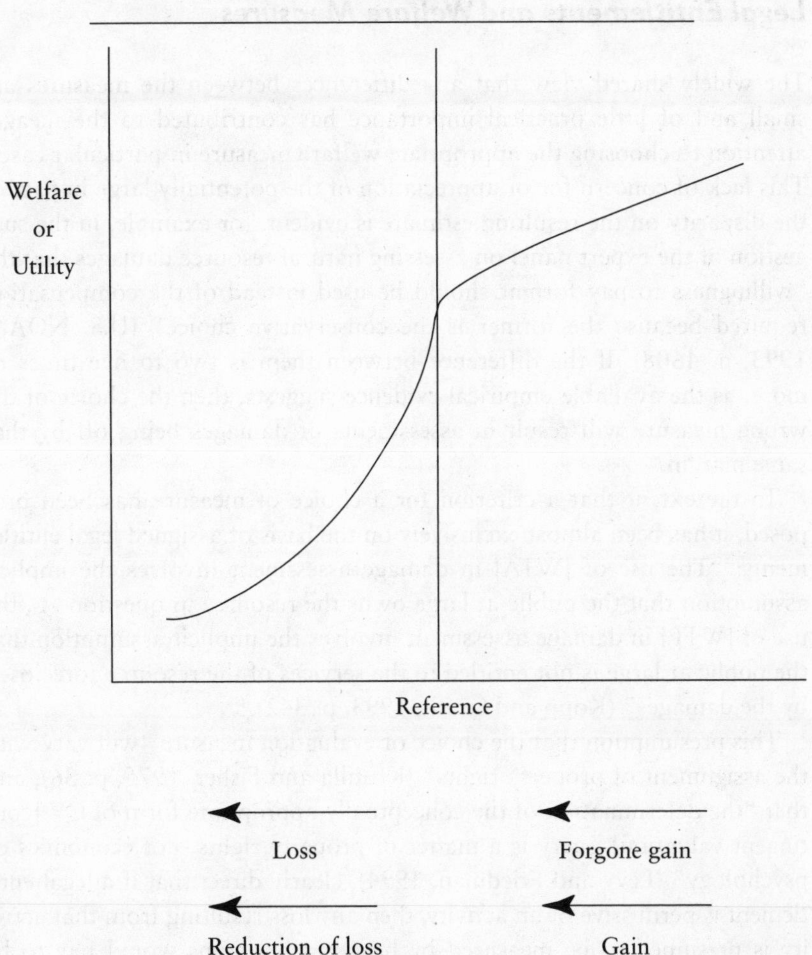

As Sunstein aptly suggests, "If all this is correct, large consequences follow" (1993, p. 230).[2] One implication of the disparity of particular interest in deriving welfare assessment criteria is that indifference curves will not be independent of the initial reference point and direction of exchange offers (Knetsch, 1989, 1992). People will commonly demand more of a good A to give up another good B than they are willing to pay of A to obtain B. This produces a discontinuity, or kink, in the indifference curve at the reference position, and (as detailed below) differing slopes over the same range of quality depending on how the change is perceived by the individual with respect to the reference level.

Legal Entitlements and Welfare Measures

The widely shared view that any differences between the measures are small and of little practical importance has contributed to the meager attention to choosing the appropriate welfare measure in particular cases. This lack of concern for or appreciation of the potentially large impact of the disparity on the resulting estimate is evident, for example, in the suggestion of the expert panel on assessing natural resource damages that the "willingness to pay format should be used instead of the compensation required because the former is the conservative choice" (U.S. NOAA, 1993, p. 4608). If the difference between them is two to five times or more, as the available empirical evidence suggests, then the choice of the wrong measure will result in assessments of damages being off by that same margin.

To the extent that a criterion for a choice of measure has been proposed, it has been almost exclusively on the basis of assigned legal entitlements: "The use of [WTA] in damage assessment involves the implicit assumption that the public at large owns the resource in question . . . the use of [WTP] in damage assessment involves the implicit assumption that the public at large is not entitled to the services of the resource foreclosed by the damages" (Kopp and Smith, 1993, p. 342).

This presumption that the choice of evaluation measure "will vary with the assignment of property rights" (Krutilla and Fisher, 1975, p. 36), and that "the determination of the conceptually appropriate form of CV [contingent valuation] query is a matter of property rights, not economics or psychology" (Levy and Friedman, 1994), clearly direct that if a legal entitlement is permissive of an activity, then any loss resulting from that activity is presumed to be measured by how much victims would pay to be relieved of the injury; alternatively, if there is a legal prohibition against an action giving rise to harms, the same losses would then be measured by the sums that would make the injuries acceptable to those adversely affected.

The near unanimity of using legal entitlements as a basis for selecting the measure to assess a loss or gain seems to stem largely from discussions, particularly among economists, of the compensating variation (CV) and equivalent variation (EV) measures of welfare impacts of price changes. The CV measure of the impact on the welfare of an individual stemming from a change in the price of a commodity has as its reference point the utility level before the price change. The justification for this choice of reference point is "the presumption that the individual has no right or claim to make purchases at the new set of prices. In contrast, the EV . . . contains the presumption that the individual has a right to the new price set and must be compensated if the new price set is not to be attained" (Freeman, 1979, p. 45). However, linking the assignment of legal entitlement to the choice between EV and CV and assuming that this determines the appropriate welfare measure in the case of environmental changes appears to be both unwarranted and misleading.

Legal entitlements, or property rules, determine whether an injured party has a cause of action against a neighbor and therefore can obtain injunctive relief or receive compensation for damages. Entitlements define what claims receive recognition by the community and determine the degree of protection offered, presumably in accord with efficiency, equity, fairness, and other community justice goals (Calabresi and Melamed, 1972). The assignment of entitlements may, for example, reflect asymmetries in avoidance costs or in the costs of enforcement and compliance; it is usually easier and cheaper, for instance, to make manufacturers of a consumer product liable for defects than to pass on responsibility to purchasers who have less information and would then need to pursue remedies individually.

The choice of economic measure involves selecting a welfare criterion that best assesses actual changes in welfare in a particular case. The extent of welfare loss associated with various injuries may well be influenced by the assignment of specific legal entitlements—rules presumably evolve to provide greater protection against more important losses. To this extent, and largely in accord with this direction of causality, property rights are related to welfare losses. However, this does not imply that the existing legal rules of entitlement determine people's reference point and thereby provide an appropriate basis for measuring those losses.

Ellickson's study (1987) of the response to differing range laws governing liability for damages to farmers' crops by straying cattle in Shasta County, California, in the United States, provides an instructive example of reference positions not varying with legal entitlements. Open range was the legal rule in half of the county, and closed range the rule in the other half. Extensive interviewing of ranchers and farmers revealed that all parties were aware of the rules, but that despite the opposite assignments of liability for crop damages caused by cattle, people in both parts of the county expected and provided similar remedies. Crops not being damaged by errant cattle was clearly deemed the reference state, and such harms were therefore considered losses for which the cattle owners were liable regardless of the legal rule.

This position of Shasta County residents appears to be consistent with other findings that actions are widely judged to be fair or unfair on the basis of comparisons with people's reference transactions, which are independent of legal restrictions. A few examples: Cutting wages is seen to be a reduction from the reference wage level and to be unfair, especially by profitable firms. Raising prices to reflect increased costs is acceptable, to reflect shortages is much less so. Reducing a yearly bonus is more acceptable than reducing salaries by a like amount (Kahneman, Knetsch, and Thaler, 1986; Shiller, Boycko, and Korobov, 1991; Frey and Pommerehne, 1993).

The reliance on nonlegal norms rather than legal entitlements in defining reference positions is also apparent in the findings of Macaulay's seminal work (1963) in the sociology of law. In cases of breaches of purchase contracts, Macaulay found that sellers uniformly believed that they ought to recover only their actual out-of-pocket costs rather than their wasted expenses plus anticipated profits to which they were legally entitled. This industry practice appears to discriminate between losses and forgone gains on the basis of a reference that, again, is independent of the legal entitlement.

A further example of legal rules accommodating reference positions, rather than values being dependent on rules, is provided by the usual treatment of adverse possession of land. A land user who over time increases ties to that land—often because of a mistake in locating a boundary fence—is commonly able to successfully assert a claim of ownership over a prior owner, an outcome seemingly dependent on the likely reference positions of the parties (Ellickson, 1989; Cohen and Knetsch, 1992). Temporary use is not rewarded, but expectations of continued use developed over many years of occupancy lead to legal rulings that recognize differences in valuations. A termination would be regarded as a loss rather than a forgone gain to a long-term current user, and would be viewed as a gain to the original holder of title; the loss would likely be valued more highly than the gain.

Rather than furthering allocative efficiency, the practice of using the property rights criterion to justify a choice of measure may well compromise this aim. For example, a municipal council might lawfully be able, without a referendum, to carry out a project yielding benefits of $100 per household, net of all costs except for one loss that householders would be willing to pay an average of $50 to avoid or would require $200 to accept. Although the municipality might enjoy legal authority allowing the development, using the WTP criterion for assessing the loss would encourage a project for which the welfare costs are far greater than the benefits—the gain ($100) would be less than the sums required ($200) for each to accept the loss. Similarly, if a private party were assessed damages of only $50 per household in such cases—on grounds, for example, of being a "conservative choice"—it could only lead to too many accidents and developments inflicting greater costs than benefits on the community.

Reference Point and Measurement Criteria

Four evaluations can be distinguished that depend on the combinations of (1) the direction of change, of having more or less of the good, and (2) the initial level relative to the reference state (Figure 2.1). A criterion for choosing an appropriate measure in each of these four cases, based on the reference state and the direction of change in the entitlement, can be illustrated with the portions of two indifference curves in Figure 2.2, where wealth, or income, is measured on the vertical axis and quantity of a good or entitlement on the horizontal. The indifference curves represent different combinations of wealth and the good that provide equal welfare to the individual and have different slopes over the same range of quantity Q1 to Q2 to reflect the greater value of losses over gains. In this illustration they have a common point to emphasize that no ranking of utility between the two "indifference" curves is implied.[3] Zero income effects, implying vertically parallel indifference curves, are assumed for convenience in indicating values in this illustration.

Evaluation 1: A Gain

The first valuation is of an increase in the quantity of the good from a reference state of Q1 to an increased quantity Q2, with W2 the initial level of wealth. This is a gain relative to the reference, evidenced in Figure 2.2 by a move from Q1 to Q2. The measure of the associated increase in welfare is the maximum sum the individual is willing to pay (WTP) for this increase—an amount up to the sum that would retain welfare at the original level. The individual would pay up to this amount but no more because paying more than this would result in being on a different indifference curve, indicating a lower level of well-being than the person had before being offered the gain. This maximum WTP is given, in Figure 2.2, by the decrease in wealth W2 minus W1.

Figure 2.2. Indifference Curves Depicting a Disparity Between Valuations of Gains and Losses, and Criteria for Choice of Measure.

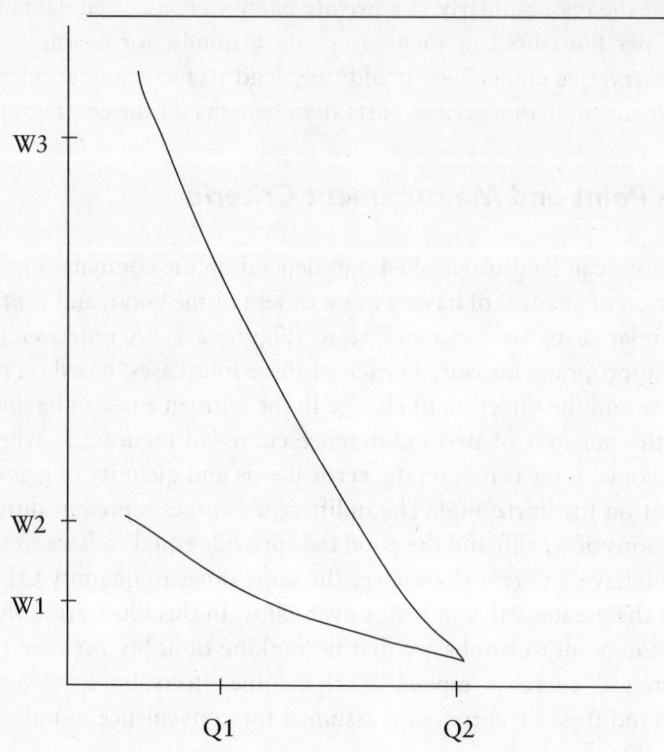

Change	*Reference*	*Perception*	*Measure*	
Q1 to Q2	Q1	Gain	WTP (to get)	W2 – W1
Q2 to Q1	Q2	Loss	WTA (to accept)	W3 – W1
Q2 to Q1	Q1	Forgone Gain	WTP (to keep)	W2 – W1
Q1 to Q2	Q2	Reduction of Loss	WTA (to forgo)	W3 – W1

Evaluation 2: A Loss

The second valuation is of a reduction in quantity from Q2 to Q1, with Q2 as the reference state and W1 the initial wealth. The welfare loss is given by the minimum compensation that the individual will accept to maintain the present level of welfare (to remain on the same indifference curve as the initial point). This WTA is given in Figure 2.2 by the difference W3 minus W1. This will normally be much larger than the difference

W2 minus W1 because of the disparity between the evaluation of otherwise commensurate gains and losses—as indicated in Figure 2.1 by the implied movement down the steep portion of the function in the domain of losses.

Evaluation 3: A Forgone Gain

This change is a reduction from an initial Q2 back to the reference Q1, with initial wealth at W1. Because the initial level is beyond the reference point, the move to Q1 is one of giving up, or forgoing, a gain. The appropriate measure of the change in welfare associated with a forgone gain is the sum which the particular individual would pay to avoid forgoing a gain above the reference, which is equivalent to obtaining a gain and is equal to W2 minus W1. It is important to distinguish this evaluation case from those in which expectations are sufficiently well formed to result in the shift of the reference point to Q2, which would cause the negative change in quantity to be treated as a loss rather than a forgone gain, and the welfare loss would then be the much larger WTA (of W3 minus W1).

Evaluation 4: Reduction of a Loss

The remaining valuation is of a positive change from Q1 to the reference state Q2, with wealth at W3. Given that the reference is Q2, the initial lower level (Q1) would be perceived as being in the losses, and an increase in quantity is then not a gain but a reduction of the current loss. The welfare measure is, therefore, the compensation that would be necessary for the individual to forgo this reduction of an existing loss—the WTA measure equal to W3 minus W1 (assuming parallel curves). This important class of cases calling for the WTA needed to accept a harm is widely misrepresented by defining elimination of a harm as a gain, or benefit, for which the WTP would be the correct measure—as is implied in the suggestion to consider "the WTP for reductions in the risks of premature mortality due to diseases with environmental causes" (Krupnick, 1993, p. 7). Similarly, although most people likely regard an oil spill as a loss, damages from spills that have already occurred are commonly assessed by using the answers to contingent valuation questions asking people how much they would pay to prevent future spills.[4] Assessing reductions in losses as gains can result in serious understatements of the value of such changes.

Choice of Measure

The impacts of the two positive and two negative changes on welfare are best assessed by either the WTP or the WTA measure, depending on whether the change is below or above the reference level. Schematically, the four cases are as follows:

DIRECTION OF CHANGE	CHANGE SHORT OF REFERENCE	CHANGE BEYOND REFERENCE
Positive	Reduce loss (WTA)	Gain (WTP)
Negative	Loss (WTA)	Forgo gain (WTP)

Whether a positive change is viewed as a gain or reduction of a loss, and a negative change is taken to be a loss or a forgone gain, depends critically on the perceived reference.

The four cases also mirror the traditional equivalent and compensating variations, or surpluses, for measuring positive and negative welfare changes. However, here the more useful distinction turns not on whether an individual "has a right to the new price set" but on the reference state from which individuals weigh gains and losses. Analogous to judging changes by the compensating variation from the point of view of present holdings, positive and negative changes in the domain of losses are measured by WTA. Analogous to judging equivalent variation changes based on anticipated holdings, pluses and minuses in the domain of gains are measured by WTP.

Welfare Measures and Definition of the Reference Point

The issue and the implications for choices and decisions can be illustrated by the choice of measure that might be used to assess the economic justification for reducing air pollution levels. If the present level of environmental quality is taken as the reference point, the benefits of control would be measured by the WTP for an improvement. Alternatively, clean air may be regarded as the norm or reference state, and the positive change in quality from the present dirty air would then be valued not as a benefit of cleaner air measured by WTP but as a reduction in the current loss and therefore assessed by the far larger WTA measure. The value of reducing pollution, and the justification for implementing control measures, would differ depending on whether the action is viewed by the beneficiaries as an improvement in current conditions or as mitigation of a present injury.

Similarly, a negative change of deteriorating water quality might be viewed as a loss, for which the WTA would be the appropriate measure, or a forgone gain most accurately assessed by the WTP measure. The decision and the choice of measure in such cases depends on which criterion most accurately reflects the actual welfare change, and therefore on the reference state that individuals use to evaluate gains and losses.

In many cases, the reference position will be fairly obvious as, for example, in the wide acceptance that being free of bodily harm is the reference whether or not a person is currently being physically assaulted.[5] In others, however, it may not be so readily apparent, as in the troublesome case of viewing the preservation of an attractive and historic building as either preventing a loss or conferring a benefit. In some cases it might be expected that some people will use one reference and some will use another. And as the case of smoking in public places in many parts of the world illustrates, reference positions may change over time.

The reference point may be taken to be the status quo in many cases, but in others it might be some other expected level regarded as normal. As Tversky and Kahneman point out, "A diversity of factors determine the reference outcome in everyday life, the reference outcome is usually a state to which one has adapted; it is sometimes set by social norms and expectations; it sometimes corresponds to a level of aspiration, which may or may not be realistic" (1981, p. 456).

The choice appears to turn largely on whether people consider themselves to be at a position without access or expectation of access to the good, or at a position in which they enjoy either current use or access to the good or the expectation that such access has, for whatever reason, some element of normalcy associated with it. As Kahneman and Miller (1986) suggest, what people perceive as normal are typically events or actions that evoke like representations—a day without an oil spill is like most other days, for example. Things that are not considered normal evoke questions about why the event or action violated the norm. "A why question indicates that a particular event is surprising and requests the explanation of an *effect,* defined as a contrast between an observation and a more normal alternative" (Kahneman and Miller, 1986, p. 148).

The departure of what occurs from what is expected prompts cognitive dissonance in affected individuals and prompts most people to construct counterfactual reasoning in which things are returned to normal (Schwarz, Wanke, and Bless, 1994). This suggests that references are closely tied to what are taken to be normal outcomes, which are often independent of the probability of an abnormal event or the possibility that victims might be able to avoid some of the consequences. People may well believe that oil spills are inevitable and cleanup equipment may be deployed along shipping routes to deal with them, but a spill is likely to still be considered an abnormal event and be treated as a loss, for which the WTA measure is appropriate. It seems at this point to be an empirical matter of when events do and do not violate norms and consequently when they are best considered to be changes in the domain of gains or in the domain of losses.

Konow's findings of people's judgments of the fairness of alternative legal responsibilities illustrate an empirical basis for determining a reference (1994). In one subsample, 80 percent of respondents indicated that they thought it unfair for a court to rule that a chemical factory was not responsible for the increased costs it imposed on a downstream user of the river water polluted by its discharge. Only 16 percent of the other subsample believed that a ruling making the chemical firm liable for the downstream costs was unfair. This seems to be evidence that clean water was the reference position of most respondents. As in the case of a firm making cuts to a reference wage, these people appear to view a deterioration from a reference water quality level as unfair and feel that the responsible party should be held liable for the change.

Gregory, Lichtenstein, and MacGregor's recent investigation (1993) of the role of past states in determining people's reference positions is another important example of an empirical basis for selecting an appropriate welfare measure. Different past histories of a variety of human health and environmental problems were presented to different groups of subjects. Half of the participants were led to view current proposals to deal with the problems as improvements over historic levels, and half to view them as attempting to restore matters to levels enjoyed in the past, as, for example, "restoring water quality in the river to its historic level." All were then asked to indicate the desirability of the improvement on a 7-point scale. The results were clear: "Presenting a proposed change as the restoration of a prior loss rather than as a gain from the status quo is shown in all five cases to have a significant effect on the evaluation of environmental, health and policy decisions" (p. 200). Such findings could materially improve selections of measures, and to the extent that measures chosen would more accurately reflect real changes in welfare, this would discourage inappropriate damage awards and inferior policy choices.

Conclusion

Many evaluation studies of the welfare changes associated with various proposed actions or policies have made fairly casual choices between willingness-to-pay and compensation-demanded measures and have, for the most part, left this as a matter of convenience. As a result, willingness-to-pay measures have been used not only to value gains, which is fully in keeping with the normal efficiency criterion, but also to assess losses and the benefits of mitigating losses, which is usually not consistent with the efficiency standard.

The recommendation to use WTP measures even where "the conceptually correct measure of lost passive-use value for environmental damage that has already occurred is the minimum amount of compensation that each individual would be willing to accept" (U.S. NOAA, 1993, p. 4603) might be justified if WTA exceeded WTP "only trivially" as ritualistically suggested by the NOAA panel (p. 4603) and others. However, as essentially all of the empirical evidence suggests that the differences are very large, the knowing use of WTP rather than WTA to assess damages because "this is the conservative choice" will almost certainly distort incentives, compromise the deterrence function of compensation awards, severely bias policy and protection choices, and undermine confidence that remedies will be fair.

Unwarranted use of the WTP measure to assess losses will create serious problems: It will unduly encourage activities with negative environmental impacts because the real value of the losses will be systematically understated. Inappropriately lax standards of environmental protection will be set because estimates of the added costs of further deterioration will be severely biased. Too few resources will be devoted to avoiding accidents and degradation. A full accounting of the costs of projects and activities having adverse environmental consequences and appropriate pricing of environmental inputs will be frustrated.

Inappropriate choices of measures that are not consistent with actual gains and losses could also be undermining confidence in resolutions of environmental conflicts and acceptance of remedial actions. If people perceive that valuations are based on a measure consistent with their preferences and notions of fairness, they may accept results that leave them less well off because they know that proper account was taken of their loss. Much of the lack of support for current policies and proposed resolutions of conflicts may be traceable to a choice of measure that does not conform to people's view of a fair accounting of losses.

An example of possible inappropriate accounting of values is the common practice of claiming that preventing deterioration of air and water quality is a "benefit" and that estimates of people's willingness to pay for this "benefit" is the appropriate value to compare with the costs of pollution control (Bromley, 1995; Lesser and Zerbe, 1995). This practice can only be justified by the dubious empirical assertion that individuals view a degraded environment as the reference, and therefore consider the degradation as forgoing clean air and water, rather than see the deterioration as a loss from present levels of environmental quality. This is parallel to assuming that not destroying a fishery is a gain, rather than considering its demise as a loss, and that not using a park for another use is a benefit, instead of such a change being taken as a loss. Such assumptions may be valid, but increasing the acceptance of policy choices based on them may require their empirical verification.

Extant legal entitlements or property claims are, of course, germane to resolving claims for compensation or other remedies by parties that might be adversely affected by actions that take or decrease the value of their holdings. However, the choice of measure used to assess the value of environmental change appears to have less to do with such legal assignments and more to do with the reference state of affected individuals. Further, the evidence of pervasive large disparities between the measures and the consequences of inappropriate choices suggest that the prevailing indifference to the choice issue is no longer easily justified.

NOTES

1. The results of some studies have indicated that the disparity may decrease, or even disappear, over repeated trials (for example, Shogren, Shin, Hayes, and Kliebenstein, 1994). However, it now appears on the basis of further tests that such results may be attributable to the failure of the Vickrey auction design, used in these studies, to accurately reveal people's valuations (Kahneman, Knetsch, and Thaler, 1995).
2. Some consequences have been suggested, for example, for economic theory (Kahneman, Knetsch, and Thaler, 1990; Knetsch, 1995b); analyses of legal relationships (Knetsch, 1984; Hovenkamp, 1991; Hoffman and Spitzer, 1993); environmental worries and policy analysis (Knetsch, 1990, 1995a); and fairness concerns (Kahneman, Knetsch, and Thaler, 1986, 1991).
3. This seeming violation of standard utility theory of economics texts is among the implications of the disparity between gains and losses (Kahneman, Knetsch, and Thaler, 1991).
4. An example of such a use of answers to one question to imply answers to a very different one is the use of valuations from the question, "What is the most your household would be willing to pay in total over the next five years in higher prices for programs that prevent oil spills, like those described above, along the West Coast over the next five years?" to provide "a measure of the damage of the Nestucca oil spill"—a spill that had already occurred (RCG/Hagler, Bailly, Inc., 1991, p. 6–3).

5. This distinction has elements in common with the harm benefit test, or criterion, for determining when compensation is due for a collective or public intervention that lowers the market value of a private holding. Actions carried out for public gain, such as acquisition of land for a park, are normally considered compensable; actions implemented to prevent a loss, such as pollution control, are commonly not deemed a "taking," and no damage payments are usually made to those required to undertake costly control measures.

REFERENCES

Benarzi, S., and Thaler, R. H. "Myopic Loss Aversion and the Equity Premium Puzzle." *Quarterly Journal of Economics,* 1995, *110,* 73–92.

Borges, B.F.J. "The Prevalence of Valuation Disparities: Within- and Between-Subject Evidence for Close Substitute Goods." Simon Fraser University Working Paper, 1995.

Boyce, R. R., and others. "An Experimental Examination of Intrinsic Values as a Source of the WTA-WTP Disparity." *American Economic Review,* 1992, *82,* 1366–1373.

Bromley, D. W. "Property Rights and Natural Resource Damage Assessments." *Ecological Economics,* 1995, *14,* 129–135.

Calabresi, G., and Melamed, A. D. "Property Rules, Liability Rules, and Inalienability: One View of the Cathedral." *Harvard Law Review,* 1972, *85,* 1089–1128.

Cohen, D., and Knetsch, J. L. "Judicial Choice and Disparities Between Measures of Economic Values." *Osgoode Hall Law Journal,* 1992, *30,* 737–770.

Ellickson, R. C. "A Critique of Economic and Sociological Theories of Social Control." *Journal of Legal Studies,* 1987, *16,* 67–99.

Ellickson, R. C. "Bringing Culture and Human Frailty to Rational Actors: A Critique of Classical Law and Economics." *Chicago-Kent Law Review,* 1989, *65,* 23–55.

Freeman, A. M. *The Benefits of Environmental Improvement.* Baltimore: Johns Hopkins University Press, 1979.

Frey, B., and Pommerehne, W. W. "International Trade in Art: Attitudes and Behaviour." *Rivista Internaxionale de Scienze Economiche a Commerciali,* 1987, *34,* 465–486.

Frey, B., and Pommerehne, W. W. "On the Fairness of Pricing—An Empirical Survey Among the General Population." *Journal of Economic Behavior and Organization,* 1993, *20,* 295–307.

Gregory, R., Lichtenstein, S., and MacGregor, D. "The Role of Past States in Determining Reference Points for Policy Decisions." *Organizational Behavior and Human Decision Processes,* 1993, *55,* 195–206.

Henderson, A. M. "Consumer's Surplus and the Compensation Variation." *Review of Economic Studies,* 1941, *8,* 117–121.

Hoffman, E., and Spitzer, M. L. "Willingness to Pay vs. Willingness to Accept: Legal and Economic Implications." *Washington University Law Quarterly,* 1993, *71,* 59–114.

Hovenkamp, H. "Legal Policy and the Endowment Effect." *Journal of Legal Studies,* 1991, *20,* 225–247.

Johnson, E. J., Hershey, J., Meszaros, J., and Kunreuther, H. "Framing Probability Distortions, and Insurance Decisions." *Journal of Risk and Uncertainty,* 1993, *7,* 728–741.

Kachelmeier, S. J., and Shehata, M. "Examining Risk Preferences Under High Monetary Incentives: Experimental Evidence from the People's Republic of China." *American Economic Review,* 1992, *82,* 1120–1141.

Kahneman, D., Knetsch, J. L., and Thaler, R. H. "Fairness as a Constraint on Profit Seeking: Entitlements in the Market." *American Economic Review,* 1986, *76,* 728–741.

Kahneman, D., Knetsch, J. L., and Thaler, R. H. "Experimental Tests of the Endowment Effect and the Coase Theorem." *Journal of Political Economy,* 1990, *98,* 1325–1348.

Kahneman, D., Knetsch, J. L., and Thaler, R. H. "The Endowment Effect, Loss Aversion, and Status Quo Bias." *Journal of Economic Perspectives,* 1991, *5,* 193–206.

Kahneman, D., Knetsch, J. L., and Thaler, R. H. "The Endowment Effect and the Vickrey Auction." University of Chicago Working Paper, 1995.

Kahneman, D., and Miller, D. T. "Norm Theory: Comparing Realities to Its Alternatives." *Psychological Review,* 1986, *93,* 136–153.

Knetsch, J. L. "Legal Rules and the Basis for Evaluating Economic Losses." *International Review of Law and Economics,* 1984, *4,* 5–13.

Knetsch, J. L. "The Endowment Effect and Evidence of Nonreversible Indifference Curves." *American Economic Review,* 1989, *79,* 1277–1284.

Knetsch, J. L. "Environmental Policy Implications of Disparities Between Willingness to Pay and Compensation Demanded Measure of Values." *Journal of Environmental Economics and Management,* 1990, *18,* 227–237.

Knetsch, J. L. "Preferences and Nonreversibility of Indifference Curves." *Journal of Economic Behavior and Organization,* 1992, *17,* 131–139.

Knetsch, J. L. "Assumptions, Behavioral Findings, and Policy Analysis." *Journal of Policy Analysis and Management,* 1995a, *14,* 68–78.

Knetsch, J. L. "Asymmetric Valuation of Gains and Losses and Preference Order Assumptions." *Economic Inquiry,* 1995b, *33,* 134–141.

Knetsch, J. L., and Sinden, J. A. "Willingness to Pay and Compensation Demanded: Experimental Evidence of an Unexpected Disparity in Measures of Value." *Quarterly Journal of Economics,* 1984, *99,* 507–521.

Konow, J. "A Positive General Theory of Economic Fairness." Loyola Marymount University Working Paper, 1994.

Kopp, R., and Smith, V. K. "Glossary Terms for Natural Resource Damage Assessment." In R. J. Kopp and V. K. Smith (eds.), *Valuing Natural Assets: The Economics of Natural Resource Damage Assessment.* Washington, D.C.: Resources for the Future, 1993.

Krupnick, A. J. "Benefit Transfers and Valuation of Environmental Improvements." *Resources,* 1993, *110,* 1–7.

Krutilla, J. V., and Fisher, A. C. *The Economics of Natural Environment.* Baltimore: Johns Hopkins University Press, 1975.

Lesser, J. A., and Zerbe, R. O. "What Can Economic Analysis Contribute to the 'Sustainability' Debate?" *Contemporary Economic Policy,* 1995, *8,* 88–100.

Levy, D. S., and Friedman, D. "The Revenge of the Redwoods? Reconsidering Property Rights and the Economic Allocation of Natural Resources." *University of Chicago Law Review,* 1994, *61,* 493–525.

Macaulay, S. "Non-Contractual Relations in Business: A Preliminary Study." *American Sociological Review,* 1963, *28,* 55–62.

Michaelman, F. I. "Property, Utility, and Fairness: Comments on the Ethical Foundation of 'Just Compensation' Law." *Harvard Law Review,* 1967, *80,* 1165–1258.

RCG/Hagler, Bailly, Inc. *Contingent Valuation of Natural Resource Damage Due to the Nestucca Oil Spill: Final Report.* Boulder, Colo.: RCG/Hagler, Bailly, Inc., 1991.

Schwarz, N., Wanke, M., and Bless, H. "Subjective Assessments and Evaluations of Change: Some Lessons from Sociological Cognition Research." *European Review of Social Psychology,* 1994, *5,* 181–210.

Shefrin, H., and Statman, M. "The Disposition to Sell Winners Too Early and Ride Losers Too Long: Theory and Evidence." *Journal of Finance,* 1985, *40,* 777–790.

Shiller, R. J., Boycko, M., and Korobov, V. "Popular Attitudes Towards Free Markets: The Soviet Union and the United States Compared." *American Economic Review,* 1991, *81,* 385–400.

Shogren, J. F., Shin, S. Y., Hayes, D. J., and Kliebenstein, J. B. "Resolving Differences in Willingness to Pay and Willingness to Accept." *American Economic Review,* 1994, *84,* 255–270.

Sunstein, C. R. "Endogenous Preferences, Environmental Law." *Journal of Legal Studies,* 1993, 22, 217–254.

Turner, R. K., Pearce, D., and Bateman, I. *Environmental Economics.* Baltimore: Johns Hopkins University Press, 1993.

Tversky, A., and Kahneman, D. "The Framing of Decisions and the Psychology of Choice." *Science,* 1981, *211,* 453–458.

U.S. NOAA Panel. "Report of the NOAA Panel on Contingent Valuation." *U.S. Federal Register,* Jan. 15, 1993, *58*(10), 4602–4614.

Willis, K., and Garrod, G. "Valuing Wildlife: The Benefits of Wildlife Trusts." University of Newcastle upon Tyne Countryside Change Unit Working Paper 46, 1993.

3

HOW PEOPLE VALUE THE ENVIRONMENT

Attitudes Versus Economic Values

Ilana Ritov and Daniel Kahneman

AMERICANS SURVEYED IN public opinion polls consistently express much concern for environmental protection (Ladd and Bowman, 1995). In 1994, for example, all but 14 percent of the people surveyed by Cambridge Reports/Research International thought that the label "environmentalist" would characterize them, at least to some degree; 63 percent identified themselves moderately or strongly with this label. Evidently, the goal of protecting the environment is widely shared. Two further questions must now be addressed: *How* do people value the environment (and other public goods, and other things)? *How much* do people value the environment and various aspects of it?

As is often the case in policy matters, the discipline of economics suggests seemingly simple answers to both these questions—although not all economists accept these answers. The economic answer to the question of how people value the environment is that there is only one way of valuing. The standard economic analysis assumes that for each individual

This research was supported by a U.S.–Israel Binational Science Foundation grant to the authors. We thank Nathan Novemsky and Shirit Kronzon for their assistance.

there exists a preference order over possible states of the world (including states of uncertainty). The objects of preference can be specified in terms of the private and public goods that are provided and the prices of these goods. The value of a good, whether private or public, is measured by the smallest monetary compensation for which the individual would agree to give it up, or approximated by the highest price that the individual would pay to acquire it. The prevailing practice is to take maximal willingness to pay (WTP) as the measure of the value of a good for an individual. This *purchase model* is the theoretical foundation for the contingent valuation method (CVM), which is currently the dominant method in attempts to measure the value of public goods. In the CV procedure the value of a public good to the public is estimated by surveys in which respondents state their willingness to pay for the good (or answer a hypothetical referendum question about a specified tax to be used for that purpose; for introductions to the controversial CVM, see Diamond and Hausman, 1994; Hanemann, 1994; Mitchell and Carson, 1989; Portney, 1994).

The economic model of value is characterized by a tight logical structure: it assumes a rational agent whose preferences conform to the highly restrictive axioms of consumer theory. The agent's preferences are also assumed to obey some principles so basic that they are usually left unstated. One of these principles is invariance: the preferences of the idealized agent are assumed to be attached to objective outcomes and to be invariant over inconsequential changes of context, formulation, or procedure (Tversky and Kahneman, 1986). For example, the willingness to pay (WTP) for a bundle of two goods (A and B) should be the sum of the WTP for A alone and the WTP for B when A has been provided (Diamond, 1996). The assumption that the same rules of value apply to lost environmental assets and to market goods underlies the applications of CVM in cost-benefit analysis and in litigation.

In criticizing these applications we have argued that standard consumer theory fails as a description of how people value the environment and that it therefore cannot provide a secure basis for measuring the value of environmental goods (Kahneman, 1986; Kahneman and Knetsch, 1992; Kahneman, Ritov, Jacowitz, and Grant, 1993; Kahneman and Ritov, 1994). We proposed instead that stated WTP is one of several correlated (but not completely interchangeable) measures of the attitude toward any environmental issue. Instead of the purchase model, we proposed that people view payments for the preservation of environmental assets from which they derive no personal benefits as *contributions*, which express the intensity of their attitudes. The present chapter elaborates this attitude model of valuation, using both new and older evidence.

Aspects of an Attitude Model

In contrast to the stark constraints imposed by the economic theory of value, the psychological interpretation of people's attachment to environmental goods can only appear vague and loose. Indeed, this attachment can be characterized in several seemingly different ways, all intuitively compelling. This section reviews previous interpretations that led to our current view of WTP as a measure of attitude.

Kahneman (1986) suggested that the statement of a positive WTP for environmental improvements can sometimes be interpreted as a symbolic action. The evidence was the early observation of the effect now known as embedding: earlier research by Kahneman and Knetsch had shown that WTP to clean up all the lakes of Ontario was only slightly larger than the WTP to clean up the lakes in any particular region of Ontario. The striking insensitivity to the scope of the intervention suggested that these WTP responses reflected a general evaluation of the act of cleaning up lakes. Unlike purchases, symbolic activities are likely to be relatively insensitive to quantity. Indeed, Baron and Greene (1996) have shown that willingness to pay for a safety device for automobiles was less sensitive to a quantitative measure of effectiveness when the device was introduced by regulation than when the same device was presented as a private good, available for purchase by individual drivers.

Kahneman and Knetsch (1992) pointed out the contrast between contributions and purchases and suggested that WTP for environmental goods is best understood as a contribution. In this context they proposed that WTP for the provision of different public goods is commensurate with the moral satisfaction (or warm glow, see Andreoni, 1990) associated with contributing to these goods. This proposal was based on Margolis's brilliant analysis (1982) of contributions to public goods. Margolis had observed that in contributions—unlike purchases—utility is derived from the act of contributing, not from its consequences. For example, a donation of $50 to public television is not motivated by a desire to see this institution have $50 more than it would otherwise have: the unexpected news that a neighbor has decided to donate $50 to public television will not cause anyone to cancel a previous plan to contribute that amount. Kahneman and Knetsch concluded that if anything is purchased by a donation, it must be a sense of moral satisfaction. (This is similar to Andreoni's analysis of seemingly altruistic gifts as motivated by "impure altruism.") The relationship between WTP and moral satisfaction was supported by two small studies in which different samples of respondents encountered a set of fourteen public causes: one sample answered a WTP question, the other rated the moral satisfaction associated with contributing to each of these causes. The rankings of the issues by average WTP and by ratings of moral satisfaction were highly correlated. The idea that contributions are driven by moral satisfaction provides a satisfactory account of the embedding effect: the intuition is that one can derive equal satisfaction from contributing to causes that vary greatly in inclusiveness, such as rehabilitating a single orphaned refugee or one hundred such orphans. This insensitivity to quantity distinguishes contributions from purchases. In a purchase model, of course, the compelling consideration is that saving one hundred orphans is much more valuable than saving one.

Subsequent studies (Kahneman and Ritov, 1994; Kahneman, Ritov, Jacowitz, and Grant, 1993) showed that the high correlation between moral satisfaction and WTP is hardly unique. The stated willingness to pay for an issue and the stated moral satisfaction associated with a contribution both belong to a cluster of correlated responses, which also includes judgments of the importance of the issue and statements of political support for public action. The entire cluster is best described as a set of expressions of the intensity of attitudes. In light of this finding, more specific interpretations (for example, that contributions are governed by moral satisfaction) appear unjustified.

The notion of attitude intensity that we sketch here is related (but perhaps not identical) to the notion of attitude strength developed by Krosnick and collaborators (see for example Krosnick and others, 1993).

The strongest evidence supporting the interpretation of WTP as one of many measures of attitude intensity was reported by Kahneman and Ritov (1994). The study elicited responses to more than thirty different topics, including a wide array of environmental problems and other public issues. The issues were presented as headlines, in which a brief description of a problem was followed by a single sentence describing a proposed intervention. An example was "DOLPHINS IN THE MEDITERRANEAN SEA ARE THREATENED BY POLLUTION. Intervention: Contribute to an international fund to save the Mediterranean Dolphin." Different groups of subjects, all visitors at the San Francisco Exploratorium, were asked to rate several issues with respect to a single measure. The measures were WTP for the proposed intervention, degree of political support for the intervention, personal satisfaction expected from making a voluntary contribution (both on a 0–4 rating scale), and a simple rating of the importance of the problem as a public issue (on a 0–6 rating scale).

As is typically the case in contingent valuation surveys, a large percentage (47 percent) of the WTP responses were zero, and a few (1.6 percent) were extremely high. To address the latter problem we winsorized WTP by adjusting to $100 all responses that exceeded that amount. Table 3.1, adapted from Kahneman and Ritov (1994), presents the means across subjects of all the above measures, for each problem. Perhaps the most striking observation about the WTP column of data is the extremely limited range of responses. The difference between average winsorized willingness to pay for the lowest-ranking problem (Spanish moss depletion in some Southern states) and the highest one (massive burning and clear-cutting, threatening the rain forest in South America) is only about $20. This difference in dollar amounts must be considered unreasonable, given the wide range of importance among the issues presented. Analyses of variance were separately performed for each questionnaire, treating both problems and respondents as random effects. The summaries of these analyses, shown at the bottom of Table 3.1, indicate that differences among problems accounted for only 4 percent of the variance of WTP responses—distinctly less than for other measures.

The main purpose of the study was to examine whether the various responses are all measures of attitude intensity. This hypothesis was tested by computing rank correlations among the mean values in Table 3.1. Table 3.2 presents these correlations. The numbers in the diagonal represent measures of reliability, obtained by a bootstrapping procedure. Table 3.2 indicates that the rankings of the issues by the different measures were very similar, with correlations ranging from .76 to .88. Furthermore, the correlations between orders derived from different measures were not substantially lower than the reliability of the individual measures. In particular, WTP correlates .84 with expected satisfaction from making a personal contribution, and .84 with rating of support for public action. These correlations are almost as high as the reliability of the separate measures. The results suggest that WTP, stated support for public intervention, and anticipated moral satisfaction from a contribution are almost interchangeable expressions of the intensity of respondents' attitudes to the issues at hand.

The correlations involving ratings of the importance of issues are of particular interest. Respondents who made the importance rating were given only the headline describing the problem, without any mention of an intervention to deal with it. The correlation of .76 between importance and WTP suggests that the problems accounted for much more of the variance of WTP than the proposed solutions (the public goods ostensibly purchased). Indeed, we proposed that WTP and the other measures collected in this study all reflect attitudes to public problems, not to particular programs or solutions. In this respect the properties of WTP for public issues depart from the standard model of WTP in consumer theory: purchases are motivated by the good that is to be acquired, but contributions (at least in

Table 3.1. Responses to All Issues.

	WTP	*Support*	*Importance*	*Satisfaction*
Animal species				
American elk	7.69	2.07	5.00	2.51
Ferret	9.55	1.66	4.92	1.62
Elephants	16.28	2.64	5.88	2.96
Marine life	13.03	2.41	6.16	2.92
Kangaroo rats	6.33	1.65	4.19	—
Florida panther	6.81	1.83	5.35	—
Falcon shell	11.21	2.13`	5.86	2.38
Dolphins[a]	12.57	1.92	5.60	—
Australian mammals[a]	8.42	1.70	4.98	2.45
Coastal reptiles[a]	3.60	1.27	5.30	1.67
Wildlife[a]	13.30	2.36	5.63	2.45
Birds	8.91	2.18	5.63	—
Spotted owl[a]	14.55	2.12	5.33	—
Plant species				
Coral reefs	12.03	2.47	5.66	2.61
Mushroom	3.63	1.36	4.51	1.56
Pine disease	5.76	2.24	4.96	2.18
Spanish moss	2.24	1.02	4.39	—
Pine trees[a]	9.79	1.71	4.65	—
Ecological damage				
Wetlands	11.49	2.29	5.47	—
CO_2 in Third World	5.44	2.03	5.53	—
CO_2—oil burning	19.88	2.68	6.19	—
Automobile pollution	18.57	2.36	5.88	2.63
Burning rain forest	23.96	2.84	6.17	—
Visibility in parks[a]	9.56	2.02	4.65	—
Toxic waste dumps[a]	20.67	2.86	6.36	2.95
Shrinking rain forest[a]	16.93	2.73	6.22	—
Toxic spills[a]	9.98	2.44	6.56	—
Solid waste[a]	15.64	2.61	6.35	—
Miscellaneous goods				
Historic buildings	5.67	1.74	5.13	2.27
Lighthouses	6.44	1.04	2.96	—
Earthquake safety	8.40	1.81	5.23	—

	WTP	Support	Importance	Satisfaction
Public health				
Power lines leukemia	17.42	2.56	6.20	2.57
Increase in anemia[a]	15.27	2.25	5.57	—
Skin cancer in farmers	12.18	2.43	5.22	2.31
Increase in myeloma[a]	12.91	2.23	5.58	2.29
AIDS in Africa[a]	10.96	1.99	5.89	—
Lead paint poisoning[a]	13.84	2.43	6.06	2.71
Variance account (%)				
Problems	4.01	8.3	15.8	12.3
Respondents	46.4	46.9	25.9	39.4
Error	49.5	44.8	58.3	48.3

Source: Adapted from Kahneman and Ritov (1994). Adapted with kind permission from Kluwer Academic Publishers.

[a]Different versions of the problem were used. Mean satisfaction rating based on one or two versions only.

the context of our study) appear to be motivated by the perceived severity of an unsolved problem or unsatisfied need.

Our argument depends on correlations between averages of different responses, computed over issues. Correlations that approach the limits set by reliability—as do those of Table 3.2—imply that the *systematic* effects of issues on different response measures are effectively identical. As in the case of other summary statistics the interpretation of these correlations is constrained by the assumption that the data are not dominated by a few individuals who produce more variance than others and who have an atypical pattern of responses. When these assumptions fail, an analysis of average responses can yield conclusions that do not represent most individuals (Nickerson, 1995). Fortunately, these concerns do not apply to the correlations of Table 3.2. Although the correlations that could be observed within individuals would surely be lower, it appears that their pattern would be the same, after allowing for the difference in reliability. For the purpose of psychological interpretation the correlations of Table

Table 3.2. Rank Correlations Between Response Measures.

	WTP	Support	Importance	Satisfaction
WTP	.87			
Support	.84	.85		
Importance	.76	.84	.88	
Satisfaction	.84	.87	.85	.90

3.2 imply that there are almost no systematic differences between measures. For the practical purpose of measurement the results imply that different measures of attitude, including WTP, may be used interchangeably to order issues by the intensity of the response they evoke in the public.

Embedding and Extension Neglect

Economic values are assumed to exhibit a form of additivity: the value of a collection of goods should be appropriately decomposable into the values successively added by each of its elements (Diamond, 1996). In violation of this essential requirement several studies have shown that WTP to deal with a problem (for example, damage to a particular species or pollution of lakes) is radically insensitive both to the quantitative dimension of the problem and to the scope of the proposed remedial action for which a payment is requested. This observation is one of the main objections to the use of the contingent valuation method for the measurement of the value of public goods (Diamond, 1996; Hausman, 1993; Kahneman and Knetsch, 1992). This flaw in the WTP measure has been studied in several research paradigms and given various names, including embedding, insensitivity to scope, symbolic response, part-whole confusion, and others. It has also been much contested (for example, see Carson and Mitchell, 1995).

A full treatment of the contentious issue of sensitivity to scope will not be attempted here. The present discussion will only attempt to analyze the phenomenon of inadequate sensitivity to the quantitative dimension of environmental problems as a special case of a general cognitive effect, which has been labeled a failure of extensional evaluation (Kahneman, 1995), and to discuss what this phenomenon can tell us about attitudes.

An ongoing project (Kahneman, 1995) is concerned with intuitive judgments in three families of tasks, which the following examples illustrate: (1) rate the overall aversiveness of a painful medical procedure; (2) judge the probability that a man named Jack, described as "charming, talkative, clever and cynical" is one of the lawyers in a set of thirty lawyers and seventy engineers from which Jack was randomly drawn; (3) determine how much you are willing to contribute to a project of covering open oil ponds with nets, which will prevent the death of twenty thousand migrating birds that would otherwise drown in these ponds. Although they appear at first glance to have little in common, the three tasks have similar structures. Each requires the evaluation of a property of a set of elements: How aversive is this set of moments of pain? Does the set of lawyers include Jack? What is the value of saving this set of birds? Each of these sets has an extensional or quantitative aspect: the duration of the medical procedure, the base-rate of lawyers in the sample, the number of birds that drown in oil. Each of these sets is also characterized by one or more *representative exemplars*: a moment of the pain, the stereotypes of a lawyer and of an engineer, the image of a bird drowning in oil.

A hypothesis of *evaluation by exemplar* has been applied to all these cases. According to this hypothesis the response to the set is determined by evaluating a corresponding property of the representative exemplar. Thus the overall pain of a medical procedure is evaluated by a representative moment, and the probability that a particular individual is a lawyer rather than an engineer is assessed by the relative resemblance of that individual to the stereotypes of the two professions. Similarly, we propose, the willingness to pay to save birds from drowning in oil is mainly determined by the response to the idea of a bird dying in this manner.

Evaluation by exemplar implies a neglect of the extensional dimension, which is stripped away when an exemplar stands for the set. There is evidence for extension neglect in diverse situations. For example, the retrospective evaluation of various unpleasant experiences has been found to be almost unaffected by the duration of these experiences (Fredrickson and Kahneman, 1993; Kahneman, Fredrickson, Schreiber, and Redelmeier, 1993); intuitive predictions have sometimes been found to be almost completely insensitive to the base rates of outcomes (Kahneman and Tversky, 1973); and WTP to prevent the drowning of birds in oil ponds did not increase significantly when the number of birds that would be saved was increased from 2,000 to 200,000 (Desvousges and others, 1992; see also Boyle and others, 1994).

The neglect of the quantitative or extensional dimension that these studies illustrate is neither universal nor absolute. It is now recognized, for example, that some experimental manipulations reliably increase the impact of base-rate information on intuitive predictions (Koehler, 1996). In particular, base-rate information is effective when the base rate is varied over successive trials (Bar-Hillel and Fischhoff, 1991). Trial-to-trial variations also induced some sensitivity to the duration of exposure to loud unpleasant sounds (Schreiber and Kahneman, 1996). However, the effect was slight, and its pattern was surprising: the effects of loudness and duration appeared to be additive, although some form of multiplicative relation would be more reasonable. Following the general strategy of searching for parallel effects in studies of extensional neglect across domains, we decided to look for a similar pattern in the response to variations in the amount of damage to threatened animal species.

In one experiment (Novemsky, Kronzon, and Kahneman, 1996), visitors to the San Francisco Exploratorium ($N = 234$) were asked to state their willingness to pay to help fund interventions for three separate environmental problems. Each problem concerned a species whose population had declined relative to historically normal values in a specified region. Respondents were asked how much they would contribute to an intervention to restore the population to its normal size. Three species that were expected to vary in importance were used (elephants, falcons, and ferrets). Three levels of population reduction were mentioned: 15 percent, 40 percent, and 65 percent. Species and damage levels were varied within respondent, so that each respondent saw each species and each damage level exactly once.

To reduce the impact of unreasonably high responses, WTP responses in excess of $100 (2.1 percent of responses) were set to that value. Figure 3.1 shows the means of winsorized WTP, plotted for each species as a function of damage level. Bootstrapping techniques were used for statistical tests. The data are quite noisy but the main effect of damage level, although small, was statistically significant. However, the expected interaction between the importance of the species and the extent of damage again failed to materialize. It would be reasonable to expect the curves of Figure 3.1 to fan out, but in fact they show a slight (and statistically reli-

Figure 3.1. Mean Willingness to Pay as a Function of Damage Level, for Three Animal Species.

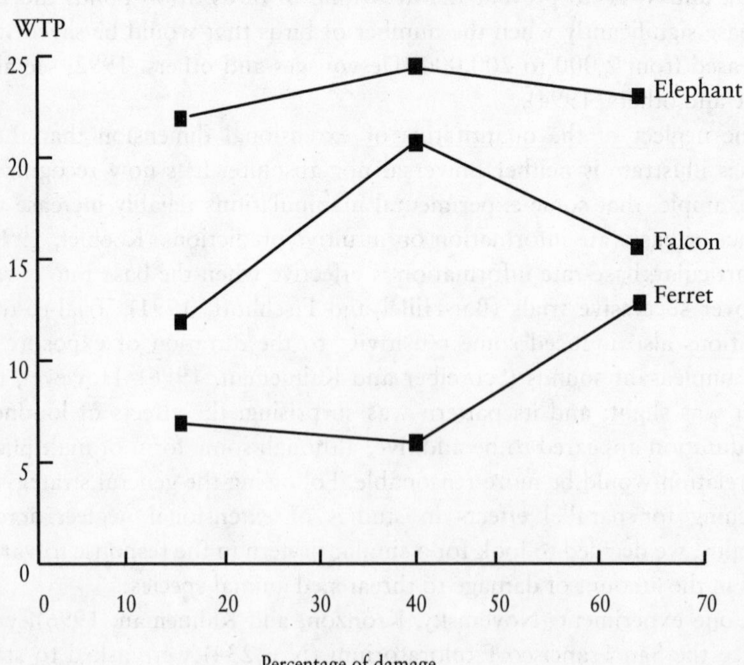

able) tendency to converge. The respondents appear to be slightly more sensitive to the extensional variable when the affected species is insignificant (ferrets) than when it matters more (falcons or elephants). The results are consistent with a slightly modified version of evaluation by exemplar, in which extensional information is used to adjust a response that is determined primarily by nonextensional considerations. Results obtained in the context of base-rate neglect and of duration neglect also conform to that pattern.

The pattern of partial extension neglect that is documented in these experiments provides a further elaboration of the attitude model that was sketched in the preceding section. We argued there that WTP and other measures of attitude to environmental issues are affected more strongly by the perceived severity of the problem than by the anticipated effect of an intervention. The present section adds the idea that the severity of an environmental problem is readily altered by variations in the intensional features of the problem (such as the salience of a particular species) and relatively impervious to manipulations of extensional aspects, such as the amount of damage or loss. Evaluation by exemplar is another difference between attitudes and economic values. Extensionality is assumed as a matter of course in economic analyses, but it is readily violated in observed preferences.

Context Dependency and Preference Reversals

The economic concept of value and the psychological concept of attitude invoke different assumptions about stability and about context independence. The preference order that is assumed in the economic analysis of value is both stable and context free. In particular the relative positions of two objects in the preference order are unaffected by the presence of irrelevant alternatives, by inconsequential details in the description of the objects, and by the procedure used to elicit the preference. Susceptibility to these effects vitiates the very notion of a preference order—and for good measure the lack of a coherent preference order is viewed as a violation of the broader assumption of economic rationality.

Some degree of stability and context independence is also assumed when the concept of attitude is invoked (Eagly and Chaiken, 1993): the main function of attitudes in psychological theory is to account for observed consistency in the response to different ofjects, on different questions and at different times. Unlike economic values and tastes, however, attitudes are assumed to be imperfectly coherent and potentially unstable. Indeed, much of the psychological research on attitudes is concerned with internal inconsistencies, transient context effects, and more enduring changes.

The notion of economic value is obviously much more powerful and constraining than the notion of attitude, which is compatible with a much larger range of observations—and therefore of more questionable value in explaining any of them. A scientist with the normal taste for simplicity would surely prefer a world in which people have preference orders over a world in which people only have attitudes. In the terms of a related distinction drawn by Fischhoff (1991), the theorist's life is simpler and more satisfying if people have articulated values (a preexisting preference order) than if they generally construct their preferences on the fly. Unfortunately, however, research has shown that the constraints of stability, invariance, and context independence are violated readily and often, which inevitably reduces the descriptive usefulness of the simpler concept of an articulated economic value. Like it or not, then, we have to make do with weaker notions, such as attitudes and constructed values. This pessimistic conclusion applies with special force to the valuation of nonmarket goods, such as environmental assets and interventions.

Preference reversals have long been recognized as a major source of evidence against the standard notion of a preference order. A preference reversal is said to occur when the proportion of respondents who appear to prefer one option over another changes substantially depending on the mode of preference elicitation. Much research has focused on reversals between choice and pricing of gambles (Lichtenstein and Slovic, 1973; Tversky, Slovic, and Kahneman, 1990). This research established that the probability of winning and the amount that can be won are weighted differently in choice and in pricing. Other studies have focused on discrepancies between the tasks of choice and of adjusting two options to equivalence, concluding that the more prominent attribute of the options is assigned more weight in choice than in matching (Tversky, Sattath, and Slovic, 1988). A third strand of research has examined discrepancies between measures of preference obtained when the objects of choice are considered one at a time or directly compared (Hsee, 1996; Blount and Bazerman, 1996).

Two types of reversals have been demonstrated in the domain of environmental goods. Irwin and others (1993) contrasted evaluation of public and private goods. Participants in their study indicated their WTP for an increment in the quality of a private good (such as a better VCR) as well as their WTP for an increment in an environmental good such as air quality. These evaluations were obtained either separately or as a direct choice. The researchers found that subjects were willing to pay more to improve the private good than the environmental good. When forced to choose, however, they tended to prefer the environmental good over the private one.

Kahneman and Ritov (1994) examined preference reversals with different types of public goods. Some participants stated their willingness to pay for a set of public interventions, considered one at a time, and under instructions to make independent evaluations. The issues included ecological problems and problems pertaining to human health or safety. Individual preferences for selected pairs of items, one from each domain, were derived from the WTP that the individual had separately stated for these items. Other participants were asked to make a choice between the same two items. Table 3.3 presents the results for seven pairs of problems.

Table 3.3. Choice and WTP: Human Safety Versus Passive Use.

	Choice	*WTP*	*Chi-Square*
Replace paint	154	47	
Elephants	57	40	10.08 $p < .001$
ties		28	
Skin cancer	72	33	
Australian mammals	31	36	8.47 $p < .01$
ties		43	
Myeloma	60	20	
Coral reefs	50	46	9.78 $p < .01$
ties		46	
Skin cancer	42	33	
Dolphins	16	40	9.77 $p < .01$
ties		40	
Earthquake safety	29	19	
Spotted owl	29	58	9.26 $p < .01$
ties		37	
Toxic spills	38	22	
Sharp visibility	18	33	8.67 $p < .01$
ties		49	
Carbon dioxide	42	29	
Mild visibility	15	32	8.40 $p < .01$
ties		51	

Source: Adapted from Kahneman and Ritov (1994).
Adapted with kind permission from Kluwer Academic Publishers.

A highly consistent pattern emerged: the relative preference for environmental interventions was substantially more pronounced in the WTP task than in direct choices between interventions that would improve the ecology and interventions that would directly affect human health or safety. For example, people were willing to pay more to save dolphins than to provide medical checkups to farmworkers threatened with skin cancer, but they tended to prefer the latter when forced to choose between the two.

Irwin and her colleagues (1993) explain the preference reversal they observed by pointing out that choice problems are often resolved by invoking arguments, "and there are many powerful, even noble, arguments in favor of one's placing higher personal value on improved environmental quality" (p. 8). Bazerman, Wade-Benzoni, and Benzoni (1995) expanded this idea, suggesting that Irwin's problems reveal a tension between what individuals want to do and what they think they should do. People want the private good but think they ought to prefer the public environmental good. The weight of the ethical considerations increases when the situation forces a choice. The weight of personal desires is stronger in the more ambiguous situation in which items are priced one at a time. The same account could be extended to the preference reversals illustrated in Table 3.3, suggesting that the following ordering applies to the moral considerations that dominate choice: human health and safety > ecological problems > inessential private goods.

Why do moral considerations have more impact in choices than in the evaluation of single options? Norm theory (Kahneman and Miller, 1986) suggests a possible answer. According to this theory an item that is presented alone evokes a context of alternatives to which it is then compared. The alternatives that are evoked tend to share the essential attributes of the target object. In the language of norm theory essential attributes are (relatively) immutable. The norm to which the object is compared consists of objects that share the immutable properties of the eliciting object and differ from it in mutable attributes. Paradoxically, this process causes the judgment of the target object to be affected primarily by attributes that are neither central nor prominent, because they are the only ones that vary. In contrast a direct comparison of two options that differ in prominent properties is likely to be strongly influenced by these differences. In other words this analysis proposes that single-object judgments (but not choices) involve a process of spontaneous categorization, which sets the reference class to which the target object is compared. Thus an ecological problem presented on its own is likely to evoke a norm that consists mainly of other ecological problems—issues of human health or possibilities of acquiring inessential private goods will not spontaneously come to

Table 3.4. Mean Rating of Problems, by Presentation Condition.

	Dolphins	***Farmworkers (Skin Cancer)***
Judged alone	4.48	2.42
Judged second	4.42	4.56

mind. The morally significant difference between these categories of problems will therefore have much less effect on single-object judgments than on choices.

The foregoing analysis suggests a strong form of context dependence in measures of attitudes, in which evaluations of objects considered alone or in direct comparisons are affected by different factors. The comparative process is sometimes evoked even when not explicitly required: if the same judgment is requested about just two items in immediate succession, for example, a comparison is quite likely to be made.

We conducted a small exercise to demonstrate this effect with ecological and health problems. The participants (seventy-five Princeton undergraduates) encountered either a single question or two questions on the same page. The questions asked for an indication of support for a public intervention to deal with a specified problem. The response was made on a 10-point rating scale anchored by "Do not support" and "Strongly support." The two issues were "high incidence of skin cancer in farmworkers," and "a threat to dolphins in some breeding locations, due to pollution." Table 3.4 presents mean ratings for each item when it was shown alone and also when it was the second item on the response form. The main result is that there was little support for an intervention addressing the health problems of farmworkers when that issue was considered on its own; there was substantially more support for the same intervention when it followed an intervention to save dolphins (the interaction effect is significant, $F(1,71) = 5.46$, $p < .02$). We surmise that the ratings of an issue presented in isolation reflect its relative standing in the context that it spontaneously evokes: the incidence of skin cancer among farmworkers probably appears to be a relatively minor public health problem, whereas the threat to dolphins appears relatively more significant in an ecological context. When the two problems are considered in immediate succession, the contrast between human and animal victims becomes salient.

Conclusion

The premise of this chapter was that we must understand how people value public issues in general and environmental issues in particular, before we can provide useful answers to the question of how values should be measured. Analyses carried out in the intellectual context of environmental economics are prone to apply the model of standard consumer theory to environmental issues—even including the value of the existence of assets that the respondent will not personally consume (known as nonuse values or passive values). We have seen that the economic concept of value, which underlies the contingent valuation method, is characterized by psychologically unrealistic logical constraints. We believe that the psychological concept of attitudes—which is inherently less constrained—provides a more useful descriptive framework.

The existing evidence that was reviewed and the new results that were introduced support the following conclusions: (1) different measures of attitude tend to yield very similar ranking of issues; (2) contrary to an economic model of value, measures of attitude (including WTP) toward public issues are mainly determined by the severity of problems, not by the features of proposed interventions; (3) extensional aspects, which are not incorporated in particular exemplars, have little effect on evaluations, perhaps because the representation of an ecological problem is dominated by images of representative exemplars; (4) ecological problems, such as damage to species, are less prominent than problems that more directly affect the welfare of humans; (5) the true importance of ecological concerns relative to other public problems is therefore likely to be overestimated when respondents are encouraged to consider ecological problems without reference to human problems.

The effects of context on evaluations raise important conceptual and methodological questions. The conceptual issue is one of selection: If the same object is evaluated differently in different contexts, which of these evaluations should count? A similar question can be raised about framing effects, where extensionally equivalent descriptions of decision problems lead to different preferences. The choice of an optimal context or frame should invoke the same general principle of rational framing: the more inclusive frames and the more inclusive contexts are likely to yield the better decisions and the sounder evaluations—unless the selection of the more extensive frame or context is biased. This principle implies that it is generally better to elicit comparative judgments or choices between competing alternatives than evaluations of isolated options, and that preferences among alternatives of different types are more informative than preferences within a homogeneous set of options. It is worth noting that these recommendations are directly contrary to the theory and practice of contingent valuation, where it is assumed that providing respondents with enough information about a particular issue is sufficient to ensure coherent evaluations.

The attitudes that we have measured are remarkably robust to one class of manipulations but highly susceptible to another. Ostensibly different attitude measures yielded highly similar orderings of issues when judgments were made one at a time. However, observed preference reversals indicated that a requirement to make explicit comparisons would yield a different ranking of issues. The two types of ranking may have different behavioral significance. Measures of attitude toward single objects may predict statements of WTP in contingent valuation exercises. They could also predict responses to other opportunities to become engaged in public issues (Krosnick and others, 1993). Choice measures, especially when they involve items from different categories, appear to provide a more adequate representation of public opinion for the purpose of policymaking.

REFERENCES

Andreoni, J. "Impure Altruism and Donations to Public Goods: A Theory of Warm-Glow Giving." *Economic Journal,* 1990, *100,* 464–477.

Bar-Hillel, M., and Fischhoff, B. "When Do Base Rates Affect Predictions." *Journal of Personality and Social Psychology,* 1991, *41,* 671–680.

Baron, J., and Greene, J. "Determinants of Insensitivity to Quantity in Valuation of Public Goods: Contribution, Warm Glow, Budget Constraints, Availability, and Prominence." *Journal of Experimental Psychology: Applied,* 1996, *2,* 107–125.

Bazerman, M. H., Wade-Benzoni, K. A., and Benzoni, F. J. "Environmental Degradation: Exploring the Rift Between Environmentally Benign Attitudes and Environmentally Destructive Behaviors." In D. M. Messick and A. E. Tenbrunsel (eds.), *Codes of Conduct.* New York: Russell Sage Foundation, 1995.

Blount, S., and Bazerman, M. H. "The Inconsistent Evaluation of Comparative Payoffs in Labor Supply and Bargaining." *Journal of Economic Behavior and Organization,* 1996, *57,* 426–441.

Boyle, K. J., and others. "An Investigation of Part-Whole Biases in Contingent-Valuation Studies." *Journal of Environmental Economics and Management,* 1994, *27,* 64–83.

Carson, R., and Mitchell, R. "The Issue of Scope in Contingent Evaluation Studies." *American Journal of Agricultural Economics,* 1995, *75,* 1263–1267.

Desvousges, W. H., and others. *Measuring Non-Use Damages Using Contingent Valuation: An Experimental Evaluation Accuracy.* Monograph 92–1. Raleigh, N.C.: Research Triangle Institute, 1992.

Diamond, P. "Testing the Internal Consistency of Contingent Valuation Surveys." *Journal of Environmental Economics and Management,* 1996, *30,* 337–347.

Diamond, P., and Hausman, D. "Contingent Valuation: Is Some Number Better Than No Number?" *Journal of Economic Perspectives,* 1994, *8,* 45–64.

Eagly, A., and Chaiken, S. *The Psychology of Attitudes.* Orlando, Fla.: Harcourt Brace, 1993.

Fischhoff, B. "Value Elicitation: Is There Anything in There?" *American Psychologist,* 1991, *46,* 835–847.

Fredrickson, B., and Kahneman, D. "Duration Neglect in Retrospective Evaluations of Affective Episodes." *Journal of Personality and Social Psychology,* 1993, *65,* 45–55.

Hanemann, M. "Valuing the Environment Through Contingent Valuation." *Journal of Economic Perspectives,* 1994, *8,* 19–43.

Hausman, J. (ed.). *Contingent Valuations: A Critical Assessment.* Contributions to Economic Analysis. Vol. 220. New York: North Holland, 1993.

Hsee, C. "The Evaluability Principle: An Explanation for Preference Reversals Between Joint and Separate Evaluations." *Organizational Behavior and Human Decision Processes,* 1996, *67,* 247–257.

Irwin, J. R., and others. "Preference Reversals and the Measurement of Environmental Values." *Journal of Risk and Uncertainty,* 1993, *6,* 5–18.

Kahneman, D. "Valuing Environmental Goods: An Assessment of the Contingent Valuation Method." In R. Cummings, D. Brookshire, and W. Schultze (eds.), *Valuing Environmental Goods: An Assessment of the Contingent Valuation Method.* Totowa, N.J.: Rowman and Allanheld, 1986.

Kahneman, D. "Extension Neglect and Violations of Monotonicity in Judgment and Preference: Three Examples." Bartlett Lecture to the Experimental Psychology Society (UK), July 1995.

Kahneman, D., Fredrickson, D., Schreiber, C., and Redelmeier, D. "When More Pain Is Preferred to Less." *Psychological Science,* 1993, *4,* 401–405.

Kahneman, D., and Knetsch, J. "Valuing Public Goods: The Purchase of Moral Satisfaction." *Journal of Environmental Economics and Management,* 1992, *22,* 57–70.

Kahneman, D., and Miller, D. T. "Norm Theory: Comparing Reality to Its Alternatives." *Psychological Review,* 1986, *93,* 136–153.

Kahneman, D., and Ritov, I. "Determinants of Stated Willingness to Pay for Public Goods: A Study in the Headline Method." *Journal of Risk and Uncertainty,* 1994, *9,* 5–38.

Kahneman, D., Ritov, I., Jacowitz, K. E., and Grant, P. "Stated Willingness to Pay for Public Goods: A Psychological Perspective." *Psychological Science,* 1993, *4,* 310–315.

Kahneman, D., and Tversky, A. "On the Psychology of Prediction." *Psychological Review,* 1973, *80,* 237–254.

Koehler, J. "The Base Rate Fallacy Reconsidered: Descriptive, Normative, and Methodological Challenges." *Behavioral Brain Science,* 1996, *19,* 1–53.

Krosnick, J., and others. "Attitude Strength: One Construct or Many Related Constructs?" *Journal of Personality and Social Psychology,* 1993, *65,* 1132–1151.

Ladd, E. C., and Bowman, K. H. *Attitudes Toward the Environment. Twenty-Five Years After Earth Day.* Washington, D.C.: AEI Press, 1995.

Lichtenstein, S., and Slovic, P. "Response-Induced Reversals of Preference in Gambling: An Extended Replication in Las Vegas." *Journal of Experimental Psychology,* 1973, *101,* 16–20.

Margolis, H. *Selfishness, Altruism, and Rationality: A Theory of Social Choice.* New York: Cambridge University Press, 1982.

Mitchell, R., and Carson, R. *Using Surveys to Value Public Goods.* Washington, D.C.: Resources for the Future, 1989.

Nickerson, C.A.E. "Does Willingness-to-Pay Reflect the Purchase of Moral Satisfaction? A Reconsideration of Kahneman and Knetsch." *Journal of Environmental Economics and Management,* 1995, *28,* 126–133.

Novemsky, N., Kronzon, S., and Kahneman, D. "Parallels Between Quantity Neglect in Willingness to Pay and Base-Rate Neglect." Poster presented at the American Psychological Society convention, San Francisco, 1996.

Portney, P. "The Contingent Valuation Debate: Why Economists Should Care." *Journal of Economic Perspectives,* 1994, *8,* 3–17.

Schreiber, C., and Kahneman, D. "Beyond the Peak and End Hypothesis: Exploring the Relation Between Real-Time Pleasure and Retrospective Evaluations." Unpublished manuscript, 1996.

Tversky, A., and Kahneman, D. "Rational Choice and the Framing of Decisions." *Journal of Business,* 1986, *59,* 251–278.

Tversky, A., Sattath, S., and Slovic, P. "Contingent Weighting in Judgment and Choice." *Psychological Review,* 1988, *95,* 371–384.

Tversky, A., Slovic, P., and Kahneman, D. "The Causes of Preference Reversal." *American Economic Review,* 1990, *80,* 204–217.

4

PREDICTING REACTIONS TO ENVIRONMENTAL CHANGE

George Loewenstein and Shane Frederick

ALL DECISIONS REQUIRE us to evaluate counterfactuals—situations other than the one we are in. Decision makers routinely ask themselves questions such as, How would I feel eating that dish, driving around in that car, married to that person, attending that school, or vacationing in that country? Questions of this type require predictions of what Daniel Kahneman calls "experience utility" (Kahneman and Snell, 1990, 1992). The accuracy of such predictions is critical for effective decision making. If we underestimate how good it will feel driving around in a nice car, we may fail to purchase that car when we should. If we overestimate how good it will feel, we may later regret purchasing it.

The accuracy of predicted experience utility (PEU) is also relevant for environmental decisions, such as whether to support environmental legislation that would raise taxes or prices, to participate in recycling programs, or to donate time or money to environmental causes. Like all other decisions, these require predictions of experience utility—for example, assessments of how bad it would be if the rain forests disappeared or if lakes became too acidified to support fish or how good it would be if air quality improved or if the California condor recovered. If such predictions

We thank Jon Baron, Baruch Fischhoff, Jack Knetsch, and the editors for helpful comments. This research was funded by the Center for the Integrated Study of the Human Dimensions of Global Change at Carnegie Mellon University.

systematically overestimate or underestimate the impact of environmental problems on experience utility, people may invest too much or too little in the environment. Furthermore, if people underestimate the effects of some problems while exaggerating the effects of others, they may misallocate scarce resources.

Appropriate public policy decisions also depend on the accuracy of PEU. In recent decades, there has been a trend toward basing public policy on private citizens' values. The best known of these efforts is Oregon's attempts to use public perceptions of the severity of different health outcomes to make rationing decisions for scarce health care dollars. In the environmental arena, new techniques such as *contingent valuation* have been developed to measure the public value of different environmental amenities. These values are used for allocating government spending, for making various types of siting and development decisions, and for guidance in litigation involving environmental degradation, such as oil or chemical spills.

Such survey-based measures of public values inevitably require predictions of experience utility; people have to imagine what it would be like to be in a different health condition or to experience an environmental state different from that currently prevailing. So the meaningfulness of measured values and the optimality of the policies based on them are constrained by the accuracy of PEU. This problem has not escaped the notice of practitioners in these areas. Consider, for example, the controversy over the siting of the federal government's high-level nuclear waste repository. Because the process of constructing and filling the repository would not be completed for another forty to sixty years, the main impacts of the repository will be delayed by almost half a century. Paul Slovic and other social scientists who have been commissioned to measure public attitudes and preferences toward the proposed repository have lamented the difficulty of eliciting preferences for such delayed outcomes. As Slovic notes, asking people to predict, for example, how the repository might affect vacation decisions to be made in the distant future might be "asking them to tell more than they can know" (Slovic and others, 1991, p. 684).

To gain insight into the accuracy of PEU for environment-related issues, one would ideally want to ask people to predict how they will feel about environmental changes that are likely to occur in the ensuing years, and then compare these predictions to actual ratings made after the projected states were experienced. For example, one might ask people to predict how much they would be disturbed by the smells emanating from a paper mill, the sounds of an airport runway, or the visual obstruction of power lines that are scheduled for construction, and then compare these predictions with their reported disturbance at different times after those facilities have been operating. Unfortunately, such a study would be infeasible for many important gradual environmental changes, such as global climate warming. In fact, even if researchers possessed the resources and patience to conduct a panel study on prediction accuracy, it is unlikely that its findings would be very revealing. With so much time passing between initial predictions and subsequent ratings, standard threats to internal validity, such as history, maturation, and instrumentation (in this case, changes in the way that respondents use the response scales), would pose formidable obstacles.

Is there any hope, then, of assessing the accuracy of PEU in environmental domains? Perhaps. Several existing studies have examined the accuracy of PEU in nonenvironmental contexts—mostly for health-related decisions—where people's future quality of life may depend critically on the accuracy of their PEU. Patients facing major medical procedures are often required to make extremely important life decisions and to provide "informed" consent, with little understanding of how the potential outcomes of alternative treatments would be experienced. Recognizing this problem, new decision aids (such as taped interviews of people who have experienced each outcome) have been developed to help inform patients about the possible outcomes of different treatments (Agre, Kurtz, and Krauss, 1994; Hopper and others, 1994).

Other researchers have begun to examine the accuracy of patients' PEU for health conditions by comparing prospective *overall health* or *quality of life* ratings with similar ratings taken after the medical treatment or procedure. Such studies attempt to determine whether patients can accurately predict the effects of medical procedures on their well-being without direct prior experience of the possible consequences. These studies and others conducted in different contexts are beginning to produce some insights into the factors that mediate experience utilities and the influences that cause people to overestimate or underestimate these utilities. The next section, "Theory and Evidence," reviews some of the findings from this emergent field of research, both in the medical and nonmedical domain, and attempts to draw out their implications for the accuracy of PEU in the environmental domain.

It is also possible to crudely test the accuracy of PEU in the environmental domain by employing a cross-sectional design rather than a prospective panel study. The research summary later in this chapter presents results from such a study, in which we asked one group of people to rate the impact on their lives of environmental changes that *have occurred* over the last decade and a second group to predict the impact of comparable changes that *may occur* in the next decade.

We close by discussing the dilemma created when accurate PEU conflicts with current preferences or values. For example, suppose evidence suggests that degradations in health or environmental conditions confer little long-term disutility. Should this information override people's current preferences that strongly oppose such deterioration? Should current opposition to increased air pollution be discounted if it partly reflects an ignorance of how rapidly or completely people adapt to reductions in air quality? We do not resolve this dilemma but do question the appropriateness of basing policy decisions *solely* on estimates of experienced utility (even when those estimates *are* accurate).

Theory and Evidence

Evidence on the accuracy of PEU is mixed. To try to make sense of the disparate findings, we have classified them into several categories, based on whether the experience being predicted is desirable or undesirable and on whether EU is accurately estimated, underestimated, or overestimated. Our intention is not to cover all cases of PEU, but only those most relevant to environmental change.[1]

Adapting to Negative Changes

The case of adapting to negative changes is most relevant to environmental decision making. Although some government programs (such as Superfund) and some individual decisions (such as removing garbage from a trout stream) are intended to produce positive changes, most environmental policies are intended to prevent further degradation. The question is whether people can accurately anticipate the effect of such degradation on their own future experience utility.

ACCURATELY PREDICTING ABILITY (OR INABILITY) TO ADAPT TO NEGATIVE CHANGES. Most studies of adaptation to negative change have been conducted in the domain of health care. Many of these studies have documented relatively accurate predictions of PEU. For example, Llewellyn-Thomas, Sutherland, and Thiel (1993) informed sixty-six laryngeal cancer patients of common outcomes of radiation therapy and asked them to predict how they would feel after four weeks of radiation therapy using direct utility rating scales and time trade-off measures of utility. Following completion of the therapy, patients described their actual end-of-therapy state and assigned a utility to it. The researchers found that the utility ratings were remarkably close to the values predicted prior to therapy. Rachman and Eyrl (1989) found that people suffering from chronic headaches were relatively accurate in predicting the intensity of future headaches. Hunter, Philips, and Rachman (1979) found that neurosurgical patients' recall of acute pain was "surprisingly accurate" up to five days after an experience of acute pain. Kent (1985) reported reasonably accurate predictions of dental pain.

Furthermore, it seems likely that the number of published studies finding no prediction bias understates the prevalence of this finding. Here, as elsewhere, biases are more interesting than accurate predictions and therefore more likely to be published. For example, a graduate student in our department collected data in small claims court to determine whether people in the heart of a dispute could predict the likely fact that they would cool off with time. She asked disputants to predict how they would feel six weeks after they won or lost the case and then followed them up six weeks later. She dropped the project when the results began to show that disputants' predictions of their own feelings were relatively accurate.

UNDERESTIMATING ABILITY TO ADAPT TO NEGATIVE CHANGES. There is very little direct evidence showing underestimation of adaptation to negative changes. However, many findings strongly suggest that people are remarkably good at adapting to or coping with deficiencies or inconveniences in the circumstances of their life. This is true generally, as when people adapt to the gradual loss of vigor as they age, and specifically, as when people get used to the noise of their computer's hard drive. In a famous study, Brickman, Coates, and Janoff-Bulman (1978) asked lottery winners, accident victims, and a control group a series of questions about past and present happiness. The lottery group consisted of twenty-two people who had recently (within the last year) won between $50,000 and $1,000,000 in the Illinois state lottery. The victim group consisted of twenty-nine people who had suffered a debilitating accident within the last year that had left them paraplegic or quadriplegic. Though accident victims did rate their current happiness as significantly lower than the control group or the lottery winners (2.96, 3.82 and 4.00, respectively, on a 5-point scale) the differences still seem small given the extremity of these outcomes. (Note that the victim group still rated their happiness as 2.96, which is above average on a 5-point scale). Although the researchers did not ask people to predict their own experience utilities beforehand (because lottery winners and accident victims cannot be identified beforehand), most people are so surprised by the results of the study that it seems likely that the respondents themselves would have underpredicted their own adaptation had they been asked.

Another set of studies has looked at how people react to good or bad news about disease states. Intuitively, one might think that having a less than 100 percent ($p < 1$) chance of a negative outcome (such as being infected with an incurable disease) would not be as bad as knowing for sure that one has the disease. Indeed, this belief seems to prevent people from getting (or performing on themselves) various medical tests, as was shown in the context of testing for Huntington's disease (for example, Mastromauro, Myers, and Berkman, 1987) and breast self-examination (Kash, Holland, Halper, and Miller, 1992). However, Brandt and others (1989) found no major disruptions in the lives of people one year after they had received an unfavorable test result for Huntington's disease (using a test for which a positive test result means a 95 percent probability of developing the disease). Wiggins and others (1992) found that people showed *less* psychopathology one year after receiving a positive HIV result than they did at the time of testing.

Thus, despite the widespread fear of adverse medical results, many studies have found that people are not only surprisingly quick to adapt to bad news but sometimes feel better after receiving it. However, none of these studies directly addressed the accuracy of PEU because none elicited such predictions. To address this gap in the literature, Sieff, Dawes, and Loewenstein (1994) conducted a study in which people who were tested for HIV predicted how they would feel about five weeks after obtaining the test results. The survey consisted of two twenty-one-item mood inventories. Subjects completed one survey based on how they would expect to feel in five weeks if they obtained a negative (favorable) result and another survey based on how they would expect to feel if they obtained a positive (unfavorable) result. The study was intended to be within-subject, but the very low rate of positive results precluded any meaningful comparisons of predicted versus actual mood among those with positive results. As a highly imperfect remedy to this problem, the researchers advertised in local newspapers for people who had received HIV test results in the last four to ten weeks, and selected a sample of positives from this group. Though the results are confounded by the noncomparability of the groups, they indicate underprediction of adaptation. As is evident from the figures in Table 4.1, respondents predicted greater misery than the people in the group that tested positive for HIV reported feeling. (They also predicted greater elation than they themselves later felt following a negative [favorable] test result.)

Table 4.1. Anticipated Versus Actual Distress Following HIV Testing.

ANTICIPATED VERSUS ACTUAL DISTRESS 4–6 WEEKS FOLLOWING UNFAVORABLE TEST RESULT (BETWEEN-SUBJECT ANALYSIS)

	N	*Mean*	*SD*	*t(df)*	*p*
Anticipated	50	94.7	22.6	2.9(69)	.005
Actual	21	77.6	21.8		

ANTICIPATED VERSUS ACTUAL DISTRESS 4–6 WEEKS FOLLOWING FAVORABLE TEST RESULT (BETWEEN- AND WITHIN-SUBJECT ANALYSIS)

	N	*Mean*	*SD*	*t(df)*	*p*
Anticipated	49	47.4	16.1	–3.9(92)	.002
Actual	54	59.1	19.4		

ANTICIPATED VERSUS ACTUAL DISTRESS 4-6 WEEKS FOLLOWING FAVORABLE TEST RESULT (WITHIN-SUBJECT ANALYSIS)

	N	*Mean*	*SD*	*t(df)*	*p*
Anticipated	25	49.8	17.8	1.5(24)	.15
Actual	25	54.7	20.7		

Note: Larger numbers signify greater distress.

OVERESTIMATING ABILITY TO ADAPT TO NEGATIVE CHANGES. People may also overpredict their ability to adapt to, adjust to, or accommodate the persistence or development of an irritation, inconvenience, imperfection, limitation, or deficiency. For example, we are often mistaken when we believe that we will get used to someone's nasal voice or eccentric habit, or cease to notice a cosmetic blemish, or become accustomed to a new inconvenience like having to separate the garbage or put the toilet seat down. However, though there seems to be abundant anecdotal evidence suggesting that we sometimes adapt less than we hope or expect, we know of little research documenting a systematic overestimation error of this type.

Tuning

For adverse outcomes, adaptation is likely to be reinforced by another process that could be called "tuning." Instead of simply passively adapting to bads, in the sense of getting used to them, people may take active steps to mold their preferences or their material circumstances to deal with such changes. For example, when people move to a new city, the initial transition is often difficult because they arrive with tastes and habits tailored to their previous location. Over time, however, tastes change, and people learn how to take advantage of the amenities offered by the new location. If the new city has great restaurants, the migrant develops an appreciation for fine food; if it offers opportunities for outdoor recreation, she takes up bicycling. Note that for undesirable changes, adaptation and tuning both have the same effect—they reduce the aversiveness of the change over time. For desirable changes, however, the two processes oppose one another; adaptation leads to a decline in utility, but tuning leads to a progressive improvement over time as people adjust their preferences or change their behavior to benefit maximally from the change.

Tuning may be important in adapting to adverse health conditions. Perhaps the paraplegics studied by Brickman, Coates, and Janoff-Bulman had already developed new interests and new friends by the time they completed the survey, and one can imagine that people in highly polluted environments develop tastes and hobbies that minimize their contact with the pollution. When people think about change, we conjecture that they imagine the new situation holding their current lifestyle constant and thereby overestimate the long-term severity of negative changes. It seems likely, therefore, that people not only underestimate how their psychological experience of a given situation will change over time but also underestimate their ability to alter which things they experience.

Adapting to Positive Changes (Satiation)

Social scientists have little understanding of why people rapidly adapt to some negative changes but become increasingly sensitized to others over time. Equally unknown are people's predictions and responses to *positive* changes—why people sometimes experience rapid satiation and other times not, and why they fail or succeed in predicting the extent of satiation.

For positive changes, rapid adaptation is a *li*ability, rather than an ability. It would clearly be preferable if newly discovered pleasures could not be satiated—if hobbies, television shows, or music albums never lost their novelty, if our romantic or sexual attraction never waned, if our elation over being promoted or receiving a favorable medical test lasted for years, rather than days or hours. Unfortunately, we rapidly adapt to many of the positive changes in our life so that they cease to bring us much pleasure. We often fail to appreciate the expanding consumption our increasing income makes possible (Scitovsky, 1976), and we may gradually take for granted the wonderful qualities of our friends or spouses. Nevertheless, not everything is subject to this phenomenon. Our new apartment's impressive view may remain impressive after millions of viewings, and there may be some people you "just can't get enough of."

How accurately can people predict their liability to adapt to positive changes? How well can they discriminate between those goods, activities, or consequences whose pleasure is fleeting and those that endure as life-long sources of pleasure? If people could accurately predict their rapid accommodation to increased influence or income, would they work as diligently for a promotion? Conversely, if people could accurately predict that the pleasure of some activities (such as musical or artistic activities) is relatively resistant to the eroding forces of adaptation, would they work harder developing the skills necessary for their enjoyment?

Only a few studies, to our knowledge, have looked at predictions of experience utility under conditions of potential satiation. Kahneman and Snell (1990) had subjects predict their future liking of either ice cream or plain yogurt, which was to be consumed every day for eight consecutive days. The subjects who ate the ice cream correctly predicted satiation—that they would enjoy the ice cream less over time. The subjects who ate the plain yogurt also expected to like it less over time but, in fact, liked it more (or disliked it less—for those subjects who considered eating plain yogurt an aversive experience).

In another pertinent study, Itamar Simonson (1990) compared the desire for variety when people choose consumption items sequentially versus simultaneously. He uncovered a phenomenon he refers to as the "diversification bias." In one condition (simultaneous choice), students chose from among six snack types the three snacks they would eat during that class and the following two classes. In the other condition (sequential choice), students chose their snacks on the same day they were to be consumed. Students chose substantially more variety when all the choices were bracketed together (the simultaneous choice condition) than when they were bracketed individually (in the sequential choice condition). In a follow-up to Simonson's paper, Read and Loewenstein (1995) replicated his effect and also showed that subjects in the simultaneous choice condition regretted opting for variety. When the second and third class meetings arose, subjects generally wished they had chosen to consume the same snack for all three days.

Surprisingly, overestimating satiation to a positive stimulus (saltiness, sweetness, nuttiness, and so on) and underpredicting adaptation to a negative stimulus (receiving an unfavorable test result) may both reflect what Read and Loewenstein (1995) call "time dilation"—the tendency to ignore or underweight time intervals occurring between consumption. If subjects imagine the three consumption episodes as occurring during a single instant (or over a very short period of time), they will overestimate the degree of satiation (for example, the extent to which eating a Snickers bar on the first day interferes with the pleasure of eating a Snickers bar on the second day).[2] Similarly, if people prospectively ignore or underweight the time interval following the receipt of bad news, they may underpredict their extent of adaptation at future times.

Research Summary

The research just discussed presents a mixed picture concerning the ability to predict future experience utility. If a systematic bias predominates, it seems to be a tendency to underestimate the strength of adaptation. One would expect this particular bias to be especially prevalent for environmental changes, due to the long periods involved and the apparent tendency to time dilate, that is, to underappreciate the length of time intervals.

Testing the Accuracy of Environmental and Nonenvironmental PEU

As noted earlier, conducting a prospective study of the accuracy of PEU is often infeasible. As a substitute, we conducted a cross-sectional study in which we asked some respondents to rate how different events that had occurred in the past decade *had affected* their quality of life, and we asked other respondents to predict how matched events that might occur in the next decade *would affect* their quality of life. Where appropriate, we also asked subjects to rate how the past or predicted change had or would "change the quality of life in this country as a whole." We chose twelve different changes, four environmental, four social, and four personal, as follows:

ENVIRONMENTAL

- Change in local air pollution
- Rain forest destruction

- Restriction of sport fishing due to pollution
- Recovery of certain endangered species

SOCIAL

- Increase in number of coffee shops and cafes
- Increase in number of television channels and selection of videotapes
- Reduced risk of nuclear war
- Increased risk of AIDS

PERSONAL

- Change in free time
- Development of pain-causing chronic health condition
- Change in household income
- Increase in body weight

In some cases, such as the increase in television channels, we knew that the event had happened for virtually everyone during the last decade and that it was almost certain to continue during the next decade. In other cases, such as weight gain, we did not know whether the individual had experienced the event during the past decade and therefore included a question to determine whether he or she had. Subjects in the prediction condition were asked to assume that they would experience such a change over the next decade (for example, that they would gain fifteen pounds). In still other cases, such as a change in free time, we asked the retrospective group whether the change had occurred and the members of the prospective group whether they expected the change to occur. We then compared the two groups, looking at subjects with matched recollections and predictions of change (for example, those who believed they had less free time than ten years ago and those who expected to have less free time ten years from now).

Method

Eighty-four adults waiting for flights at the Pittsburgh International Airport in November of 1995 were randomly assigned to complete one of the two surveys. Forty-one completed the retrospective survey and forty-three completed the prospective survey. Subjects received a chocolate bar for completing the self-administered survey. The survey began by eliciting demographic information—gender, age, household income, city of residence, and whether the respondent had lived in that city for at least ten years. Subjects then saw a quality of life "ladder" with rungs labeled from 0 ("worst life imaginable") to 100 ("best life imaginable"), and they were asked to position themselves on the scale. Subjects in the retrospective condition were asked whether the air quality in their city had *improved significantly, deteriorated significantly,* or *remained about the same* over the past ten years. Subjects in the prospective condition were asked to predict how (or if) the future air quality in their city would change, using the same three response options. Both groups were then asked to rate (or predict) how changes in air quality would affect the quality of their life. The response scale shown here is for the retrospective condition. (The scale for the prospective group was identical except for tense—for example, "has decreased" was replaced by "will decrease.")

How much has [described scenario] changed the quality of your life? (Circle one of the following, using the key shown below.)

L M S 0 S+ M+ L+

L = has *decreased* the quality of my life by a *large* amount (over 10 points on the ladder)

M = has *decreased* the quality of my life by a *moderate* amount (between 5 and 10 points on the ladder)

S = has *decreased* the quality of my life by a *small* amount (between 0 and 5 points on the ladder)

0 = has *not affected* the quality of my life at all, or does not apply to me.

S+ = has *increased* the quality of my life by a *small* amount (between 0 and 5 points on the ladder)

M+ = has *increased* the quality of my life by a *moderate* amount (between 5 and 10 points on the ladder)

L+ = has *increased* the quality of my life by a *large* amount (over 10 points on the ladder)

Results

Fifty-three percent of the respondents were male; the mean age was forty-six (SD = 15). Of the sixty-two subjects who responded to the income question, 65 percent had an income less than $20,000, and the remainder had incomes between $20,000 and $40,000. Given the surprisingly low income range, we can only speculate that people with higher incomes were less likely to answer this question. Sixty percent of the sample had lived in the same city for the last ten years. The mean quality of life was 76 on the 100-point scale (range from 12 to 100; SD = 17). The prospective and retrospective groups were similar on every dimension except income, for which the prospective group was marginally higher ($p < .10$).

The general pattern of results shown in Table 4.2 can be summarized as follows: people generally expect changes in their environments to have a greater impact on their quality of life than they actually seem to experience (or report experiencing). Seven of the eight significant or marginally significant differences in the table reflect this pattern (the increase in television channels shows the opposite pattern.) This pattern is most consistent with respect to the environmental problems; three out of three display the pattern of greater anticipated than experienced change. (Air quality was not included because the small numbers of respondents either reporting or

Table 4.2. Experienced Versus Predicted Impact on Life Satisfaction.

Description	*Experienced*	*Predicted*	*Significance (p <)*
Environmental			
Rain forest destruction	–.4	–1.2	.01
Restricted sport fishing due to pollution	–1.2	–1.8	.10
Recovery of certai endangered species	+.3	+.7	.11
Social			
Increase in coffee shops and cafes	+.2	0.0	n.s.
Increase in number of television channels and selection of videotapes	+.6	0.0	.02
Reduced risk of nuclear war	+.9	+.9	n.s.
Increased risk of AIDS	–.4	-1.0	.02
Personal			
Increase in free time	+.8	+1.8	.05
Decrease in free time	–.6	–.1	n.s.
Development of pain-causing chronic health condition	–1.7 (n = 8)	–1.6 (n = 37)	n.s.
Increase in body weight	–.6 (n = 18)	–1.2 (n = 37)	.10

predicting positive or negative changes in air quality precluded any comparison between the two groups.)

Change in income is excluded from Table 4.2 because a t test was not the appropriate analysis. Because we asked subjects how much their income had increased (or was expected to increase), we regressed change in quality of life against change in income. To test whether changes in income had a differential impact on quality of life when viewed retrospectively or prospectively, we modeled the interaction between condition and change in income as an independent variable. If people conform to the general pattern of exaggerating the impact of changes prospectively, we would expect to observe a positive interaction term. The actual estimated equation was

$$\textit{CHANGE}\text{ IN LIFE QUALITY} = .76 + .000015 \times CI + .000028 \times CI \times PROSP$$

$$p < .01 \qquad\qquad p < .10 \qquad\qquad R^2 = .27$$

where CI stands for change in income, and $PROSP$ is a dummy variable designating the prospective condition. Notice that although the interaction term is only marginally significant, the combined magnitude of the CI effect is roughly three times as high in the prospective condition (.000043 = .000015 + .000028) as in the retrospective condition (.000015). Stated simply, people expected income to influence their quality of life about three times as much as it actually seems to.

Table 4.3 presents comparisons between the impact on personal quality of life and the impact on the quality of life in the country for the five changes for which we included both kinds of impact. For all five changes, both negative or positive, people expected the impact on quality of life to be greater on the country than on themselves.

Table 4.3. Impact of Events: Self Versus Country.

Description	*Impact on Self*	*Impact on Country*	*Significance (p <)*
Rain forest destruction	–.8	–1.1	.05
Restricted sport fishing due to pollution	–.8	–1.4	.0001
Recovery of certain endangered species	+.6	+1.1	.0002
Reduced risk of nuclear war	+.9	+1.5	.0001
Increased risk of AIDS	–.7	–2.2	.0001

Discussion

Our results point to two major patterns. First, people seem to expect changes in their circumstances to affect their quality of life in the future more than equivalent things have affected their quality of life in the past. We can think of two possible reasons for this effect. First, and consistent with much of the evidence reviewed in the previous section, people may underestimate their own tendency to adapt to change. Second, they may overestimate the impact of any one factor on their quality of life. Clearly, quality of life depends on a wide variety of things, any one of which is likely to have only a small impact. However, perhaps when a respondent's attention is focused on a particular type of change (such as opportunities for fishing), he or she exaggerates its overall importance. Either of these mechanisms could explain the discrepancy between prospective and retrospective evaluations, and both predict that people exaggerate the overall impact of adverse and favorable changes in a particular area of their life.

The second major pattern we observe is a tendency to view the changes as having a greater effect on the country as a whole than for oneself. This effect could have a trivial cause; perhaps people simply increase their assessment to account for the numbers of people affected. But this seems unlikely to us because any such adjustment would be difficult to even represent on the 7-point scale in the questionnaire. An alternative, and we believe more plausible, explanation for this effect is that people answer the question about other people much as they answer questions about their own future selves—tending to underestimate the power of adaptation.

Clearly, the findings of this study should be interpreted cautiously. The cross-sectional methodology is a poor approximation of the within-subject panel study that one would ideally want to run. The cross-sectional methodology has two major pitfalls. First, it is difficult to equate the magnitude of changes that have occurred in the past with changes that will occur in the future. Subjects either may not view a given change as equally severe (for example, any further reduction in rain forests may seem more severe given that so many have already been depleted) or may simply not believe the assumptions posited in the survey (for example, that the risk of nuclear war has dramatically declined in the last ten years). However, it seems unlikely that the failure to equate past and future changes could account for the highly systematic discrepancies that we observed, unless future changes are typically expected to be more dramatic than past changes. The second major limitation is the failure to account for age effects. Given that the mean age of subjects in our two experimental conditions is equivalent, when we ask them to either look back on the last ten years or look forward to the next ten years, we are implicitly comparing two different decades of their lives. For example, in the retrospective condition, a thirty-year-old is being asked about the decade between ages twenty and thirty, whereas in the prospective condition, he or she is being asked about the decade between ages thirty and forty. To partly investigate the severity of this problem, we looked at the correlation between age and judgments of change in quality of life and found no significant relationship. We also ran regressions for each type of change in which the dependent variable was impact on quality of life and the independent variables were condition and age. In no case was the age coefficient significant. We also ran similar regression in which we added ten years to the ages of people in the prospective condition to take account of the fact that their questions dealt with a period one decade later. Again, controlling for age did not change the basic pattern of results.

Conclusion

In a seminal paper, James March noted that "rational choice involves two kinds of guesses: guesses about the future consequences of current actions and guesses about future preferences for those consequences" (1978, p. 589). Making decisions on the basis of biased assessments of how one will *feel* about outcomes is no less problematic than making decisions based on inaccurate assessments of the outcomes themselves. In the environmental domain, as in others, both types of predictions are important, but the lion's share of research has focused on the latter—on predicting the objective consequences of current actions, such as global warming, ozone depletion, and so on. There has been very little research looking at the accuracy of PEU in any domain and, to our knowledge, virtually none that focuses on the environment. This chapter is a first attempt to address this gap in the literature.

Predicting future preferences and values is difficult. Kahneman and Snell (1990) have shown that people have different intuitions regarding the dynamics of hedonic experience and that they often cannot predict their own future experience (much less the experience of individuals in future generations). This evidence has important implications. If people do not know what is good for them, we cannot assume that their choices maximize their utility (*utility* here means some measure of the hedonic quality of experiencing an event or its outcome; Kahneman and Varey, 1991).

However, although accurate PEU may be necessary for rational choice, it is far from clear that decisions should be based solely on PEU, even if accurate measures were available. Consider the following examples:

- There is some evidence that the inhabitants of poorer cities (Schneider, 1975), regions (Liu, 1970), or countries (Easterlin, 1973) are no less happy than the inhabitants of wealthier places. Suppose these studies are correct. Should we therefore conclude that economic development is a misguided goal? Similarly, if we discover that individuals with Down's syndrome are actually happier than average, should society discontinue research aimed at preventing it, or even find ways of inducing it *in utero*?
- If consequences are evaluated solely by the experienced utility of humans, should we conclude that environmental degradation is acceptable if it goes unnoticed by current and future generations? Should the government conceal or misrepresent the degree of environmental damage to minimize the detrimental effect of negative emotions on experienced utility? Conversely, should we conclude that the increased awareness of knowledge about some area (or some animal species) resulting from media coverage of some environmental calamity represents an increase in people's existence value and that the degradation is therefore beneficial? (How many people had even heard of Prince William Sound prior to the *Exxon Valdez* spill?)

There are (at least) two ways to reconcile apparent discrepancies between utilities inferred from actual choice or stated preference and the utilities reported in subjective measures of well-being. First, it is possible that the discrepancy is illusory because analyses of experience utility neglect the utility of transitions. *In the long run,* lottery winners may be no happier (nor paraplegics any sadder), but the brief period of ecstasy (or agony) immediately after winning the lottery (or becoming paralyzed) may justify the intense attraction of (or aversion to) those outcomes. Consider, for example, the aversiveness of getting a tooth drilled without anesthesia, or the horror of the final moments preceding an airplane crash, when the passengers realize that all is lost; it may not be unreasonable to place a large value on a relatively brief period of misery.

Second, the discrepancy might be caused by a type of *responsibility effect.* As Shefrin and Statman postulate (1984, p. 269), people may feel worse about an outcome when they have chosen it than when it just occurs (or just "is"). For example, an alternative world which has always lacked desert pupfish would be indistinguishable from the world we currently live in, where such species exist in small numbers in isolated places and are rarely seen or even known about by anyone (thereby lacking characteristics that affect people's choiceless experience utility). (See Loomes and Sugden, 1982, and Sugden, 1985, for a discussion of choice utility versus choiceless utility.) However, once a person is made aware of such a species and his or her attention is temporarily focused on its plight, that person may be willing to sacrifice considerable amounts of money to prevent the feeling that he or she stood by and chose not to help while the species went extinct.

The preceding discussion highlights the difficulty of reconciling experience and choice utility. Sometimes the discrepancy simply reflects errors in judgment that we should strive to eliminate. Do we really want to base public policy on the uninformed judgments of people who have never experienced the relevant outcomes? Do we want to base health rationing decisions on people's inaccurate assessments of the utility of different health states or base environmental policy on people's stereotypical, misguided images of the effects of different types of environmental degradation? At other times, however, the discrepant experience- and choice-based evaluations may reveal distinct aspects of human values. Thus, although most decision makers would surely want to consider how people experience outcomes, few would feel comfortable bequeathing a world so polluted that natural trees are replaced with plastic ones, even if the plastic trees are acceptable to (or even preferred by) future generations. We find ourselves persuaded by Tribe (1974, pp. 1325–1326), who argues that it is a mistake to value the environment solely in terms of how well it satisfies human preferences: "Policy analysts typically operate within a social, political, and intellectual tradition that regards the satisfaction of individual human wants as the only defensible measure of the good, a tradition that perceives the only legitimate task of reason to be that of consistently identifying and then serving individual appetite, preference, and desire. . . . To insist on the superiority of natural trees in the teeth of a convincing demonstration that plastic ones would equally well serve human purposes may seem irrational—yet the tendency to balk at the result of [such an] analysis remains."

We believe that the best resolution to this dilemma lies in informing people about the consequences of their decisions in the fullest, deepest manner possible. As we note, this is already a major trend in medical decision making, where new methods have been developed to make sure that informed consent really is informed. Acquiring and communicating understanding about changes in experience utilities will likely prove difficult for many environmental decisions because many of the consequences are uncertain, unfamiliar, delayed, or protracted. For now, perhaps the best that can be done is to educate private individuals and policymakers about what has been learned about general principles that mediate temporal changes in experience utility.

NOTES

1. One important topic relating to PEU is the ability to predict future emotions, drives, and somatic sensations such as hunger and pain. Loewenstein (1996) refers to these influences as "visceral factors" and discusses in detail two types of pervasive prediction errors: First, people seem to underestimate the impact of visceral factors when they are not experiencing them in the present. For example, when one is not hungry after lunch, it is difficult to appreciate the motivational force of the temptation one experiences if peanuts are available just before dinner. Second, when currently experiencing a visceral factor, people often have difficulty imagining themselves not experiencing it. When angry, it is difficult to imagine that one will cool off quickly; when hungry, it is difficult to imagine oneself satiated—hence the danger of grocery shopping "on an empty stomach."
2. Notably, when Read and Loewenstein emphasized the time intervals between class meetings, the discrepancy between sequential and simultaneous choice was significantly reduced.

REFERENCES

Agre, P. A., Kurtz, R. C., and Krauss, B. J. (1994). "A Randomized Trial Using Videotape to Present Consent Information for Colonoscopy." *Gastrointestinal Endoscopy,* 1994, *40*(3), 271–276.

Brandt, J., and others. "Presymptomatic Diagnosis of Delayed Onset Disease with Linked DNA Markers. The Experience in Huntington's Disease." *Journal of the American Medical Association,* 1989, *261*(21), 3108–3114.

Brickman, P., Coates, D., and Janoff-Bulman, R. "Lottery Winners and Accident Victims: Is Happiness Relative?" *Journal of Personality and Social Psychology,* 1978, *36,* 917–927.

Easterlin, R. "Does Money Buy Happiness?" *Public Interest,* 1973, *30,* 3–10.

Hopper, K. D., and others. "Interactive Method of Informing Patients of the Risks of Intravenous Contrast Media." *Radiology,* 1994, *192,* 67–71.

Hunter, M., Philips, C., and Rachman, S. "Memory for Pain." *Pain,* 1979, *6,* 35–46.

Kahneman, D., and Snell, J. "Predicting Utility." In R. M. Hogarth (ed.), *Insights in Decision Making: A Tribute to Hillel J. Einhorn.* Chicago: University of Chicago Press, 1990.

Kahneman, D., and Snell, J. "Predicting a Changing Taste: Do People Know What They Will Like?" *Journal of Behavioral Decision Making,* 1992, *5,* 187–200.

Kahneman, D., and Varey, C. "Notes on the Psychology of Utility." In J. Roemer and J. Elster (eds.), *Interpersonal Comparisons of Well-Being.* Cambridge, England: Cambridge University Press, 1991.

Kash, K. M., Holland, J. C., Halper, M. S., and Miller, D. G. "Psychological Distress and Surveillance Behaviors of Women with a Family History of Breast Cancer." *Journal of the National Cancer Institute,* 1992, *84,* 24–30.

Kent, G. "Memory of Dental Pain." *Pain,* 1985, *21,* 187–194.

Liu, D. *The Quality of Life in the United States.* Kansas City, Mo.: Midwest Research Institute, 1970.

Llewellyn-Thomas, H., Sutherland, H., and Thiel, E. "Do Patients' Evaluations of a Future Health State Change When They Actually Enter That State?" *Medical Care,* 1993, *31*(11), 1002–1012.

Loewenstein, G. "Out of Control: Visceral Influences on Behavior." *Organizational Behavior and Human Decision Processes,* 1996, *65,* 272–292.

Loomes, G., and Sugden, R. "Regret Theory: An Alternative Theory of Rational Choice Under Uncertainty." *Economic Journal,* 1982, *92,* 805–824.

March, J. "Bounded Rationality, Ambiguity and the Engineering of Choice." *Bell Journal of Economics,* 1978, *9,* 587–608.

Mastromauro, C., Myers, R. H., and Berkman, B. "Attitudes Toward Presymptomatic Testing in Huntington's Disease." *American Journal of Medical Genetics,* 1987, *26,* 271–282.

Rachman, S., and Eyrl, K. "Predicting and Remembering Recurrent Pain." *Behavioural Research and Therapy,* 1989, *27*(6), 621–665.

Read, D., and Loewenstein, G. "Diversification Bias: Explaining the Discrepancy in Variety Seeking Between Combined and Separated Choices." *Journal of Experimental Psychology: Applied,* 1995, *1*(1), 34–49.

Schneider, M. "The Quality of Life in Large American Cities: Objective and Subjective Social Indicators." *Social Indicators Research,* 1975, *1,* 495–509.

Scitovsky, T. *The Joyless Economy: An Inquiry into Human Satisfaction and Consumer Dissatisfaction.* New York: Oxford University Press, 1976.

Shefrin, H., and Statman, M. "Explaining Investor Preferences for Cash Dividends." *Journal of Financial Economics,* 1984, *13,* 253–282.

Sieff, E. M., Dawes, R. M., and Loewenstein, G. F. "Anticipated Versus Actual Responses to HIV Test Results." Working Paper, Carnegie Mellon University Department of Social and Decision Sciences, 1994.

Simonson, I. "The Effect of Purchase Quantity and Timing on Variety Seeking Behavior." *Journal of Marketing Research,* 1990, *32,* 150–162.

Slovic, P., and others. "Perceived Risk, Stigma, and Potential Economic Impacts of a High-Level Nuclear Waste Repository in Nevada." *Risk Analysis,* 1991, *11,* 683–696.

Sugden, R. "Regret, Recrimination and Rationality." *Theory and Decision,* 1985, *19,* 77–99.

Tribe, L. H. "Ways Not to Think About Plastic Trees: New Foundations for Environmental Law." *Yale Law Journal,* 1974, *83,* 1315–1348.

Wiggins, S., and others. "The Psychological Consequences of Predictive Testing for Huntington's Disease." *New England Journal of Medicine,* 1992, *327*(20), 1401–1405.

PART TWO

BARRIERS TO ENVIRONMENTALLY FRIENDLY BEHAVIOR

5

ENVIRONMENTAL DISPUTES

Competition for Scarce Resources and Clashing of Values

Leigh L. Thompson and Richard Gonzalez

ENVIRONMENTAL DISPUTES ARE often difficult to resolve because they involve scarce resources and touch on people's core ideological beliefs. Everyone is a stakeholder in the use of the environment and its resources. Consider the dispute over the Arctic National Wildlife Refuge, nineteen million acres in the northwest corner of Alaska designated by President Jimmy Carter in 1980 that environmentalists called the last intact and protected Arctic ecosystem. The refuge, the chief calving ground for the porcupine caribou herd, 150,000 of which migrate to the shores of the Arctic Ocean during the summer, was also believed to be the last chance for a major oil strike in the United States, according to Alaskan leaders and oil-industry officials. The dispute over oil drilling in the refuge

We thank Craig Fox, Andy Hoffman, Laura Kray, Vicki Medvec, and the participants in the conference on Psychological Perspectives to Environmental and Ethical Issues in Management for helpful insights and comments. The research in this chapter was supported by National Science Foundation (NSF) grants SES-9210298, SES-9110572, and PYI-9157447. Portions of this chapter were completed while Leigh Thompson was a fellow at the Center for Advanced Study in the Behavioral Sciences, supported by NSF SBR-9022192.

focused on the potential effects of development on the caribou and the impoverished Gwich'in Indians, who depended on the herd for food.

The dispute appeared to be a complex tangle of issues, parties, values, beliefs, information, and ideology. Bob Childers, advocate for Alaska's Gwich'in Indians, opposed the drilling. The state of Alaska struggled for more than two decades to open the refuge to oil and gas exploration, which would improve the lives of Alaskans. Polls indicated, however, that a majority of Americans opposed developing a remote refuge that few would ever see. The Republican Congress approved the drilling for oil in the preserve in a measure intended to raise $1.3 billion to reduce the deficit. But a dispute developed within the Republican ranks. Moderate Republicans showed weak support for the drilling, and a disagreement over how to split the drilling revenues erupted. The economic arguments against drilling were bolstered when the U.S. Geological Survey halved its initial estimate of how much oil lay beneath the land.

There were benefits to oil drilling. Neighbors of the Gwich'in, the Inupiat people, who initially feared environmental damage from drilling, began to fear that they would lose the benefits from the $120 million in oil-related revenues each year from the Alaskan pipeline. As Isaa Akootchook, a village leader for the Inupiat, said as he watched Monday Night Football on his TV, "We used to be against [oil development] because we didn't know about these things. This [drilling] will be good for the Inupiat people" (Delios, 1995, p. 1).

The refuge battle was carried out with extensive direct-mail campaigns and full-page ads in far-off newspapers. This Alaskan refuge battle is an example of how the environment is a symbol for our self- and world-views as well as a resource to be allocated. As with most important issues, one's position on environmental issues provides a medium for the expression of fundamental values, beliefs, and ethics concerning the world. In this chapter, we suggest that environmental disputes are different from other types of conflicts most commonly dealt with in the negotiation literature. We have both a theoretical and a practical mission. In the sections that follow, we analyze environmental disputes from a behavioral negotiation point of view, identify the key obstacles to effective dispute resolution, and show how to create movement in seemingly intractable environmental disputes. We provide a review of the key concepts and elements of behavioral negotiation research and relate those concepts to the analysis of environmental disputes. We do not attempt to review environmental issues and the foundations of the ideologies that underlie them (see Hoffman and Ehrenfeld, 1995; Susskind, 1990; Egri and Pinfield, 1994; Colby, 1989; Gladwin, Kennelly, and Krause, 1995, for overviews).

Behavioral Negotiation Framework

Negotiation is a joint decision-making process through which interdependent persons mutually decide how scarce resources will be allocated. *Mutual* decision making is a necessary component of negotiation. If one party has complete authority over the other party, negotiation cannot occur. Whereas environmental disputes can occur even when only one party gets to make the decision, negotiations require that more than one party have decision-making power. Negotiations must also involve a range of feasible outcomes. If one person must choose between total victory or yielding completely, no bargaining can occur.

Key Elements

According to Thompson and Hastie (1990a), the key elements of a negotiation include the parties, the issues, the parties' interests concerning the resources at stake, the communication that occurs between parties, and the outcomes of the negotiation. The parties are people who have a stake in the negotiation and who have decision-making authority. The parties represent their own interests or the interests of a constituency; a party may be a team, group, or larger collective. In the Alaskan preserve dispute, the parties included the native Gwich'in Indians, the oil companies, Congress, the president, and the American people. The *issues* were the concerns held by each party in the dispute, such as the type of drilling, extent of drilling, and its effects on wildlife and on indigenous persons.

The *interests* of parties refer to their preferences for the issues to be resolved (for example, the Republican Congress is interested in development to minimize the national debt; the Gwich'in Indians and other environmentalists want to preserve their natural way of life). In most negotiation situations, people do not have complete, perfect information about the interests of the other parties involved. For this reason, most negotiation situations are characterized by each party's having *incomplete information.* People may exchange information about their interests, but they cannot verify with certainty the other person's preferences; in this sense, people negotiate in ignorance with respect to the other party's preferences. In a negotiation situation, people have the opportunity to *communicate.* Finally, a critical element of negotiation is the *outcome.* Negotiations may end in mutual agreement or impasse. Mutual agreements may be evaluated in terms of their joint profitability and in terms of parties' outcomes.

Key Principles

We briefly discuss key principles from behavioral negotiation theory (for more extensive treatments, see Neale and Bazerman, 1991; Thompson, 1996), relate them to disputes over environmental issues, and discuss what we view as the main obstacles for the successful application of behavioral negotiation principles.

The Bargaining Zone

Probably the most important question to address in any dispute is whether an agreement is feasible. That is, is it possible for parties to reach a settlement, and is it wise for each party to do so? The answer to this question is determined by the size of the bargaining zone, which represents the overlap between parties' reservation points. A *reservation point* is the point that represents the least acceptable terms a party would be willing to accept. When the bargaining zone is positive—each party's reservation point is potentially acceptable to all other parties—agreement is feasible. It is in both parties' interests to reach agreement, especially if there are costs involved in prolonging the negotiation. For example, consider a simple negotiation situation involving the management of a lumber company and union workers. The union has determined that the lowest hourly wage increase that is acceptable before it goes on strike is five cents; the management has determined that it would be willing to increase hourly wages by seven cents. In this case, the bargaining zone is positive: any wage settlement between five and seven cents is viable, and it is in both parties' interests to agree on a settlement.

Distributive Component

The bargaining zone only tells us whether it is possible for parties to agree. It does not tell us exactly what agreement will be reached. Obviously, it is in each party's interest to reach a settlement that is closer to the other party's reservation point and nearer to its own target point. A *target point* is what parties would like to have (not what they would be willing to live with). In most cases, it is not possible for negotiated settlements to satisfy both parties' target points, which may be unrealistically optimistic. This question of who gets how much of the resources to be divided is the *distributive* component.

A distributive component is present even in negotiation situations that contain exclusively *compatible* issues, because parties must allocate resources. Further, parties may or may not be aware of the presence of compatible interests. For example, consider a house sale where, unbeknownst to the seller, the buyer would like the seller to leave the hardware materials in the basement. The seller, however, hires a company to clean out the entire basement. The hardware gets thrown away, resulting in less profit for the buyer.

Integrative Component

It is commonly known that every negotiation situation has a distributive component. It usually comes as a surprise that most negotiation situations also contain an *integrative* component, or how the resources available to the parties are expanded. It may seem odd to think of people creating resources in negotiation, but most negotiation situations are not purely fixed sum. Rather, through a variety of mechanisms, people can expand the total pie of resources to be created (see Pruitt and Carnevale, 1993). For example, consider a situation in which citizens want a local manufacturing company to minimize its waste products. The citizens are concerned with maintaining the purity of their waterways; the company is concerned with gaining community endorsement for its products. An integrative agreement is reached when the company minimizes waste and the local newspaper prints a series of full-page endorsements. This example illustrates the principle of nonspecific compensation.

The resource pie can be expanded in various ways (see Rubin, Pruitt, and Kim, 1994; Pruitt and Carnevale, 1993, for overviews). One way is by making *trade-offs* among issues (Raiffa, 1982). For example, consider a negotiation between a city and community residents concerning an airport expansion. The city desires the revenue increase that would come with expansion; the community residents are opposed because of the noise and added traffic. Because both parties feel entitled, on some level, to their own views, the dispute may seem intractable. An agreement may be possible, however, if the pie is expanded by adding other issues and providing opportunities for trade-offs. The city may have long-term growth needs, while the community has immediately pressing medical and education needs. A mutually beneficial trade-off may involve providing the citizens with a new hospital and school facilities in exchange for airport expansion that will take several years to plan and develop. Further, the city may respond to the concerns of the community by enhancing ground transportation to alleviate the projected traffic and placing restrictions on flight patterns to minimize noise.

There are many other ways to construct and enact integrative agreements. Differences more than similarities between people pave the way toward integrative agreement. Because parties to disputes are not identical in their tastes, forecasts, and endowments, they may have something to offer that is relatively less valuable to them than to those with whom they negotiate. Lax and Sebenius (1986) note five dimensions of difference that negotiators may exploit to capitalize on integrative agreement: differences in valuation for the negotiation issues, differences in expectations for uncertain events, differences in risk attitudes, differences in time preferences, and differences in capabilities. The relative resource gains produced by leveraging resources can vary widely.

Usually, though not always, people must have information about each other's preferences for integrative solutions to be developed. Probably the most serious hindrances to the development of mutually beneficial tradeoffs are faulty perceptions people hold about the interests of others. Most negotiators who have not received special training or expertise have a *fixed-pie perception* (Bazerman and Neale, 1983; Thompson and Hastie, 1990b). That is, they perceive the other party's interests to be completely opposed to their own. This faulty perception is present at the outset of most negotiation situations (Thompson and Hastie, 1990b) and is remarkably persistent, even in the face of disconfirming information (Thompson and DeHarpport, 1994). The fixed-pie perception is at the root of a particularly unfortunate negotiated outcome: the lose-lose agreement (Thompson and Hrebec, 1996). The lose-lose agreement occurs when people mutually agree to an outcome that is worse for both of them than some other readily available outcome. Lose-lose outcomes characterize those negotiation situations in which parties fail to realize that they have compatible interests—such as the case with the home buyer and seller. Although in a sense all pareto-inefficient outcomes (those in which there does not exist another outcome that would improve at least one party's utility without reducing the other's utility) could be considered lose-lose agreements, we use lose-lose to refer to pareto-inefficient agreements where compatible issues exist, so that superior outcomes are readily available (Thompson and Hrebec, 1996). The lose-lose outcome occurs in over 20 percent of conflict situations, and over 50 percent of negotiators who do not fall prey to lose-lose outcomes nevertheless erroneously believe that their interests are opposed when they are not. Further, the lose-lose effect is not limited to laboratory investigations; Balke, Hammond, and Meyer's analysis (1973) of a labor strike at a chemical company revealed faulty perceptions about preferred wage increases. Failure to realize that parties have compatible *interests* is different than the failure to realize that parties have different *priorities,* which may be mutually traded off. In most cases, people are not aware that they have unnecessarily wasted resources. Inefficient agreements such as this are costly not only for the parties involved but also for the larger community (Rubin, Pruitt, and Kim, 1994) that pays the price of increased waste, underutilization of human capital, and a mounting federal deficit.

Integrative agreements offer a number of important advantages for parties to environmental conflicts. First, via integrative agreements people can get more of what they want and therefore may be more satisfied with the outcome. Second, the creation of resources makes it more likely that parties' interests can be effectively resolved and an impasse avoided (especially if the created resources are easy to distribute). For instance, if two parties are negotiating over how to distribute resource A, an integrative agreement might solve the impasse by redefining the situation so that each party feels as though it is gaining what it seeks and not giving up what it desires. Finally, integrative agreements serve the interests of the community by minimizing the likelihood that one or more parties will renege, requiring renegotiation, and by making more efficient use of scarce resources.

We believe that as in other conflicts, integrative agreements are possible in virtually all environmental disputes. In saying this, we do not mean to imply that all parties can attain outcomes that satisfy their target points but rather that some agreements create more added value than others. (See Hoffman and Ehrenfeld, 1995; Porter, 1985, for different perspectives about the feasibility of integrative agreements.)

In the environmental domain, the question of integrative agreements has become one of whether *win-win* agreements are possible. The answer to this question, of course, depends upon how win-win is defined. We define win-win agreements as those that capitalize on parties' interests so as to increase added value. Win-win agreements are usually misconstrued in two serious ways. First, they are construed to mean that both parties to a negotiation achieve their target points. When viewed in this way, win-win agreements are not possible (if they were possible, then there would not be a negotiation problem). In most cases, however, parties may reach agreements that are much better than their reservation points if they focus on the potential for integrative agreement. Further, we believe that some settlements are better for all the parties involved than are others.

Win-win agreements have also been interpreted to mean that people are *happy* with the outcomes they obtain in negotiation. But using subjective perceptions like happiness and satisfaction as an index of the efficiency of negotiated outcomes is problematic for several reasons. First, people's subjective perceptions and evaluations are highly context dependent. The same objective outcome may be viewed quite differently, as a function of arbitrary aspects of the context. For example, people report greater life satisfaction on days when the weather is sunny than when the weather is cloudy (Schwarz and Clore, 1988). Second, subjective perceptions are influenced by social comparison information. That is, people feel more successful about negotiated interactions when they perceive the other party to be disappointed with the outcome than when the other party seems pleased (Thompson, Valley, and Kramer, 1996). Finally, people often confuse what they regard as "fair" outcomes with integrative outcomes. That is, people feel that if the allocation of resources is equal or equitable, the agreement is good. Compromise, or the even division of resources, is often viewed as a fair procedure for allocating resources. However, "fair" settlements may be inefficient. The equal division of resources in no way guarantees that resources have not been unnecessarily wasted. Furthermore, compromise agreements work against the development of mutually beneficial trade-offs. Another problem is that there is no universal or absolute index of fairness. In a dispute, there are likely to be as many fair solutions as there are parties to the negotiation (Messick, 1992; Bazerman, 1993).

We believe neither of these definitions of win-win is useful. Rather, we regard a win-win outcome to be one that is efficient—meaning that there is no other outcome parties could reach that at least one party would prefer without reducing the other party's utility.

A Framework for the Analysis of Disputes

It is useful to distinguish conflicts of interest from conflicts that arise from different conceptualizations of the situation. Game theory (von Neumann and Morgenstern, 1947; Gibbons, 1992) and cognitive negotiation theory (Neale and Bazerman, 1991; Thompson, 1990, 1996) have been used to analyze how well various compromise strategies work in reaching satisfactory solutions to conflicts of interest. However, many conflicts arise not because of competing interests but because parties do not share the same conceptualization of the situation. This may occur because of divergent ideologies, values, or cognitive structures. The mode of resolution for such conflicts is not joint compromise, concessions, or the integrative bargaining model we have discussed. Resolution requires an altered understanding of the situation by one or both people. Unlike conflicts of interest, conflicts over values and ideology may not have a "best" or optimal solution but instead may be assessed in terms of the accuracy of people's perceptions of the other side (Hammond, Stewart, Brehmer, and Steinmann, 1975) and the preservation of values.

The social psychological and organizational literature on conflict has been divided into two streams that have developed independently. One focuses on conflicts of interest, also known as scarce resource competition; the other focuses on conflicts of ideology, understanding, and value. (Values differ from beliefs, but they have not been treated separately in the literature.) To our knowledge, Rapoport (1960) was the first to distinguish conflicts of interest, or what he called *games* (encounters designed for playing out conflicts of interest), from conflicts of ideology, or *debates* (encounters designed for the discussion of ideological differences). According to Rapoport, the objective of games is to outwit one's opponent, whereas the objective of debates is to convince one's opponent. (Rapoport also discussed fights, in which the goal is to harm the opponent.) Aubert (1963), Hammond (1965), Marwell (1966), Kelley and Thibaut (1969), and Glenn, Johnson, Kimmel, and Wedge (1970) made similar distinctions between scarce resource competition and value conflict.

Using the distinction between scarce resource conflict and ideological conflict, we pose a general framework for the analysis of disputes. Figure 5.1 presents a four-cell structure for analyzing the nature of conflict. For any given conflict, people's interests concerning scarce (tangible) resources may be at stake, or their beliefs about the nature of the world may be in conflict, or both. Of course, it could be argued that all conflicts of ideology involve implications for resources and that scarce resource conflict has its roots in ideological differences, but our concern is the *focal* issues in conflict and how they are *subjectively perceived* by individuals. Cell A is the *no conflict* case: parties agree both on ideology and the distribution of resources. Cell B is the *scarce resource conflict* case: people share an understanding of the situation but disagree on the allocation of resources. This cell is the one most often studied by game theorists, behavioral decision theorists, and negotiation theorists. Cell C is the *ideological conflict* case: people disagree (at least immediately) concerning their ideologies or the facts of the situation but do not have to apportion scarce resources. Cell D is the *complex conflict* case: people are in disagreement concerning their ideologies, and scarce resources are at stake. We suspect that most conflicts concerning environmental issues are of the complex type in cell D.

The central thesis of our chapter is that environmental conflicts, such as the one over the Arctic natural preserve, involve both conflict over scarce resources and clashes of ideology. Resources and fundamental values are at stake. This may occur in two ways. In some instances, parties may have values in conflict and simultaneously compete for perceived scarce resources. In other cases, one party may perceive the conflict in terms of

Figure 5.1. Analyzing the Nature of Conflict.

Conflict of values (ideology)	Conflict of interest (scarce resources): No	Conflict of interest (scarce resources): Yes
No	Cell A: No Conflict Parties in agreement on issues and ideology	Cell B: Scarce Resource Conflict Parties in disagreement about apportionment of resources but agree Ideologically about the nature of the dispute
Yes	Cell C: Ideological Conflict Parties in disagreement about nature of world, correct view, what should or ought to be; no disagreement concerning apportionment of resources	Cell D: Complex Conflict Parties in disagreement about resources and about ideology

values; the other may regard the situation in terms of resources. We suspect that this occurs in environmental disputes when developers base their position on interests and environmentalists base their position on values. The game theory and the behavioral negotiation models can only take us so far in understanding how these complex conflicts may be effectively resolved.

Keeney (1992) has addressed the issue of how values should affect decision making. Keeney encourages making decisions and resolving disputes through the explicit discussion of values. His model, however, cannot paint a complete portrait of the negotiation processes because it fails to take into account the interdependent processes occurring in a negotiation. It is our goal in this chapter to identify social psychological processes that prevent efficient dispute resolution. We also use the social psychological framework to suggest ways to resolve disputes that include conflict over fundamental beliefs and values, like those found in environmental disputes.

Obstacles in the Effective Resolution of Conflict

We propose that environmental conflicts involve both competition for scarce resources and clashes of ideology. The behavioral negotiation framework previously described provides insight into how integrative solutions might permit trade-offs in environmental disputes, but it avoids the issue of how values and ideology (which are present in environmental disputes) influence conflict. What problems might the parties involved, or third parties, encounter as they attempt to fashion trade-offs among issues in environmental disputes? In this section, we highlight what we regard to be some of the key social psychological obstacles to the development of mutually beneficial, integrative agreements in environmental disputes. Our analysis is primarily speculative and awaits empirical validation. The problems we cite all have the common denominator of conflict over values and ideology. We do not mean to imply that these obstacles are exclusive to environmental conflicts. Rather, we view these as major impediments to the successful resolution of environmental disputes as well as other kinds of conflicts that involve values. We also note that the following obstacles might interact in the sense that factors that produce one obstacle may also lead to other obstacles as well; hence the entries in this list of obstacles are not independent.

Sacred Values and Taboo Trade-Offs

The trade-off principle is ideal for dealing with scarce resources conflicts containing issues that are independent and fungible, that is, available for trade-offs. The behavioral negotiation framework assumes that people are able and willing to place value on resources to compare them or are at least able to make apple and orange comparisons among resources and trade them in a way that maximizes their outcomes. But the notion of trading becomes unconscionable in some conflict situations (Tetlock, Peterson, and Lerner, 1996). That is, in some conflicts people are reluctant and often refuse to place a monetary value on a good or even think of trading it. Tetlock, Peterson, and Lerner call such issues *sacred issues* and distinguish them from their fungible cousin so common in the negotiation paradigm, *secular issues*. Sacred issues are those that the decision maker deems unavailable for compromise, trade, or even questioning. Although a behavioral decision theorist might account for sacred values by attaching a very high monetary value, this does not address psychological aversion to trade. In a dispute concerning the construction of a dam in Arizona that would remove native Indians from their ancestral land, a Yavapai teenager said, "The land is our mother. You don't sell your mother" (Espeland, 1994).

Sacred issues are puzzling to the behavioral negotiation theorist who assumes that acts can be ordered and that all resources may be placed on a single utility metric and then traded accordingly. According to Tetlock, Peterson, and Lerner (1996), sacred issues lead to "taboo trade-offs," wherein people are reluctant or refuse to trade. They note that attaching a monetary value to a bottle of wine, a house, or the services of a gardener can be a cognitively demanding task but raises no questions about the morality of the individual. In contrast, attaching monetary value to human life, familial obligations, national honor, and the ecosystem seriously undermines one's social identity or standing in the eyes of others (Schlenker, 1980). For the environmentalist, proposals to exchange sacred values (such as environmental resources) for secular ones (for example, money, time, or convenience) constitute taboo trade-offs. To the list of sacred values, we add the porcupine caribou, the wildflowers, and the bird species that inhabit the Alaskan refuge. What makes these sacred is not the tangible resource they represent but the symbolic meaning attached to them—they represent a way of life that is threatened.

Given the inherently sacred values that operate in environmental disputes, the familiar notion of trading, so important to the theory of behavioral negotiation, is likely to be considered unacceptable and reprehensible to the environmentalist. But we believe that sacred and secular issues are contextually defined. That is, the social perceiver, by virtue of key features of social context, attributes sacred status to certain issues (Tetlock, Peterson, and Lerner, 1996). For example, the presence of referent groups that derive their self-identity through their association with certain values and the similarity of the dispute to other disputes that involve sacred issues may lead people to view an issue as sacred. Sociocultural norms also affect sacredness of certain positions, such as smoking, which is now generally considered baneful. The sanctity of issues is also influenced by the labels and names used to define conflicts. For example, in 1994, all three members of Alaska's congressional delegation began referring to the part of the Arctic National Wildlife Refuge that would be subject to oil exploration as the "Arctic Oil Reserve." The group believes this term is more accurate because that part of the refuge is not officially classified as either wilderness or refuge. Environmentalists object to this term and even to the use of the acronym ANWAR (Arctic Natural Wildlife Refuge) because they worry that unless the words *wildlife refuge* are clearly stated the public will not understand the value of the land.

We use the term *sacred* to describe people's preferences on issues on which they view themselves as uncompromising. It immediately becomes obvious, however, that sacred issues may be a profitable strategy. That is, it is to one's advantage in a negotiation situation to be viewed as uncompromising (perhaps even fanatical). By anointing certain issues as sacred, and removing them from bargaining consideration, a negotiator may increase the likelihood of an individually favorable settlement. The strategy is similar to the irrevocable commitment strategy (Schelling, 1960).

We refer to issues that are not really sacred but positioned as such as *pseudo-sacred* (we are indebted to Max Bazerman for this term). There are two variants of pseudo-sacredness that hinge upon the deliberateness of one's strategy. The first variant is that some people may believe their values prohibit any discussion of trade, but presented in the appropriate context a proposal that traded a sacred issue might be considered and chosen. The second variant involves deliberate misrepresentation. We believe that the greatest impediments to resolving environmental disputes stem from the first variant. Perhaps people view themselves as having greater purity of conviction than is actually the case. Thus, for example, if the Yavapai Indians would trade one acre of land for a hospital, a new school, or money, then the land is not truly sacred but pseudo-sacred.

At this point, it could be argued that truly sacred values cannot exist because everyone has his price. That is, with sufficient compensation, people are willing to trade off a sacred value. We think the critical distinction to be drawn is not the amount that one must be compensated but the social-cognitive factors that operate to affect parties' views of sacredness.

Affiliation Bias and Reactive Devaluation

The affiliation bias refers to the tendency of people to evaluate a person's actions based on the person's alleged party affiliation rather than on the merits of the behavior itself. Consider, for example, a hypothetical case: both a chemical company and an environmental advocacy group leave a park area picnic without disposing of their waste products. Which group is judged most harshly? The affiliation bias would suggest that the chemical company group would be judged more harshly than the environmental group—even when their actions are identical.

The common belief is that actions speak louder than words. The implication is that all of us use people's behaviors as an insight into their real attitudes (for example, Jones and Davis, 1965). Certainly, most of us would like to believe that we evaluate a person's behaviors at face value and make judgments about the person's underlying values on the basis of an objective analysis of his or her behavior. Although actions may speak louder than words, a person's party affiliation may speak loudest of all, setting up a directional tendency for observers to make inferences about underlying ideology.

A classic example is the one provided by Hastorf and Cantril (1954) of the differing perceptions of the infractions by different team members in a football game. The perceived aggressiveness of the infractions was entirely predictable by students' team affiliations. Another example is Oskamp's examination (1965) of people's perceptions of a number of international diplomacy behaviors. Half of the respondents evaluated actions that were attributed to the United States; the other half evaluated the identical action, this time purportedly taken by the Soviet Union. (That is, one respondent would read, "The U.S. has established rocket bases close to the borders of Russia," and the other would read, "Russia has established rocket bases close to the borders of the U.S."). People's perceptions of the action differed dramatically as a function of the perceived agent of the action, the United States or Russia, but not of the actual action. This suggests that people perceive the same objective behavior as either sinister or benign merely as a consequence of the agent's affiliation.

In a similar vein, Ross and Stillinger (1991) describe the *reactive devaluation* effect as the tendency for people on opposite sides in a conflict to devalue the proposals offered by the other side as a mere consequence of their having been offered; when the same proposal is offered by one's own side or a neutral party, the acceptability of the proposal increases dramatically. The side on which one sits at the negotiation table defines one's affiliation with or against a proposal.

Reactive devaluation can be an obstacle to negotiation. If an environmentalist is willing to concede five hundred acres of forest to a logging interest, we predict that the logging interest will devalue the concession. What is wrong with those trees? Why are "they" willing to give up these trees? Thus a good faith effort on the part of the environmentalist to demonstrate a willingness to negotiate could backfire because it is devalued by the other side.

Punctuation of Conflict and Causal Chunking

A basic tenet of social psychology is that social interaction can be understood as a fairly continuous stream of causes and effects, with each person's actions influencing the subsequent actions of his or her interaction partners (for example, Jones and Gerard, 1967). Indeed, to an outside observer, a series of communications is viewed as an uninterrupted sequence of interchanges. People who are actively engaged in social interaction, especially conflict situations, do not always see things this way, however. Instead, they organize their interactions into a series of discrete causal chunks. Whorf (1956) terms this process the "punctuation of the sequence of events."

According to Swann, Pelham, and Roberts (1987), people simplify their perceptions of their interactions by organizing them into discrete causal chunks. These chunks influence the extent to which people are aware of their influence on others as well as their impressions of others. Swann,

Pelham, and Roberts distinguish between two kinds of chunking patterns: self-causal and other-causal. People form self-causal chunks (for example, my action causes my partner's action) when they are on the offensive and other-causal chunks when they are on the defensive.

Similarly, Kahn and Kramer (1990) describe the biased "punctuation of conflict" as a tendency for people involved in conflict to interpret interactions with their adversaries in self-serving and other-derogating terms. Thus an actor, A, perceives the history of conflict with another actor, B, as a sequence of B-A, B-A, B-A, in which the initial hostile or aggressive move was made by B, causing A to engage in defensive and legitimate retaliatory actions. Actor B punctuates the same history of interaction as A-B, A-B, A-B, however, reversing the roles of aggressor and defender.

Disagreement about how to punctuate a sequence of events and a conflict relationship is at the root of many environmental disputes. When each side to the dispute is queried, people on each side explain their frustrations and actions as defenses against the acts of the other party. As a result, conflict can escalate unnecessarily but cannot be readily defused.

Perceived Efficacy of Coercion and Conciliation in Conflicts

The successful resolution of environmental conflicts depends on accurately predicting the effectiveness of our social influence strategies. That is, to modify another person's actions, it is important to distinguish between the actions that would facilitate such a change and the ones that would inhibit change in the desired direction.

Rothbart and Hallmark (1988) analyzed the nightly broadcasts from London by the American journalist Edward R. Murrow, who reported on the psychological and physical consequences of the Nazi bombing of British cities (Murrow, 1941). Contrary to Nazi intent, the bombing did not move the British toward surrender. It had quite the opposite effect, strengthening rather than diminishing their resolve to resist German domination. Shortly after the United States entered World War II, the Americans joined the British in launching costly bombing raids over Germany. In part, the intent was to decrease the German people's will to resist. Later research reported by the Office of Strategic Services compared lightly and heavily bombed areas and found only minimal differences in civilians' will to resist. Similarly, in environmental disputes the erroneous perception that the opposition will weaken in the face of heavy attack often encourages aggressive rather than constructive action.

In addition to that World War II example, Rothbart and Hallmark cite others, including Pearl Harbor, South Africa, and North Vietnam. Each instance reveals large differences in countries' perceptions of what will be effective in motivating an enemy and what will be effective in motivating themselves or their allies. The general principle appears to be that coercion is viewed as more effective with our enemies than with ourselves, whereas conciliation is viewed as more effective with ourselves than with our enemies.

Rothbart and Hallmark cite three explanations why this principle might be true. First, the multiple goals interpretation suggests that a preference for punitive strategies with one's enemies may reflect a desire to inflict injury or pain as well as a desire to influence behavior in a desired direction. The relative preference for punishment is based on an incompatible desire to both injure and modify the behavior of the enemy. The symbolic value explanation suggests that people are inclined to use more coercive strategies with an opponent because the appearance of toughness conveys information about our own motives and intentions, which in the long run may bring about the desired result. A third approach, social categorization, suggests that the mere creation of mutually exclusive, exhaustive social categories leads to different assumptions about category members, with more favorable attributes assigned to in-group than to out-group members (Brewer, 1979; Tajfel, 1970). We suspect that social categorization processes are particularly powerful in environmental disputes because of the well-defined camps.

With this literature in mind, one cannot help but wonder whether some of the tactics used in environmental disputes may raise the hurdle that needs to be overcome for a successful negotiation. Tactics such as chaining oneself to a fishing boat or placing metal spikes in trees to damage logging equipment might strengthen the resolve of the other side.

Exaggeration and Polarization of Others' Views

In many instances, people exaggerate the difference between their own and others' belief systems in a way that promotes conflict. Ross and Ward's principle of naive realism describes a psychological process that leads to the exaggeration of differences. According to Ross and Ward (1994), people believe that their own views are unbiased and assume that others are reasonable people like themselves. When confronted with what appears to be a difference in views and opinions concerning a sociopolitical matter, people initially assume that the other side lacks the information that led them to their own reasoned and objective viewpoint. If one supplies the other side with information that seems abundantly clear but the other party still does not come around, the perceiver regards the opponent to be an irrational, ideological extremist.

Robinson, Keltner, Ward, and Ross (1994) examined people's perceptions of the other side in a variety of sociopolitical issues, such as racial incidents and school curriculum reform. The pattern of results was striking. People exaggerated the viewpoints held by the other party in a way that made differences in ideology appear larger than they really were. People tended to perceive the other side's views as more uniform and their own views as more varied and heterogeneous. Thus ideological conflict is often exacerbated unnecessarily as a partisan construes the other person's values to be more extremist and unbending than they really are. We expect this tendency to be further exacerbated to the extent that perceivers homogenize all members of the other party—that is, perceive minimal variability in views held by the other side (Linville, Fischer, and Salovey, 1989).

Sinister and Fanatical Attribution Errors

Ross (1977) described the fundamental attribution error as the tendency for social perceivers to explain the causes of the behavior of others in terms of their underlying dispositions and to discount the role of situational factors. We think that the fundamental attribution error operates in environmental conflicts as well. But Ross did not specify what kind of dispositional attribution people would make. Jones and Davis (1965) suggested that people will make correspondent inferences; attitudes are seen as corresponding to the overt behavior. We believe that the attributions people make in environmental disputes take a particular form that is not symmetric. Many environmental disputes involve a group that is believed to be interested in the economic *development* of the environment and an opposing group that represents the interests of the *ecosystem.* We believe that when each group is asked what they believe to be the cause of the dispute, each will attribute the negative aspects of conflict to the dispositions of the other party.

Our analysis of sinister and fanatical attributions complements Fiske's account (1993) of attributional behavior in power relationships. Fiske argues that people in low-power positions are dependent on the behaviors of more powerful others and will spend more time considering the behavior of powerful others than vice versa. People in low power positions often attribute sinister intentions to the actions of others. Kramer (1995) describes the sinister attribution error as the tendency for people in less powerful positions to ascribe malicious intent to the behavior of others. Applying the work of Fiske and Kramer to the content of environmental disputes, we predict that the environmental group will tend to attribute evil and sinister motives to the development group, whereas the development group will tend to regard the environmentalists as fanatic lunatics. This perception was comically noted by a Republican congressman George Gekas of Pennsylvania, who was accused by the opposing partisan party of anti-environmental attitudes. The angered Gekas mocked the accusation, "Mr. Speaker and members of the House, I hate clean air. I don't want to breathe clean air. I want the dirtiest air possible for me and my household and my constituents. That's what the supporters of this motion want people to believe about our position on these riders. Now, you know that's absolutely untenable" (*Morning Edition,* 1995).

Heartfelt Versus Calculated Interests

Understanding the relationship between a person's values and interests is also important for overcoming obstacles to conflict resolution. We pose two simple models for understanding the psychological interplay between values and interests: value-driven interests and interest-driven values. The most common way to view this relationship is the *value-driven interests* model, wherein a person's interests reflect his or her underlying values. In the *interest-driven value* framework, a person's interests drive or dictate his or her values. The difference between these two models is based, in short, on whether one's values are *heartfelt* or *calculated.* The distinction rests on whether one's interests are driven by social and moral values that are independent of self-interest, or whether self-interest shapes one's values. We believe that either model can hinder the effective resolution of conflict. We further believe that many people view their interests to be an expression of their values, unless economic interest is a cornerstone value. We will make the point later that people tend to view their adversaries' values as calculated.

Most people view their values as dictating and shaping their interests but view others as expressing values that serve their self-interest. Thus we may view the values held by our opponents as being slaves to their unbridled greed and self-interest but regard our own interests as an expression of our underlying values. Consequently, we tend to believe that others' values are more capricious than our own. In a sense, people believe that at the right price others can be bought or persuaded, but that they are committed to their own value system. We suspect that environmentalists' and developers' views of one another are not symmetric. That is, environmentalists may very well accuse developers of harboring evil, calculated interests, and developers may view environmentalists as naive and idealistic. Why do people tend to see their own interests as heartfelt and others' as calculated? There are several reasons.

It is difficult for people to grant that there may, in fact, be more than one valid view of the world. That is, although people allow others to have different preferences and tastes, there is only one set of "right" or correct views. The presence of more than one value system is psychologically disturbing for the person who wants to believe that there is a single, objective reality. A second reason why people regard their own views as heartfelt is that they view themselves as guided by conscience and feeling, rather than cold cognition. The primacy of affect over cognition has been supported in research (for example, Zajonc, 1980). Self-presentation concerns may also lead us to justify our interests as arising from values. Indeed it is generally socially inappropriate to make arguments on the basis of self-interest.

Outsmarting Versus Convincing

When we negotiate over tangible resources and we manage to make a gain (say, in our salary or the price of a house), we often feel that we have been successful in *outsmarting* the other person. When we manage to get a fence sitter to see our point of view on a controversial subject, we often feel that we have been successful in *convincing* the other person. In which case do we feel more satisfied? With some exceptions, the most satisfaction comes from our use of rational, persuasive argument rather than clever tricks (Rapoport, 1960). This belief is not without empirical support. French and Raven's analysis (1959) of bases of power indicates that more compliance occurs when power is legitimate or expert rather than coercive. Convincing someone about the correctness of our own views seems to confirm not only those views but also ourselves as rational, thoughtful people. Convincing others also confirms the naive realism view that if people on the other side had the "proper" information they could come to view the situation in the same way (Ross and Ward, 1994). Furthermore, rational argument serves a person's own interests: changing someone's underlying views has a more lasting impact than if one person just gets another person to give in to him or her on a single occasion. For these reasons, we suspect that in most environmental disputes, which tend to involve sacred values, people desire to convince, rather than outsmart, others. In highly emotionally charged disputes, people want others (especially their opponents) to appreciate their point of view.

The problem is that most people are not terribly persuasive spokespersons for their own ideology. One reason is that people mostly interact with others who have similar viewpoints, and thus receive confirmation of their own views without focusing on the other side's arguments. A second reason is that people tend to confuse ideology with rational argument.

Tetlock, Peterson, and Lerner (1996) note that when people are pressed to justify their political preferences, all inquiry ultimately terminates in the expression of values that people find ridiculous to justify any further. We suspect that the same is true for environmental issues: in the Arctic oil-drilling controversy, environmentalists consider protection of the environment a self-evident need just as pro-drilling Republicans consider economic development a self-justifying explanation. When questioned about why they hold a given view, people tend to restate their view rather than provide reasons for holding it. According to Rokeach (1973), values represent core beliefs. Conversely, we view our own beliefs as persuasive because they reinforce our basic values. The problem is that when others present us with their ideology, we view it as unmitigated propaganda, and we often accuse the other side of talking around the issues and not dealing with the conflict squarely.

Elster (1995) distinguished between two strategic uses of argument. These two correspond to the general distinction we draw between conflict of interest and conflict of understanding. Elster argued that people can induce agreement either by *bargaining* or through *rational* argument. When people bargain, they make threats and promises with a claim to credibility; when people argue, they make assertions with a claim to validity. Elster posed the question, Why argue at all? That is, why don't people simply bargain through the use of threats and demands? Elster ultimately concluded that argument serves at least five useful purposes and that all serve to maximize self-interest. First, if others believe that a person is truly arguing from principle, they may be more willing to back down because they regard the other as willing to suffer a loss rather than accept a compromise (Frank, 1988). Second, the use of ideology and principle is often a subterfuge, used for political purpose to hide what is in reality a deal among special interests. The third purpose is for persuasion and is related to the concept of informational influence (Deutsch and Gerard, 1955). Fourth, social norms often prescribe that people should take positions that are beneficial to the collective. Discussions of values and principles provide an acceptable text for dialogue when the social context does not tolerate the discussion of interests. Finally, parties to a dispute might use arguments out of fairness to avoid humiliating an opponent. That is, if the stronger party articulates an impartial reason that allows the weaker party to save face, both gain.

Prescriptive Implications

Having focused on the factors that make environmental disputes resistant to the principles of negotiation, we can ask what steps may be taken to create positive movement in environmental disputes.

As a first step, the environmental scholar needs to realize that environmental disputes involve values as well as interests. The implication is that both values and interests must be considered when studying the problem of resolving environmental disputes. A second step is to examine ways of creatively allocating resources in a manner that satisfies parties' values using the integrative bargaining principles already described. It is unrealistic, however, to assume that solutions can always be crafted that satisfy parties' underlying issues. Assuming that these basic approaches have not been successful in moving the resolution of the dispute forward, what may be done? Following are several strategies we suggest could facilitate effective dispute resolution. Our ideas are primarily speculative and await empirical examination.

Using Resources to Change Values

Depending upon one's view of it, the approach of using resources to change values is a form of bribery or seduction. In short, opponents are offered a taste or allowed to experience the positive aspects of the change they are reluctant to negotiate, in the hope that they will be reluctant to give up a resource they have enjoyed. The idea is connected to the endowment effect (Thaler, 1980), in which people are more reluctant to part with something once it is in their possession. This was the case of the Inupiat Indians in Alaska, who were initially opposed to the drilling but have come to enjoy the amenities of modern life made possible by oil exploration in their community. People are motivated to bring their beliefs in line with their behavior. This strategy of allowing the other side to experience a resource may help alleviate the sacred value obstacle because it facilitates viewing the value as something that can be traded.

Psychological theories of cognitive dissonance (Festinger, 1957) and self-perception (Bem, 1967) state that people bring their beliefs in line with their behavior. Thus the endowment effect might reflect several psychological processes in addition to the notion of loss aversion that is usually thought to drive the endowment effect. This strategy could backfire, however. The key obstacles to overcome when implementing this strategy are issues of face saving (Brown, 1968) and the maintenance of self-identity. That is, people do not want to look like they can be bought or have sold out (see the section "Perceived Efficacy of Coercion and Conciliation" earlier in this chapter).

Learning the Necessity of Trade-Offs

No one can live without making choices among sacred issues. For everything that a person chooses, something is not chosen. Even in the case of the Gwich'in Indians, achieving their goal of continuing to hunt caribou in the pristine wilderness means that the longevity of tribe and children will be reduced (without the benefits of formalized medicine and education that development brings). Why is it so hard for people to realize the trade-offs they make? The answer may be that they do not cognitively code the choices they make in terms of sacrifices. They focus on the road taken instead of the road not taken. A potentially useful strategy for facilitating negotiation is to reframe the issue from a political, environmental, or social one to one of economics and cost-benefit analysis. The idea is to make it clear that trade-offs are inevitable—that people constantly make decisions that affect others' welfare. When people eat beef, they affect the food chain; when people use cloth diapers, they affect the water supply; when they use plastic, they affect landfills. It is impossible not to affect the welfare of others. People's views of their own choices and how they involve trade-offs is myopic; the best approach is to learn to be cognizant of the trade-offs people do make and how best to weigh the issues.

Another problem stands in the way of getting negotiators to focus on trade-offs. Even if we convince people that they do in fact make trade-offs in their role as *decision makers,* they may still be reluctant to make trade-offs as *negotiators.* Negotiation is often viewed as a strategic take-and-do-not-give-up enterprise rather than a creative give-and-take enterprise.

Creating a Sticky Slope

One reason that movement is blocked in environmental conflict is that people fear a slippery slope—that if they give in on one issue even a little bit they eventually lose all ground. Often the slippery slope concerns the perception of what events are likely to take place in the future. However, with so much uncertainty, future conditions are hard to reliably foresee. If a person or a party could receive assurance that a concession in one area would not start an avalanche of capitulation, it might be possible to develop more creative and mutually beneficial negotiated agreements. A sticky slope, the conceptual opposite of a slippery slope, means assuring the party who makes a concession that further ground is not also imperiled. The trick, of course, is creating meaningful sticking points. Raiffa (1982) suggests a number of methods for creating contingent contracts that provide insurance to parties reluctant to take risks. When parties have different perceptions about the state of the world, instead of arguing about what is or will likely be, they can bet on their differences. For example, consider a conflict involving developers' desire to build a bridge in a wetlands area and environmentalists' concerns that the construction will harm wildlife. The developers do not believe that the construction will have adverse effects. The parties may fashion a bet in which the animal population will be monitored following construction. If a critical number of animals have suffered adverse effects, then the developers will remove the bridge and, furthermore, donate money to special habitat preserves. If the animal population has not been endangered, however, additional development exploration is allowed. The essential feature of such a bet is that uncertainty about future conditions is used to leverage agreement. Most important, the people on each side of the dispute get an insurance policy that protects them from losing all ground should things go awry.

Changing the Sociopolitical Context

The social context often determines whether trade-offs are taboo or not. As we noted earlier, affiliation tendencies can block potentially beneficial trade-offs. Thus one way to facilitate negotiation is to remove accountability pressures. In general, when people anticipate that their decisions and actions will be scrutinized by others, they are more attuned to sociopolitical pressures. Although being attuned to sociopolitical issues and information is important, the resulting pressure may hinder decision-making quality. It may be possible to create teams of decision makers to diffuse responsibility or task forces to absorb blame. Thus one way of altering the sociopolitical context is to create scapegoats and mutual enemies.

Introducing a Common Goal

The introduction of a common goal does two things: it removes the perception that the other party's interests can be completely opposed, and it builds a new value representing a higher-order principle that both parties find acceptable and perhaps superior to their previously espoused values. This prescription guards against attributional obstacles such as exaggerating the other party's view, attributing sinister motives to the other side, and perceiving the other party as calculating.

In Sherif and others' classic studies at Robber's Cave (1961), two opposing factions were brought together by a common goal. In environmental disputes, the common goal may take the form of a new paradigm or ideology that encompasses developers' interests and environmentalists' goals: sustainable development. Hoffman and Ehrenfeld (1995) outline the components for the creation of a paradigm shift that would encompass two opposing value systems. In particular, they argue that eco-development, sustaincentrism, or more commonly, sustainable development as an ideology would be compatible with both frontier economics and deep ecology, two currently opposing ideologies. Although Hoffman and Ehrenfeld's proposed paradigm shift is not dependent on the introduction of an enemy, such shifts might be more palatable for parties with the creation of a party or position that threatens both parties.

Setting a Precedent of Agreement

An interesting phenomenon occurs when people are asked to solve brainteasers or puzzles: effort and persistence are much greater when people believe a solution exists than when they doubt that it does. We argue that a precedent of agreement in a dispute context creates the very mechanisms necessary for agreement: persistence and creativity. The status quo can also provide an interesting norm. If solutions to disputes have always been reached in the past, this sets a precedent for solving the present negotiation. No one wants to be in the party that broke tradition. For example, we are aware of a psychology department that has a history of unanimous agreement on hiring decisions. The desire not to disturb the norm of unanimity is quite powerful at silencing any minority view.

Reframing Ideological Illusions

It is amusing to nonpartisan observers that partisans of both sides in presidential debates usually claim victory. Of course, it is a logical impossibility that both sides can win on an issue. Nevertheless, with enough rhetoric, bolstering, and selective perception, both sides can be quite confident that they won and can maintain their dual illusion. Likewise, mediators may facilitate trade-offs that maintain the illusion that values have been preserved. The key is to reframe values in terms of general principles, not as specific positions. This will provide sufficient ambiguity to allow parties to be flexible about the means of achieving their values, especially when accountability to a constituency is critical. This strategy attempts to eliminate the outsmarting versus convincing obstacle discussed earlier.

Conclusion

We are not the first to examine the relationship between scarce resource competition and ideological conflict. Notable predecessors include Walton and McKersie's attitudinal structuring model (1965), Raiffa's analysis (1982) of the Camp David negotiations, Fisher and Ury's admonition (1981) to separate people from the problem, Pruitt and Carnevale's treatment (1993) of the values that underlie interests, and Keeney's work (1992) on value-focused thinking. In each of these approaches, parties are encouraged to be flexible about their means to achieving an end. But most of the previous approaches circumvent the problem of engaging parties in dialogue. The assumption is that interests flow from people's underlying values, that values may be served by an array of several different outcomes, and that the best solution is to keep goals intact and find interests that coincide with both parties' goals. This is a nice idea for the negotiation of landlord and tenant disputes, car sales, and employment relations, but it is often unrealistic for environmental disputes. The negotiation literature, in a sense, conveniently sidesteps the problem of values by focusing on trade-offs of interests among parties who are already in agreement on the basic nature of the dispute.

We have suggested some of the complexities that arise in what we call complex conflicts and how the behavioral negotiation model cannot address these problems. We have suggested some ways of overcoming these problems and facilitating integrative agreements in environmental conflicts. Our ideas are admittedly speculative and require empirical examination, but we have reported relevant literature where possible.

Some could accuse us of arguing that people should be willing to negotiate anything and that people must place an economic price on core values. Certainly, it would seem that some things in life cannot have a price. We have argued that the refusal to consider trading certain things is part of a deeply rooted value system. But we have also argued, in line with Tetlock, Peterson, and Lerner (1996), that whether people are aware of it or not they do make choices that involve trade-offs. They may not realize that they can do this; nor do they usually frame the choices they make in terms of trade-offs. Instead, it appears that when values are involved, people fall into a lexicographic decision mode, which can affect negotiation. In the lexicographic decision mode, values drive the choice so that tradeoff does not seem relevant—the individual picks the option that appears best on the important value without regard to other values and their trade-offs. Our list of prescriptive suggestions can be interpreted as procedures to move individuals away from a lexicographic decision strategy to a more compensatory strategy.

The central message in this chapter is that people's interests are influenced by beliefs and values and that values often serve as self-justifying systems for the pursuit of interests. By pulling down the value smoke screens that hide the choices and trade-offs that people make, we may pave the way toward more effective conflict resolution, even in such complex and heated debates as those involving environmental issues.

REFERENCES

Aubert, V. "Competition and Dissensus: Two Types of Conflict and Conflict Resolution." *Conflict Resolution,* 1963, *7,* 26–42.

Balke, W. M., Hammond, K. R., and Meyer, G. D. "An Alternate Approach to Labor-Management Relations." *Administrative Science Quarterly,* 1973, *18,* 311–327.

Bazerman, M. H. "Fairness, Social Comparison, and Irrationality." In K. Murnighan (ed.), *Social Psychology in Organizations.* Englewood Cliffs, N.J.: Prentice Hall, 1993.

Bazerman, M. H., and Neale, M. A. "Heuristics in Negotiation: Limitations to Effective Dispute Resolution." In M. H. Bazerman and R. J. Lewicki (eds.), *Negotiating in Organizations.* Thousand Oaks, Calif.: Sage, 1983.

Bem, D. "Self-Perception: An Alternative Interpretation of Cognitive Dissonance Phenomena." *Psychological Review,* 1967, *74,* 183–200.

Brewer, M. "In-Group Bias in the Minimal Intergroup Situation: A Cognitive-Motivational Analysis." *Psychological Bulletin,* 1979, *86,* 307–324.

Brown, B. "The Effects of Need to Maintain Face on Interpersonal Bargaining." *Journal of Experimental Social Psychology,* 1968, *4,* 107–122.

Colby, M. *The Evolution of Paradigms of Environmental Management in Development.* Washington, D.C.: Strategic Planning Division, Strategic Planning and Review Department, World Bank, 1989.

Delios, H. "Arctic Preserve Focus of Symbolic Battle." *Chicago Tribune,* Nov. 15, 1995, p. 1.

Deutsch, M., and Gerard, H. B. "A Study of Normative and Informational Social Influence upon Individual Judgment." *Journal of Abnormal and Social Psychology,* 1955, *51,* 629–636.

Egri, C., and Pinfield, L. "Organization and the Biosphere: Ecologies and Environments." In *Handbook of Organizational Studies.* London: Sage, 1994.

Elster, J. "Strategic Uses of Argument." In K. Arrow and others (eds.), *Barriers to Conflict Resolution.* New York: Norton, 1995.

Espeland, W. "Legally Mediated Identity: The National Environmental Policy Act and the Bureaucratic Construction of Interests." *Law and Society Review,* 1994, *28*(5), 1149–1179.

Festinger, L. *A Theory of Cognitive Dissonance.* New York: HarperCollins, 1957.

Fisher, R., and Ury, W. *Getting to Yes: Negotiating Agreement Without Giving In.* Boston: Houghton Mifflin, 1981.

Fiske, S. T. "Controlling Other People: The Impact of Power on Stereotyping." *American Psychologist,* 1993, *48,* 621–628.

Frank, R. H. *Passions Within Reason: The Strategic Role of the Emotions.* New York: Norton, 1988.

French, J., and Raven, B. "The Bases of Social Power." In D. Cartwright (ed.), *Studies in Social Power.* Ann Arbor: University of Michigan Press, 1959.

Gibbons, R. *Game Theory for Applied Economists.* Princeton, N.J.: Princeton University Press, 1992.

Gladwin, T. N., Kennelly, J. J., and Krause, T. "Shifting Paradigms for Sustainable Development: Implications for Management Theory and Research." *Academy of Management Review,* Oct. 1995, pp. 874–907.

Glenn, E. S., Johnson, R. H., Kimmel, P. R., and Wedge, B. "A Cognitive Interaction Model to Analyze Culture Conflict in International Relations." *Journal of Conflict Resolution,* 1970, *14,* 34–48.

Hammond, K. "New Directions in Research on Conflict Resolution." *Journal of Social Issues,* 1965, *11,* 44–66.

Hammond, K., Stewart, T., Brehmer, B., and Steinmann, D. "Social Judgment Theory." In M. Kaplan and S. Schwartz (eds.), *Human Judgment and Decision Processes.* Orlando:, Fla. Academic Press, 1975.

Hastorf, A., and Cantril, H. "They Saw a Game: A Case Study." *Journal of Abnormal and Social Psychology,* 1954, *49,* 129–134.

Hoffman, A. J., and Ehrenfeld, J. R. "Deconstructing Corporate Environmentalism: Or, What Are We Really Talking About Here?" Paper presented at the fourth conference of the Greening of Industry Network, Toronto, Nov. 1995.

Jones, E. E., and Davis, K. E. "From Acts to Dispositions: The Attribution Process in Person Perception." In L. Berkowitz (ed.), *Advances in Experimental Social Psychology.* Orlando, Fla.: Academic Press, 1965.

Jones, E. E., and Gerard, H. B. *Foundations of Social Psychology.* New York: Wiley, 1967.

Kahn, R. L., and Kramer, R. M. "Untying the Knot: De-Escalatory Processes in International Conflict." In R. L. Kahn and M. N. Zald (eds.), *Organizations and Nation-States: New Perspectives on Conflict and Cooperation.* San Francisco: Jossey-Bass, 1990.

Keeney, R. *Value-Focused Thinking.* Cambridge, Mass.: Harvard University Press, 1992.

Kelley, H., and Thibaut, J. "Group Problem Solving." In G. Lindzey and E. Aronson (eds.), *Handbook of Social Psychology.* New York: Random House, 1969.

Kramer, R. "Dubious Battle: Heightened Accountability, Dysphoric Cognition, and Self-Defeating Bargaining Behavior." In R. Kramer and D. Messick (eds.), *Negotiation as a Social Process.* Thousand Oaks, Calif.: Sage, 1995.

Lax, D. A., and Sebenius, J. K. *The Manager as Negotiator.* New York: Free Press, 1986.

Linville, P. W., Fischer, G. W., and Salovey, P. "Perceived Distributions of Characteristics of In-Group and Out-Group Members: Empirical Evidence and a Computer Simulation." *Journal of Personality and Social Psychology,* 1989, *57,* 165–188.

Marwell, G. "Conflict over Proposed Group Actions: A Typology of Cleavage." *Journal of Conflict Resolution,* 1966, *14,* 135–175.

Messick, D. "Equality as a Decision Heuristic." In B. Mellers and J. Baron (eds.), *Psychological Perspectives on Justice: Theory and Applications.* New York: Cambridge University Press, 1992.

Morning Edition, National Public Radio, Nov. 3, 1995.

Murrow, E. R. *This is London.* New York: Simon & Schuster, 1941.

Neale, M. A., and Bazerman, M. H. *Cognition and Rationality in Negotiation.* New York: Free Press, 1991.

Oskamp, S. "Attitudes Toward U.S. and Russian Actions: A Double Standard." *Psychological Reports,* 1965, *16,* 43–46.

Porter, M. *Competitive Advantage.* New York: Free Press, 1985.

Pruitt, D. G., and Carnevale, P. J. *Negotiation in Social Conflict.* Pacific Grove, Calif.: Brooks/Cole, 1993.

Raiffa, H. *The Art and Science of Negotiation.* Cambridge, Mass.: Harvard University Press, Belknap Press, 1982.

Rapoport, A. *Fights, Games, and Debates.* Ann Arbor: University of Michigan Press, 1960.

Robinson, R., Keltner, D., Ward, A., and Ross, L. "Actual Versus Assumed Differences in Construal: 'Naive Realism' in Intergroup Perception and Conflict." *Journal of Personality and Social Psychology,* 1994.

Rokeach, M. *The Nature of Human Values.* New York: Free Press, 1973.

Ross, L. "The Intuitive Psychologist and His Shortcomings: Distortions in the Attribution Process." In L. Berkowitz (ed.), *Advances in Experimental Social Psychology.* Vol. 10. Orlando, Fla.: Academic Press, 1977.

Ross, L., and Stillinger, C. "Barriers to Conflict Resolution." *Negotiation Journal,* 1991, *8,* 389–404.

Ross, L., and Ward, A. "Psychological Barriers to Dispute Resolution." In M. Zanna (ed.), *Advances in Experimental Social Psychology.* Vol. 27. Orlando, Fla.: Academic Press, 1994.

Rothbart, M., and Hallmark, W. "In-Group and Out-Group Differences in the Perceived Efficacy of Coercion and Conciliation in Resolving Social Conflict." *Journal of Personality and Social Psychology,* 1988, *55,* 248–257.

Rubin, J. Z., Pruitt, D. G., and Kim, S. H. *Social Conflict: Escalation, Stalemate and Settlement.* (2nd ed.) New York: McGraw-Hill, 1994.

Schelling, T. *The Strategy of Conflict.* Cambridge, Mass.: Harvard University Press, 1960.

Schlenker, B. R. *Impression Management.* Pacific Grove, Calif.: Brooks/Cole, 1980.

Schwarz, N., and Clore, G. L. "How Do I Feel About It? The Informative Function of Affective States." In K. Fiedler and J. Forgas (eds.), *Affect, Cognition, and Social Behavior.* Toronto: Hogrefe, 1988.

Sherif, M., and others. *Intergroup Conflict and Cooperation: The Robber's Cave Experiment.* Norman: University of Oklahoma Press, 1961.

Susskind, L. E. "A Negotiation Credo for Controversial Siting Disputes." *Negotiation Journal,* Oct. 1990, pp. 309–314.

Swann, W. B., Pelham, B. W., and Roberts, D. C. "Causal Chunking: Memory and Inference in Ongoing Interaction." *Journal of Personality and Social Psychology,* 1987, *53*(5), 858–865.

Tajfel, H. "Experiments in Intergroup Discrimination." *Scientific American,* 1970, *223,* 96–102.

Tetlock, P. E., Peterson, R., and Lerner, J. "Revising the Value Pluralism Model: Incorporating Social Content and Context Postulates." In C. Seligman, J. Olson, and M. Zanna (eds.), *Values: Eighth Annual Ontario Symposium on Personality and Social Psychology.* Hillsdale, N.J.: Erlbaum, 1996.

Thaler, R. "Toward a Positive Theory of Consumer Choice." *Journal of Economic Behavioral Organization,* 1980, *1,* 39–60.

Thompson, L. "Negotiation Behavior and Outcomes: Empirical Evidence and Theoretical Issues." *Psychological Bulletin,* 1990, *108,* 515–532.

Thompson, L. *Negotiation Theory, Research, and Basic Principles.* Unpublished manuscript, Northwestern University, 1996.

Thompson, L., and DeHarpport, T. "Social Judgment, Feedback, and Interpersonal Learning in Negotiation." *Organizational Behavior and Human Decision Processes,* 1994, *58,* 327–345.

Thompson, L., and Hastie, R. "Judgment Tasks and Biases in Negotiation." In B. H. Sheppard, M. H. Bazerman, and R. J. Lewicki (eds.), *Research in Negotiation in Organizations.* Greenwich, Conn.: JAI Press, 1990a.

Thompson, L., and Hastie, R. "Social Perception in Negotiation." *Organizational Behavior and Human Decision Processes,* 1990b, *47,* 98–123.

Thompson, L., and Hrebec, D. "Lose-Lose Agreements in Interdependent Decision Making." *Psychological Bulletin,* 1996, *120*(3), 396–409.

Thompson, L., Valley, K., and Kramer, R. "The Bittersweet Feeling of Success: An Examination of Social Perception in Negotiation." *Journal of Experimental Social Psychology,* 1996, *31,* 467–492.

von Neumann, J., and Morgenstern, O. *Theory of Games and Economic Behavior.* (2nd ed.) Princeton, N.J.: Princeton University Press, 1947.

Walton, R. E., and McKersie, R. B. *A Behavioral Theory of Labor Relations.* New York: McGraw-Hill, 1965.

Whorf, B. L. "Science and Linguistics." In J. B. Carroll (ed.), *Language, Thought, and Reality. Selected Writings of Benjamin Whorf.* New York: Wiley, 1956.

Zajonc, R. "Feeling and Thinking: Preferences Need No Inferences." *American Psychologist,* 1980, *35,* 151–175.

6

THE DYSFUNCTIONAL ASPECTS OF ENVIRONMENTAL STANDARDS

Ann E. Tenbrunsel, Kimberly A. Wade-Benzoni, David M. Messick, and Max H. Bazerman

MANY OF THE DECISIONS businesses face affect the environment, including decisions about whether to use scarce resources, develop dysfunctional by-products, expose employees to risky substances, and market profitable but potentially harmful products. As illustrated in the recent collapse of the northeastern fishery, neglecting the environment in these decisions can result in severe and potentially irreversible consequences, not only for the businesses themselves but also for the stockholders, the employees, and the consumers. Regulation has been the solution of choice for these environmental problems. Environmental law is now an institutionalized response to such environmental concerns, with global efforts to deal with environmental problems hinging on the willingness to follow rules (Plater, Abrams, and Goldfarb, 1992). The popularity of regulation has resulted in a regulation "flood" (Plater, Abrams, and Goldfarb, 1992), with a staggering number of environmental laws (Orts, 1995).

Regulation has been popular for a good reason: legal standards can and do produce positive results. Lack of regulation can result in rampant

The authors would like to thank George Loewenstein for his insightful comments and the Center for the Study of Ethical Issues in Business, the Kellogg Environmental Research Center, and the Kellogg Dispute Resolution Resource Center for supporting this research.

destruction as individuals and corporations abandon their social responsibilities. Legislation provides individuals with guidelines for acceptable behavior that can minimize self-interested, destructive choices and enhance the welfare of our society (Plater, Abrams, and Goldfarb, 1992). By regulating the behaviors of individuals and firms that may have undesirable consequences, legal standards can create a just process and raise consciousness about destructive practices (Rosenbaum, 1991; Plater, Abrams, and Goldfarb, 1992). Indeed, regulation has been cited as one of the reasons we have seen a decrease in the use of chemical substances, such as the reduction of PCBs, a decrease in the use of pesticides such as DDT and known carcinogens, and the gradual elimination of asbestos and fluorocarbons (Rosenbaum, 1991).

Legal standards are indisputably beneficial and necessary. The benefits, however, should not blind us to the costs nor deter us from diagnosing problems that may arise from a regulatory approach to environmental problems. Despite the successes we have noted, existing standard-and-enforcement programs are generally not working, and it is this failure that may be the biggest challenge faced by environmentalists (Rosenbaum, 1991; Anderson and Leal, 1991). As Rosenbaum (1991) states, "No problem casts a larger shadow over the second environmental era than the continuing failure of environmental institutions and policies to achieve many essential regulatory goals" (p. 301). Given the increased environmental problems faced by this society, it is imperative that the causes for regulatory failures be not only determined but also understood theoretically and investigated empirically so that potential corrections may be identified.

Our purpose is to use a psychological perspective to investigate the problems associated with standards without denying their benefits. Many economists, environmentalists, and business executives have begun to espouse a nonregulatory approach to environmental problems (Anderson and Leal, 1991). It is not our goal to promote this approach. Rather, we seek to understand psychologically the problems that may arise from a standard-based approach. Only after the problems are identified and empirically investigated can a more informed comparison be made about the advantages and disadvantages of a regulatory approach.

Legal standards, although directing and mobilizing effort toward solving environmental problems, can and do have negative side effects. Realizing the costs of the current system may help this society devise more effective and efficient environmental protection. We propose that one of the main sources of these costs is that legal standards become an independent force, taking on a life of their own, leaving rationality, innovation, and societal interest behind. In this chapter, we first provide evidence of the suboptimal outcomes that can result from an adherence to standards. We then suggest that this suboptimality is due to a tendency for standards to direct attention toward the law itself and away from the purpose of the law. In a previous paper, we argued that one explanation for this misdirected attention is the cognitive distortions that standards can produce (Tenbrunsel, Wade-Benzoni, Messick, and Bazerman, 1996). In this chapter, we suggest that there is also a motivational explanation, namely that standard-based systems can change the incentive systems for individuals and promote self-interested rather than societally based behavior. We suggest that the suboptimal outcomes that result are the product of (1) unintentional actions on the part of the decision maker, where rules are being followed as they were intended, and (2) intentional actions, where decision makers purposely engage in undesirable behaviors in order to beat the system. Finally, we argue that the uncertainty of legal standards provides the opportunity for justifying self-interested behavior at the expense of societally beneficial behavior.

Suboptimal Outcomes: Anecdotal and Empirical Evidence

Suboptimal outcomes resulting from a focus on complying with a legal standard, rather than on achieving the objective underlying the standard, are numerous. Consider the following two examples.

In an effort to reduce sulfur dioxide emissions, Congress followed historical tradition by requiring strict adherence to a "best available technology" standard for new coal-fired generating plants. This standard forced owners of such plants to install expensive stack-gas scrubbers when an alternative of using cleaner, low-sulfur western coal was available. The end result: adherence to the best available technology standard resulted in a solution that was more expensive and less effective, costing businesses and ultimately consumers in the form of increased electricity costs (Anderson and Leal, 1991).

A state is having a problem with pollution. A consensus has emerged that less pollution would be desirable, and as a result, a pollution standard has been specified. The solution to this problem specification requires manufacturers to use "tall stacks." Tall stacks send the pollution a larger distance, diminishing the effect on the local citizens. Unfortunately, this behavior by U.S. firms disperses pollutants into the upper atmosphere where they are "air mailed" to Canada (Rosenbaum, 1991).

Similar problems are echoed in Howard's *The Death of Common Sense* (1994), which presents many stories and arguments that testify to the problems created by environmental, legal, and building standards. One example concerning toxic waste cleanup helps drive home the point.

> Under one requirement, before industrial land with any toxic waste can be used, it must be cleaned up to almost perfect purity. It sounds great, but the effect is to drive industry out to virgin fields, where it encounters no such costs. Instead of cleaning up one dirty lot, the strict law creates a second dirty lot [p. 8].

These common stories emphasize that standards often lead to a focus on how to meet that standard, rather than a focus on how to optimally deal with the underlying problem. Many corporate environmental officers argue that employee time is entirely used up meeting legal standards, not allowing them to create truly meaningful environmental changes. Our point is not to apologize for corporations but to theoretically and empirically investigate the downside of environmental standards.

Tenbrunsel, Wade-Benzoni, Messick, and Bazerman (1996) empirically explored whether standards lead decision makers to depart from optimal decisions. It was argued that most decisions are presented to decision makers one at a time; for example, Is this company making an appropriate effort to reduce pollution? The presence of standards in an assessment of multidimensional behavior was predicted to result in a more favorable evaluation of suboptimal behavior that meets a standard than of optimal behavior that violates the standard; however, it was argued that this would occur only when the decision maker was assessing one option at a time. It also argued that when decision makers choose between two or more options, they see the superiority of optimal behavior that violates the standard over suboptimal behavior that meets a standard. This set of predictions was based on a recent line of research on preference reversals (Blount and Bazerman, 1996; Bazerman and others, 1994; Irwin, Slovic, Lichtenstein, and McClelland, 1993; Kahneman, Ritov, Jacowitz, and Grant, 1993) suggesting that individuals exhibit preference inconsistencies in single (one option evaluated at a time) versus multiple-choice (multiple options evaluated together) contexts.

Tenbrunsel, Wade-Benzoni, Messick, and Bazerman (1996) placed subjects in the role of a citizen advisory board member who had been asked to evaluate arsenic emissions of a copper plant. The copper plant's three component processes were emitting arsenic, believed to cause arsenic-related cancers. The relationship between the level of emissions from the component processes and related cancers was described as linear, so that any reduction in the emission of arsenic would result in a corresponding decrease in the number of related cancers. Subjects were told that in order to reduce the dangers of copper smelters, the Environmental Protection Agency (EPA) has set regulations governing emissions, specifically setting a limit of no more than 100 tons per year per component process.

As board members, subjects were told that they were to rate one or more proposals submitted by the plant to reduce the current emissions. Subjects were placed into one of three conditions: (1) Single "meets standard": subjects evaluated a single plan in which every component process met the EPA regulation by emitting no more than 100 tons per year. (2) Single "does not meet standard": subjects evaluated a single plan in which although only one component process met the EPA regulation, the total emissions were less than that of the single "meets standard" plan. (3) Multiple: subjects evaluated both the single "meets standard" plan and the single "does not meet standard" plan.

The plant's previous emissions, emissions under the EPA recommendations, and emissions under the company's proposals, listed in Table 6.1, were then provided to the subjects. Subjects were not given the labels of "meets standard" and "does not meet standard" plan but rather were asked to evaluate the "plan" (single-condition subjects) or "plan A and plan B" (multiple-condition subjects). Subjects in the single condition saw data for only one of the plans. Subjects in the multiple condition saw the entire set of data. In the single condition, they were asked if the plan should be approved by the EPA (yes or no). In the multiple condition, they were asked which plan, if either, the EPA should approve (plan A, plan B, or neither). The overwhelming number of subjects who were in the single "meets standard" condition thought that the plan should be approved (twenty-seven versus four). Fifteen subjects in the single "does not meet standard" condition thought the plan should be approved, and fourteen thought it should not. However, subjects who saw both plans overwhelmingly favored the "does not meet standard" plan: five thought the "meets standard" plan should be approved, nineteen thought the "does not meet standard" plan should be approved, and one individual thought neither plan should be approved.

Thus, for plans presented singly, the approval rate for the smaller reduction "meets standard" plan was almost nine to five over the greater reduction "does not meet standard" plan; however, when the plans were presented together, the approval ratio was almost four to one in favor of the greater reduction "does not meet standard" plan. Ratings of acceptability of the plans followed a similar pattern, with ratings of acceptabil-

Table 6.1. Data for Emissions from Three Component Processes at a Copper Plant as Presented to Study Subjects.

Component Process	Previous	EPA Standards	"Meets Standard" Plan	"Does Not Meet Standard" Plan
1	200	100	97	108
2	200	100	91	115
3	200	100	95	9
Total	600	300	283	232

ity slightly higher for the smaller reduction "meets standard" plan in the single condition but much higher for the greater reduction "does not meet standard" plan in the multiple condition. Here we see that when assessing one option at a time, decision makers evaluate suboptimal choices that adhere to a standard more highly than optimal choices that violate the standard.

Environmental Standards: Changing the Motivators

The anecdotal and empirical evidence presented suggests that adherence to legal standards can lead to suboptimal results. A focus on the legal standard can lead to a neglect of the purpose behind the standard, encouraging environmentally unfriendly (or less friendly) behavior. In an attempt to understand the process by which suboptimal outcomes result from the presence of legal standards, we propose that regulation may change the incentive structure system for individual decision makers.

Standard-based systems, by setting up criteria that one should adhere to, narrow the decision objective to one of compliance with the standard. The "law itself, not the goals to be advanced by law, is now our focus . . . law's original goal is lost" (Howard, 1994, p. 49). We argue that the suboptimal outcomes that can result from this narrow focus are due both to unintentional actions on the part of decision makers who are just following the rules of the system, and intentional actions whereby decision makers attempt to "beat the system."

Just Follow the Rules

People who desire to do the right thing by focusing on the purpose of the legal standard rather than the standard itself are discouraged, and potentially penalized, for attempting to do so. As Howard (1994, p. 50) states, "Rules preclude initiative. Regimentation precludes evolution." Indeed, the focus on complying with existing rules has been pinpointed as a force against innovation and creativity in solving environmental problems. Take the thwarted creative attempt by Amoco as an example of this problem (Dowd, 1994). Amoco, in a joint effort with the EPA, determined that it could achieve a far greater percentage reduction in benzene emissions through a $6 million expenditure that would change the method by which gasoline was loaded into barges than through a $30 million expenditure that would upgrade its wastewater treatment system. The problem: the EPA regulations only addressed sewage systems and did not address barges. Consequently, the innovative technique was not an option. Current farm regulation is also seen as encouraging compliance and discouraging creative solutions. Current farm programs, including subsidized irrigation and crop insurance, arguably send the wrong signals to farmers by encouraging them to break prairie sod and plant crops in arid regions rather than to develop creative solutions (including no farming in certain regions) that may more effectively solve the problem (Anderson and Leal, 1991). Similarly, Superfund dollars, from a regulated enterprise that oversees and helps finance waste site cleanup, are seen as decreasing the incentive for polluters to develop new and better technology (Anderson and Leal, 1991).

The incentive to attend to the legal standard may not only discourage innovation but may also promote self-interested behavior. Anderson and Leal (1991) provide an illustration of this phenomenon in their discussion of private property. They describe a regulatory situation in which property owners who wish to leave some of their entitled water in the stream for the fishes, rather than divert it all to their property as they are entitled to do, would lose claim to the water because the use would not be considered beneficial. This "use it or lose it" structure creates a paradoxical situation, forcing individuals to look out for their best interests whether they desire to or not.

The resulting "follow the rules" mentality may lead to a more permanent motivational change whereby individual responsibility for societal problems is dramatically diminished. Specifically, the excessive use of legal standards to govern behavior may replace one's intrinsic motivation to behave in an environmentally friendly manner with an extrinsic motivation driven by legal standards. Deci's work (1971) on motivation supports this idea. Deci suggested that the presence of an extrinsic source of motivation may actually decrease or undermine intrinsic motivation. In particular, Deci (1975) discovered that extrinsic factors that were perceived as controlling, rather than informational, were associated with a shift to extrinsic motivational processes.

Applying Deci's research to environmental regulation, it may be that the intrinsic motivation to do what is optimal or what is right is replaced by the extrinsic motivation to do that which is enforced and controlled by the standard. We propose that the shift in motivational forces may result in a "no law against it" mentality, which may actually increase environmentally unfriendly behavior in unregulated situations. Specifically, if intrinsic environmental ethics are replaced by extrinsic law-governed values, what happens when one faces a situation where there is no regulation? Deci's work suggests that one's undesirable behaviors might actually increase in these situations because the extrinsic factor (the legal standard) is missing. If, for example, the government regulates one type of carcinogenic emissions (type A), but does not regulate another (type B) for political reasons, a business may wash its hands of responsibility and emit type B in vast quantities because there is no law that says it cannot do so. In this sense then, regulation can foster a "no law against it" mentality that encourages undesirable behaviors in unregulated situations.

Beating the System

The preceding discussion focused on suboptimal outcomes that resulted from the system itself: attention is focused on the standard, which may decrease effort to develop more innovative solutions to the problem and may increase undesirable actions in areas not currently governed by legal standards. In these situations, decision makers are not intentionally engaging in behaviors that produce suboptimal outcomes. Rather, as Darley (1994) states, a person, "with the best will in the world, does what optimizes his or her performance measurements, without realizing that this is not what the system really intended" (pp. 18–19).

A standard-based system can have another, more ethically questionable and at least as destructive side effect. Individuals faced with a legal environmental standard may cheat the system by exploiting its weaknesses (Darley, 1994). Thus, perhaps even worse than shifting people's motivations away from protecting the environment and toward adherence to a standard, legal standards and their accompanying measures may actually induce decision makers to influence the measures without regard to what is happening to the environment, potentially producing destructive results. The following illustration was relayed to one of the authors in an MBA class by a student who had been a naval jet pilot instructor.

The instructor's responsibility was to train young men and women to fly combat jets. Each month, the squadron was allocated jet fuel on the basis of the amount of fuel it had used in the previous month. Following a month in which there had been bad weather and in which there had been few training missions, the squadron risked receiving less fuel than it might have the opportunity to use if the weather in the following month was good.

The squadron leader who told this story considered not flying in good weather because of a lack of fuel to pose a great risk because the lack of training could jeopardize the students if they were in combat. To insure against this risk, at the end of each month he filled the squadron's fuel tanks, flew into the upper atmosphere, and dumped the jet fuel, thereby qualifying for a full allocation for the following period. A perfectly reasonable-appearing method of measuring fuel use (and need) had the effect of polluting the atmosphere and incurring unnecessary fuel costs.

The example illustrates how the presence of legal standards and measures may induce a reaction in people to try to beat the system. Cialdini's theoretical discussion (1996) on surveillance technology lends support to this notion. Cialdini asserts that the placement of surveillance technology can replace an individual's intrinsic motivation for behaving appropriately because "it is the right thing to do" with an extrinsic motivation for behaving appropriately because "the system is watching." This switch in motivations is posited to result in individuals attempting to trick or bypass the surveillance mechanisms (Deci and Ryan, 1987; Cialdini, 1996). Thus, if one knows how pollution is detected, one may conceal the pollutants rather than eliminate them. If one knows how inspections are done, one may try to deceive the inspectors rather than reduce hazardous substances. If there is a system that fines polluters, one may try to avoid being fined rather than avoid polluting.

Procedural rules and standards are seen as creating perfect opportunities for "slick operators" (Howard, 1994). Originally intended to ensure that society behaved responsibly, standard-based systems and processes have instead been used to create devices that allow for manipulation and extortion. The end result is a system with unintended, and often ignored, costs.

Ambiguity and Self-Serving Actions

The preceding sections explored the ways in which standards might change the incentive system for individuals, thereby creating dysfunctional outcomes. We argue in this section that ambiguity may only exacerbate the problem by creating an opportunity for individuals to seek self-serving outcomes.

Ambiguity surrounding the regulation process can promote unintended problems that lead to the failure of regulatory systems. Susskind (1994) argues that uncertainty allows for loose interpretation of standards. The lack of clarity that results from this uncertainty is in turn seen as one of the reasons for overexploitation (Anderson and Leal, 1991) of natural resources.

Environmental standards tend to be surrounded by uncertainty in several ways. First, there is uncertainty about the behavior of the natural environment. Second, there is uncertainty about the process of determining legal standards, and the levels at which to set them. Third, there is often uncertainty in the interpretation of the legal standard itself. These sources of uncertainty may provide individuals with a justification for self-interested rather than environmentally conscious behavior.

Much of the ecological debate over such issues as the use of fisheries or the maintenance of clean air concerns the definition of "safe" levels of resource use (Messick, 1991) or pollution discharge. The point at which exploitation will endanger future access to a resource is often unclear. For example, it may be difficult to determine when a heavily harvested renewable resource will collapse, or how long it will take to recover, or if recovery is possible at all. Similarly, it is difficult to predict the level at which pollutants will cause adverse effects on humans. The behavior of the natural environment frequently surprises us, and there is much that is unknown about our interrelationship with nature. We sometimes inadvertently disrupt the elegant balance of ecological systems, often with the good intention of improving the world. Such was the case with the creation of chlorofluorocarbons (CFCs), global warming, and the draining of the wetlands. In fact, it is a rare case when we can predict with absolute certainty the behavior of the natural environment. We are even frequently surprised by the weather, despite tenacious efforts invested in forecasting it.

Uncertainty regarding the behavior of the natural environment leads to uncertainty about establishing environmental legal standards. If we are unsure about a resource's ability to replenish itself, how do we know what level of harvesting is sustainable? Our environmental standards seem to imply that safe levels of environmental contaminants can be found. For example, the Clean Air Act requires the EPA to provide "an adequate margin of safety . . . requisite to protect public health" in setting National Ambient Air Quality Standards (Portney and Harrington, 1995). One can imagine the problems in interpreting such vague and ambiguous language. A lower ambient concentration of a particular pollutant almost always implies a lower risk of adverse health effects. In the case of air pollution, even very low levels of pollutants pose some risk of adverse reactions in children and the elderly with chronic respiratory disease. Thus it would seem that no safe level is likely to exist for pollutants. Portney and Harrington (1995) point out that if air quality standards are required by law to provide an adequate margin of safety, and if even weak concentrations of pollutants pose some risk to some individuals, then it would appear that only zero concentrations could be permitted under law. However, we know that total elimination of pollution is impossible and pollution standards are rarely set at zero. Thus we can deduce that the process by which legal standards are set involves more than just safety considerations. When setting standards, rather than ask, What is safe? we are more likely to ask, What is safe *enough*? What is politically, financially, and technically feasible? What is reasonable? or What is appropriate? Recalling an eight-hour briefing on fine particulate standards, Rosenbaum (1991), citing William Ruckelshaus, former administrator of the EPA, elucidates how regulation is open to technical controversy and litigation, thus making the management of chemical waste problematic: "Our scientists told me that we can defend any standard between 150 and 250 parts per million. So pick a number" (p. 142).

The uncertainty about the behavior of the natural environment and its effects on us leads to uncertainty in the establishment of appropriate legal standards, which in turn augments the uncertainty in the interpretation of standards. If one knows that a legal standard has been established in accordance with the "pick a number" method, one is likely to question the importance of meeting it with precision—especially if meeting the legal standard conflicts with one's self-interest. To illustrate, we will briefly describe an observation from our classrooms that is consistent with this effect.

In a four-party social dilemma simulation case that we use in our negotiations classes, we observe students actually perceiving different levels of uncertainty surrounding a standard depending on how hard it is to solve the dilemma. Students play the role of fishers who are collectively overharvesting a particular fishery. They are told that marine scientists have assessed their fishery and determined that it is overfished. A species is overfished if it is reduced to a level that is too low to enable the species to sustain its existence over time. The maximum annual catch that can be taken from a fishery without diminishing its overall size is called the maximum sustainable yield, or MSY. MSY is determined by the size of the group, annual growth rates, and the age structure of the group. Thus a level of harvesting that is greater than the MSY level means that in the long run, the fish population will not be able to reproduce itself and will eventually become commercially extinct. In the classroom simulation, parties are informed that estimates of their fishery reveal that their total collective catch level is significantly higher than the MSY, and thus the fishery's viability as a commercial resource is at risk. Participants are told that the MSY is half of the total current collective harvest.

The constraints of the dilemma are such that the four parties benefit more from mutual cooperation in one version of the case than in a second version. In the first version, where the dilemma is easier to solve, students accept the MSY that is given to them and use it as a goal. In the second version, where the problem is harder to solve, students question the MSY and bring up the issues of uncertainty in the standard-setting process and in the recovery capabilities of the resource. They tend to decide as a group that a higher collective harvest is a better goal, acceptable because of the uncertainty surrounding the MSY. Students see and focus on uncertainty in the standard when the standard is harder to meet, whereas uncertainty surrounding the standard does not come up as an issue when the standard is relatively easy to meet. The standard (MSY) is the same objective level in both cases. In addition, the definition of MSY and the standard-setting process are described precisely the same way in both cases. Thus there is no more objective uncertainty in one case than in the other.

In this example, it seems that uncertainty is sought out and embraced because it provides a justification for self-serving behavior. In real-life resource dilemmas, there is ambiguity about the resource's future—how fast it will replenish itself and how each party will be affected. Such ambiguity makes it difficult to determine safe levels of harvesting. When people are faced with so much ambiguity, their judgments tend to be biased in a manner that favors themselves (Thompson and Loewenstein, 1992).

Humans have a well-developed capacity for rationalization. Self-interest is one of the most important nonobjective influences on information processing and it is well established that people tend to conflate what is personally beneficial with what is fair or moral (Loewenstein, 1995). Uncertainty, by providing a justification, can encourage self-interested (Hsee, 1994) and unethical (Tenbrunsel, 1995) choices. Recent research by Hsee (1994) points directly to the prevalence of rationalization in situations involving uncertainty. When exposed to a decision involving trade-offs between normatively justifiable options and options more attractive to the decision maker, subjects opt for the more justifiable alternative when the attributes of the options are precisely defined. However, when uncertainty is introduced, there is a strong preference in favor of the more personally attractive option.

The current ambiguity of legal standards is seen as exacerbating the incentive structure problems described previously. By providing individuals with the opportunity to interpret regulatory constraints as they see fit (Kaplan and Harrison, 1993), individuals are given an additional reason or justification for behaving in a self-interested manner. Thus ambiguity helps to tip the self-and-society pendulum away from environmentally friendly behaviors and toward environmentally unfriendly behaviors.

Policy Implications

Our argument against dysfunctional standards could easily be taken out of context and be used to suggest that we are anti-regulation, which is certainly not the case. Rather, we believe that society should move toward wiser regulations—an obviously moderate political position without an effective sponsor.

Unfortunately, some people use the term *regulatory reform* to mean gutting regulation to enrich big business. We think that regulations should be reformed so as to improve the economic environment while simultaneously creating a better regulatory environment. In many cases, wiser regulation could allow for greater environmental improvement at a lower economic cost than current regulation. We see the need for a bipartisan search for wiser regulations that eliminate dysfunctional standards and provide better standards that business and environmental groups can rally behind. In this way, our purpose is similar to that of many business leaders, local officials, and angry citizens who are arguing that new rules should be based on sound science and solid economics (Dowd, 1994).

This argument contradicts the win-lose mentality that is widespread in the environmental debate. What we hear and read are anecdotes that support the need for more or less regulation. We read about a silly regulation that wastes millions of dollars to provide trivial environmental benefit,

Figure 6.1. The Current Economic-Environment Debate.

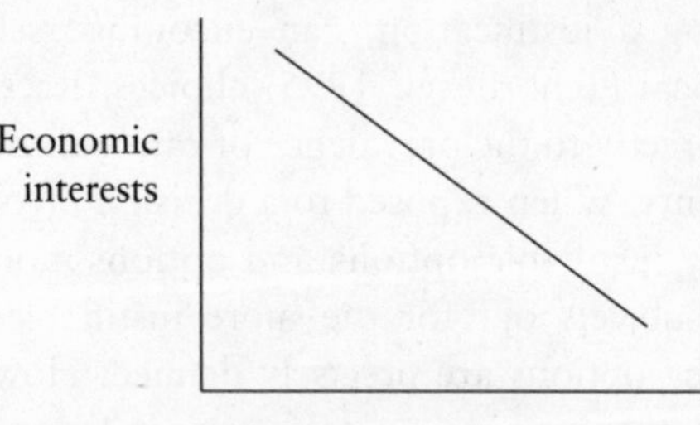

and we read about companies that abuse the environment and need to be regulated. Why? These anecdotes provide good soundbites to politicians, while destroying our economic and environmental interests. Currently, the debate pits economic interests against environmental interests, as in the diagram in Figure 6.1. We argue that wiser regulation would change the debate to a creative search for solutions that reward both economic and environmental interests, moving the plotted line to the northeast on the diagram in Figure 6.2. Once we create great gains to the northeast, the debate can continue along the efficient economic-environment frontier. Effective political solutions result in finding trade-offs in which each party gives up something less important in return for something more important to it. However, the wrong environmental debate emerges when both sides assume that "What is good for the other side is bad for us," capturing the essence of the mythical fixed pie.

Figure 6.2. Wiser Regulations Support a More Efficient Economic-Environment Frontier.

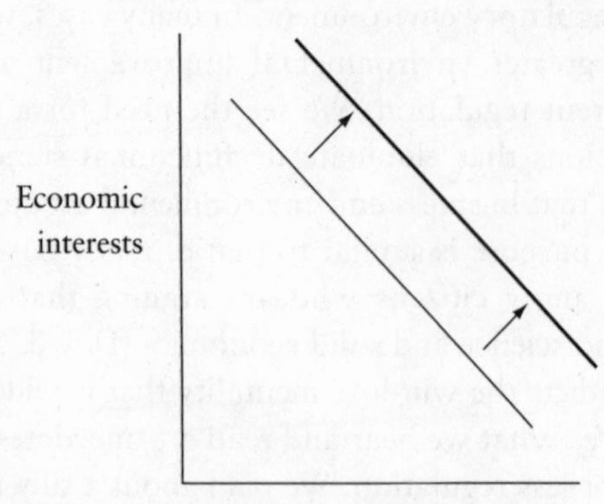

Conclusion

Our goal in this chapter was to begin an examination of why regulatory systems can fail. We wanted to respond to the call for regulation based on sound science by taking a psychological perspective to investigate why regulation might not achieve promised environmental benefits and, in some cases, why it might actually harm the environment. We proposed that regulation can actually change the incentive structure for individual decision makers, encouraging self-interest at the expense of societal interest, in turn producing suboptimal outcomes. In situations characterized by legal standards, it appears that innovation is discouraged and even penalized. In addition to a situation-by-situation influence, we also asserted that there may be a more permanent shift in motivational forces. Specifically, we asserted that a regulation mentality can shift one's motivation away from intrinsic, environmentally friendly behaviors and attitudes toward extrinsic, standard-based actions. The extrinsic emphasis on the legal standard can in turn promote environmentally unfriendly behaviors, both by creating a gaming system whereby decision makers' focus becomes one of beating the system and by institutionalizing a "no law against it" mentality. Finally, we argued that the shift toward self-interest is further exacerbated by the inherent ambiguity characteristic of the regulatory system.

Empirical investigation of these ideas is one step toward answering the call for environmental standards based on sound science. One recommendation that may come from empirical support for these ideas is a need to change the regulatory incentive system to harness self-interest without diminishing the positive effects that environmental legal standards can and do have. One of the ways to do this may be to bridge the incentive structures for the regulated with that of the regulator. Browner, the EPA administrator, has begun to realize the need for such an alignment: "We need to create incentives for plant managers in companies all across the country to look for ways to get the most out of pollution control for the least amount of money. I need those guys working with me" (Dowd, 1994, p. 100).

We believe that understanding the problems of the current system is the first step in constructing such a bridge.

REFERENCES

Anderson, T. L., and Leal, D. R. *Free Market Environmentalism.* San Francisco: Pacific Research Institute for Public Policy, 1991.

Bazerman, M. H., and others. "The Inconsistent Role of Comparison Others and Procedural Justice to Hypothetical Job Descriptions: Implications for Job Acceptance Decisions." *Organizational Behavior and Human Decision Processes,* 1994, *60,* 326–352.

Blount, S. B., and Bazerman, M. H. "The Inconsistent Evaluation of Comparative Payoffs in Labor Supply and Bargaining." *Journal of Economic Behavior and Organization,* 1996, *57,* 426–441.

Cialdini, R. B. "Social Influence and the Triple Tumor Structure of Organizational Dishonesty." In D. M. Messick and A. E. Tenbrunsel (eds.), *Codes of Conduct: Behavioral Research into Business Ethics.* New York: Russell Sage Foundation, 1996.

Darley, J. "Gaming, Gundecking, Body Counts, and the Loss of Three British Cruisers at the Battle of Outland: The Complex Moral Consequences of Performance Measurement Systems in Military Settings." Paper presented to the fourteenth Biennial Applied Behavioral Sciences Symposium, Colorado Springs, Colo., 1994.

Deci, E. L. "Effects of Externally Mediated Rewards on Intrinsic Motivation." *Journal of Personality and Social Psychology,* 1971, *18,* 105–115.

Deci, E. L. *Intrinsic Motivation.* New York: Plenum, 1975.

Deci, E. L., and Ryan, R. M. "The Supports of Autonomy and the Control of Behavior." *Journal of Personality and Social Psychology,* 1987, *53,* 1024–1037.

Dowd, A. R. "Environmentalists Are on the Run." *Fortune,* Sept. 19, 1994, pp. 91–100.

Howard, P. K. *The Death of Common Sense.* New York: Warner Books, 1994.

Hsee, C. "The Elasticity Effect: Uncertainty-Allowed Choice Shift Toward a Tempting but Task-Irrelevant Direction." Working paper, University of Chicago, Graduate School of Business, 1994.

Irwin, J. R., Slovic, P., Lichtenstein, S., and McClelland, G. H. "Preference Reversals and the Measurement of Environmental Values." *Journal of Risk and Uncertainty,* 1993, *6,* 5–18.

Kahneman, D., Ritov, I., Jacowitz, K. E., and Grant, P. "Stated Willingness to Pay for Public Goods: A Psychological Perspective." *Psychological Science,* 1993, *4,* 310–315.

Kaplan, M. R., and Harrison, J. R. "Defusing the Director Liability Crisis: The Strategic Management of Legal Threats." *Organization Science,* 1993, *4,* 412–432.

Loewenstein, G. "Behavioral Decision Theory and Business Ethics: Skewed Tradeoffs Between Self and Other." In D. M. Messick and A. E. Tenbrunsel (eds.), *Ethical Issues in Managerial Decision Making.* New York: Russell Sage Foundation, 1995.

Messick, D. M. "Social Dilemmas, Shared Resources, and Social Justice." In H. Steensma and R. Vermunt (eds.), *Social Justice in Human Relations.* Vol. 2. New York: Plenum, 1991.

Orts, E. W. "Reflexive Environmental Law." *Northwestern University Law Review,* 1995, *89,* 1–139.

Plater, Z.J.B., Abrams, R. H., and Goldfarb, W. *Environmental Law and Policy: Nature, Law, and Society.* St. Paul, Minn.: West, 1992.

Portney, P. R., and Harrington, W. "Health-Based Environmental Standards: Balancing Costs with Benefits." *Resources,* 1995, *120,* 7–10.

Rosenbaum, W. A. *Environmental Politics and Policy.* Washington, D.C.: Congressional Quarterly, 1991.

Susskind, L. E. *Environmental Diplomacy.* New York: Oxford University Press, 1994.

Tenbrunsel, A. E. "Justifying Unethical Behavior: The Role of Expectations of Others' Behavior and Uncertainty." Unpublished doctoral dissertation, Northwestern University, Evanston, Ill., 1995.

Tenbrunsel, A. E., Wade-Benzoni, K. A., Messick, D. M., and Bazerman, M. H. "The Dysfunctional Aspects of Standards: A Psychological Explanation and Empirical Demonstration of When Standard-Based Systems Produce Suboptimal Outcomes." Working paper, 1996.

Thompson, L., and Loewenstein, G. "Egocentric Interpretations of Fairness and Interpersonal Conflict." *Organizational Behavior and Human Decision Processes,* 1992, *51,* 176–197.

7

ATTITUDES, ATTITUDE STRUCTURE, AND RESISTANCE TO CHANGE

Implications for Persuasion on Environmental Issues

Alice H. Eagly and Patrick Kulesa

AS THE TWENTIETH century draws to a close, environmental issues are increasingly the subject of media attention and a focus of social action. After a rapid increase in environmental awareness and concern in the late 1960s and some decrease in the 1970s, public support for environmental protection increased again in the 1980s and remains relatively high (Dunlap and Scarce, 1991). In 1990, slightly over 20 percent of Americans who were surveyed listed the environment as the first or second most important problem facing the United States, and 78 percent endorsed the sentiment that a major effort should be made to try to improve the quality of the environment (Dunlap and Scarce, 1991). In the European Community in 1992, 85 percent of respondents considered protecting the environment and fighting pollution to be urgent problems (Finger, 1994).

Consistent with this general concern about the environment, issues such as the logging of old-growth forests in the Pacific Northwest and the building of dams on rivers capture public attention from time to time and illustrate the conflict between human use of environmental resources and the preservation of natural environments. As such issues have emerged, attempts to influence the public have accelerated. Winning the support of large segments of the population is essential in such debates because public policy on controversial issues ultimately reflects public perceptions of the advantages and disadvantages of various courses of action. Communications directed to the general public are important, not only because they may influence public opinion and therefore have an impact on public policy, but also because they are potentially effective in inducing individuals to engage in behaviors that can lessen the destructive impact of humans on the environment. For example, persuasive communications on transportation issues have the potential to induce changes in thinking that foster increased use of public transportation, to the extent that they portray positive consequences of using public transportation (such as reduced pollution) and discount negative consequences (such as inconvenience). Indeed, to change public policies and citizen behavior, environmental activists have little practical alternative to influencing the public through communications presented in the mass media.

A first question to address is whether persuasive communications can change attitudes and behaviors sufficiently that environmental problems could be alleviated. Although some scholars have argued that mass communication has little effect on public attitudes (for example, McGuire, 1985), the modern view is that media have sizable impact under limited conditions, especially when the public is repeatedly exposed to messages advocating a particular view. For example, communications through the media are no doubt important in inducing the increasing participation in environmental actions such as recycling (33 percent participation reported in 1972 versus 80 percent in 1990; see Dunlap and Scarce, 1991). However, the most striking example of an exceptionally effective persuasion campaign is the campaign against smoking, which began in 1964 with the publication of the report of the U.S. Surgeon General's Advisory Committee on Smoking and Health. Persuasive materials carried by the media emphasized the unhealthful consequences of smoking, and compulsory health warnings were introduced on tobacco advertisements and cigarette packages. In addition, policy shifts included increases in excise taxes on tobacco and restrictions on the locations where smoking is allowed. These changes made smoking considerably more expensive and less convenient. As a result of this antismoking campaign and associated changes in public policy (Hu, Sung, and Keeler, 1995), smoking has declined substantially (see also Nelson and others, 1995).

In this chapter, we apply theories of attitudes and attitude change to understand how attitudes and beliefs about environmental issues might be influenced by persuasive appeals. Important to designing effective appeals is an understanding of attitude structure, especially the link between environmental attitudes and important social values. In addition, modes of effective persuasion are discussed, including the use of fear-inducing appeals. We also consider relations between attitudes and behavior in order to understand the conditions under which changed attitudes would promote environmentally friendly behavior. Throughout our analysis, we emphasize that attitude theory and research have very useful practical implications for the design of effective communications on environmental issues.

Attitude Structure

To introduce attitude theory, we first explain what attitudes are and then examine aspects of attitude structure that are especially relevant to persuasion on environmental issues. There is general agreement among contemporary attitude theorists that an *attitude* is a psychological tendency that is expressed by evaluating a particular entity with some degree of favor or disfavor (Eagly and Chaiken, 1993). Expressed succinctly, attitudes are people's evaluations of entities, which are called *attitude objects* in the parlance of attitude theory. Attitude objects can be virtually anything—that is, any entity that is distinguished in an individual's mind.

Although individuals may have predispositions to respond positively or negatively to certain classes of stimuli, an attitude does not exist until the entity in question has elicited an evaluative response. Evaluative responding, whether it is covert or overt, can produce a psychological tendency to respond with a particular degree of evaluation when subsequently encountering the attitude object. If this tendency to respond is established, the person can be said to have formed an attitude toward the object.

An overall evaluation of an attitude object may be stored in memory and subsequently retrieved (such as "recycling cans and bottles is good"), or the tendency to evaluate may be carried forward to new situations by memories that are more episodic and less abstract (such as the good feel experienced last week when recycling cans). The experiences that produced the evaluative tendency are also stored. The perceiver may represent these experiences as associations that link the attitude object with the relevant aspects of her or his prior experience. We use the term *intra-attitudinal structure* for this aspect of attitude structure (Eagly and Chaiken, 1993).

To understand intra-attitudinal structure, readers might think about a citizen who moves to a community that has a curbside recycling program in place. Reading a pamphlet about the program would allow the citizen to encode some characteristics of the program and would perhaps produce affective reactions as well (such as a feeling of pride about the program), and these cognitions and affective reactions would remain associated with the curbside program in the person's mind. Cognitions representing the attributes or characteristics of curbside recycling are known as *beliefs* in attitude theory. Simultaneously, the evaluative content of these beliefs and of the affective reactions could be abstracted by the person to produce an overall attitude toward the recycling program. Furthermore, the evaluative content of the behaviors the citizen engaged in as he or she participated in recycling could contribute to his or her overall attitude, and representations of these behaviors could remain associated with the attitude. Subsequent experiences, both direct and indirect, would provide additional associations. With repeated experiences, associations concerning the attitude object would become more abstract and thereby summarize many past experiences. For example, repeated experience with placing the recycling bin at the curb might produce the belief that the program is "convenient." In this manner, the citizen's personal history of responding to recycling on a cognitive, affective, and behavioral basis imparts to this attitude its internal (or intra-attitudinal) structure.

The term *structure* also implies relationships between attitudes and thus refers to molar structures that encompass more than one attitude. We have termed these properties of attitudes *inter-attitudinal structure* (Eagly and Chaiken, 1993). Attitudes thus become linked to one another when one attitude implies another attitude psychologically. Such links may be established on diverse bases. Sometimes logical analyses forge relations between attitudes (for example, if I am in favor of reducing air pollution, I ought to support investing tax money to improve public transportation). Sometimes links between attitudes are created by observing a conjunction between two attitude objects, when, for example, a communication source (say, Bob Dole) advocates a position on an issue (such as repealing the gasoline tax). Such a conjunction may place in a molar structure one's attitude toward the source and one's attitude on the issue. Observations of covariation between attitudinal positions could establish connections between attitudes as well (for example, I observe that people favorable to animal rights generally support environmental conservation).

Often inter-attitudinal structures are hierarchical in the sense that more abstract and general attitudes encompass more concrete and particular attitudes. For example, one's attitude toward environmental preservation is more general than one's related attitudes toward waste recycling or wilderness protection. The attitude object associated with a more general attitude can be viewed as a category that contains more specific attitude objects as components, implying that the specific attitudes would have the same valence as the more general attitude. Some theorists have in particular emphasized more abstract attitudes that they term *values,* which are defined as representations of general goals or end states of human existence (Rokeach, 1968, 1973). Indeed, the external structure of attitudes on controversial social issues may often be hierarchical in the sense that these attitudes are linked to general values.

Intra-attitudinal and inter-attitudinal structure reflect contrasting ways that attitudes are formed. One can form an attitude experientially based on evaluative responding to the attitude object. This cognitive, affective, or behavioral responding can occur as a part of direct experience consisting of interaction with the attitude object itself or as a part of indirect experience consisting of exposure to cues that denote the attitude object. This intra-attitudinal mode of forming attitude structure entails storing the information produced by one's responses as mental associations between the attitude object and these responses.

Alternatively, one can form an attitude at least in part by establishing links between one attitude object and other attitude objects. The links between the target attitude and other attitudes are stored, along with the target attitude itself. Often this approach to forming attitudes entails an abstract inference by which an attitude is an implication of a more general attitude that has already been formed. As Stern, Dietz, Kalof, and Guagnano (1995) argued in relation to environmental attitudes, people may fall back on their values to develop a position when faced with a specific environmental dilemma. Indeed, Wood, Prislin, and Pool (1995) provided an excellent experimental demonstration of the participants' deduction of a novel attitude from their attitudes toward a much broader issue. When attitudes are deduced from values and other broad attitudes, they are generalizations from more abstract attitudes. In contrast, by the alternative intra-attitudinal logic that we have described, attitudes can also be generalizations from associations that are formed from evaluative responding to the object of the attitude.

Intra-Attitudinal Structure of Environmental Attitudes

The aspect of the intra-attitudinal structure of environmental attitudes that has been studied most extensively is issue-relevant knowledge—that is, the factual beliefs that people hold about environmental issues. Consistent with Finger's research (1994) on the Swiss, the majority of citizens of North American and European countries probably have substantial general knowledge of environmental issues gleaned from watching television and reading magazines and newspapers. They know about recycling and the likely sources of air and water pollution. Many citizens are aware of and concerned about phenomena such as the ozone hole, global warming, and acid rain. However, knowledge in this form would not necessarily foster positive attitudes toward environmental preservation because it is the evaluative content of these beliefs that should determine attitudes. Nonetheless, some studies of concentrated direct experience with the natural environment (for example, wilderness exposure) have shown a positive impact of such experience on such attitudes (see Ham, 1983; Miles, 1991).

Wood (1982; Wood, Rhodes, and Biek, 1995) examined knowledge about environmental issues in several studies of students' reactions to persuasive communications. She assessed students' working knowledge of environmental preservation by having them list beliefs and prior experiences relevant to this issue. Although these respondents differed considerably in the number of items they wrote down, on the average students listed approximately four beliefs and three prior experiences. These findings suggest that underlying students' attitudes toward environmental preservation is an intra-attitudinal structure that encompasses beliefs about environmental preservation and representations of their past environment-relevant behavior.

Inter-Attitudinal Structure of Environmental Attitudes

The aspect of the inter-attitudinal structure of environmental attitudes that researchers have investigated most thoroughly is the relations between these attitudes and values. The best-known research of this type, by Stern and his colleagues (Stern, Dietz, and Kalof, 1993; Stern and Dietz, 1994; Stern, Dietz, Kalof, and Guagnano, 1995), examined values associated with a general attitude that they termed *environmental concern,* which expresses one's evaluation of environmental preservation and endorsement of the kinds of beliefs generally advocated by environmentalists. In factor analytic studies, they derived measures of three values that were positively or negatively correlated with this attitude. They termed one of these values *egoistic* because it consisted of a commitment to maximize personal well-being and one's own outcomes. In addition, Stern and his collaborators maintained that environmental attitudes may be driven by an *altruistic* value, which consists of concern for the costs and benefits that accrue to others rather than oneself. Finally, they showed that environmental attitudes are also correlated with a *biospheric* value, by which costs or benefits are viewed in relation to the ecosystem or the biosphere as a whole.

Other theorists have proposed a very similar tripartite division of the values relevant to environmental attitudes. Axelrod's parallel classification

(1994) identified an *economic* value, referring to goals such as economic security, material rewards, and avoidance of costs; a *social* value, referring to the consequences that one's actions have for others; and a *universal* value, referring to contributions to the betterment of the world in general. In yet another rendition of this value trio, Merchant (1992) delineated three grounds for environmental ethics: *egocentric,* referring to the maximization of self-interest, *homocentric,* referring to the maximization of outcomes for the greatest number of people, and *ecocentric,* referring to the stability, diversity, and harmony of the ecosystem. What is consistent in these and related formulations (for example, Dunlap and Van Liere, 1978) is the view that to some extent U.S. citizens hold an egocentric value representing priority assigned to personal outcomes, and to some extent they hold altruistic and biospheric values representing their valuing of outcomes for other humans, other species, and the biosphere. Of course, the balance between these three values would vary substantially between individuals. The egocentric value is correlated with opposition to environmentalist measures that make one's personal life substantially less convenient or more expensive but correlated with support of measures that protect aspects of the environment that have direct personal impact. Although the biospheric value is generally positively related to support for environmentalism, the altruistic value can be deployed in support of or opposition to environmentalism, depending on the specifics of the particular environmental issue. For example, people valuing altruism might be favorable to actions that would preserve the environment for future generations but unfavorable to actions that would threaten workers' employment opportunities.

Research suggesting that environmental attitudes are embedded in a network of broader values has much in common with research on attitudes toward other controversial social issues. For example, both racial attitudes and attitudes toward welfare have been linked to two values: one of these values expresses an individualistic work ethic, and the other expresses a mix of humanitarianism and egalitarianism. In a study of whites' attitudes toward blacks, Katz and Hass (1988) demonstrated that endorsement of the work ethic value was correlated with holding negative beliefs about blacks, whereas endorsement of a humanitarian and egalitarian value was correlated with holding positive beliefs about blacks. Research by Kulesa (1995) has shown similar relationships for attitudes toward welfare. Beliefs opposing welfare benefits for the poor were associated with support for the work ethic, whereas beliefs favoring welfare were associated with valuing humanitarianism-egalitarianism. In research by Shaw-Barnes (1994), attitudes toward gays and lesbians were linked to three other social values. Specifically, negative beliefs about gays and lesbians were associated with valuing fundamentalist religion and the traditional family, whereas positive beliefs about these groups were associated with valuing civil rights and liberties.

Using Persuasive Communications to Change Strong Attitudes

Our treatment of attitude structure yields a definition of attitude strength, a property of attitudes that renders them difficult to change but increases their impact on information processing and behavior. Attitudes are strong to the extent that they are well embedded in an existing attitudinal structure. Consequently, attitudes can be strong in two senses: They can have an extensive intra-attitudinal structure—that is, they can be supported by many associations arising from direct and indirect experience. They can also have an extensive inter-attitudinal structure—that is, they can be inferentially linked to other attitudes and in particular can be linked to more abstract attitudes, including values.

Research on resistance to attitude change has repeatedly shown that it is more difficult to change attitudes to the extent that they are strong—that is, embedded in a knowledge structure on an intra-attitudinal or inter-attitudinal basis (see Eagly and Chaiken, 1995). Strong attitudes are not readily changed by limited exposure to persuasive messages. Yet, even on important social issues, the average citizen's attitudes may not be so strongly held that influence is completely prevented. Our own research on abortion attitudes recently provided a demonstration of this point (Eagly and others, 1995). In this study, persuasive messages on the abortion issue were presented to introductory psychology students who were preselected to be either prochoice or prolife, and to members of campus prochoice and prolife activist groups. These students were randomly assigned to listen to a carefully reasoned presentation that argued for either a prolife or prochoice position and were thus exposed to a proattitudinal or counterattitudinal appeal. The activist students showed no attitude change either immediately following the message or two weeks later during a follow-up session. In contrast, among the psychology students, those who listened to a counterattitudinal message changed their attitudes toward the message, whereas those exposed to a proattitudinal appeal moved slightly away from their own position. The attitude change toward the counterattitudinal messages was still detectable two weeks later. Nonetheless, attitude strength predicted extent of persuasion. To the extent that participants' attitudes were strong, as assessed by a pretest self-report measure of attitude strength, they were less influenced by the counterattitudinal appeal. Moreover, appropriate data analyses suggested that the greater resistance to persuasion of the activists, compared with the psychology students, should be attributed to their greater attitude strength.

Persuasion through the presentation of verbal appeals thus can be effective in inducing change in important attitudes, even attitudes on widely discussed and controversial social issues, at least to the extent that attitudes are not extraordinarily strong. However, persuasion in the context of relatively strong attitudes demands persuasive techniques that take the likely sources of attitude strength into account.

Changing Attitudes That Have an Extensive Intra-Attitudinal Structure

Because citizens typically do have at least moderate prior knowledge on environmental issues, the designers of persuasive communications need to be aware of this knowledge. As a general rule, extensive knowledge about a particular issue (that is, intra-attitudinal structure) protects people from changing their attitudes on that issue, in part for the simple reason that the new information must compete with the beliefs people already hold. Moreover, knowledgeable message recipients tend to process new information in a way that maintains their attitudes (see Eagly and Chaiken, 1995; Wood, Rhodes, and Biek, 1995). Findings consistent with the general principle that resistance to change is greater to the extent that an attitude has an extensive internal structure are many. For example, several studies have shown that providing participants with information that adds beliefs to their intra-attitudinal structure confers resistance to subsequent communications (for example, Himmelfarb and Youngblood, 1969; Lewan and Stotland, 1961). Most relevant to our focus on the environment are the demonstrations by Wood (1982; Wood, Rhodes, and Biek, 1995) that high levels of working knowledge about environmental preservation increase resistance to counterattitudinal communications.

As Wood, Rhodes, and Biek (1995) argued, the relation between knowledge and attitude change is actually more complex than the simple idea that knowledgeable people are closed-minded and resistant to change. Knowledge also increases the ability to receive new information and to evaluate it critically. For example, Wood and Kallgren (1988) found that participants with more environmental knowledge were more influenced by the content of counterattitudinal messages (and less influenced by the likability of the source) than were less knowledgeable participants; recall and thought-listing data confirmed that more knowledgeable recipients processed the message more effectively. Although the improved message reception and heightened criticality that knowledge produces may often result in resistance to change, they could as well create susceptibility to especially valid and cogent arguments.

Given that a target audience is likely to be at least somewhat knowledgeable on environmental issues, the most obvious suggestions for effective persuasion are to formulate strong, cogent arguments and in addition to attempt to add a substantial amount of intra-attitudinal structure consistent with the attitudinal position that the persuader desires to instill. Change induction techniques should provide people with a very large amount of new experience with the attitude object. To the extent that many new associations were added, the attitude abstracted from the new and pre-existing associations would be heavily influenced by the new associations, especially given their advantage of recency. Repetition of the new structural elements may be important as well. Thus abundant inputs would be recommended to those interested in changing attitudes that already have extensive intra-attitudinal structure, especially inputs that span the range of possible types of associations, from cognitive through affective through behavioral.

From this perspective, it is interesting that well-documented successes in changing strong attitudes have involved bombarding the target audience with a large amount of information consistent with the desired attitude(s) and, at least sometimes, isolating these individuals from competing influences. Psychotherapy thus often involves frequent contact with a therapist over a relatively long period of time. Religious conversions may involve placing potential converts in a community of religious people who are somewhat isolated from the larger society (Conway and Siegelman, 1978; Lofland, 1977). In the case of the campaign against smoking, citizens received large amounts of antismoking information, much of which, such as the warnings on advertisements and cigarette packages, exposed them to countless repetitions of the same message. To the extent that persuasion in these natural settings can be attributed to the information that target persons received, the lesson for persuasion on environmental issues is to communicate lots of information and to repeat it frequently.

Changing Attitudes Whose Inter-Attitudinal Structure Links Them with Values

When attitudes are strong because they are linked to values, effective persuasive appeals often contain arguments that address or invoke the values to which the issue is commonly linked in people's minds. In our research on abortion attitudes (Eagly and others, 1995), for example, the content of our largely value-based appeals was derived from the arguments most commonly used by prolife and prochoice groups; leaders of activist groups assisted us in writing communications that presented their views effectively. Although these messages were not written systematically to invoke particular values, an analysis of their arguments from the perspective of attitude structure would reveal that they did indeed invoke values that are commonly linked to the abortion issue in citizens' minds (for example, Kristiansen and Zanna, 1988). Thus the prochoice message appealed to individual freedom and self-determination, and the prolife message appealed to the sanctity of life and traditional family values.

The embeddedness of environmental attitudes in values provides explicit guidance for designing persuasive appeals. As we have already suggested, the most obvious value-based persuasive technique consists of invoking the values commonly associated with attitudes on environmental issues. For example, an appeal designed to promote the use of public transportation could focus on the idea that the resulting reduction in air pollution would be a positive benefit for everyone. Such an argument would call on the altruistic or social value that may often underlie positive attitudes toward environmental preservation. In general, invoking values that are ordinarily linked to environmental attitudes provides a blueprint for designing argumentation on these issues.

This principle that persuasive messages should invoke widely shared values has already been put into practice by the writers of appeals on environmental issues. We are able to illustrate these value-based appeals from Lange's description (1993) of the rhetoric used in the debate on protecting the forest habitat of the northern spotted owl (see also Satterfield, forthcoming). This dispute pits the timber industry, which provides employment for a significant portion of the population of the area, against environmental groups, who argue that the loss of an indicator species like the spotted owl demonstrates that the health of the forest is in jeopardy. Both sides of the dispute framed information to connect their own positions to the values that are commonly associated with environmental issues. For example, environmentalists contended that the forest is a finite resource to be preserved for future generations and that lumber workers can and should be retrained for alternate occupations. This appeal invokes the altruistic value in the argument that maintaining the forest would benefit others in the future; it also attempts to deflect a criticism that would be damaging from an altruistic perspective—namely, that the loggers' interests would be sacrificed. Also, the focus on the forest as a finite resource invokes a concern for the integrity of the biosphere. In response, the representatives of the timber industry emphasized the need to maintain employment for loggers and to support the local communities; they also argued that the forest is a renewable resource. The timber industry thus based its appeal on altruistic concerns for forestry employees and their communities and also sought to portray itself as reasonably attentive to biospheric issues.

As Lange (1993) pointed out, simple, readily comprehended slogans and images were used to communicate positions in the debate on the northern spotted owl. This strategy not only directs attention away from the complexity of the issue but also captures favorable associations with widely shared values. For example, the timber industry has promoted an "owls versus people" mentality in the media that portrays the controversy as a simple case of jobs for people versus habitat for one seemingly less important species. In this slogan, altruistic concerns for the jobs of people were placed in juxtaposition with a biospheric concern for a little-known species of owl—surely a comparison whose persuasive power would favor the logging interests. Environmentalist groups responded by conjuring up images of millions of acres of wasteland that once housed a healthy forest and countless species of wildlife. This image of devastation conveyed the importance of protecting the biosphere and thereby produced an appeal to the very value that the logging interests attempted to discount in their owls versus people slogan. Also implicit in these messages is the attempt by each side to represent the opposing side as callously unconcerned about important values—another value-based persuasive technique. Thus the logging industry portrayed the environmentalists as completely insensitive to the altruistic concerns inherent in the jobs issue, and the environmentalists portrayed the logging industry as completely insensitive to the biospheric concerns inherent in prevailing logging practices.

The timber industry's attempt to simplify the Pacific Northwest debate by portraying the issue as one of owls versus people exemplifies yet another aspect of value-based persuasive techniques: decoupling an attitude from a value to which it has become attached (Eagly and Chaiken, 1995). By suggesting that concern for the owl should receive little weight within this debate, the significance of the biospheric value in this debate is directly challenged. By making biospheric concerns less relevant, the timber industry's advocacy implies that attitudes should be based on altruistic concerns, which focus attention on jobs for people.

Another strategy for value-based argumentation is to reframe the views of one's opponents as linked to unacceptably extreme versions of values, which would be rejected by most members of the target audience. This use of values can be seen in the northern spotted owl controversy in the components of rhetoric that Lange (1993) termed vilification. For example, environmentalists have been portrayed by the logging industry as radicals or eco-terrorists who intend to preserve the environment by preventing any form of access to its resources. This accusation invokes an extreme form of the biospheric value that would not be endorsed by the general public. In like manner, environmental activists have responded by portraying the timber industry as a small group of giant corporations whose unlimited resources are directed at destroying the environment, without concern about the consequences for the planet or even timber workers (see also Satterfield, forthcoming). This argument depicts the timber industry as representing an extreme form of egoism in the service of corporate interests. In this manner, each side is characterized as holding views that follow from extremist versions of the values that are ordinarily associated with environmental issues in people's minds.

This influence tactic is not unique to environmental issues. For example, Vanderford's case study (1989) of rhetoric on the abortion issue showed that each side attempts to depict the other as an enemy with the power to impose its own unacceptable values. Thus prochoice rhetoric portrays a minority group of Catholic Church officials who are determined to thwart the separation of church and state and to restrict a woman's right to choose, whereas in parallel fashion prolife rhetoric points to an elite group of media, business, and political leaders who use their power and influence to promote a radically egoistic agenda that elevates convenience and freedom of choice over any concern for the life of the unborn child.

Another value-based influence technique consists of merely priming values held by message recipients rather than referring to them directly or indirectly in persuasive argumentation. Priming can produce attitude change, of at least a temporary sort. In their research on whites' racial attitudes, Katz and Hass (1988) demonstrated that priming one of the values relevant to attitudes toward blacks caused predictable changes in attitudes toward this social group. Priming was accomplished by the simple device of having participants respond to a set of items that assessed the value. Priming humanitarian and egalitarian values resulted in increased endorsement of pro-black beliefs, whereas priming the individualistic work ethic value resulted in increased endorsement of anti-black beliefs. These findings suggest that merely activating a value may strengthen the aspect of an attitude that is linked to this value, without the presentation of a persuasive message. In the context of the debate on the northern spotted owl, priming the biospheric value should promote negative attitudes toward the logging industry because this value is associated with preservation of the forest and its species. On the other hand, priming the altruistic value would lead to positive attitudes toward timber industry policies to the extent that these values bring workers' jobs to mind.

Other value-based persuasive techniques were discussed by Katz (1960) as part of his functional theory of attitudes. Katz, along with other attitude theorists, maintained that one of the functions that attitudes serve is to allow people to express their strongly held values and that such expression yields personal satisfaction. Thus a person who is dedicated to the health of the biosphere and draws self-esteem from this identity should be motivated to hold attitudinal positions that appropriately reflect this value. To change such attitudes, Katz suggested using persuasive techniques that involve changing values, rather than merely emphasizing existing values and enhancing or attacking their links with an issue.

One of these techniques involves inducing dissatisfaction with important values. Katz cited as an example the so-called brainwashing tactics used by Chinese Communists to convert American prisoners of war in Korea. This approach involved undermining support for prisoners' values and attempting to replace democratic values with a new value system consistent with Communist principles. The prisoners' captors thus tried to exploit the deductive process through which attitudes (for example, toward the Chinese people) follow from values by fashioning a new Communist value system from which the desired attitudes would then be deduced. Although the vivid term *brainwashing* and the military context of the Korean War may conjure up images of evil persuaders, the tactic of attempting to change values is common in political and religious persuasion, because the influencing agents typically desire to produce not merely change in a single attitude but generalized change in a large number of attitudes. For example, becoming a Mormon or a Black Muslim would entail accepting many interrelated attitudes.

The second approach to change described by Katz targets the attitudes themselves rather than the values. In this method, new experiences with attitude objects create intra-attitudinal structures that change the attitudes. By changing a number of the attitudes connected to a given value, support for the value itself would erode, and new attitude-value structures would begin to form. For example, representatives of the logging industry might attack attitudes linked to the biospheric value (for example, by arguing that many different actions that are intended to preserve the environment produce serious economic damage).

Both of Katz's techniques presume considerable control over the informational environment of the target persons. Moreover, undermining existing values and substituting new values would no doubt be a lengthy process, and changing a number of attitudes linked to a value would also require extensive persuasive efforts.

As we noted when we first introduced the tripartite analysis of the values commonly associated with attitudes on environmental issues, these values often have opposite implications for evaluative responding. The egoistic value may typically foster anti-preservation attitudes, although when citizens' environmental attitudes arise from their concerns about their personal health and safety, this value may foster favorable attitudes toward restricting some environmentally harmful actions. The biospheric value ordinarily fosters pro-preservation attitudes. As our discussion of the northern spotted owl controversy illustrates, the altruistic value may be captured by either side in environmental debates—that is, by the environmentalists who argue that everyone gains from preservationist actions or by the exploiters of resources who argue that everyone gains from the expansion and preservation of jobs and the growth of industry. Despite these complexities, a citizen holding egoistic and biospheric values might nonetheless be, for example, sympathetic to an increase in gasoline taxes on biospheric grounds but unsympathetic on egoistic grounds. Given these conflicting sentiments, such an individual would be described as *ambivalent* by attitude theorists (for example, Thompson, Zanna, and Griffin, 1995). Ambivalence thus consists of having simultaneously a positive and a negative orientation toward an attitude object—that is, holding positive and negative beliefs, experiencing favorable and unfavorable affects, and engaging in approach and avoidance behaviors. One of the important consequences of this ambivalence may be greater vulnerability to persuasive arguments in the form of appropriately designed value-based appeals directed at either side of the issue. Moreover, arguments advocating either preservationist or anti-preservationist positions might be readily accepted, because beliefs consistent with both sides of the issue would be represented cognitively and could be made accessible in the context of appropriate argumentation.

According to Tetlock's *value pluralism model* (1986, 1989), people whose beliefs on an issue are integratively complex (that is, they have multiple beliefs that are linked by logical and causal bonds) tend to endorse values that have conflicting evaluative implications for the issue. For example, people who are integratively complex on the issue of maintaining profitable trade relations with countries that deny basic civil liberties might perceive that this policy would enhance one of their values and diminish another one. The enhanced value might be "maintaining a comfortable and prosperous life," and the diminished value might be "ensuring that people have individual freedom." If, as in this illustration, one value fosters a positive attitude on an issue and the other value fosters a negative attitude, bringing both values to bear on the issue should induce complex thinking and more moderate attitudes, at least to the extent that people who hold both values try to reconcile their conflicting implications. On environmental issues, people who endorse, for example, both egoistic and biospheric values are likely to have integratively complex attitudes toward an issue such as increasing the gasoline tax to reduce automobile travel. These integratively complex individuals should have somewhat moderate attitudes and be somewhat vulnerable to appeals based on either egoistic or biospheric concerns.

Implications of Persuasion Theory for Environmental Issues

Now we turn to another theme important in contemporary attitude theory, the psychological mechanisms or processes through which persuasion occurs. In general, theorists have proposed two major types of processes by which attitudes can be modified by persuasive communications: a demanding process that involves understanding and cognitively elaborating the semantic content of persuasive argumentation, and a less demanding process (or processes) that does not depend on the careful scrutiny of persuasive arguments (Chaiken, Wood, and Eagly, 1996; Eagly and Chaiken, 1993). One well-known dual-process theory is the heuristic-systematic model (Chaiken, 1980, 1987; Chaiken, Liberman, and Eagly, 1989), which considers a less demanding process by which simple decision rules or *heuristics* mediate persuasion. A related dual-process theory is the elaboration likelihood model (Petty and Cacioppo, 1986a, 1986b), which considers several less demanding processes in its *peripheral route* to persuasion. These theories can be considered important members of a family of dual-process theories that have been proposed in the literatures on attitudes and social cognition (for example, Fazio, 1990; Fiske and Neuberg, 1990; Gilbert, 1989; Tetlock, 1985; Smith, 1994).

The effectiveness of most of the persuasive methods that we have discussed in this chapter presumes that message recipients process the content of argumentation with some care and that their understanding and elaboration of this content affect their attitudes. Petty and Cacioppo (1979) referred to this effortful scrutiny of message arguments as a *central route* to persuasion, whereas Chaiken (1980) has labeled such cognitive processing *systematic*. This systematic processing is required if communications change attitudes by adding new intra-attitudinal structure (such as new beliefs). Most of the value-based persuasive techniques that we discussed also require systematic processing to be effective. For example, if the timber industry's biospheric argument about the forest as a renewable resource is to be effective, it must be fleshed out by a description of logging operations and the steps by which forests renew themselves. To be persuaded by such an argument, recipients must understand it and presumably engage in favorable elaboration of its details.

A few of the value-based techniques we have described are less dependent on systematic processing. For example, the owls versus people slogan and photographs of clear-cut forests presumably require little detailed processing, although some elaboration of the slogan or image is required in order that the audience draw the intended conclusion. Also, priming values is a technique that does not in itself depend on elaborative processing but that may bias subsequent systematic processing in the direction implied by the value.

Underlying the assumption that people do not necessarily process messages systematically is the least effort or "cognitive miser" idea that people process information superficially and minimally unless they are motivated to do otherwise (see Eagly and Chaiken, 1993). Therefore, dual-process theories of persuasion emphasize that recipients of messages must have sufficient motivation to engage in more effortful, systematic forms of processing. In addition, recipients must have the capacity or ability to engage in this more deliberative form of processing that involves careful evaluation of persuasive argumentation.

Consequences of Systematic and Heuristic Processing

What does the dual-process approach have to offer those who design persuasive appeals on environmental issues? One central lesson is that persuasion induced by systematic processing is more persistent than persuasion induced by heuristic processing. A number of studies have confirmed this prediction about the enduringness of change (including Chaiken, 1980; Chaiken and Eagly, 1983, Experiment 2; Mackie, 1987; Petty, Cacioppo, and Heesacker, reported in Petty and Cacioppo, 1986a). The principle underlying this greater persistence is that systematic processing yields a structure of beliefs that supports the changed attitude; these beliefs then allow people to defend their attitudes from subsequent attack. Persuasion accomplished by heuristic processing and other peripheral mechanisms that are not based on scrutiny of persuasive arguments would not provide message recipients with beliefs to support their newly adopted or revised attitudes.

Because systematic processing has the potential to produce long-term shifts in attitudes, designers of persuasive appeals should facilitate such processing by attempting to ensure that recipients have sufficient motivation and ability to engage in this relatively effortful processing. Sufficient motivation may be achieved by making appeals personally relevant (see Johnson and Eagly, 1989). For example, antipollution appeals that focus on the consequences of pollution for local residents and provide suggestions for improving local conditions may motivate careful scrutiny of message arguments. In terms of the abilities demanded for systematic processing, most persuasive messages presented in the media are relatively undemanding for more educated citizens, but many presentations, especially if they are relatively technical, could readily exceed the abilities of less educated citizens. Moreover, ability to process information can be limited by situational factors such as time pressure (Kruglanski, 1989) and distraction (Petty and Brock, 1981). In general, effective persuasion by systematic processing presumes understandable messages presented in situations that do not seriously restrict recipients' ability to process them. Therefore, environmental activists should tailor their messages to the educational level and cognitive abilities of their target audience and present these messages in a context in which audience members are likely to pay attention to them.

One important issue is the extent to which persuasive efforts should feature message characteristics that are associated with heuristic processing of messages. Such characteristics would include, for example, the expertise of the message's source, a cue that could produce persuasion by the simple decision rule that "experts are always right." Consensus cues, such as implied or explicit agreement from other people, can also serve as a persuasion heuristic, as can other classes of cues (see Chaiken, Liberman, and Eagly, 1989). If attitudes were changed by persuasion heuristics and systematic processing of message arguments failed to occur, only a fairly superficial type of change would take place. Indeed, numerous experiments have shown that heuristic cues influence persuasion when recipients elaborate a message only minimally, whereas message content (that is, the quality of the arguments) affects persuasion when recipients engage in more extensive cognitive elaboration (see reviews by Petty and Cacioppo, 1986a, 1986b; Eagly and Chaiken, 1993). Although this logic might seem to advise against the introduction of heuristic cues, the lessons from the persuasion literature are actually considerably more complex.

As Petty, Cacioppo, and their colleagues maintained (Petty and Cacioppo, 1984; Petty, Kasmer, Haugtvedt, and Cacioppo, 1987; Petty and Wegener, forthcoming), certain persuasion variables may serve multiple roles. For example, they argued that the roles for source cues are the following: (1) when motivation and ability to process message content are low, source variables may indeed act as peripheral cues or heuristics;

(2) when motivation and ability are high, people may merely be less influenced by source cues, or source cues might themselves act as persuasive arguments; (3) when motivation and ability are at some moderate level, source cues may enhance or reduce systematic processing. Thus, from the perspective of elaboration likelihood theory, positive peripheral cues such as a high level of source expertise would often have positive impact (but sometimes no impact), and the route through which this impact occurs depends on level of elaboration. Therefore, psychologists who understand the complexity of these relationships cannot offer environmental activists any simple rules about whether to include heuristic cues such as high source expertise in their persuasive messages.

In the context of the heuristic-systematic model, Chaiken and her colleagues (for example, Eagly and Chaiken, 1993; Chaiken, Liberman, and Eagly, 1989) argued that systematic and heuristic processing can exert both independent and interdependent effects on judgment. As an illustration of interdependence of the two forms of processing, heuristic processing of a source cue might lead message recipients to form expectancies about message validity, and these expectancies could bias systematic processing in a positive or negative direction, depending on whether the source cue was positive (such as having high credibility) or negative (low credibility). Chaiken and Maheswaran (1994) obtained such findings when a persuasive message was ambiguous. With unambiguous messages, more conventional findings were obtained: when task importance was low, source credibility influenced participants' attitudes, but argument quality did not; when task importance was high, only argument quality affected attitudes. In summary, heuristic cues affect persuasion by a variety of processing routes: they can exert independent effects as simple persuasion heuristics (especially when systematic processing does not furnish information that contradicts their validity); they can bias systematic processing; and their impact can be attenuated by systematic processing. The bottom line for inclusion of heuristic cues is thus not a simple prediction: such cues can produce rather superficial persuasion, but they might enhance or reduce enduring persuasion or have no impact whatsoever, depending on a variety of moderating conditions such as recipients' level of elaboration of the message.

Threat Appeals

Given the very serious dangers posed by environmental problems like air pollution and depletion of the ozone layer, it is not surprising that many persuasive appeals stress the negative consequences of failing to ameliorate environmental problems. Such appeals may well arouse fear or anxiety in their recipients. Whether fear and other negative emotions would facilitate or inhibit persuasion has been the focus of considerable research in social psychology. In recent years, psychologists have examined this issue from a dual-process perspective.

To remind readers of the history of research on fear appeals, we note that early research by Janis and his colleagues (see Hovland, Janis, and Kelley, 1953) was based on the idea that fear is a negative drive state and that behaviors that mitigated this state, which would include accepting a message's reassuring recommendations, would be reinforced. Although this drive-reduction model was short on empirical support, the approach and associated empirical work (Janis and Feshbach, 1953) addressed basic issues about how fear influences information processing and persuasion. In subsequent years, social psychologists proposed several important theories of the persuasive impact of fear appeals (Janis, 1967; Leventhal, 1970; McGuire, 1969; Rogers, 1983; Sutton, 1982). In addition, many empirical studies were published, and in general, these studies have shown that higher levels of threat lead to greater persuasion (Boster and Mongeau, 1984; Eagly and Chaiken, 1993).

Dual-process theories have raised new questions about the processes through which fear may affect persuasion. Specifically, research by Jepson and Chaiken (1990) and Gleicher and Petty (1992) showed that participants exposed to fear appeals processed messages less systematically than those exposed to less threatening appeals. For example, Jepson and Chaiken found that recipients who were chronically fearful about cancer detected fewer logical errors in a message about cancer checkups and listed fewer issue-related thoughts than recipients who were less fearful. Consequently, the more fearful recipients were more persuaded, presumably because of their reduced capacity or motivation for thinking critically about the logically flawed message. However, other evidence has shown that fear arousal can increase systematic processing of communications (Baron and others, 1994). Because fear thus remains a variable whose impact on persuasion depends on various moderating conditions, the designers of persuasive appeals on environmental issues should use fear-provoking appeals with caution and be especially attentive to the possibility that they may reduce systematic processing.

In analyzing the potential for using threat appeals on environmental issues, one especially important consideration is that the fear appeals typically used in research have described threats that could be substantially alleviated through personal behavior (for example, health threats that can be addressed by prudent preventive behaviors). In contrast, threats to the quality of the environment cannot be meaningfully reduced merely through one's own behavior. An individual can do little to solve the problems of industrial pollution or ozone layer depletion, for example. Therefore, fear appeals could leave audience members with feelings of powerlessness and lack of control. To the extent that message recipients believe that they cannot alleviate the danger portrayed in the message, the appeal will be unpersuasive (Janz and Becker, 1984; Rippetoe and Rogers, 1987).

To address the issue posed by the lack of efficacy of personal behavior, researchers should examine threat appeals that encourage collective action to solve environmental problems. Whereas an individual's actions have little impact on environmental problems, collective actions can be more effective. Illustrating this approach, Hine and Gifford (1991) found that exposing participants to a fear-inducing antipollution editorial that included a visual slide presentation produced more commitment to engage in relevant social action and to donate money and time to an environmental organization than exposure to a message not accompanied by fear-arousing content. In addition, Shelton and Rogers (1981) demonstrated that a threat appeal that presented the suffering of whales led to stronger intentions to support anti-whaling organizations than a less threatening appeal. These studies thus suggest that threat appeals may successfully induce actions that are collective in the sense that they support organizational efforts to address environmental problems. Such organizations (for example, Greenpeace and Sierra Club) coordinate and deploy the time, effort, and money contributed by individuals.

Attitudes as Predictors of Environmental Behavior

The implicit or explicit reason that activists desire to change environmental attitudes is that they believe that these attitudes have a directive and dynamic impact on environmentally relevant behavior. Although research on attitudes is fully supportive of attitudes' causal role in relation to behavior, research on the attitude-behavior relation shows that simple expectations about strong attitude-behavior relations will typically be disconfirmed. As researchers have repeatedly demonstrated, general environmental attitudes such as the popular environmental concern variable are usually only weakly correlated with particular environmentally friendly behaviors, such as participating in curbside recycling (see Finger, 1994; Oskamp and others, 1991; Stern, 1992). However, consistent with the claim that general environmental attitudes affect one's general tendency to engage in environmentally relevant behaviors, considerably larger attitude-behavior correlations are obtained if measures of a number of different attitude-relevant behaviors are aggregated and then correlated with the attitude (Fishbein and Ajzen, 1974). In an excellent demonstration of this point, Weigel and Newman (1976) assessed citizens' attitudes toward environmental preservation at one point in time and obtained unobtrusive measures of several ecologically oriented behaviors several months later. Whereas the attitude was only weakly related to single behaviors, it was highly related to an index that aggregated all of the behaviors into a more comprehensive behavioral index.

Another principle that can be gleaned from attitude-behavior research is that specific behaviors such as recycling can be predicted quite effectively from attitudes that are more specifically tailored to the particular behaviors that a researcher desires to predict. According to this principle of the compatibility (or correspondence) of attitudes and behaviors, attitudes toward behaviors are the best predictors of behavior (Ajzen, 1988; Ajzen and Fishbein, 1977). For example, attitudes toward participating in an upcoming Earth Day rally would predict participation much better than environmental concern or attitudes toward the environmental movement. Although the superior prediction of behavior from attitudes toward behaviors may seem obvious, this prediction is psychologically meaningful to the extent that these attitudes have a causal role in relation to behavior, as claimed by Fishbein and Ajzen's theory (1975) of reasoned action. In this theory, attitudes toward behavior (and subjective norms) produce intentions to behave, and these intentions in turn cause behavior. From the perspective of this popular theory, persuasive messages that aim to change behavior should target attitudes toward behavior, and change in these attitudes requires change in the perceived consequences of behavior (Ajzen and Fishbein, 1980; Fishbein and Ajzen, 1981; see Eagly and Chaiken, 1993, forthcoming). This theory of attitude-behavior relations thus provides specific advice for the design of persuasive appeals that are intended to change behavior.

Another issue important for psychologists and activists is understanding what attitudes actually come to mind—that is, are accessible—in situations that call for a behavioral response. This issue arises independently of the correspondence principle by which more specific attitudes are more predictive of behavior. For example, when people are given an opportunity to donate money to an environmental organization, the accessibility issue concerns the likelihood of an attitude coming to mind spontaneously: would a general concern about the environment come to mind, as opposed to more specific environmental attitudes (toward water or air pollution, for example)? Attitudes that have been frequently and recently activated are more accessible and therefore are likely to come to mind, as Fazio and his colleagues have argued (for example, Fazio, 1990).

Heightened accessibility makes an attitude more likely to influence action, regardless of the specificity of the attitude. Fazio (1986) has further maintained that highly accessible attitudes are activated automatically upon mere exposure to the attitude object. The importance of accessibility has been demonstrated, not only in numerous laboratory experiments but also in a field study of voting behavior (Fazio and Williams, 1986). In this study, participants who responded faster to attitudinal measures concerning presidential candidates (indexing these attitudes' greater accessibility) showed more consistency between their attitudes and their actual voting behavior than those who responded more slowly to the attitude measures.

As Bamberg (1996) argued, a variety of environmentally relevant attitudes may come to mind but not function as direct determinants of behavior. Illustrating that high accessibility of an attitude is not sufficient to induce a strong attitude-behavior relation, research by Snyder and Kendzierski (1982; see also Borgida and Campbell, 1982) showed that the attitude must in addition be perceived as relevant to the behavior. Especially in natural settings offering multiple ways of expressing an attitude, a particular attitude will induce a particular behavior only to the extent that people believe that the behavior offers an appropriate way to express the attitude.

The practical implications of research on the accessibility and relevance of attitudes are readily apparent: effective persuasive appeals should not only activate attitudes but also argue that these attitudes call for environmentally responsible behaviors. For example, an appeal that effectively induces behavior might first activate citizens' negative attitudes toward politicians who allow corporations to ignore environmental standards and then call for citizens to turn their anger into action by writing to a particular representative, supporting a rival candidate, and boycotting certain products. Activating appropriate attitudes and suggesting that they are relevant guides for behavior thus provides another blueprint for environmental advocacy.

Finally, cognitive dissonance theory has provided important insights that can enable activists to induce people to act on their pro-preservation attitudes (Festinger, 1957). One of the paradoxes of the psychology of environmentalism is that citizens generally hold pro-preservation attitudes but routinely engage in environmentally unfriendly actions, such as driving to work instead of using public transportation. Dissonance theory has long emphasized the motivating power of inducing behavior that is inconsistent with attitudes, an induction that makes people feel hypocritical. Ordinarily, such an induction consists of having research participants freely choose to engage in behavior that has undesirable consequences, and the dependent variable of interest is attitude change (Cooper and Fazio, 1984). However, in a less common application of dissonance theory directed to changing behaviors in natural settings, researchers have made participants aware that their chronic environmentally relevant behavior has undesirable consequences. For example, Kantola, Syme, and Campbell (1984) informed a group of Australian citizens that they consumed a large amount of electricity and reminded them that on an earlier survey they had indicated that citizens have a duty to save electricity. Similarly, Dickerson, Thibodeau, Aronson, and Miller (1992) made a group of college students aware of their positive attitudes toward water conservation and of the wastefulness of their showering behavior (and also publicly committed them to taking shorter showers). In comparison to appropriate control treatments, the dissonance-inducing treatments used in these studies produced greater conservation of energy and water.

The practical lesson from this research is that the potentially distressing discrepancies between people's environmentally unfriendly behaviors and their pro-environmental attitudes are ordinarily not brought to mind in daily life. Psychologists can design inductions that do bring such discrepancies to mind, and the resulting discomfort can motivate behavioral change.

Conclusion

Our attitudinal perspective on environmental issues yields a number of extremely important insights. In particular, this perspective provides activists with principles for designing persuasive communications that influence environmentally relevant behavior. We have thus argued that environmental attitudes are often strong because they have at least moderately elaborated intra-attitudinal and inter-attitudinal structure. Therefore, persuasive communications need to take into account the structural bases of these attitudes. We thus recommend providing extensive and repeated communicative input, and these persuasive appeals should address the values to which environmental attitudes are ordinarily linked. Taking a dual-process perspective, the designers of persuasive appeals should attempt to elicit systematic processing by ensuring that message recipients have sufficient motivation and ability to process environmental communications systematically. Persuasion cues that might serve as persuasion heuristics should be introduced with the awareness that the direction and extent of their impact depend on several moderating conditions. Similarly, fear appeals should be approached with care because of their potential to interfere with systematic processing. Finally, persuaders who desire to change behaviors should consider several additional suggestions that follow from research on the attitude-behavior relation: they might target attitudes toward behaviors; they might attempt to heighten the accessibility of environmental attitudes and their perceived relevance for environmental action; and they might induce feelings of hypocrisy by capitalizing on the frequent discrepancies between citizens' pro-environmental attitudes and their environmentally unfriendly behaviors.

To fully understand the social psychology of environmental action, many other factors need to be considered, especially the relation of individual attitudes to organizational behavior, governmental policy, and social movements (Ungar, 1994). Because collective action is required to redress environmental problems, a much more powerful environmental social movement must emerge for a profound shift to occur toward a preservationist society. Such a movement would unite scattered environmentalist groups and focus the energies of a large number of citizens. The collective actions that would follow would profoundly influence governmental policy and the actions of organizations and individuals.

REFERENCES

Ajzen, I. *Attitudes, Personality, and Behavior.* Chicago: Dorsey, 1988.

Ajzen, I., and Fishbein, M. "Attitude-Behavior Relations: A Theoretical Analysis and Review of Empirical Research." *Psychological Bulletin,* 1977, *84,* 888–918.

Ajzen, I., and Fishbein, M. *Understanding Attitudes and Predicting Social Behavior.* Englewood Cliffs, N.J.: Prentice Hall, 1980.

Axelrod, L. J. "Balancing Personal Needs with Environmental Preservation: Identifying the Values That Guide Decisions in Ecological Dilemmas." *Journal of Social Issues,* 1994, *50,* 85–104.

Bamberg, S. "Allgemeine oder spezifische Einstellungen bei der Erklaerung umweltschonenden Verhaltens? Eine Erweiterung der Theorie des geplanten Verhaltens um Einstellungen gegenueber Objekten" [General or specific attitudes in explaining ecologically responsible behavior? An enlargement of the theory of planned behavior by the concept of attitudes toward objects]. *Zeitschrift fuer Sozialpsychologie,* 1996, *27,* 47–60.

Baron, R. S., and others. "Negative Emotion and Message Processing." *Journal of Experimental Social Psychology,* 1994, *30,* 181–201.

Borgida, E., and Campbell, B. "Belief Relevance and Attitude-Behavior Consistency: The Moderating Role of Personal Experience." *Journal of Personality and Social Psychology,* 1982, *42,* 239–247.

Boster, F. J., and Mongeau, P. "Fear-Arousing Persuasive Messages." In R. N. Bostrom (ed.), *Communication Yearbook*. Vol. 8. Thousand Oaks, Calif.: Sage, 1984.

Chaiken, S. "Heuristic Versus Systematic Information Processing and the Use of Source Versus Message Cues in Persuasion." *Journal of Personality and Social Psychology,* 1980, *39,* 752–766.

Chaiken, S. "The Heuristic Model of Persuasion." In M. P. Zanna, J. M. Olson, and C. P. Herman (eds.), *Social Influence: The Ontario Symposium*. Vol. 5. Hillsdale, N.J.: Erlbaum, 1987.

Chaiken, S., and Eagly, A. H. "Communication Modality as a Determinant of Persuasion: The Role of Communicator Salience." *Journal of Personality and Social Psychology,* 1983, *45,* 241–256.

Chaiken, S., Liberman, A., and Eagly, A. H. "Heuristic and Systematic Processing Within and Beyond the Persuasion Context." In J. S. Uleman and J. A. Bargh (eds.), *Unintended Thought*. New York: Guilford Press, 1989.

Chaiken, S., and Maheswaran, D. "Heuristic Processing Can Bias Systematic Processing: Effects of Source Credibility, Argument Ambiguity, and Task Importance on Attitude Judgment." *Journal of Personality and Social Psychology,* 1994, *66,* 460–473.

Chaiken, S., Wood, W., and Eagly, A. H. "Principles of Persuasion." In E. T. Higgins and A. Kruglanski (eds.), *Social Psychology: Handbook of Basic Principles*. New York: Guilford Press, 1996.

Conway, F., and Siegelman, J. *Snapping: America's Epidemic of Sudden Personality Change*. New York: Lippincott, 1978.

Cooper, J., and Fazio, R. H. "A New Look at Dissonance Theory." In L. Berkowitz (ed.), *Advances in Experimental Social Psychology.* Vol. 17. Orlando, Fla.: Academic Press, 1984.

Dickerson, C. A., Thibodeau, R., Aronson, E., and Miller, D. "Using Cognitive Dissonance to Encourage Water Conservation." *Journal of Applied Social Psychology,* 1992, *22,* 841–854.

Dunlap, R. E., and Scarce, R. "The Polls—Poll Trends: Environmental Problems and Protection." *Public Opinion Quarterly,* 1991, *55,* 651–672.

Dunlap, R. E., and Van Liere, K. D. "The New Environmental Paradigm: A Proposed Measuring Instrument and Preliminary Results." *Journal of Environmental Education,* 1978, *9,* 10–19.

Eagly, A. H., and Chaiken, S. *The Psychology of Attitudes.* Orlando, Fla.: Harcourt Brace, 1993.

Eagly, A. H., and Chaiken, S. "Attitude Strength, Attitude Structure, and Resistance to Change." In R. E. Petty and J. A. Krosnick (eds.), *Attitude Strength: Antecedents and Consequences.* Hillsdale, N.J.: Erlbaum, 1995.

Eagly, A. H., and Chaiken, S. "Attitude Structure and Function." In D. Gilbert, S. Fiske, and G. Lindzey (eds.), *The Handbook of Social Psychology.* (4th ed.) New York: McGraw-Hill, forthcoming.

Eagly, A. H., and others. *Attitudes and Attitude Strength as Determinants of Memory for Attitude-Relevant Information.* Unpublished manuscript, Northwestern University, 1995.

Fazio, R. H. "How Do Attitudes Guide Behavior?" In R. M. Sorrentino and E. T. Higgins (eds.), *Handbook of Motivation and Cognition: Foundations of Social Behavior.* New York: Guilford Press, 1986.

Fazio, R. H. "Multiple Processes by Which Attitudes Guide Behavior: The MODE Model as an Integrative Framework." In M. P. Zanna (ed.), *Advances in Experimental Social Psychology.* Vol. 23. Orlando, Fla.: Academic Press, 1990.

Fazio, R. H., and Williams, C. J. "Attitude Accessibility as a Moderator of the Attitude-Perception and Attitude-Behavior Relations: An Investigation of the 1984 Presidential Election." *Journal of Personality and Social Psychology,* 1986, *51,* 505–514.

Festinger, L. *A Theory of Cognitive Dissonance.* New York: HarperCollins, 1957.

Finger, M. "From Knowledge to Action? Exploring the Relationships Between Environmental Experiences, Learning, and Behavior." *Journal of Social Issues,* 1994, *50,* 179–197.

Fishbein, M., and Ajzen, I. "Attitudes Toward Objects as Predictors of Single and Multiple Behavioral Criteria." *Psychological Review,* 1974, *81,* 59–74.

Fishbein, M., and Ajzen, I. *Belief, Attitude, Intention, and Behavior: An Introduction to Theory and Research.* Reading, Mass.: Addison-Wesley, 1975.

Fishbein, M., and Ajzen, I. "Acceptance, Yielding, and Impact: Cognitive Processes in Persuasion." In R. E. Petty, T. M. Ostrom, and T. C. Brock (eds.), *Cognitive Responses in Persuasion.* Hillsdale, N.J.: Erlbaum, 1981.

Fiske, S. T., and Neuberg, S. L. "A Continuum of Impression Formation, from Category-Based to Individuating Processes: Influences of Information and Motivation on Attention and Interpretation." In M. P. Zanna (ed.), *Advances in Experimental Social Psychology.* Vol. 23. Orlando, Fla.: Academic Press, 1990.

Gilbert, D. T. "Thinking Lightly About Others: Automatic Components of the Social Inference Process." In J. S. Uleman and J. A. Bargh (eds.), *Unintended Thought*. New York: Guilford Press, 1989.

Gleicher, F., and Petty, R. E. "Expectations of Reassurance Influence the Nature of Fear-Stimulated Attitude Change." *Journal of Experimental Social Psychology,* 1992, *28,* 86–100.

Ham, S. H. "Cognitive Psychology and Interpretation: Synthesis and Application." *Journal of Interpretation,* 1983, *8,* 11–27.

Himmelfarb, S., and Youngblood, J. "Effects of Factual Information on Creating Resistance to Emotional Appeals." *Psychonomic Science,* 1969, *14,* 267–270.

Hine, D. W., and Gifford, R. "Fear Appeals, Individual Differences, and Environmental Concern." *Journal of Environmental Education,* 1991, *22,* 36–41.

Hovland, C. I., Janis, I. L., and Kelley, H. H. *Communication and Persuasion: Psychological Studies of Opinion Change*. New Haven, Conn.: Yale University Press, 1953.

Hu, T., Sung, H., and Keeler, T. E. "Reducing Cigarette Consumption in California: Tobacco Taxes Versus an Anti-Smoking Media Campaign." *American Journal of Public Health,* 1995, *85,* 1218–1222.

Janis, I. L. "Effects of Fear Arousal on Attitude Change: Recent Developments in Theory and Experimental Research." In L. Berkowitz (ed.), *Advances in Experimental Social Psychology.* Vol. 3. Orlando, Fla.: Academic Press, 1967.

Janis, I. L., and Feshbach, S. "Effects of Fear-Arousing Communications." *Journal of Abnormal and Social Psychology,* 1953, *48,* 78–92.

Janz, N. K., and Becker, M. H. "The Health Belief Model: A Decade Later." *Health Education Quarterly,* 1984, *11,* 1–47.

Jepson, C., and Chaiken, S. "Chronic Issue-Specific Fear Inhibits Systematic Processing of Persuasive Communications." *Journal of Social Behavior and Personality,* 1990, *5,* 61–84.

Johnson, B. T., and Eagly, A. H. "The Effects of Involvement on Persuasion: A Meta-Analysis." *Psychological Bulletin,* 1989, *106,* 290–314.

Kantola, S. J., Syme, G. J., and Campbell, N. A. "Cognitive Dissonance and Energy Conservation." *Journal of Applied Psychology,* 1984, *69,* 416–421.

Katz, D. "The Functional Approach to the Study of Attitudes." *Public Opinion Quarterly,* 1960, *24,* 163–204.

Katz, I., and Hass, R. G. "Racial Ambivalence and American Value Conflict: Correlational and Priming Studies of Dual Cognitive Structures." *Journal of Personality and Social Psychology,* 1988, *55,* 893–905.

Kristiansen, C. M., and Zanna, M. P. "Justifying Attitudes by Appealing to Values: A Functional Perspective." *British Journal of Social Psychology,* 1988, *27,* 247–256.

Kruglanski, A. W. *Lay Epistemics and Human Knowledge: Cognitive and Motivational Bases.* New York: Plenum, 1989.

Kulesa, P. *The Link of Ambivalent Attitudes to Values and Political Cognition: A Potential Implication for Persuasion.* Unpublished master's thesis, Purdue University, 1995.

Lange, J. I. "The Logic of Competing Information Campaigns: Conflict over Old Growth and the Spotted Owl." *Communication Monographs,* 1993, *60,* 239–257.

Leventhal, H. "Findings and Theory in the Study of Fear Communications." In L. Berkowitz (ed.), *Advances in Experimental Social Psychology.* Vol. 5. Orlando, Fla.: Academic Press, 1970.

Lewan, P. C., and Stotland, E. "The Effects of Prior Information on Susceptibility to an Emotional Appeal." *Journal of Abnormal and Social Psychology,* 1961, *62,* 450–453.

Lofland, J. *Doomsday Cult: A Study of Conversion, Proselytization, and Maintenance of Faith.* New York: Irvington, 1977.

Mackie, D. M. "Systematic and Nonsystematic Processing of Majority and Minority Persuasive Communications." *Journal of Personality and Social Psychology,* 1987, *53,* 41–52.

McGuire, W. J. "The Nature of Attitudes and Attitude Change." In G. Lindzey and E. Aronson (eds.), *Handbook of Social Psychology.* Vol. 3. (2nd ed.) Reading, Mass.: Addison-Wesley, 1969.

McGuire, W. J. "Attitudes and Attitude Change." In G. Lindzey and E. Aronson (eds.), *Handbook of Social Psychology.* Vol. 2. (3rd ed.) New York: Random House, 1985.

Merchant, C. *Radical Ecology: The Search for a Livable World.* New York: Routledge, 1992.

Miles, J. C. "Teaching in Wilderness." *Journal of Environmental Education,* 1991, *22,* 5–9.

Nelson, D. E., and others. "Trends in Cigarette Smoking Among U.S. Adolescents, 1974 Through 1991." *American Journal of Public Health,* 1995, *85,* 34–40.

Oskamp, S., and others. "Factors Influencing Household Recycling Behavior." *Environment and Behavior,* 1991, *23,* 494–519.

Petty, R. E., and Brock, T. C. "Thought Disruption and Persuasion: Assessing the Validity of Attitude Change Experiments." In R. E. Petty, T. M. Ostrom, and T. C. Brock (eds.), *Cognitive Responses in Persuasion.* Hillsdale, N.J.: Erlbaum, 1981.

Petty, R. E., and Cacioppo, J. T. "Issue Involvement Can Increase or Decrease Persuasion by Enhancing Message-Relevant Cognitive Responses." *Journal of Personality and Social Psychology,* 1979, *37,* 1915–1926.

Petty, R. E., and Cacioppo, J. T. "Source Factors and the Elaboration Likelihood Model of Persuasion." *Advances in Consumer Research,* 1984, *11,* 668–672.

Petty, R. E., and Cacioppo, J. T. *Communication and Persuasion: Central and Peripheral Routes to Attitude Change.* New York: Springer-Verlag, 1986a.

Petty, R. E., and Cacioppo, J. T. "The Elaboration Likelihood Model of Persuasion." In L. Berkowitz (ed.), *Advances in Experimental Social Psychology.* Vol. 19. Orlando, Fla.: Academic Press, 1986b.

Petty, R. E., Kasmer, J. A., Haugtvedt, C. P., and Cacioppo, J. T. "Source and Message Factors in Persuasion: A Reply to Stiff's Critique of the Elaboration Likelihood Model." *Communication Monographs,* 1987, *54,* 233–249.

Petty, R. E., and Wegener, D. T. "Attitude Change: Multiple Roles for Persuasion Variables." In D. Gilbert, S. Fiske, and G. Lindzey (eds.), *The Handbook of Social Psychology.* (4th ed.) New York: McGraw-Hill, forthcoming.

Rippetoe, P. A., and Rogers, R. W. "Effects of Components of Protection-Motivation Theory on Adaptive and Maladaptive Coping with a Health Threat." *Journal of Personality and Social Psychology,* 1987, *52,* 596–604.

Rogers, R. W. "Cognitive and Physiological Processes in Fear Appeals and Attitude Change: A Revised Theory of Protection Motivation." In J. T. Cacioppo and R. E. Petty (eds.), *Social Psychophysiology: A Sourcebook.* New York: Guilford Press, 1983.

Rokeach, M. *Beliefs, Attitudes, and Values: A Theory of Organization and Change.* San Francisco: Jossey-Bass, 1968.

Rokeach, M. *The Nature of Human Values.* New York: Free Press, 1973.

Satterfield, T. A. "Pawns, Victims, or Heroes: The Negotiation of Stigma and the Plight of Oregon's Loggers." *Journal of Social Issues,* forthcoming.

Shaw-Barnes, K. *Social Values and Attitudes Toward Gays and Lesbians.* Unpublished master's thesis, Purdue University, 1994.

Shelton, M. L., and Rogers, R. W. "Fear-Arousing and Empathy-Arousing Appeals to Help: The Pathos of Persuasion." *Journal of Applied Social Psychology,* 1981, *11,* 366–378.

Smith, E. R. "Procedural Knowledge and Processing Strategies in Social Cognition." In R. S. Wyer and T. K. Srull (eds.), *Handbook of Social Cognition.* (2nd ed.) Hillsdale, N.J.: Erlbaum, 1994.

Snyder, M., and Kendzierski, D. "Acting on One's Attitudes: Processes for Linking Attitudes and Behavior." *Journal of Experimental Social Psychology,* 1982, *18,* 165–183.

Stern, P. C. "Psychological Dimensions of Global Environmental Change." *Annual Review of Psychology,* 1992, *43,* 269–302.

Stern, P. C., and Dietz, T. "The Value Basis of Environmental Concern." *Journal of Social Issues,* 1994, *50,* 65–84.

Stern, P. C., Dietz, T., and Kalof, L. "Value Orientations, Gender, and Environmental Concern." *Environment and Behavior,* 1993, *25,* 322–348.

Stern, P. C., Dietz, T., Kalof, L., and Guagnano, G. A. "Values, Beliefs, and Proenvironmental Action: Attitude Formation Toward Emergent Attitude Objects." *Journal of Applied Social Psychology,* 1995, *25,* 1611–1636.

Sutton, S. R. "Fear-Arousing Communications: A Critical Examination of Theory and Research." In J. R. Eiser (ed.), *Social Psychology and Behavioral Medicine.* Chichester, England: Wiley, 1982.

Tetlock, P. E. "Accountability: The Neglected Social Context of Judgment and Choice." In L. L. Cummings and B. M. Staw (eds.), *Research in Organizational Behavior.* Vol. 7. Greenwich, Conn.: JAI Press, 1985.

Tetlock, P. E. "A Value Pluralism Model of Ideological Reasoning." *Journal of Personality and Social Psychology,* 1986, *50,* 819–827.

Tetlock, P. E. "Structure and Function in Political Belief Systems." In A. R. Pratkanis, S. J. Breckler, and A. G. Greenwald (eds.), *Attitude Structure and Function.* Hillsdale, N.J.: Erlbaum, 1989.

Thompson, M. M., Zanna, M. P., and Griffin, D. W. "Let's Not Be Indifferent About (Attitudinal) Ambivalence." In R. E. Petty and J. A. Krosnick (eds.), *Attitude Strength: Antecedents and Consequences.* Hillsdale, N.J.: Erlbaum, 1995.

Ungar, S. "Apples and Oranges: Probing the Attitude-Behavior Relationship for the Environment." *Canadian Review of Sociology and Anthropology,* 1994, *31,* 288–304.

Vanderford, M. L. "Vilification and Social Movements: A Case Study of Pro-Life and Pro-Choice Rhetoric." *Quarterly Journal of Speech,* 1989, *75,* 166–182.

Weigel, R. H., and Newman, L. S. "Increasing Attitude-Behavior Correspondence by Broadening the Scope of the Behavioral Measure." *Journal of Personality and Social Psychology,* 1976, *33,* 793–802.

Wood, W. "Retrieval of Attitude-Relevant Information from Memory: Effects on Susceptibility to Persuasion and on Intrinsic Motivation." *Journal of Personality and Social Psychology,* 1982, *42,* 798–810.

Wood, W., and Kallgren, C. A. "Communicator Attributes and Persuasion: Recipients' Access to Attitude-Relevant Information in Memory." *Personality and Social Psychology Bulletin,* 1988, *14,* 172–182.

Wood, W., Prislin, R., and Pool, G. J. "Attitude Formation: Structural Consistency and the Deduction of Novel from Existing Attitudes." Unpublished manuscript, Texas A&M University, 1995.

Wood, W., Rhodes, N., and Biek, M. "Working Knowledge and Attitude Strength: An Information-Processing Analysis." In R. E. Petty and J. A. Krosnick (eds.), *Attitude Strength: Antecedents and Consequences.* Hillsdale, N.J.: Erlbaum, 1995.

8

WASTE HEURISTICS

The Desire Not to Waste Versus the Desire for New Things

Hal R. Arkes and Laura Hutzel

IN THIS CHAPTER, we attempt to resolve a paradox that has significant environmental implications. On the one hand, people dislike being wasteful. Their dislike of being wasteful is so great that they will occasionally act contrary to their own self-interest in order to avoid behaviors that they think promote wastefulness. For example, many of us have closets bulging with clothes we have not worn in years, yet we just can't seem to discard them. It seems wasteful to throw out all those very thin ties and bell-bottom trousers when there is obviously a lot of use left in those relics.

On the other hand, even though people dislike being wasteful, they will discard or abandon minimally used items in order to procure a brand-new item. Many people replace their current computer with one that is capable of performing more than they need at a speed that is vastly greater than they require. Such lack of conservation results in the underutilization of many products and the overutilization of many landfills. How can people both dislike wastefulness and yet prefer new items to perfectly good but used ones?

Extract on p. 156 from H. R. Arkes, "The Psychology of Waste," *Journal of Behavioral Decision Making*, 1996, 9, 213–224, reprinted by permission of John Wiley & Sons, Ltd.

Our search for the resolution of this paradox has led us to perform three series of experiments, which we present here. In the first group of studies, we demonstrate that people will go to surprising lengths so as not to be wasteful. For example, many people pay for a tank of gas when they pick up a rental car. This prior purchase entitles the customer to bring the car back with hardly any gas in the tank. Such renters often assiduously drive around town before turning in their car in order to use the gas they have paid for. To pay for fuel and then not use it seems wasteful to these people. We should point out that the definition of *waste* used by such consumers might not be one endorsed by economists, but we will present some colloquial definitions of waste that we hypothesize people do use.

In our second group of experiments, we suggest that one reason people prefer a new over a used item is the fear that a used item might be a "lemon" (Akerlof, 1986). In other words, the used item might have some hidden defects that become apparent only after the item has been purchased. Overgeneralization of this lemons principle causes people to prefer new to used items, even when used items have little potential to go sour.

The desire not to be wasteful can often dominate the desire to replace used items with new ones. In our third category of research, we show that when the natural features of an item are cued, people choose to preserve rather than replace. This finding is particularly important because it suggests a way to increase people's willingness to interact in a more friendly way with their environment. We also suggest that money and natural resources are not perceived to be in limitless supply, contrary to the perceived supply of most commodities. Thus waste is less of an issue for most commodities than for money and natural resources, and therefore the desire for new items dominates the desire not to waste in this domain.

The Desire Not to Be Wasteful

When we began this research, we consulted several elementary economics texts for the definition of *waste*. None of the texts contained a definition of this term. Although there might not be a well-accepted "official" definition of waste, Larrick, Morgan, and Nisbett (1990), Hirst, Joyce, and Schadewald (1994), and Arkes (1996) have suggested that people follow various colloquial maxims in order to guide their economic behavior. Arkes (1996, p. 214) proposed two such maxims that laypersons may use to define wastefulness:

- *Wastefulness occurs when a person spends more on an item than is necessary.* It is extremely annoying to find out that the person sitting next to you on the airplane paid only half of what you paid for a seat on that flight. If one buys a product and then find out that the item could have been purchased at a lower price, one feels that money has been wasted.

- *Wastefulness occurs when a person does not fully utilize the item that has been purchased.* As Thaler (1980) has pointed out, no matter how sore one's tennis elbow, a player will try to get full use of a tennis club membership by heroically playing tennis every week. To sit at home after having paid tennis club dues is wasteful because the membership would not be fully utilized.

Arkes (1996, Experiment 1, pp. 215–316) presented the following scenarios to forty-eight undergraduates.

> Mr. Munn and Mr. Fry each live in an apartment near the local movie theater. Mr. Munn can go to the movies only on Monday night. Mr. Fry can go to the movies only on Friday night. Each movie costs $5, no matter which night it is shown. Each movie generally is shown for a whole week.
>
> Since Monday night is generally a pretty "slow" night at the movies, the manager of the theater offers a package to those who go to the movies on Mondays. Although tickets are $5, the manager will sell a three-pack for $12. The three-pack can be used on any three Mondays during the next month. Mr. Munn looks over the schedule for the next month and sees only two movies he is interested in seeing. So he [decides] not to buy the three-pack. Instead he pays $5 on each of the first two Mondays of the month to see a movie. Mr. Fry also pays $5 on each of the first two Fridays of the month to see a movie.
>
> Then there is a change in the schedule. One of the movies that was supposed to come that month cannot be obtained. Instead, the manager substitutes a new movie that both Mr. Munn and Mr. Fry are somewhat interested in seeing. Had Mr. Munn bought the three-pack, he could have seen this new movie without paying any more money than the extra $2 he would have needed to buy the $12 three-pack. Since he didn't buy the three-pack, both Mr. Munn and Mr. Fry will have to pay $5 to see the new movie.

Respondents were then asked if Mr. Munn or Mr. Fry would be more likely to pay to see the new movie or if the two men were equally likely to do so. Of the forty-eight respondents, thirty-four thought that Mr. Fry would be more likely than Mr. Munn to see the movie. Of course, this is contrary to a standard economic analysis. According to the latter, since Mr. Munn and Mr. Fry would have identical marginal costs and benefits if they saw the movie, the two men should be equally likely to attend. However, an analysis of the reasons provided by the subjects for their responses suggested that many subjects thought that Mr. Munn would think it wasteful to pay $5 to see the movie, given that he could have seen it for only $2 had he purchased the three-pack. Such sentiments are congruent with the spirit of the first maxim: wastefulness occurs when a person spends more on an item than is (or was) necessary. We repeat: this maxim might not be congruent with a definition of wastefulness endorsed by an accountant or economist. However, it is a heuristic whose application generally would result in prudent economic behavior. It is easily understood, and it is easily applied.

The second maxim is that wastefulness occurs when a person does not fully utilize an item that has been purchased. Arkes (1996, Experiment 2) questioned two groups of subjects concerning their willingness to buy a computer program that calculated both federal and state income taxes. Both groups were told that they had purchased such a program last year but, due to a change in the tax laws this year, the old program is now obsolete. Subjects in one group were told that the current year's $80 program was on sale for $50. The subjects in the other group were told that they could trade in last year's program to get a $30 reduction in the price of the current year's $80 program. The two groups therefore would pay equal out-of-pocket amounts to purchase the program. Nevertheless, a significantly greater proportion of participants in the latter group were willing to buy the new program. Arkes suggests that the obsolete program could be more fully utilized if it could be used to obtain a price reduction in this year's program. This heightened the willingness of the subjects in the "trade-in" group to purchase the new computer program. Arkes also suggests that the subjects who could not use their old program to obtain a price reduction thought it was wasteful to buy a new program because the old program had such abbreviated use.

The prior questionnaire studies have demonstrated that people do not want to waste. Even though Mr. Munn might enjoy the third movie just as much as Mr. Fry would, to go to that movie would be wasteful, at least according to the first maxim. To buy a new computer program very similar to the old one when the old one has been used only once also seems wasteful, according to the second maxim. Given the evidence from these studies that people are waste-phobic, we might predict they would wring every iota of use out of an item before discarding it in favor of a replacement item. However, we will now present evidence that the propensity to utilize an item fully is not universal.

The Desire for New Things

We hypothesize that the desire not to be wasteful can be overridden by the desire for new things. The latter desire can cause items of good quality to be discarded too hastily. Often we replace items that function perfectly well just to obtain the newer or more modern version. For example, although Volvos are built to withstand substantial use and abuse, one of the authors knows a man who replaces his Volvo relatively often. These purchases appear to be motivated either by the desire to have the newest model or the unfounded belief that the old car has the potential to fall apart in the near future.

The preference for new items is of concern because it has obvious detrimental effects on the environment, as raw materials are required to sustain these replacements. To investigate the preference for the new over the old, we have run several questionnaires with the same general methodology. A used item that is usually expensive is currently available for the same price as an inferior new item. Both items are covered by warranties for the same period. Nevertheless, the used item is rejected in favor of the inferior new item. The following questionnaire illustrates this situation.

Suppose that you will be in Athens next summer, so you decide to shop at a local appliance store for a dehumidifier. You have two options.

The first option is a relatively inexpensive dehumidifier for $150. It has a five-year warranty, so you know that you can get it repaired for free should anything go wrong with it during the next five years.

The second option is a two-year-old used dehumidifier that originally cost quite a bit more than $150, but in its used condition, the price is now $150. It initially had a seven-year warranty, but the store is willing to honor the last five years on that warranty. Thus you know you can get it repaired for free, like the other model, should anything go wrong with it during the next five years.

You have checked the dehumidifier ratings in *Consumer Reports*, and you have concluded that there is very little chance that either model will need to be fixed. Both dehumidifiers are very durable.

The question is, Which dehumidifier do you prefer to buy?

The new model was preferred by twenty-eight of the thirty-four undergraduates who answered this question. We have also run analogous questionnaires with other products. If the warranties and prices are equal, the majority of subjects preferred the new model to the used one, even if the used item was initially superior. In order to heighten the allure of the used item, we had to go to extreme lengths. For example, if someone bought a compact disc player a few days ago but returned it because he found out that he was being transferred to another city, and the returned compact disc player had never been taken out of its plastic wrapper, then our respondents were willing to try the nominally "used" higher quality product.

One reason why new items might be preferred to perfectly good used ones is suggested by Akerlof's lemons principle (1986), which helps to explain why a car decreases radically in value as its front tires leave the new car lot.

A buyer of a new car initially does not know whether the car is a lemon. After the car has been driven for a short time, the owner of the now-used car has ascertained whether it indeed is a lemon. If the owner wishes to sell the car for any reason, potential buyers will not know whether it is a lemon. Whether it is a gem or a lemon, the seller will represent it as a good car. As a result, the potential buyer requires that the used car be sold at a relatively low price to compensate for the possibility that the car is a lemon. Note that both the high-quality used cars and the lemons are sold for this low price because the buyer cannot with any certainty determine the status of the car under consideration. Thus there is a sensible reason why a used car, even if barely used, costs much less than a new car. The used car has more lemon potential.

We initially thought that a complete warranty on a high-quality used item would alleviate this problem. However, a complete warranty on a high-quality used item never replaced the confidence the respondents placed in a new item. Furthermore, low confidence in a used item may even be generalized to items that have only been used and owned by the buyer making the decision, in which case the possibility of concealed defects may be less than if someone else had owned the item. This is because the inner workings of a used product, even if owned only by the decision maker, may be complex or unfamiliar enough that it still might have lemon potential. The possibility that hidden flaws might manifest themselves and create future problems was a major concern to our respondents. For example, 45 percent of the respondents who preferred a new building over a completely renovated old one thought the new structure would somehow be better, more durable, more efficient, more attractive, or a combination of those.

Our hypothesis, then, is that people generalize Akerlof's lemons principle to areas where it might be less applicable. Such overgeneralization might contribute to people's hasty replacement of old items and to a sentiment that old or used items are not of sound quality.

One factor that may fuel use of the lemons principle is that people might regret their choice if they select an old item and it proves to be deficient. The potential of anticipated regret lowers the attractiveness of the old item (Landman, 1993). Even with full warranties covering both items, respondents still believed that the old item would fall apart sooner, so they opted for the new item. Another factor favoring the new item might have been that although a full warranty might prevent a financial loss, it would not eliminate the hassle of repairing a used item.

Our first group of studies provided evidence that people do not want to be wasteful, and our second group of studies provided evidence that people prefer new to perfectly good but used items. Our third group of studies was designed to pit these two tendencies against each other. Under what circumstances would people prefer to conserve the old, and under what circumstances would they prefer to abandon the old in favor of the new?

This third group of studies consisted of five pairs of questionnaires, each pair having exactly the same format. The first member of each pair was the "one-property" version. An example follows.

> Suppose you own a small amount of stock in a company. The company is facing an issue that requires a vote by the stockholders. Please consider the issue, and then we'll ask you how you would vote on it.
>
> The vote concerns a factory that is in a very bad state of repair. The equipment is outdated, and the building is in very bad condition. There are two options, each of which would cost exactly the same amount of money.
>
> Option #1 is to completely renovate the old factory. Modern equipment would be purchased, and the building would be totally modernized.
>
> Option #2 is to abandon the old factory and build a totally new one at the very same location. Brand-new equipment would be put in the new building.
>
> If you had to choose between the two options, which would you choose? (Select one option, please.)

The second member of each pair of questionnaires was the two-property version. The two-property questionnaire paired with the one-property version already given was identical to it except for the second option:

Option #2 is to abandon the old factory and build a totally new one across the street on land the company already owns. Brand-new equipment would be put in the new building.

In the one-property version, the respondents made the expected choice: they strongly preferred the construction of a new factory (option #2). However, we were surprised to find that respondents to the two-property version preferred renovation. This was a rare instance in which people eschewed the new in favor of preserving the old. After examining the reasons the respondents wrote down for their choice, we hypothesized that the two-property version fostered renovation because the respondents did not want to waste the land under the abandoned factory. Of the respondents who chose to renovate the old factory, 47 percent mentioned that they were concerned about the waste of land or materials, expressed environmental misgivings, or stated that there would be a better use for the other piece of land. Respondents to the one-property version mentioned waste or environmental concerns only 9 percent of the time; apparently they did not mind wasting the usable portions of the old factory. They were very much in favor of demolishing the old structure. Note that land waste was not an issue in the one-property questionnaire because renovation and demolition would both result in the use of the single property on which the factory was situated. Only in the two-property version did our subjects become preservationists.

We hypothesized that the abandonment of land seemed wasteful because land is a natural resource. To test this hypothesis, we ran four more pairs of questionnaires in addition to the original factory version. These four varied in the extent to which natural resources were cued in the questionnaires. An important pair was one that was identical to the original factory version except that the natural resources that went into the factory's construction were mentioned. The following is the second paragraph of this new one-property version:

The vote concerns a factory that is in a very bad state of repair. The equipment is outdated, and the building is in very bad condition. Because the building is old, it has pine floors, oak walls, and clay bricks—all natural materials.

Note that this version is identical to the original factory questionnaire except that the pine, oak, and clay materials used to construct the factory are all mentioned. We could determine the extent to which respondents increased their propensity to preserve rather than demolish by comparing this nature-cued version to the original factory version.

The other three pairs of questionnaires included a nature museum, a wildlife refuge, and a park with a skating rink. They were identical in format to the original pair of factory questionnaires.

One group of subjects simply rated these five topics (for example, the nature museum) on a 1–100 scale: "How much does this make me think of nature?" A one-way analysis of variance revealed statistically significant differences among the five topics' scores ($p < .001$). In particular, the two factory pairs differed significantly ($p < .001$).

The five pairs of questionnaires—ten questionnaires in all—were each given to ten different groups of subjects. In order to determine the "preservation propensity" of each of the five topics, we created a very simple preservation propensity index (PPI):

Preservation propensity index =

$$[(\text{renovate}_1 - \text{rebuild}_1)/n_1] \div [(\text{renovate}_2 - \text{rebuild}_2)/n_2]$$

In the one-property version:

Renovate_1 = number of people who prefer to renovate

Rebuild_1 = number of people who prefer to rebuild

n_1 = number of respondents

In the two-property version:

Renovate_2 = number of people who prefer to renovate

Rebuild_2 = number of people who prefer to rebuild

n_2 = number of respondents

The divisor is the difference in the proportion of people who preferred to renovate versus build a new item when two properties were involved.

Table 8.1. Preservation Propensity Index (PPI) of Five Structures and the Extent to Which Each "Makes Me Think of Nature."

	STRUCTURE				
Variable	*Factory*	*Factory with Materials Cued*	*Park with Skating Rink*	*Nature Museum*	*Wildlife Refuge*
"Think of nature"	10.6	40.3	53.1	80.3	88.8
PPI	–2.45	0	–.10	.83	1.0

With two properties, land waste is an issue, and people are generally conservationists. They want to renovate because to rebuild means to waste the original property. The divisor thus represents the propensity to conserve when land waste is obviously at issue.

The real test of conservation occurs when only one property is under consideration. In this situation waste is not obvious. The dividend of the PPI represents the extent to which people want to renovate rather than rebuild under these one-property circumstances. Our hypothesis is that the desire to renovate is generally less when only one property is at issue, so the PPI will generally be less than unity. However, if the structure being considered for renovation or replacement makes people think of nature, then people may be equally conservation-oriented in the one- and two-property situations. Table 8.1 contains the data for the relationship between the cueing of nature and the PPI; Figure 8.1 depicts the relationship.

It is apparent that to the extent a topic cues nature, the respondents to our questionnaires preferred not to waste over having new items. A linear function between the magnitude of nature cueing and the PPI accounts for over 88 percent of the variance. The fact that the two pairs of factory questionnaires differ so dramatically in their PPI is important for three reasons.

First, merely mentioning the natural materials in the factory increased the magnitude of "nature cueing" from 11 to 40 on our 1–100 scale, and it increased the PPI from –2.5 to 0. Furthermore, cueing of the natural components of the factory increased the proportion of respondents who mentioned waste and environmental concerns from 3 percent to 17 percent.

Second, although all five pairs of questionnaires were identical in format, the nature museum, wildlife refuge, and park pairs differed on a number of factors, such as presence of animals, number of manufactured objects, and many other dimensions. Therefore their varying levels of the PPI might be attributed to a number of potential factors. However, the

Figure 8.1. Relation Between the Magnitude of Nature Cueing and the Preservation Propensity Index.

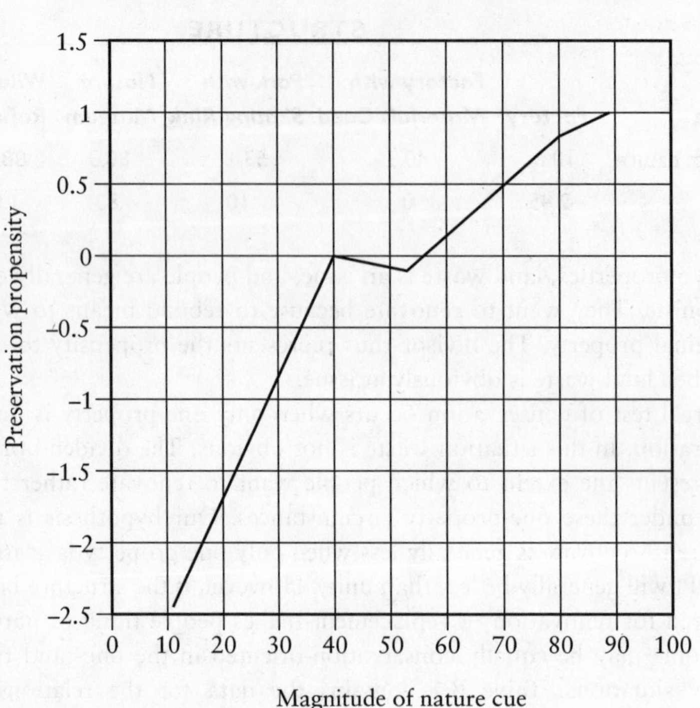

two factory versions were identical except for the cueing of the natural constituents of the factory itself. This was sufficient to increase the PPI to a significant degree. This heightens our confidence in our hypothesis that the cueing of nature is responsible for the varying levels of the PPI in the other questionnaires. Of course, the very strong relation between cueing of nature and the PPI depicted in Figure 8.1 is also supportive of this hypothesis.

Third, the two factory questionnaires rule out an alternative explanation that might have applied to the other three pairs. Perhaps people were less willing to demolish when two properties were at stake not because they abhorred land waste but because the abandoned entity would constitute an eyesore. Renovation might be preferred in the two-property case simply to avoid this eyesore, which would be present if a new structure were built. Because both of the factory "two-property" versions would have left an eyesore if subjects chose to abandon the old property and build anew, the significant difference between the two factory pairs of questionnaires must be due to some factor other than the avoidance of an eyesore.

Our conclusion is straightforward. To the extent natural resources were cued, our respondents were willing to reject the new; instead they preferred to preserve the old.

Conclusion

The first group of studies suggests that people do not want to waste. Such motivation should foster conservation. The second group of studies suggests that people desire new things. Such motivation should foster consumption and replacement. The final study shows that cueing nature fosters conservation over replacement when both courses of action are possible. In this section, we offer a conjecture as to the cause of this final result.

The first group of studies pertains to the potential waste of money. For example, our participants thought that Mr. Munn did not want to pay $5 when he could have purchased the tickets previously for $2. In the final experiment the participants who read the nature-cued factory questionnaire were told that the old factory had old oak, pine, and clay components. These natural components, as well as money, are all in limited supply. They cannot easily be replaced. In such situations, our participants did not want to waste.

However, when our participants considered a nondescript factory or a dehumidifier, they did not mind discarding the old. The new option cost no more, and there seems to be an endless supply of factories, as well as dishes, books, CD players, and all the other consumer products we have used in our questionnaires. As long as the object under consideration seems to be in abundant supply, waste does not play a role in participants' decisions. In such cases, people desire new things.

Overgeneralization

The questionnaire studies we have reviewed contain two examples of the overgeneralization of sensible rules.

First, the maxims "Don't spend more on an item than is necessary" and "Fully utilize any item" seem to be eminently reasonable. Yet, as we have seen, misapplication of these maxims can result in behavior contrary to one's best interests. For example, Mr. Munn languishes at home rather than attending a movie he's somewhat interested in seeing. Other authors, such as Larrick, Morgan, and Nisbett (1990) and Arkes (1991), also have noted that sensible maxims like "Waste not, want not" can be misapplied, leading to such errors as the honoring of sunk costs.

These maxims provide two main advantages: they are simple, and they usually foster prudent economic behavior. However, such maxims have a disadvantage: like many rules, they can be overgeneralized. It should be noted that the problem of overgeneralization is by no means unique to economic rules. For example, perhaps the central issue in the psychology of problem solving is the overgeneralization of simple rules into domains in which they are no longer appropriate (Luchins, 1942).

A second example of overgeneralization is the misapplication of Akerlof's lemons principle (1986). There are good reasons why used items should cost less than new ones. For the same reasons, new items should generally be preferred to used ones if the prices are identical. In our questionnaire studies, we were never able to tempt subjects into breaking this last "rule," even when we attempted to eliminate the factors upon which this rule is based. Minimally used higher-quality items with a full warranty were never preferred to lower-quality new items selling at the same price. We suggest that this represents an overgeneralization of the lemons principle, which is cognitively simple, generally prudent, but not necessarily universal.

We have recently noted an example that may represent a third type of overgeneralization, in this case, overgeneralization of the desire not to waste. It involves the popularity of recycling, which we could consider testimony to people's desire not to waste because it alleviates the problems of overflowing landfills and growing energy usage. Are recycling efforts paying off?

Undoubtedly recycling efforts in our communities are generally worthwhile and beneficial. However, at one point the recycling industry in Cincinnati was not able to process all the newspapers that were being collected (Lithen, 1991). The collected papers simply became another pile of trash. In fact, collection of the papers resulted in substantial consumption of gasoline and required considerable financial support. Amalgamating the citizens' newspapers into one pile would seem to be of questionable benefit to the environment if the recycling industry could not use the papers. Nevertheless the newspaper collection continued.

The Role of Cueing

In our final study, we demonstrated that when items that cued nature were under consideration, subjects became conservationists. For example, in one pair of the factory questionnaires, we blatantly cued the natural components. This technique is a common one in the social-cognition area. For example, Chaiken and Baldwin (1981) used a linguistic technique to cue prior pro- or anti-ecology behaviors. Participants starting with weakly defined environmental attitudes expressed postmanipulation attitudes congruent with the cueing. Sometimes the cueing can be done quite surreptitiously. For example, Feinberg (1986) found that merely having a credit card logo present in the vicinity caused subjects to assign higher prices to various products.

More closely related to our finding is research by Northcraft and Neale (1986), who investigated under what circumstances people would choose "to throw good money after bad." Northcraft and Neale (1986) found that when they mentioned alternative uses for the money under consideration, subjects in their experiment were less likely to invest more funds in a failing course of action. Instead the subjects were more likely to spend the funds on an alternative. Cueing alternatives thus significantly altered the subjects' economic decisions.

In a similar fashion, we suggest that by mentioning the natural components of the factory and, for other participants, by presenting such topics as a wildlife refuge or nature museum, we cued a new and important basis upon which the replace-versus-renovate decision would be made. Because natural resources are in limited supply, the participants adopted a "waste not" course of action.

This final study thus has a rather optimistic tenor. To the extent that the natural components are cued, we might be enticed to become environmentally more friendly.

REFERENCES

Akerlof, G. A. "The Market for 'Lemons': Quality Uncertainty and the Market Mechanism." In J. B. Barney and W. G. Ouchi (eds.), *Organizational Economics: Toward a New Paradigm for Understanding and Studying Organizations.* San Francisco: Jossey-Bass, 1986.

Arkes, H. R. "Costs and Benefits of Judgment Errors: Implications for Debiasing." *Psychological Bulletin,* 1991, *110,* 486–498.

Arkes, H. R. "The Psychology of Waste." *Journal of Behavioral Decision Making,* 1996, *9,* 213–224.

Chaiken, S., and Baldwin, M. W. "Affective-Cognitive Consistency and the Effect of Salient Behavioral Information on the Self-Perception of Attitudes." *Journal of Personality and Social Psychology,* 1981, *41,* 1–12.

Feinberg, R. A. "Credit Cards as Spending Facilitating Stimuli: A Conditioning Interpretation." *Journal of Consumer Research,* 1986, *13,* 348–356.

Hirst, D. E., Joyce, E. J., and Schadewald, M. S. "Mental Accounting and Outcome Contiguity in Consumer-Borrowing Decisions." *Organizational Behavior and Human Decision Processes,* 1994, *58,* 136–152.

Landman, J. *Regret: The Persistence of the Possible.* New York: Oxford University Press, 1993.

Larrick, R. P., Morgan, J. N., and Nisbett, R. E. "Teaching the Use of Cost-Benefit Reasoning in Everyday Life." *Psychological Science,* 1990, *1,* 362–370.

Lithen, R. "Recycling Popular, but Costly." *Cincinnati Enquirer,* Jan. 4, 1991, p. 2.

Luchins, A. S. "Mechanization in Problem Solving." *Psychological Monographs,* 1942, *54* (entire issue 248).

Northcraft, G. B., and Neale, M. A. "Opportunity Costs and the Framing of Resource Allocation Decisions." *Organizational Behavior and Human Decision Processes,* 1986, *37,* 348–356.

Thaler, R. "Toward a Positive Theory of Consumer Choice." *Journal of Economic Behavior and Organization,* 1980, *1,* 39–60.

PART THREE

MENTAL MODELS OF THE ENVIRONMENT

9

KNOWLEDGE AND ACTION

Cultural Models of Nature and Resource Management in Mesoamerica

Scott Atran and Douglas L. Medin

IN THE MAYA LOWLANDS of northern Peten in Guatemala and the southern Yucatan peninsula of Mexico, Maya communities have existed for two millennia in a neotropical rain forest that outside forces have, within just a few decades, brought to the edge of extinction. The sudden turn from sustainable to unsustainable forest use suggests differences in how native Maya and immigrant communities conceive of and manage forest resource systems in the same area. This chapter reports the progress of ongoing research into what those differences are. Our design uses detailed case studies and comparisons of the ways such groups structure, communicate, and implement knowledge of common-pool resources (CPRs) over time. Here we present a preliminary assessment of some of the social and cognitive factors affecting the alarming cycle of deforestation, loss of biodiversity, and community breakdown in lowland Mesoamerica.

This chapter was prepared with the assistance of Elizabeth Lynch, Norbert Ross, Edilberto Ucan Ek', and Valentina Vapnarsky. The work described in this chapter is supported by National Science Foundation grant SBR 94–22587. We would like to thank Tom Simpson, John Coley, Willet Kempton, and the editors for helpful comments on earlier drafts of this chapter.

The research centers on three questions: (1) What is the structure and content of local ecological knowledge (such as biodiversity) that enables successful commons management? (2) What is the character of communication networks that make possible assimilation, distribution, and implementation of the information? (3) To what extent is loss of local knowledge and disruption of communication networks related to a breakdown of the commons? Another issue motivating this research, but not subject to direct empirical test, is, What lessons do microlevel approaches to commons systems hold for the future of global commons, such as the earth's forests, ranges, water, and air?

Breakdown of Mayaland Commons

It will hardly be news to the reader that the rain forests of Mesoamerica, rich in biodiversity, are being destroyed in a steady, systematic manner. Less obvious but perhaps equally important is loss of cultural diversity: cultural knowledge and traditions identified with the rain forest and the management of its biodiversity are also disappearing from the face of the earth. For the past several years, we have been studying folkbiological knowledge among the Itzaj Maya of northern Guatemala—an area where a long-standing rain forest and the indigenous culture it has long harbored are disappearing.

Our initial goal was a comparative study with an eye to determining universal and culturally varying aspects of categorization of and reasoning about the biological world. The pairing of these investigations with undeniable evidence of rain forest destruction led us to believe that knowledge and action may be closely linked. Before describing these observations and their relevance to the present project, we first need to place the issue of resource management in the specific contexts of Mayaland and the commons.

Mayaland

Our study targets two sites: northern Peten (Guatemala) and the southern Yucatan peninsula (Quintana Roo, Mexico). Both sites lie within the forested region of neotropical Mesoamerica known as the Maya lowlands. For more than two thousand years, lowland Mayan speakers have inhabited the area. During the first millennium, a great forest civilization developed in Peten (and, to a lesser extent, in Yucatan). At its height, this classic Maya civilization supported a population of perhaps three million people in Peten (thirty-five thousand square kilometers). Following its collapse toward the end of the first millennium, a postclassic civilization arose in Yucatan (and, to a lesser extent, in Peten) that maintained many of the classic traditions while incorporating elements of Toltec and Aztec cultures. Although the Spanish succeeded in exterminating the Maya priesthood and nobility, Mayan language and (to a recognizable degree) agro-forestry customs survive to the present day.

The demise of classic Maya civilization is associated with archaeological evidence of spiraling population growth, unrelenting warfare, acute nutrient deficiency in human populations, and geometrically increasing rates of deforestation. Dense forest covers reappeared in the postclassic period, when population levels had declined by about an order of magnitude. The Spanish conquest reduced the native Maya population of Peten yet another order of magnitude. From the Spanish conquest until the early 1960s, Peten's population did not exceed 30,000. Since then, government support of logging and agricultural colonization has again increased Peten's population to some 400,000; however, the last remaining native Maya community is now reduced to a few hundred souls. Forest cover has already declined by about half. After some two millennia of recognizable continuity, northern Peten-Maya language and forest culture verges on extinction.

Granted, there may be a causal connection between rising population and deforestation at the end of the classic period. The fact remains that native Maya sustained fairly dense forest cover for the better part of two thousand years with populations at least equal to, and probably much greater than, immigrant populations today. By contrast, the current immigrant population of Peten is poised to destroy the remaining forest within two decades. In the Yucatan peninsula, there are still a few hundred thousand lowland Mayan speakers. But the colonization, privatization, and commercialization of the forest is driven by a much greater influx of people and capital than in Peten, so that the rate of deforestation and degeneration of biodiversity is even more rapid.

In postconquest Peten, access to the forest was implicitly restricted by a combination of natural and cultural constraints—colonists found the forest inhospitable and the harvesting of its products practically worthless to European tastes and the accumulation of wealth (Atran, 1993b). More recently, pressures to "harvest" trees have increased and the Itzaj Maya of Peten have taken steps to legally and physically bound (by firebreaks) areas of the forest they wish to reserve exclusively for their community's use.

In south central Quintana Roo, Yucatec Maya "rebels" were intermittently successful in guarding their forests against intrusion by Spanish speakers until the beginning of the twentieth century. The Mexican Revolution produced a constitution that provided some legal protection (Article 27) against open access to colonists, raiders, and "free riders" by vesting community rights of land possession and use rights in a commons institution known as the *ejido*. Today, however, the *ejidos* are beginning to break up under privatization pressures consequent to implementation of the North American Free Trade Agreement and the corresponding abrogation of Article 27 of the Mexican Constitution.

Tragedy of the Commons

A commons is a public resource pool that individuals use to physically sustain themselves. As such, a commons is typically subject to overuse if people individually act to maximize their personal gains. Indeed, Hardin's parable (1968) of the tragedy of the commons has framed much of the debate about how to deal with environmental degradation and its human consequences, where "rational" calculation of gains and losses for individual decision makers leads inexorably to overuse and ruin of resources. Individuals have little motivation to conserve if others are simply allowed to "free ride" and reap the fruits of that individual's labor. Actually, it is in that individual's self-interest to maximize (over)use, even though the collective outcome is disaster (see White, 1994, for a recent demonstration).

On the surface, the devastation of tropical forests seems to fit the bill exactly. The rain forest is being treated as a commons, and it is rapidly disappearing, despite increasing attention from the United Nations and other nongovernmental organizations. This attention has been paired with debates concerning how to preserve the forest in the face of realities driven by maximizing utility. In almost every case, two candidate solutions emerge: the imposition of some constraining central authority or privatization of the commons (North and Thomas, 1977; Liebrand, Messick, and Wilke, 1992).

There are, however, empirical problems with each of these alternatives. The problems are not unrelated to the inability of utility theories, with all externalities internalized and values measured and negotiated, to account for even the simplest human-environment interactions in small-scale societies, much less the diverse and complex behaviors in large-scale societies (Rappaport, 1979; Martinez-Alier, 1987; Costanza, 1991). For example, there seems to be no principled way to measure the future preferences of subsequent generations in a world of ever-changing values or to assign negotiable values to sacred or inviolable prescriptions. (Note that an inviolable prescription in society, such as "Do not sell your children," may be violated in practice but the violator is reckoned a sociopath, not a wrong-headed negotiator). In important respects, we believe that the commons discussion needs to be turned on its head; that is, we shall argue that the "normal" state of affairs is often successful management of the commons and that the commons breakdown should be analyzed accordingly, rather than as an inevitability. To make this point, we begin with a brief historical perspective on the commons.

Historical and Contemporaneous Background

In the first place, thousands of cases of local commons management have been catalogued (Martin, 1992), with numerous comparative studies of successful commons management by anthropologists and political scientists (McCay and Acheson, 1987; Berkes, 1989; Ostrom, 1990; Bromley, 1992). Until the forced enclosures at the dawn of the industrial revolution, most of Europe was organized in terms of commons (Stahl, 1969; Yelling, 1977; Rowley, 1981). In fact, until the expansion of the market economy to remote corners of the world, much of the world was so organized. Along with the industrial revolution came political revolution, as a "tragedy of enclosures" forced the breakup and displacement of English and French peasant communities (Darby, 1940; Bruhnes, 1978). In short, the tragedy of the commons is not everywhere and at all times a natural and inevitable state of affairs.

Second, while the debate rages over whether to privatize or collectivize, the track record for each of these options has so far been one of abysmal failure. Collectivization of the commons, as in parts of central Europe and the Soviet Union, for example, has often led to extreme impoverishment. Privatization schemes, as in forced titling of Middle East commons from the Atlantic coast of Morocco to the Swat Valley of Pakistan, has frequently led to the breakdown of social organization, environmental degradation, the rise of factionalism, and famine (Atran, 1986).

Nowhere is the debate over the commons and what to do about them more current or compelling than in Mesoamerica today. Although Mexico, for example, adopted many aspects of the Napoleonic Code, it rejected France's provision against maintenance of the commons *(nul n'est tenu de rester en indivision)* in order to preserve some vestige of the indigenous commons, or *ejidos* (Eckstein, 1966). In this last decade of the twentieth century, however, Mexico and Central American governments have decided to dismantle these enduring commons in order to encourage open access to the market and privatization. Coincidentally, the environments and the cultures that reside within them are suffering ever-increasing rates of devastation and upheaval. Open-market access, unrestricted immigration, and enclosure may be the most powerful constellation of factors in contemporaneous rain forest destruction in Mesoamerica and elsewhere.

As mentioned earlier, the tropical forests of the Central Maya lowlands once supported a population at least an order of magnitude greater than today's population and sustained it for hundreds of years, or orders of magnitude longer than current rates of deforestation allow. At least on a relative time scale, there simply is no corresponding record of success for either collectivization or privatization of common-pool resources. Nor is it the case the successful commons are possible only under conditions of low population density.

Implications for Mayaland Commons

These observations—of historical continuity and contemporary demise—point to the possibility, directly contradictory to Hardin's thesis, that breakdown of commons occurs not because they are inherently unmanageable but because the long-standing conditions for their management are being destroyed. The challenge is to identify the conditions for successful commons management before this form of management is eliminated from the planet. Given that no other form of management has proven sustainability, it may be a rich source of ideas for successful global sustainability.

Elinor Ostrom and others have done case and experimental studies of the institutional conditions for successful commons, such as rule configurations for appropriating resources, monitoring access, and sanctioning violators (Ostrom, Gardner, and Walker, 1994). Our research focus is more on process than structure, that is, on the mix of psychological, cultural, and ecological factors that condition successful or unsuccessful commons behavior. We believe that a process focus is a good strategy for identifying factors that are candidates for generalization to other contexts.

Current Context

This section describes the populations we studied and their agro-forestry practices. It then outlines our present research focus.

Setting

We are looking at a number of populations that live off the same area or biotope, the lowland Maya forests of southern Mexico and northern

Guatemala. We selected these populations because they differ in their ability to sustain themselves in the same environment. So far we have begun looking at four groups of people: two groups of native Maya Indians and two groups of immigrant Ladinos. Ladinos is the term used to refer to people of mixed or Indian origin that no longer speak their native Maya tongue. The native groups are the Yucatec Maya in south central Quintana Roo, Mexico, and the Itzaj, who are the last Maya native to the Peten forest of Guatemala—once the center of classical Maya civilization. Each of the two immigrant groups is the closest settlement to its respective native group. The immigrant Ladinos that live near the Itzaj have been around on the average for more than one decade but in most cases less than two; immigrants in the group that live near the Yucatec Maya have been around on the average for less than a decade.

Itzaj Maya claim that Ladinos do not recognize that their behavior violates the "natural" rights and duties incumbent upon people and the forest to tend to one another because "there is no heartfelt affection for land they were not born to and which they will abandon." Immigrants, they feel, are detached from their roots *(u motz)* and lineage *(u ch'ib'aloo'),* with Maya using *roots* and *lineage* as interchangeable terms in both organic and social contexts. As a result, the Itzaj feel compelled for the first time in living memory to establish institutionalized mechanisms for delimiting boundaries and for monitoring and sanctioning intruders or freeloaders who appropriate the fruits of another's efforts. In the past, the Maya's cohesive social networks alone may have sufficed to rapidly convey the necessary information and sustain vigilance for forest maintenance.

In Yucatan, the state-supported structure of the *ejidos* helped local communities to maintain closed access until quite recently. Now, the government is forcing the *ejidos* to privatize common agricultural lands while encouraging the communities to "selectively cut" their vestigial forest lands with the aid of private logging concerns. Native Maya communities are attempting to resist in various ways, with sporadic success. A key aspect of social control is the community's periodic assignment of individuals to tend particular trees. These individuals may cut their assigned trees if mature, but premature or excessive cutting can lead to sanctions and loss of tree assignments.

With the reduction of the remaining forests, and the consequent rise in timber prices, the most valuable "high grade" trees (mahogany and tropical cedar) are being cut to the vanishing point. Secondary trees, which are still underexploited in Peten, have become prime timber in the Yucatan (for example, *tzalam,* or *Lysiloma bahamense,* and *chechem,* or *Metopium brownei*). Immigrant communities are felling these at an awesome rate. Many of these immigrant groups, including influential elements in the community we are studying, are petitioning the government to declare the entire area cattle pasture *(zona ganadera)* so that all constraints on clear-cutting might be lifted. As it is, chain saws can be heard in the village throughout the day, as can the trailers that surreptitiously cart out the felled timber at night.

It is interesting to note that the Guatemalan Ministry of Agriculture is attempting to emulate the Mexican Forestry Department in encouraging selective cutting of remaining forest stands. Local and regional nongovernmental organizations (NGOs) operating in Peten have been granted concessions ostensibly designed to "sustainably develop" the forested areas inhabited by immigrant communities. Using the area of Yucatan that figures in our study as an example of "successful management," these NGOs are strenuously soliciting bids from logging companies to selectively harvest the stands under their "protection." So far, the Itzaj have declined the "protection" of the vice-minister of agriculture and many of the NGOs, but the political and economic pressure on them to "rationally develop" what little remains of a once mighty heritage is great and unrelenting.

Thus, together with the internal cognitive and social makeup of our populations, external political and economic conditions are clearly at work in determining the present and future course of commons management. As long as these external, market-driven pressures dominate, commons management will inevitably run down, although the pace of cultural and biological destruction will likely be different for different groups. Our study of internal factors may not indicate how destruction can be avoided in the face of these seemingly overwhelming external factors, but it might reveal modes of resistance and even recovery should those external factors change.

Groups and Practices

Both the Maya and Ladino groups practice a form of agro-forestry (increasingly supplemented by nontraditional sources of subsistence based on a money economy) and make use of wood in construction. The mainstay of subsistence for each group is so-called slash-and-burn, or swidden, agriculture. In the forest where this technique is applied, the trees are cut and the land fired and cleared so that crops can be planted for a few years, that is, until exhaustion of the nutrients released into the soil from the initial burning of trees and undergrowth compels the cultivator to move on to another section of the forest.

Rates of decomposition are very high in such moist, hot conditions, resulting in lack of humus formation and storage in the top soil (as in temperate forests). Instead, nutrients are cycled between living organisms and recently dead organisms, a network of fine roots and mycorrhiza absorbing mineral nutrients as they are released by decomposers. The result is a nutrient-rich litter layer overlying a nutrient-poor mineral soil with little storage capacity.

Slash-and-burn agriculture addresses two ecological problems inherent in agricultural production: plant competition (weeds) and nutrient recycling (Vandermeer and Perfecto, 1995). By burning off competitors before seeding a plot, the farmer provides an initial advantage to crop plants. Through burning, the nutrients normally stored securely in plant materials are released en masse to provide a rich growing environment for the crops.

A brand-new crop layer is able to use up only a portion of the nutrients suddenly released from a multistoried old-growth forest patch. After the first burning, there are usually enough excess nutrients to allow rapid regeneration of "weeds." If there were no further burning, the forest would also regenerate at close to a normal pace, that is, at about the rate of regeneration that follows a light gap in the canopy by natural processes of tree fall.

More often, the initial weed growth is burned or mulched to provide nutrients for yet another crop cycle. Additional burning further reduces the already diminished capacity of the forest floor to hold the nutrients. If the normal nutrient-cycling process of the forest continues to be interrupted in this way, runoff and leaching will produce a net export of nutrients and an inability to support vegetative growth. The land must be abandoned and new fields cleared and burned. With broad-scale clearing and forest degradation, remaining surface nutrients are rapidly leached by sun and rain, the few seeds that sprout die in the hot sterile soil of the clearings, massive species extirpation occurs (about ten to thirty animal species for every plant species), and soon the land is no longer able to sustain appreciable human population (Gomez-Pompa, Vazquez-Yanes, and Guevara, 1972; Hecht and Cockburn, 1990).

There are, however, at least six critical differences between Maya and Ladino swidden practices that lead to differences in sustainability (Atran, 1993b). In what follows, the "Maya" practices are most pronounced in the case of the Itzaj, and the "Ladino" practices most pronounced for the Yucatan group; nevertheless, such differences are also more or less discernible for the Yucatec Maya and Peten Ladino groups (see Nations and Nigh, 1980, for a similar distinction with respect to the Lakantun Maya of Chiapas).

1. Ladinos burn the crown of hills. This greatly impedes forest regeneration because hillside soils wash out more easily, exposure to sun is higher, and the wind-borne dispersal of seeds is reduced (seeds borne higher up disperse farther and wider through random weighted motion). The Maya, in contrast, spare hill crowns.
2. Ladinos build large fires that are often hard to control. The Maya, in contrast, clear an area with several smaller fires. Smaller, cooler fires may volatilize less nitrogen, a limiting nutrient for plant growth (Tom Simpson, personal communication). Moreover, Maya fires are calibrated to the requirements of different types of tree stands, which are interspersed throughout their agricultural plots, or milpas. (In fact, the Itzaj Maya have tried to provide Ladinos instruction in how to set proper fire breaks around and within their plots.)
3. The Maya habitually allow longer fallow periods (five to seven years) than Ladinos (two to three years) and traditionally leave a forest patch to recover to maturity after it has been alternately used and left fallow for the span of a person's lifetime (about fifty years).
4. The Maya avoid broad clearing by ensuring that the extent of forest surrounding a clearing is at least several times greater than the clearing. In Peten, the area of forest a given Itzaj tends is usually anywhere from five to twenty-five times the area of the clearing. This tended forest "reserve" is harvested for wood and other (nontimber) forest products but neither burned nor clear-cut. Where Ladino and Maya plots touch, the Maya ensure that tree stands *(t'ool~che')* ring their milpa plots.
5. In some cases, Maya forgo successive burning and shifting altogether. After the first burn, an Itzaj farmer may stay on the same milpa plot for a working lifetime (in one case, forty-six years to date), using mulch from weeds to provide a low but constant level of productivity. This is much more labor-intensive than burning but also much more sustainable in the long run.
6. Maya plant a greater multiplicity of crops, which probably supports a greater degree of associated biodiversity (such as insects and other animals). To an appreciable extent, the structure of a Maya plot emulates the layered and diverse structure of the surrounding forest. This provides the Maya a richer and more resistant stock of staples while also facilitating forest regeneration.

In short, unlike the Maya, the Ladinos tend to deplete the rain forest until it is no longer renewable. This is not to say that the Ladinos do not appreciate the value of the forest or the future to themselves or their families. Like other developing-world colonists, they may well understand their dependence on biological diversity far more accurately and acutely than urban North Americans do and in ways that compare favorably with native peoples. As we shall see, however, this understanding of human-animal-plant interdependency may be asymmetrical, with little concern for or awareness of how reciprocity between people, animals, and plants sustains biological diversity and cultural survival. By contrast, Maya understanding of human-plant-interactions tends to be more symmetrical, involving reciprocal dependencies.

Research Focus

Why do the Ladino immigrants and Maya differ in their treatment of the rain forest? We are trying to understand these differences in behavior by experimentally probing a mix of psychological, cultural, and ecological variables. Our initial hypothesis was that the two groups had very different understandings of the rain forest, understandings that are tied to action. These understandings can be thought of as *tacit theories* (Medin, 1989) or *mental models* (Gentner and Stevens, 1983), that is, structured forms of causal knowledge that can be used to guide reasoning and make predictions. Specifically, we thought that the Ladinos might be destroying the forest not deliberately but rather through a form of ignorance, in other words, behaving in accordance with a mental model that, if it were accurate, would lead to sustainability. The problem from this perspective would be that they have the wrong mental model, either because it is insufficiently informed or because it qualitatively fails to capture the kinds of human-nature interactions that would actually sustain those interactions.

Of course, a variety of other possibilities may give rise to differential behavior in the Maya and Ladino groups. For example, we are also looking at differences in social networks. Differences in social structure may be tied both to cultural obligations (such as social sanctions for inappropriate land use) and to the diffusion of knowledge concerning practice. In addition, we have been attempting to develop measures of cultural and moral commitment to the rain forest: for example, perceptions of mutually shared obligations in tending the forest.

The general idea from the perspective of mental models is that the less you know about the natural world, the more you are liable to destroy it, either through ignorance or intention. Also, the denser your social network, the more redundant and assimilable the information about proper and improper ways of dealing with the environment; but the more varied your social network, the greater the possibility of a cognitive division of labor and the more flexibly and efficiently information can be dealt with. In other words, there may be optimal forms of diverse but overlapping communication networks for processing and acting upon information (see, for example, Granovetter, 1973, Hammer, 1983). Finally, a moral—perhaps even sacred—concept of tending the forest, as a counterpart to the concept of the forest tending people, encourages awareness and action toward a mutually shared future.

Our project is at an early stage. We have some initial observations that reveal some surprising similarities across groups as well as some striking differences. This chapter represents a progress report, and we are far from any definitive conclusions. Nonetheless, our initial findings are quite intriguing. Before describing our research in detail, however, we further motivate it by placing it in the context of a more general project of studying people's understanding of the biological world.

We came to study the commons by a somewhat circuitous route. Our original focus was on universal principles of folkbiology, but this research led us inexorably to questions of culture and ecology. In particular, our previous and ongoing research on folkbiology among Maya and people who live in North America (specifically the Midwestern United States) suggested to us that Maya seamlessly integrate cognitive, cultural, and ecological factors whereas the Midwesterners do not.

For example, although both cultures seem to categorize and rank biological species in taxonomies that correlate significantly, and in almost identical fashion, with the Linnaean taxonomies used by biological systematists, the two cultures reason from their taxonomies differently. Our measure of reasoning is category-based induction (Rips, 1975). A number of phenomena associated with category-based induction have been identified (Osherson and others, 1990), and we focus on three of them. The first phenomenon is similarity, and the judgments of both groups conform to it: the closer the taxonomic distance between two categories, the more likely it is that people will believe that the two categories share some novel or unfamiliar biological property (such as susceptibility to some novel disease). For example, if people are told that eagles have some novel biological property, they are more likely to believe that falcons also have this property than that ducks do. The other two phenomena differ in character across cultures (Lopez and others, forthcoming).

First, consider typicality. Both groups more readily project properties to a whole category from properties of a typical category member than from an atypical one. For example, North Americans believe that novel properties true of sparrows are more likely to be true of all birds than are novel properties of atypical birds like turkeys. Itzaj also show typicality, but the basis for typicality is different. For the North Americans, typical birds are medium-sized birds similar to lots of other birds. In other words, typicality is based on central tendency. For Itzaj Maya, typicality is more like an ideal (see also Barsalou, 1985). For example, the wild turkey is the most typical Itzaj bird, whereas sparrowlike birds are judged atypical. So a novel property true of wild turkeys is more likely to be judged true of all birds than is a novel property true of sparrowlike birds.

For all plant and animal life forms, Itzaj Maya judge typicality on the basis of a combination of morphological, cultural, and ecological factors. Typical animals and plants, such as the jaguar and the guano palm, have high cultural value, but no single cultural dimension defines that value: jaguars are lords of the forest; guano palms are sources of shelter and food. Animals and plants judged to be typical tend to be large and otherwise physically striking, but size or physical salience alone does not suffice: cows are bigger than jaguars, but they are not typical. All typical animals and plants have notable roles in Maya conceptions of human ecology: the jaguar's home range, forty to fifty square kilometers, defines a forest section; the wild turkey's presence means that game abounds (in ecological terms, wild turkeys are "sentinel species"), and where guano palm is abundant, human settlement can be assured. In sum, for the Maya, cultural, ecological, and morphological properties are part of a single organizational scheme.

This does not mean that the Maya assign predefined special purposes or functional signatures to taxonomies and make inferences based on them. Instead, it implies a sound conceptual infrastructure for the widest range of human adaptation to surrounding environmental conditions. In other words, the aim appears to be to maximize the relevance of the biological world to human understanding. This is not the case with the North Americans' judgments using taxonomically based inferences. As with scientific systematics, for the North Americans the ideal goal appears to be to maximize inductive potential regardless of human interest. In other words, the motivating idea is to understand nature as it is "in itself." For Itzaj, and arguably for other small-scale societies, their structure works to maximize inductive potential relative to human interests.

The third phenomenon is diversity (see, for example, Osherson and others, 1990). Itzaj "fail" to apply the so-called diversity principle to biological reasoning with animal (such as mammal) and plant (such as palm) taxa, and concern with ecology is one key factor responsible for the results. According to the diversity principle, if other things are equal (as when taxa are equally typical), then a biological property shared by two taxonomically close taxa (for example, a wolf and a coyote) is less likely to be shared by a superordinate group of taxa (such as mammals) than a property shared by two taxonomically distant taxa (for example, a wolf and a gopher). The diversity principle corresponds to the fundamental principle of induction in biological systematics: that is, a property found in any two organisms is likely found in the smallest or lowest-ranked taxon containing the two. Suppose, for example, that you find a property in a turkey and in the bacterium *E. coli.* Using the diversity principle, you can justifiably attempt to project that property to the lowest taxon containing *E. coli* and turkeys, namely, all organisms.

North American folk seem to use their biological taxonomies much as scientists do when using unfamiliar information to infer what is likely in the face of uncertainty. Informed that goats and mice share a hitherto unknown property, they are more likely to project that property to mammals than if informed that goats and sheep do. By contrast, Itzaj tend to use similarly structured taxonomies to search for causal ecological explanations of why unlikely events should occur: to give one example, bats may have passed on the property to goats and mice by biting them, but a property would not likely need an ecological agent to be shared by goats and sheep. In short, common properties among ecologically associated but taxonomically distinct things imply a transfer of properties through a mediating agent, whereas common properties among taxonomically closely associated things imply inherent similarity. This seems to be a way Maya spontaneously think, but not a way people in the United States usually think. In other cases, the Maya employ a form of ecological diversity (which pair comes into contact with more other organisms), which is not necessarily correlated with morphological diversity. Apparently, context-sensitive causal concerns about the relationships between taxa serve to block context-free uses of diversity-based reasoning across taxonomies.

It is not that Itzaj do not understand the diversity principle. In tests with diversity-based reasoning in other domains, Itzaj performed successfully as a group. For example, when asked whether a person should spend a fixed amount of time visiting one part of a forest or many parts in order to determine if that forest should be settled or cultivated, Itzaj invariably opted for the latter alternative.

Note that in both the U.S. and Itzaj cases, similarly structured taxonomies are providing the distance metrics over which biological induction takes place. For the North Americans, taxonomic distance indicates the extent to which underlying causes are more likely to predict shared biological properties than are surface relationships. For Itzaj, taxonomic distance suggests the extent to which ecological agents are likely to be involved in predicting biological properties that do not conform to surface relationships. A priori, either stance might be correct. For example, diseases are clearly biologically related; however, distribution of a hitherto unknown disease among a given animal population could well involve epidemiological factors that depend on both inherent biological susceptibility and ecological agency.

More generally, what "counts" as a biological cause or property may be different for folk, like the Itzaj, who necessarily live in intimate awareness of their surroundings and those, like North American folk, whose awareness is less intimate and necessary. For Itzaj, awareness of biological causes and properties may directly relate to ecology, whereas for most North American folk the ecological ramifications of biological causes and properties may remain obscure. Historically, the West's development of a worldwide scientific systematics explicitly involved disregard of ecological relationships and of the colors, smells, tastes, and textures that constitute the most intimate channels of recognition and access to the surrounding living world (Atran, 1990).

These results have led us to believe that ecological knowledge is crucial to Maya reasoning about the natural world. This understanding gives rise to two questions. First, to what extent is knowledge of the natural world, particularly ecological knowledge, influenced by cultural factors that are particular to the Maya? Second, to what extent are the behavioral differences that exist between the Maya and the Ladinos with regard to agroforestry (sustainability) driven by differences in knowledge and associated mental models? Our observations also suggest that ecological sensibility among the Maya is integrally bound up with cultural significance, though not in any direct utilitarian or functional sense. We aim to make corresponding observations among the Ladino populations.

Initial Measurements and Preliminary Results

To explore how ecological knowledge is culturally embedded, we devised a series of tasks. In one, we asked a set of informants in each population to tell us which kinds of plants and animals are most necessary for the forest to live. In another, we asked for explicit judgments concerning dependencies between plants and dependencies between animals. In a third task, we asked for dependencies between plants and animals. For all these tasks, we asked people to justify their answers at every point.

Biological Knowledge

KEY PLANTS AND ANIMALS FOR THE RAIN FOREST. To our surprise, we found that the overwhelming majority of informants in each of the four populations, inhabiting an area covering fifteen thousand square kilometers and thousands of species, name the same two dozen or so species as most important for the rain forest. For plants, the nominees are overwhelmingly canopy trees, followed by understory palms and tree vines. Nearly all of the nominated plants and animals have high cultural value; however, the reasons the Maya informants give for their choices almost always include ecological value.

Consider, for example, the small *Chamaedorea* palms called *xate* in Spanish and *ix-xyaat* in Maya. These have no traditional cultural value for Maya. Their current value is to the cash economy, where they are collected from the deep forest for export to Florida and elsewhere for use in floral arrangements. The locals have no idea what they are used for. Many informants mention *xate* as necessary for the forest to live but justify its choice in purely ecological terms: *xate* is a small palm that covers and protects the forest floor, preserving the humidity that allows the other plants to thrive and thereby ensuring that the animals, in turn, are fed and sheltered by the plants. Although from a scientific standpoint many other species would fit the bill, for the Maya there are no grounds for isolating cultural from ecological significance. A given species is vital to life in the forest—including, crucially, human life—only if it exhibits both dimensions. In other words, social or economic value renders salient the ecological value of certain species, and these species are represented in both cultural and ecological terms.

In a second task, we asked informants to describe what happens when each of these salient species disappears. Each folk species mentioned in the previous task was paired with every other species in its domain (plants with plants, animals with animals). Our purpose was to test whether these cultures make use of the notion of a keystone species. A species is a keystone of a given ecological community if its removal leads to a drastic change in the community's makeup and if its reappearance leads the community to recover something like its original state (Wilson, 1992). For each pair of species, we asked if the disappearance of one would positively or negatively affect the other, or not at all.

These three alternatives allow each species pair to be represented in terms of one of six ecological relationships. For example, if disappearance of one species negatively affects the existence of a second species and vice versa, then the relation is one where both partners derive benefit (something like the ecologist's notion of symbiotic mutualism, but perhaps at another level). If disappearance of the first species negatively affects the second but disappearance of the second species does not affect the first, then the relation is one where one partner derives benefit and the other is not harmed (akin to symbiotic commensalism). If disappearance of the first species negatively affects the second but disappearance of the second species positively affects the first, then the relation is parasitic with respect to the second species, and so on.

Again to our surprise, of the thousands of possible species interrelationships that could be represented in this way, only a very few species were deemed vital to the well-being of other species, and the species chosen were much the same in the four human populations. For animals, only the jaguar had a significant positive or negative role. For plants, only the broad relationships that directly reflect the storied structure of the forest were mentioned, that is, relationships between upper-story canopy trees as a group, understory palms as a group, and connecting-story vines as a group. In all the human communities we studied, there was evident ecological awareness of forest plants as structures for distributing shade and water.

These findings suggest two intriguing possibilities: First, at least certain first-order aspects of ecological understanding seem to be common to all the native and immigrant groups in our study and not dependent on longstanding tradition or cultural life in the forest. Second, the notion of keystone species is not particularly relevant to this understanding. Indeed, the whole organic metaphor of nature that is current in popular Western thinking about ecology seems to be entirely alien to these people. Ladinos never describe the forest as a living being, consisting of essential parts that are necessarily dependent upon one another, where some parts—or species—are so essential that the whole dies without them (Kempton, Boster, and Hartley, 1995).

ANALOGIES AND MENTAL MODELS OF THE RAIN FOREST. Among Ladinos, there is no view of the environment as being similar to the human body, which consists of integrated parts that vitally depend upon one another (for example, the spleen vitally depends upon the heart, but only disappearance of the heart leads to death of the body). This is basically true for Maya as well, except in the case of the jaguar, who gives order to the forest through his lordly rule and vies with man for the title of master of the forest *(u yumil k'aax)*. But the jaguar is essential not because it is a keystone species but because it is a mediator between animal and human relationships to the forest.

Instead, the model that both Maya and Ladino informants tend to use when they imagine the forest is more like a house or household. In fact, the Maya cosmos is classically represented as a house (*itzam-naj, itzam*-house). In this worldview, the parts are vitally linked to one another but not in any essential way. The kitchen and living room may be more important than the storage room or pantry, but you could always sleep in the rafters or cook in the pantry if you had to. Unlike the popular view of ecology current in the United States and Europe, neither the Maya nor the Ladino conception of the environment is something akin to a delicately balanced house of cards. Rather, the Maya and the Ladinos see the forest as naturally robust and recoverable, unless subject to sustained external disruption. In this, their views may be closer to ecological science than North American lay thinking.

Take the Itzaj Maya view of the tapir and the breadnut tree *(Brosimum alicastrum)*. The Itzaj refer to the tapir as the "animal of the seven fleshes" and the breadnut tree as the "milpa of the animals." Both the tapir and the breadnut tree are currently priority items in Itzaj attempts to preserve a vestigial section of their traditional forest, known today as the "Bio-Itzaj" Reserve. Itzaj acknowledge that people and jaguars will have other flesh to eat should the tapir vanish, and that the twoscore species of mammals and birds that feed off breadnut fruits and leaves can move on to a host of other trees and herbs should the breadnut disappear. But should the tapir vanish, "nobody will know what it's like to have the seven fleshes together"; and should the breadnut tree disappear, so many animals will never be found together again.

Both Ladinos and Maya say that the forest is structured like a household, with canopy plants protecting understory plants like parents protecting children. Moreover, both groups talk of the forest as a house in a more directly functional way: walking in the forest, one sees and obtains everything one needs to physically make a house, and looking about a house, one sees in its materials much of the variety and structure of the forest (hardwood from the canopy trees providing the frames; palms providing thatch; grasses, earth, and understory softwoods for the marl walls; vines for the ties, and so on).

But there are differences between the groups. Maya, but not Ladinos, say that the animals that move within the forest also see their homes in the forest and the forest in their homes (nests, lairs, and so on). As one man put it: "The forest is like a house because it is life, shade, cool air. Its animals and trees live as a family lineage. There is everything that is necessary, like where to rest and also happiness" *(A'k'aaxej je'b'ix a'naj mentik yanil kuxtal, b'o'oy, siis ik'. U b'a'al~che'iloo' u cheoo' b'ayil uchib'aloo kuxutaloo'. Yan tulakal b'a'al kuk'ab'etil je'b'ix tu'ux kuwenel b'ay xan kiyolal).*

Moreover, the Maya say that people and animals need the forest to live just as the forest needs people and animals to live. For example, in one study in Peten, we found that 73 percent of the Maya said humans are much more likely to help rather than hurt plants, compared to 45 percent of the Ladinos. The forest is a place that satisfies not only material wants but also the desire to see beauty *(yutzilil)*. For Maya, then, the forest is not just a metaphorical house but literally "our home" *(ki wotoch)*.

INTERACTIONS BETWEEN PLANTS AND ANIMALS. Perhaps the most striking group differences arise for the descriptions of interspecies relationships. Even for the few nominated integral species like the jaguar and the vines on the one hand and other animal and plant species on the other hand, native Maya tend to consider these relationships to be reciprocal, whereas Ladinos tend to view them asymmetrically. Ladinos explicitly deny that birds and animals help the rain forest, whereas native Maya believe that the animals, the birds, and the trees tend to one another. The Maya groups generally and the Itzaj in particular also have a tighter cultural consensus than do the immigrant groups in their understanding of plant-animal interactions. We use factor analysis in order to measure consensus, that is, levels of agreement and disagreement between and across subjects (Romney, Weller, and Batchelder, 1986).

An interesting illustration of the relationship between scientific and folk-ecological principles is the case of the strangler fig (*Ficus involuta,* Maya = *kopo',* Spanish = *amate* or *matapalo,* which means tree-killer). Unlike most trees, the strangler fig does not grow from the ground up but germinates arboreally far above the ground. After germinating, it sends out aerial roots that drop downward into the vascular system of the host tree. In time, the roots reach the ground and graft together. The strangler roots envelop the host tree, gradually killing it by reducing its ability to transport nutrients.

Like other pioneering trees that are adapted to rapidly fill light gaps in the forest, the strangler has a high rate of growth and fecundity, producing numerous small-seeded fruits. Unlike the large-seeded species, whose exemplars are widely scattered so as to avoid nonspecific competition for scarce resources, small-seeded pioneering species rely on a large seed shadow. This increases the plant's ability to get a seed into an appropriate spot so as to take advantage of virgin resources as soon as possible (Forsyth and Miyata, 1995). As a result, the strangler can be found almost everywhere that the climax forest has been disturbed. It is often seen dominating secondary growth areas and frequently found climbing over the limestone face of an ancient Maya temple.

Only the Maya believe that this tree can help people, and that animals can help this tree. Like tank bromeliads and certain lianas, which live or originate above the ground where water is hard to capture, the strangler's vinelike roots evolved to store water. This makes the strangler an important emergency water source for Maya in northern Peten, where there is a dry season (February through April) and few permanent water sources. The Maya also use the strangler's sticky sap to poultice swellings and to block up the skin holes made by burrowing botfly larvae (so as to suffocate them before they pose a serious health threat).

The Maya, however, do not cite the strangler as one of the most important trees to the forest just because of these advantages. Many other trees that are not cited have more important nutritional or medicinal functions. Rather, the strangler is singled out because of the large range of animal life it supports. Its broad canopy attracts many birds, bats, and monkeys, which feed on its sweet and pulpy fruit. Its creviced trunk and base serve to host and protect numerous species of lizards, insects, and small rodents. Peccaries and large rodents, such as agoutis and pacas, congregate around the base to eat the ripe figs that the monkeys and larger birds drop or knock to the ground.

Unlike temperate forest trees, most tropical forest trees use fleshy fruits to disperse their seeds instead of wind or hook. Only canopy trees can take much advantage of the wind, and even they tend to rely on frugivory, or fruit eating. This is because the intense competition in the rain forest makes it unlikely that members of a single species can cluster sufficiently in a given area to profit from the random wind-borne dispersal of pollen or seed. As a result, mobile animals like birds, bats, and monkeys are indispensable to effective seed dispersal and rain forest survival.

Maya notions of reciprocity appear to acknowledge these basic facts about tropical rain forest ecology. Although individual informants may differ significantly in their ideas of which animals help or hurt a given tree like the strangler, there is an overall sense of reciprocity. Thus for the Itzaj, bats, birds, monkeys, peccaries, and large rodents may both help and hurt the strangler, depending on whether they destroy the seed when they eat the fruit (with bats considered the least destructive and peccaries and large rodents the most destructive).

Even agoutis and pacas, which usually eat and destroy the seed, may be faced at times with such an abundance of fruit and seed that they hide away a few and then neglect them, as squirrels do with acorns. This is the principle of predator satiation or saturation. Such saturation can result from the absence or scarcity of other (fruit) predators: if some of the fruit eaters are no longer around, then there may be too many fruits left over for the remaining fruit eaters. (Note that mast fruiting—the huge production of seeds at irregular intervals that characterizes oaks and other temperate forest trees—is rare in tropical rain forests because the weather fluctuations that trigger the process are usually not severe enough).

Like rain forest tree species, no rain forest animal species are overly abundant in the neotropics. This makes obligatory dependencies between species potentially disastrous; for if one partner vanishes the other is also liable to disappear. Fortunately, nutrient and seed dispersal systems in the tropical forest are buffered. If a given tree species is no longer available, the animals that feed on it can usually find other food sources in nearby trees. And should any animal species become scarce for any reason, then the seeds of a given tree species can be dispersed by the remaining animal species. The metaphor of the forest as the "Maya house," with partially redundant and substitutable parts, clearly accords with this buffered nature of the tropical rain forest.

Social and Knowledge Networks

Another data-driven observation is that the social networks within which information concerning the environment is conveyed are structured differently for Maya and Ladinos. In our ongoing research, we use variations of standard techniques for elicitation and analyses of social networks (Wellman, 1979; Scott, 1988). For each population, we selected an initial set of informants and asked them: (1) "Outside of your household, who are the people you most depend upon in your life?" For each informant, we then elicited an extended social network from the persons ranked most important and least important by that informant. We are looking at different kinds of networks, including networks of mutual dependence in everyday life versus networks geared solely to getting information about the forest, for example: (2) "Who do you talk to about the forest?" and (3) "Who do you go to when you want to find out something you don't know about the forest?" Each person listed is scored on a coding sheet for sex, age, occupation (farmer, logger, and so on), social role (kin, workmate, friend, and so on), location (same or other neighborhood, village, province, place of origin as informant), and frequency of contact (for example, twice daily equals 720 contacts per year).

For both the Maya and Ladino groups, the responses intimate a social division of cognitive labor (see, for example, Ford, 1976, for a comparable social division of medical knowledge in a small-scale Amerindian society).

Most everyday information seems to circulate among people cited in answer to question 1; most highly specialized information about the forest is obtained from people cited in answer to question 3; much everyday information about the particular topic of the forest is obtained from those people in question 1 that the informant considered most knowledgeable, and from those people in question 3 considered most accessible. There is a great overlap in Maya responses to question 3; that is, the experts cited tend to be the same across Maya informants. There is considerably less overlap in Ladino responses to question 3; however, in Peten much of what overlap Ladinos report is owing to the fact that the majority of Ladinos cite Itzaj experts. By contrast, no Maya ever cites a Ladino as an expert.

In the Maya case, individual networks elicited from question 1 tend to be more kin-based than Ladino networks. Immigrant networks tend to be less densely and more diversely composed (neighbor, congregation, workmate, Itzaj) and the different networks do not seem to overlap as much, despite the fact that the Ladino communities in our study are smaller than the Maya communities. Thus, even if the right information were to enter one part of the overall network, it would more likely be lost before it became entrenched throughout the community as a whole.

Nevertheless, there is some evidence that Itzaj experts provide a steady source of information that affects Ladino knowledge and behavior concerning the forest. The Peten immigrants overwhelmingly cite native Maya as expert sources of information about the forest. The Peten immigrants often describe the manner in which people help (or should help) plants in ways that are often explicitly attributed to Itzaj. So far, however, the fundamental Maya belief about the reciprocal relations between plants and animals has not taken hold in either of the Ladino immigrant groups.

In sum, there are intriguing indications of important relationships between some of the kinds of ecological information (reciprocal, nonreciprocal) and social communication networks (densely overlapping, diverse) pertinent to successful or unsuccessful commons management. On the one hand, there is a main effect in our studies of population: native Maya and immigrants differ significantly with regard to ecological information and social networks (assuming the Yucatec data turn out to show corresponding differences). For Maya, but not Ladinos, ecological interactions are reciprocal. The ultimate sources of information about the forest are virtually all native Maya, at least in Peten. On the other hand, there may also be a main effect of significant differences between the Guatemalan groups and the Mexican groups. For example, preliminary analyses suggest that the Itzaj subjects may have more pervasive and detailed beliefs than the Yucatec subjects about how animals help plants, especially in regard to seed dispersal. The Peten Ladinos appear to differ from immigrants in the Yucatan in their belief that people help many important plants and that important animals interact with important plants (albeit mostly in harmful ways). Peten Ladinos also crucially incorporate native Maya into their communication networks whereas preliminary data suggest that the Yucatan immigrants do not.

These differences appear to be associated with differences in how the actors actually treat the forest. Although our studies of forest practices have just begun, it is already clear that native Maya make greater efforts to preserve their forest as a closed-access system (discussed in the next section) and are relatively more successful than immigrant populations in preserving the forests they use. Also, Peten groups are apparently more knowledgeable and successful than the Yucatan groups in sustaining the human-plant-animal interactions that they believe are important to the forest and their life within it. In other words, grades of success (or failure) in commons management may be differentially linked to conditions of culture and environment, with the positive role of lowland Maya culture being strongest in more richly forested Peten.

Other Observations: Moral Commitment as a Semantic Value

Other factors, possibly interrelated with ecological knowledge and social networking, may be responsible for the commons breakdown in Mayaland. For example, native Maya readily conceive of the forest as a closed-access system (see Ciriacy-Wantrup and Bishop, 1975). A closed-access system has aspects of both the private and public domains of classical economists but is not exclusively one or the other. Like public domain, all (and only) members of the community have rights of usufruct. But as in the private domain, the fruits of one's labor cannot be appropriated by another (note that this dual aspect of the commons renders it opaque to the theoretical and legal apparatus of both individual-based and collective-based economies and worldviews). Peten Ladinos, however, refer to the forest as "land for anyone's taking" (*tierra agarrada de nadie*); that is, they define it as open access. They have a nomadic view of the forest, so that what would be considered cheating or free riding in a closed-access system would not be perceived as such in an open-access system.

So far, one might be tempted to argue that our observations demonstrate cultural differences in discounting the future rather than having concern for others. Almost by definition there are differences in discounting, but we have reservations about the explanatory value of this perspective. Managing forest commons is related to both discounting and concern for others. Much of the data we provide seems directly related to discounting, which may be explainable in terms of perceived ownership of the land (Maya case) versus temporarily using it (Ladino case). Yet no Maya feels that the land belongs to him or her alone; rather, it is shared with the community that defines the rights and obligations of each member. Maya do not imagine the future in terms of individual agents, or atoms, disconnected from a meaningful social context. Rather, they see the long-term relationship between forest and community as a contract of mutual assistance, which individuals today may or may not "freely" chose to follow. If they do not, they have no valor *(chich muk)*.

For Ladinos, a jaguar is a striking, powerful, and significant animal. For native Maya, the jaguar made the first sound of the world. When you ask Maya, "How do you know whether the forest will survive?" they answer, "Listen for the sound of the jaguar. When there are no more jaguars, there will be no more forest and there will be no more Maya." Ladinos say nothing of the kind. True, Ladinos admire jaguars or fear them for the livestock. Yet the Ladinos would no more cease to be who they are should the jaguar vanish than people in the U.S. would cease to be who they are should the bald eagle disappear. In other words, no purely extensional value can be assigned to culturally important or "sacred" resources. These resources also appear to have intensional, or semantic, value that utility theories have no principled way of capturing.

We would also like to develop indices of cultural "closeness" to the rain forest. For example, we asked informants how they learned what they know about the rain forest. The Ladinos frequently mentioned parents and other people, whereas the Maya mentioned these but also frequently said they obtained their knowledge by walking alone in the forest. Obviously, some cultural intervention is needed if one is to learn culturally appropriate linguistic labels, so the Maya answer may reveal a sense of closeness more than anything else.

Further evidence comes from people's beliefs concerning how important stories and legends about the rain forest are to understanding the forest. All the Maya, but less than half the Ladinos, said that stories were important. For the Maya especially, forest legends were never "false" but always carried a message about what a person should expect when walking in the forest and how the animals, spirits, and ancestors would expect that person to behave with respect and valor so as to profit from the forest while avoiding misadventure and misfortune. Interestingly, the only repeated stories of the forest told to us by Ladinos were variations on

Hansel and Gretel (which conveys the idea that the forest is scary and that you can get lost in it), and stories of how Maya turn themselves into animals (the Maya themselves believe that there are *waay* among them who can transform themselves into animals in order to carry out witchcraft). A systematic exploration of the stories and justifications associated with species interactions may allow us to operationally tease out a sense of moral commitment as a factor in sustainable commons management.

A final observation was made only for Peten. When asked what the greatest change is among the people of Peten, including Ladinos as well as the younger generation of Spanish-speaking Itzaj, Itzaj elders tend to reply that "people no longer know how to walk in the forest" and that "people no longer know how to talk and visit with one another." Itzaj say that for people who know how to walk in the forest and talk "the true tongue" (*jach t'an,* that is, Maya), the forest is "truly beautiful" *(jach yutzil).* Unlike Ladinos, they express no fear of the forest, which is simply called Mayaland *(u-lu'um-il maayaj).*

Thus, in addition to data that appear to demonstrate differences in discounting the future (with the Maya striving not to compromise the future), justifications of their own and others' behaviors suggest that what defines Maya readiness to preserve their commons is a moral commitment to the living kinds they live with, including concern for other Maya. This commitment may account for the differences in behavior associated with the striking similarities and subtle differences in the kinds of first-order ecological knowledge (see also Rappaport, 1979). In other words, a commitment to context, culture, and identity may be so mutually defining in Maya eyes that one could no more conceive of cheating on the forest or the community, or living within a web of entirely nonreciprocal human-plant-animal interactions, than a mother could imagine starving her children for some marginal utility, such as another bit of meat. This moral commitment could be expressed as a sacred obligation to preserve the cognized structure of the forest. Unlike a theory, which may be more or less responsive to changes in fact and negotiable, a sacred scenario would be fairly immune to changes in fact and nonnegotiable.

To be sure, given the momentous changes occurring, actors that failed to be cognizant of change would be doomed. Yet to abandon sacred obligations could equally condemn a long-standing way of life to oblivion. There may be compromise solutions to this dilemma. Traditionally sacred prescriptions and unavoidable monetary negotiations might be "hybridized," with the sacred rendered less than absolute and the edges taken off raw calculations of utility. Or actors might learn to operate simultaneously in both of these very different worlds, sometimes behaving from one vantage and sometimes from the other. These alternative solutions, although distinguishable in principle, may require a much more nuanced appreciation of the role of cosmology in the structuring of fact and action than current notions of folk theory insinuate.

Our native Maya groups do appear to operate with hybridized or distinct sets of values. Individuals often appear to be consciously aware of what they are doing when distinguishing what the ancestors would undoubtedly do from what they may now be forced to do by novel circumstances. Use of Maya versus Spanish may also play a role, because sacred obligations generally are couched in Maya alone. As the younger generations rely more on Spanish than Mayan, sacred cultural prescriptions may recede into the background. In other words, the relationship between language loss and cultural practice bears further scrutiny.

Discussion

Current Picture

The preliminary nature of our observations precludes any strong conclusions. On a first pass, nominations of important species as well as first-order interactions within plants and within animals reveal comparable results for the Ladino and Maya populations. Furthermore, this common pattern reflects both cultural importance and biological reality. Finally, both populations depart from a normative ecological model in favor of a mental model where the rain forest is seen as being like a house.

A second pass reveals important differences. The Ladinos almost uniformly reject the idea that animals help the forest whereas Maya see the relationships between plants and animals as being more symmetrical. The analogy of the forest to a house can accommodate both positions because the house metaphor is fairly abstract. Other observations suggest that the Ladinos think of the forest as more like a rental property than a permanent home; but it is too early to tell how widespread and entrenched the house analogy is in either population.

The same must be said for the social and knowledge networks. Here we find that the Ladino networks are more diffuse and show less overlap than those of the Maya populations. This certainly sets the stage for significant differences in the transmission of knowledge and social values; however, we have yet to show that this is a difference that makes a difference with respect to agro-forestry practice. These cautions notwithstanding we can begin to see the outlines of group differences in models of biological knowledge and action.

Cultural Models of Knowledge and Action

Consider the forest as a network of persons and nonhuman animal and plant species that help or harm one another. The persons and species are the nodes or agents of the network. The life-support interactions, notably the food-web interactions, are the pathways that link together the nodes (Holland, 1989). Through the pathways flow the nutrients and other resources that humans and nonhuman agents process in the forest network.

Two important and interrelated properties characterize the flows and agents, respectively, of the tropical forest network: recycling and diversity. Although science still knows little about the mechanics of how tropical forests maintain themselves, ecologists generally agree that recycling and diversity are mutually sustaining in complex ways. A diverse array of agents is much better than any single agent at capturing and recycling resources before they are removed from the network (leached, extracted, and so on). Reciprocally, the more resources that are retained, the more they can be exploited in varied ways and provide multifarious niches for diverse agents. Moreover, the combined effect of recycling and diversity is nonlinear: the cycling of resources by an aggregate of diverse kinds of agents yields a much richer product than the sum of individual actions (Holland, 1995).

A rich ecological system, such as a tropical forest, differs from a less rich system in that it supports a higher degree of adaptation through agent (for example, species) substitution. Convergence and mimicry are two examples of adaptation through agent substitution. Substitution occurs when one kind of agent becomes temporarily or permanently absent from the system and another agent moves in to occupy its niche. A niche in a rich system is characterized by the multiple interactions centering on each kind of agent. When the pattern of interactions is disturbed or sundered, the multiplicity of vestigial connections tends to favor the rapid emergence of a substitute—an agent that will quickly "fill the gap" and provide most of the missing interactions. Such biological substitution is almost never a process of mere replacement but involves manifold subtle changes that are crucial to further adaptation, evolution, and diversification of life (Wilson, 1988).

Suppose that these are among the basic facts about life in the tropical forest. To sustain itself in such an environment, an agent would need some sort of internal structure that would enable it to appropriately respond to the relevant facts. At the very least, an agent's internal structure would have to capture regularities in its environment's stimulus-structure.

Furthermore, it would have to capture them in such a way as to anticipate consequences likely to follow from encountering—or failing to encounter—those regularities.

For people, the appropriate internal structure plausibly includes a mental model. In this regard, a mental model is an internal structure that allows the agent (and other people who inspect the agent's model, including researchers) to infer something about the environment. It also motivates the agent's actions. Such a model includes criteria (rules) for input selection, inference, and performance. These criteria may be tacit or overt. If the resulting behavior effectively anticipates future consequences for the environment, then the agent has a sustainable model; otherwise the model is unsustainable (see, for example, Holland, 1995).

In light of the preliminary results of our study of resource management in lowland Mesoamerica, it is tempting to say that native Maya have a more or less sustainable model of the forest and that immigrants have a more or less unsustainable one. Assuming that the results of our tasks capture relevant aspects of these models, and given the statistical consensus in each of our populations on the tasks, we may use our results to recreate Maya and Ladino "cultural models." Thus far, there appear to be four outstanding candidate elements of the Maya model: (1) selecting crucial input (that is, relevant species) jointly on the basis of perceptual (morphology), cultural (function), and ecological (dominance) salience; (2) inferring recycling through the reciprocal interactions between humans, plants, and animals; (3) inferring the substitutability of agents through the image of the forest as the "Maya house"; and (4) performing in accordance with an effective understanding of the forest through milpa practices that emulate and maintain forest biodiversity and the recycling of nutrients.

First, native Maya select the species that are most important to the life of the forest in ways similar to the selection of those species considered most typical, or "true." We have yet to determine whether this also applies to Ladinos. Criteria for what is typical or true seem to be very different for native Maya and urbanized North Americans, although we have still to inquire into North American selection criteria for ecologically important species.

Second, the reciprocal relationships that Maya infer between themselves and nonhuman species evince at least some awareness of resource flow and recycling. For the Itzaj, the most common rule of inference is that those animals that eat or play with the fruit of certain plants but do not digest the seeds help to spread those plants around the forest and to fertilize them. Ancillary inferences are made on the basis of the size and hardness of the fruit and seed relative to the animals that interact with them.

A more common rule of inference among Yucatec Maya is related to the ecological notion of saturation. Saturation occurs when a plant species produces more than enough fruits for an animal species that feeds on it. For example, over time oak trees tend to produce more acorns than local squirrel populations can consume. By scattering and hiding acorns that they will not eat, the squirrels help to spread and generate oaks. For the Yucatec Maya, certain animals help certain plants by hiding away excess fruit and otherwise preparing the ground for growth and the spread of the plants throughout the forest.

Quite possibly neither Itzaj notions of seed fertilization by animals nor Yucatec notions of ground cleaning by animals are completely accurate by scientific standards. But the appreciation that animals and plants help one another by channeling resources necessary to life and growth may represent an effective "truth" about the tropical forest that has other important concomitants in inference and performance. This, of course, is a matter for further study.

A third candidate element in the cultural model of native Maya is the conception of the forest as a house, ruled by people and jaguars. Recall that none of our subject populations seemed to isolate species that are akin to the ecologist's notion of keystone species. Rather, they appeared to view the ecological structure and content of the forest as a house, with (partially) substitutable agents, connectors, and resources. A legitimate question arises as to whether this conception of convergent species is more appropriate to understanding the stability of tropical forests than the concept of keystone species (the latter, perhaps being more apposite to temperate environments). Where native Maya and immigrants differed was in their appreciation of reciprocal interactions and of the moral obligations required to sustain these interactions indefinitely.

A fourth element concerns the realm of performance, although the putative connection between knowledge and action is presently more conjectural than causal or even correlational. Earlier on we alluded to the difference between Ladino and Maya agriculture in terms of recycling. Ladino agriculture tends not to recycle resources. The forest is clear-cut and burned, and little effort is made to retain the surface nutrients that tropical downpours then swiftly leach from the shallow soil. By contrast, Maya agriculture tends to recycle resources. Examples include ringing agricultural plots with trees to prevent nutrients from being washed away; letting weeds have more fallow time to reuse nutrients; emulating the forest's biodiversity structure with multiple crops in storied arrangements (for example, root crops with low-lying vine crops, cereal crops, and fruit trees); protecting and tending some of the forest trees and animals, thus allowing them to also recycle critical nutrients (for example, Itzaj are currently deepening natural water holes in shaded areas so that jaguars and tapirs will not venture out of the Maya reserve in the dry season, where they are more liable to be shot by immigrants).

To be sustainable, these and other critical elements of the model would have to cohere under change. How this might happen is a long-term goal of our research. Should the native Maya possess a sustainable cultural model (or class of models) of the tropical forest—capable of anticipating and adapting to forest cycles—then lowland Maya culture might prove to be a privileged agent in the maintenance of the forest's integrity. If sustainable, such a cultural model would be privileged over the internal structures of nonhuman agents simply because it is a mental model that can infer, anticipate, and accommodate prior to any action taking place. Such a sustainable model would be a potentially dynamic factor in the evolution of forest biodiversity because of the range of interactions it could conceivably represent and help to implement.

Historical and archaeological evidence provides intriguing suggestions to this effect. If so, then the relationship between the survival of cultural diversity and the survival of biological diversity in Mesoamerica may be as close as the Maya themselves suggest: if the Maya and the forest do in fact live by and for one another, then neither might long endure without the other. Maya anticipation that this is indeed the case may be a critical aspect of a sustainable model that others lack. Again, this strong conclusion awaits further systematic investigation.

Projections for Research

Perhaps it is a bit naive to expect simple answers to complex questions. At this point, the reader may despair of possibilities for future progress in this research, for it seems that we are going to be confronted with a host of differences between the native and immigrant groups and that any of the differences, either alone or in combination with other factors, may be critical. How do we proceed?

We believe that there are three strategies that can be profitably be pursued. First of all, we need to move our analyses to a more specific level of detail and to tie them to action. In one extension, in ongoing work we are using the overlapping species lists already elicited as "important for the forest to live." In this task, we place all of the nominated animal cards in front of the informant and then, for each plant, we ask which animals depend on that plant for shelter, food, or shade or in any other way the informant considers vital to the animal. This allows us to identify plant-mediated ecological networks among animals, and animal-mediated ecological networks among plants. We will then compare these ecological networks to the plant and animal taxonomies that we have already elicited and continue to elicit among these populations. This will allow us to get a closer look at the largest difference in ecological knowledge that we noted between the two populations.

We will also target probes at the ecological significance of specific agro-forestry practices. It is possible that the reason that Ladinos are destroying the forest is that they simply do not know enough about how it works. Just as physicians distinguish between physiology and pathophysiology, we intend to extend observations on normal forest ecology to situations of disturbance, where (human) interventions upset normal conditions. Ladinos and Maya may differ in their appreciation of and monitoring for abnormal conditions. In short, our goal is to move to a level of detail where mental models can be potentially linked to agro-forestry practice.

The second research strategy is to look for populations and contexts that may serve to disentangle what otherwise might be confounded factors. Thus, in order to control for the combined effects of social networks and ecological knowledge, we will be testing immigrant Maya groups who have moved into the lowlands from the highlands. We expect that their social networks will look very much like native Maya networks in terms of an interlocking clan-based structure, and very unlike the Ladino networks, which are based on residence, church affiliation, and work. The immigrant Maya, however, should not have the detailed ecological knowledge seen in our indigenous Maya groups. One possibility is that the immigrant Maya will initially engage in destructive agro-forestry practices but quickly assimilate more sustainable practices when appropriate knowledge is introduced into the social and cosmological structure. Language and cosmology are decidedly more robust among Kekchi immigrants than Itzaj. An initial encounter between Itzaj and Kekchi Maya immigrants resulted in an exchange of Itzaj forest knowledge for Kekchi prayers (see Atran, 1993a).

Another possibility is that the closed character of immigrant Maya social networks will continue to impede learning from native groups. Recent satellite imagery gathered by Conservation International tends to confirm our preliminary observations that the slash-and-burn practices in Peten of the Kekchi Maya, who originate from the highlands of Alta Vera Paz, are significantly more destructive than the practices of certain groups of immigrant Ladinos. It also appears that these immigrant Ladinos have more intense and redundant social contacts with native Maya in matters concerning forest knowledge and practice than do Kekchi. Immigrant Ladinos are beginning to understand and employ certain Itzaj agroforestry techniques such as protecting valuable trees, whereas the Kekchi are not. If these trends prove significant and enduring, that will suggest that sustainable management may depend more on (ecologically) context-sensitive versus context-free cultural traditions than on indigenous versus nonindigenous cultural traditions (compare Arizpe, Paz, and Velázquez, 1996). In fact, there is long-standing evidence of cultural borrowing and exchange between "Petenero" Ladinos and native Maya. Some families that primarily identify themselves as Ladino have Itzaj surnames that antedate the Spanish conquest, and even more have orchards and milpas that are virtually indistinguishable from those of the Itzaj (see Schwartz, 1990).

Another set of populations we plan to look at consists of lowland Lakantun Maya and highland Tzeltal Maya immigrants in the Sierra Lacandon of Chiapas. The Lakantun have preserved significantly more of their cosmological system than the other lowland Maya groups. A number of Lakantun still refuse to be Christianized, to sport Western garb, or to abandon the sacred rituals associated with farming and hunting. Accordingly, the role of cosmology should be more important, or at least more salient, in Lakantun community conceptions and practice of agroforestry than in all of our other groups. The influence of the Lakantun on the Tzeltal (and vice versa) may also reveal differences between those Tzeltal who are allied with the Lakantun in attempting to preserve the Lacandon forest as joint commons and those Tzeltal seeking to enter the forest reserves in order to clear them for agriculture and pasture.

The third research strategy involves a combination of systematic observations with laboratory research. In some parts of southern Mexico, the forest commons have closed access and are managed by formally institutionalized *ejido* councils. These common-pool resource councils represent communities of varying social compositions of Ladinos, native Maya, and immigrant Maya. A sampling of these local councils provides variation on dimensions such as group composition and size, and nature of resource. The group decisions with respect to timber sales can thus provide a natural dependent variable, and *ejido* discussions represent a rich source of less formal observations.

In the long term, our plan is to bring these various factors into the laboratory so that they can be systematically manipulated in well-controlled experiments. Most laboratory studies of resource dilemmas have used participants who do not know each other, and the studies do not attend to variables such as degree of moral commitment to some resource. But there is no principle that would bar these sorts of considerations from laboratory studies. Furthermore, these studies can be conducted with higher fidelity than has been common. For example, studies of island biogeography suggest that biodiversity can be calculated on the basis of the fourth power of the land area (Myers, 1988). These observations can be built into resource dilemmas and further validated by field observations (using remote sensing), linking biological inventories to amount and quality of forest cover.

Implications for Global Conservation and Development

Today, remaining commons regimes—even those that have survived centuries and perhaps millennia—are very unlikely to endure far into the next millennium, or even next century. They are largely unacceptable to leading world legal, political, and economic institutions, which concentrate instead on exclusively private or public management. Most conservation and development projects have focused on physical rather than human capital, thus allowing the accumulated human capital to rapidly deteriorate. But with the disappearance of this social capital comes the need to learn from scratch how to match cultural institutions to the physical environment and how to make commitments of mutual trust in joint undertakings related to common survival. Given the exponential rate of deforestation, species loss, and population growth, learning from scratch how to manage commons problems is plausibly not the best strategy.

There is no obvious solution to the problem of upscaling the lessons of the local commons to a worldwide context. Opening access to a multicultural world with myriad values and reference schemes seems to undermine the very foundations of successful commons management, which are based on closed access, shared values, and a common system of reference. Moreover, there is strong empirical evidence that traditional local commons generally have not been able to physically survive the intrusion of the world market for very long. Thus we do not expect that conditions for acquisition and exchange of information relevant to successful commons management in Maya forests can be automatically extended to the diverse ecological zones that span the globe.

Nevertheless, we do envisage findings that will be practically and theoretically instructive. Practically, they may better equip us to avoid the likely failure of many of the more expensive conservation and development schemes that are unwittingly designed to take the place of local commons regimes, albeit on an empirically less firm but more grandiose scale.

For those schemes that do seek grass-roots involvement, our research might show that prescriptions for including local peoples make little sense and may even be counterproductive unless they include an informed assessment of variations in local knowledge and belief. Theoretically, we may be able to discover to what extent mismatches in mental models are hazardous to cross-group cooperation, and what properties of social networks are most likely to predict the success of commons solutions.

More generally, suppose for the sake of argument that humans are not solely, or even by evolutionary design, self-interest maximizers in the narrow senses of utility theories. Consider, instead, that under certain empirically identifiable conditions humans are cognitively disposed to share resources, risks, reference systems such as language, and plans for the future. Imagine, that is, that maximization of self-interest asserts itself not so much by nature as by default, when ordinary ties with the environment and community are severed. Even then, people may sense the moral failure of a rationally unassailable Faustian bargain.

Consider this analogy. Context-free, extensional theories of rational choice and marginal utility may be related to context-sensitive, intensional theories of value and decision making much as formal logic is related to the natural logic of everyday language. Like formal logics, extensional theories of choice involve a rather coherent, limited set of explicit assumptions and axioms. Any formal logic initially derives its limited syntax of conjunctions and rules of inferences from the richer but more complex "natural logic" of everyday language and then manipulates these derivative forms to enhance clarity and inferential power in rhetoric or the sciences. Similarly, extensional theories of choice may derive assumptions and axioms from richer, more complex forms of "natural reasoning," where loss and gain are not equal, the future is not discounted, and so on, in order to enhance the precision and predictive power of decision making in government or markets. Nothing else around rivals formal logic for clear communication or utility theory for precise prediction. Nevertheless, clarity and precision may not be the only, or even the primary, conditions for successful communication or resource-use decisions in everyday life. Other considerations of relevance may be important and even paramount (see Sperber and Wilson, 1986).

If so, then the lessons of local commons for global problems may be something like the lessons of representational grammars for learning unfamiliar natural languages or relearning impaired ones. The grammars of schools are not themselves natural grammars, they are—ideally—lawfully related to natural grammars and derivative from them, but they are much harder to use and master than natural grammars. Education and insight are required—education about what should come naturally to us, if only the normal triggering conditions of physical sensitivity to stimuli and social intercourse were readily available.

Conclusion

What is the overall perspective of this project? We are trying to understand the cognitive and cultural processes that drive people to preserve or destroy their common resources. We hope this focus on process will yield insights that can be applied to global commons, although we are well aware of inherent problems in upscaling the lessons of successful local commons to a wider planetary context. One of the lessons our data seem to show is that whatever the final mix of factors responsible for successful commons management among Maya in the rain forest, it does not consist exclusively or primarily in calculations of marginal utility, unless one could assign a uniform measure of utility that conveys substitutability across one's children, community, and the species one lives with.

To put it another way, on the surface it may seem to make sense to talk about how people value things in terms of extensional measures like utilities. But that does not seem to hold much promise for getting at the meaning of the forest to the Maya or even to ourselves. If utility represents a syntax for comparisons, then a severe limitation is that it does not get at the intensional semantics of human interaction with the natural world.

REFERENCES

Arizpe, L., Paz, F., and Velázquez, M. *Culture and Global Change: Social Perceptions of Deforestation in the Lacandona Rainforest in Mexico.* Ann Arbor: University of Michigan Press, 1996.

Atran, S. "Hamula [Patriclan] Organisation and Masha'a [Commons] Tenure in Palestine." *Man,* 1986, *21,* 271–295.

Atran, S. *Cognitive Foundations of Natural History: Towards an Anthropology of Science.* Cambridge, England: Cambridge University Press, 1990.

Atran, S. "The Bio-Itza." *Anthropology Newsletter,* Oct. 1993a.

Atran, S. "Itza Maya Tropical Agro-Forestry." *Current Anthropology,* 1993b, *34,* 633–700.

Barsalou, L. "Ideals, Central Tendency, and Frequency of Instantiation as Determinants of Graded Structure in Categories." *Journal of Experimental Psychology: Learning, Memory, and Cognition,* 1985, *11,* 629–654.

Berkes, F. (ed.). "Common Property Resources." London: Belhaven Press, 1989.

Bromley, D. (ed.). *Making the Commons Work.* San Francisco: ICS Press, 1992.

Bruhnes, J. *Human Geography.* Skokie, Ill.: Rand McNally, 1978.

Ciriacy-Wantrup, S., and Bishop, R. "'Common Property' as a Concept in Natural Resource Property." *Natural Resources Journal,* 1975, *15,* 713–727.

Costanza, R. (ed.). "Ecological Economics: The Science of Management and Sustainability." New York: Columbia University Press, 1991.

Darby, H. *The Draining of the Fens.* Cambridge, England: Cambridge University Press, 1940.

Eckstein, S. *El ejido colectivo en Mexico* [The collective *ejido* in Mexico]. Mexico City: Fondo de Cultura Económica, 1966.

Ford, R. "Communication Networks and Information Hierarchies in Native American Folk Medicine: Tewa Pueblos, New Mexico." In W. Hand (ed.), *American Folk Medicine.* Berkeley: University of California Press, 1976.

Forsyth, A., and Miyata, K. "Tropical Nature: Life and Death in the Rain Forests of Central and South America." New York: Touchstone, 1995.

Gentner, D., and Stevens, D. *Mental Models.* Hillsdale, N.J.: Erlbaum, 1983.

Gomez-Pompa, A., Vazquez-Yanes, C., and Guevara, S. "The Tropical Rainforest: A Nonrenewable Resource." *Science,* 1972, *177,* 762–765.

Granovetter, M. "The Strength of Weak Ties." *American Journal of Sociology,* 1973, *78,* 1360–1380.

Hammer, M. "'Core' and 'Extended' Social Networks in Relation to Health and Illness." *Social Science Medicine,* 1983, *17,* 405–411.

Hardin, G. "The Tragedy of the Commons." *Science,* 1968, *162,* 1243–1248.

Hecht, S., and Cockburn, A. *The Fate of the Amazon.* New York: HarperCollins, 1990.

Holland, J. *Adaptation in Natural and Artificial Systems.* Cambridge, Mass.: MIT Press, 1989.

Holland, J. *Hidden Order: How Adaptation Builds Complexity.* Reading, Mass.: Addison-Wesley, 1995.

Kempton, W., Boster, J., and Hartley, J. *Environmental Values in American Culture.* Cambridge, Mass.: MIT Press, 1995.

Liebrand, W., Messick D., and Wilke, H. (eds.). *Social Dilemmas: Theoretical Issues and Research Findings.* Oxford, England: Pergamon Press, 1992.

Lopez, A., and others. "The Tree of Life: Universal and Cultural Features of Folkbiological Taxonomies and Inductions." *Cognitive Psychology,* forthcoming.

Martin, F. *Common-Pool Resources and Collective Action: A Bibliography.* Bloomington: University of Indiana (Workshop in Political Theory), 1992.

Martinez-Alier, J. *Ecological Economics.* Oxford, England: Blackwell, 1987.

McCay, B., and Acheson, J. *The Question of the Commons.* Tucson: University of Arizona Press, 1987.

Medin, D. "Concepts and Conceptual Structure." *American Psychologist,* 1989, *44,* 1469–1481.

Myers, N. "Tropical Forests and Their Species." In E. O. Wilson (ed.), *Biodiversity.* Washington D.C.: National Academy Press, 1988.

Nations, J., and Nigh, R. "Evolutionary Potential of Lacandon Maya Sustained-Yield Tropical Forest Agriculture." *Journal of Anthropological Research,* 1980, *36,* 1–30.

North, D., and Thomas, R. "The First Economic Revolution." *Economic History Review,* 1977, *30,* 229–241.

Osherson, D., and others. "Category-Based Induction." *Psychological Review,* 1990, *97,* 185–200.

Ostrom, E. *Governing the Commons.* Cambridge, England: Cambridge University Press, 1990.

Ostrom, E., Gardner, R., and Walker, J. (eds.). *Rules, Games, and Common-Pool Resources.* Ann Arbor: University of Michigan Press, 1994.

Rappaport, R. *Ecology, Meaning, and Religion.* Berkeley, Calif.: North Atlantic Books, 1979.

Rips, L. "Inductive Judgments About Natural Categories." *Journal of Verbal Learning and Verbal Behavior,* 1975, *14,* 665–681.

Romney, A. K., Weller, S., and Batchelder, W. "Culture as Consensus: A Theory of Culture and Informant Accuracy." *American Anthropologist,* 1986, *88,* 313–338.

Rowley, T. (ed.). *The Origins of Open-Field Agriculture.* London: Croom Helm, 1981.

Schwartz, N. *Forest Society: A Social History of Peten, Guatemala.* Philadelphia: University of Pennsylvania Press, 1990.

Scott, J. "Trend Report: Social Network Analysis." *Sociology,* 1988, 22, 109–127.

Sperber, D., and Wilson, D. *Relevance*. New York: Blackwell, 1986.

Stahl, H. *Les anciennes communautés villageoises roumaines*. Paris: Centre National de la Recherche Scientifique (CNRS), 1969.

Vandermeer, J., and Perfecto, Y. *Breakfast of Biodiversity: The Truth About Rainforest Destruction.* Oakland, Calif.: Institute for Food and Development Policy, 1995.

Wellman, B. "The Community Question: The Intimate Networks of East Yorkers." *American Journal of Sociology,* 1979, *84,* 1201–1231.

White, S. "Testing an Economic Approach to Resource Dilemmas." *Organizational Behavior and Human Decision Processes,* 1994, *58,* 428–456.

Wilson, E. O. (ed.) *Biodiversity.* Washington, D.C.: National Academy Press, 1988.

Wilson, E. O. *The Diversity of Life.* New York: Norton, 1992.

Yelling, J. *Common Field and Enclosure in England 1450–1850.* London: Macmillan, 1977.

10

MENTAL MODELS OF POPULATION GROWTH

A Preliminary Investigation

Dedre Gentner and Eric W. Whitley

WITH THE INCREASING dominion of the human species over the planet's ecology, the study of human cognition has taken on new significance. The growth of human population and activities now affects the general ecology to a significant extent (Erlich, 1988; McMichael, 1993; Nisbet, 1991). For this reason, the ways in which people reason and make decisions have become matters of global import. As a striking indicator of where we rank on the scale of global cataclysms, consider the rate of species extinction. According to Kempton, Boster, and Hartley (1994, p. 27), "With human-caused intervention, current rates of extinction are estimated to be somewhere between four thousand and twenty-seven thousand per year" (against an estimated background rate of less than one per year) (also see Wilson, 1992; World Resources Institute, 1992, p. 128; Peters and Lovejoy, 1990). They note that this rate of extinction is typically associated with transitions from one geological age to another. By this criterion, the current explosion of human population and human activities assumes a magnitude formerly reserved for major geological events.

In order to understand and affect these processes, we must first establish the current forms. This chapter presents some initial studies of mental

This research was supported by NSF grant BNS-87-20301 and ONR grant N00014-92-J-1098.

models of human population growth and its effects on the environment. We chose population growth as our topic because of its importance in the question of whether human activities can be brought into balance with our planet's ecology.

A mental model is a representation of the world that allows people to understand, predict, and solve problems in the domain (Gentner and Stevens, 1983; Johnson-Laird, 1983; Kempton, Boster, and Hartley, 1994). Such models are typically based on systems of long-standing beliefs. For example, in Patrick Hayes's classic paper (1985) on the naive physics of liquids, roughly eighty axioms are used to characterize the representations involved in understanding liquids: the possible states a liquid can take and the possible transitions between states. These axioms capture the knowledge that predicts when a liquid will flow, stand still, or spread into a thin sheet on a surface. But mental models are not always correct. Kempton, Boster, and Hartley (1994) discuss the example of global warming. They found that individuals often perceived global warming as the result of pollution of the atmosphere by industrial substances, particularly chlorofluorocarbons (CFCs) from aerosol cans. They appeared to have merged the greenhouse effect with the ozone depletion effect. In the greenhouse effect, less heat *escapes* from the earth (because visible light striking the earth and radiating back as heat (infrared light) is absorbed on its way out by greenhouse gases in the atmosphere), thus warming the atmosphere. In the ozone depletion effect, more ultraviolet light *enters* the atmosphere because of depleted ozone in the atmosphere. Furthermore, people conceived of gases as particles that could be filtered; this view, combined with the idea that artificially created substances are the sole source of the problem, further contributes to an incorrect model of global warming. With this model, people assume that minimizing the release of chemical pollutants—for example, by banning aerosol cans and incorporating filters at production sites—would best mitigate the global warming problem. They neglect the factors of energy efficiency, fuel consumption, and land clearing that have large effects on levels of carbon dioxide and other greenhouse gases.

Why should environmentalists care about mental models? One reason is to understand and anticipate people's behavior. It must be conceded there are often substantial inconsistencies between people's stated beliefs and their behavior, or between their decisions given different framings of what appears to be the same information (for example, Bazerman, 1994; Kahneman, Slovic, and Tversky, 1982). Yet there is also considerable evidence that people's beliefs about a domain influence their decisions. Another reason to study mental models, apart from their uses in predicting behavior, is the issue of communication. As Morgan and others (1992, p. 2050) point out, "Communicators need to know the nature and extent of a recipient's knowledge and beliefs if they are to design messages that will not be dismissed, misinterpreted, or allowed to coexist with misconceptions."

The long-term goals of this research are (1) to identify the mental models and belief systems that people are using within a set of ecologically relevant domains and to characterize the conditions for access and use of these models, (2) to trace cultural changes in the models across time, and (3) to investigate methods of creating conceptual change so that models consonant with long-term welfare will inform people's day-to-day behavior. In this chapter, we first briefly review research on the properties of mental models. Then we present the results of a preliminary investigation of current mental models of population growth conducted using electronic forums. Finally, we consider some possible ways to change mental models.

Mental Models

Mental models are related to several other kinds of representational structures. Although all the following categories shade into one another, and although their uses are variable across researchers, there is a rough division as follows. *Schemas* (or *schemata*) are general belief structures. *Scripts* are schemas summarizing event sequences; they are characterized by a chiefly linear temporal order. *Naive theories* or *folk theories* are global systems of belief encompassing whole domains such as biology. *Mental models* tend to be smaller in scope than are theories. They are typically restricted to arenas of knowledge for which the person possesses a densely interconnected system of relations, usually causal but sometimes also (or instead) spatial or mathematical. Another aspect of mental models is that, by tradition, mental models research is more likely to include an explicit representation of the knowledge than is research on schemas or theories.

Mental models have informed research on the representation and use of causal and scientific knowledge (Forbus and Gentner, 1986; Glenberg, Meyer, and Lindem, 1987; McCloskey, 1983; Stevens and Collins, 1980) in areas including naive physics (Collins and Gentner, 1987; Hayes, 1985; Williams, Hollan, and Stevens, 1983), the development of astronomical knowledge (Vosniadou and Brewer, 1992), spatial representation (Forbus, 1983, 1990; Glenberg and McDaniel, 1992; McNamara, 1986; Tversky, 1991) and navigation (Hutchins, 1983), analogical problem solving (Bassok, 1990; Clement, 1983, 1994; Gentner and Gentner, 1983;

Halford, 1989, 1993; Holyoak and Koh, 1987; Novick and Holyoak, 1991; Keane, 1985, 1988), the comprehension of physical mechanisms (de Kleer and Brown, 1983, 1984; Forbus, 1984; Hegarty, 1992; Hegarty and Just, 1993; Kempton, 1986; Kieras and Bovair, 1984; Miyake, 1986; Proffitt, Gilden, Kaiser, and Whelan, 1988; Schumacher and Gentner, 1988a, 1988b; Schwartz and Black, 1996), and the interaction of people with computers and other devices (Adelson, 1981; Burstein, 1986, 1988; Chee, 1993; Norman, 1983, 1988).

Mental models can facilitate problem solving and reasoning in a domain. Gentner and Gentner (1983) gave novice subjects questionnaires about electricity and categorized them according to whether their models of electric circuits were based on analogies to water flow or to moving crowds (two analogies commonly used to understand electricity). When the subjects were given new electric circuit problems involving combinations of parallel or serial resistors and batteries, their patterns of performance could be predicted from their reported model.

Mental models are used in comprehension of text, as noted by Johnson-Laird (1983) and his colleagues. This approach to mental models differs from other research cited in this chapter in that it postulates minimal working memory sketches: temporary data structures set up for the purposes of immediate comprehension and reasoning tasks (for example, Mani and Johnson-Laird, 1982). This work includes research on propositional inference (Byrne, 1989; Johnson-Laird, Byrne, and Schaeken, 1992), spatial inference (Byrne and Johnson-Laird, 1989), and quantificational inference (Johnson-Laird and Bara, 1984; Johnson-Laird, Byrne, and Tabossi, 1989). (See Johnson-Laird and Byrne, 1991, for a review of this research. See also Rips, 1986, and Norman, 1983, for general discussions and critiques.) The focus on immediate comprehension and working-memory tasks in this approach has led to a relative lack of emphasis on long-term knowledge and causal relations. However, there is considerable potential overlap, as shown by recent evidence suggesting that long-term causal mental models can influence the working-memory representations that people use, even in speeded tasks (Hegarty, 1992; Hegarty and Just, 1993; Schwartz and Black, 1996).

Mental models can facilitate learning, particularly when the structure of the new learning is consistent with the model. For example, Kieras and Bovair (1984) showed that subjects could operate a simulated device more accurately and could diagnose malfunctions better when they had a causal mental model of its functioning rather than a merely procedural grasp of how to operate it. Similarly, Gentner and Schumacher (1986; Schumacher and Gentner, 1988a, 1988b) showed that subjects were better able to transfer an operating procedure from one device to another when they had a causal model of the operation of the first device rather than just a set of procedures. In this instance, as in the case of the electricity analogs discussed above, the degree of facilitation depended greatly on the match between the original model and the new material. These and many convergent results show that prior models must be taken into account in predicting and designing learning interventions.

There is evidence that mental models can influence real-life environmental decision making. Kempton, Boster, and Hartley (1994) note that mental models "give an underlying structure to environmental beliefs and a critical underpinning to environmental values." For example, Kempton (1986) proposed on the basis of interviews that people use two distinct models for home heating systems and that these are reflected in different methods of regulating their thermostats. In the *threshold model,* the thermostat is viewed as setting the goal temperature but not controlling the rate at which the furnace operates. In the (incorrect) *valve model,* the thermostat is viewed as a valve that regulates the rate at which the furnace generates heat. Having derived these two models from interviews, Kempton examined the thermostat records collected by Socolow (1978) from real households. The patterns of thermostat settings provided indirect evidence that people were using these two kinds of models to operate their home furnaces. In particular, some families set their thermostat only twice a day—low at night, higher by day, consistent with the threshold model—whereas others constantly adjusted their thermostats between very high and very low temperatures. This is an expensive strategy but one consistent with the valve model as articulated by Kempton's interviewees, who compared the furnace to a gas pedal or a faucet (both valve devices) and suggested, for example, that you need to "turn 'er up high" if you want the house to get warm fast.

Identifying Mental Models of the Effects of Human Population Growth Using Electronic Forums

Methods of studying mental models vary in their directness. The initial elicitation of mental models is normally done by the direct method of interviews or questionnaires that explicitly ask people about their beliefs (for example, Collins and Gentner, 1987; Kempton, 1986) or by analyzing think-aloud protocols collected during reasoning (Ericksson and Simon, 1984; Klahr and Dunbar, 1988). Once the mental models are at least roughly known or guessed, indirect methods can be used: materials can be designed such that people's mental models can be inferred from observations of behavior during reasoning and problem solving. For example, researchers note patterns of correct and incorrect responses, response times, eye movements, or particular errors made (for example, Chi, Feltovich, and Glaser, 1981; Gentner and Gentner, 1983; Hegarty, 1992; Hegarty and Just, 1993; Schwartz and Black, 1996) or patterns of retention for new materials in the domain (Bostrom, Atman, Fischhoff, and Morgan, 1994; Morgan and others, 1992).

The typical course of research is to begin with fairly direct elicitation of the models and then move to indirect validation of the proposed mental models. However, there are sometimes complications in directly asking about mental models. First, people may have quite different models for phenomena within what experts would call the same domain. Collins and Gentner (1987) and Gentner (1980) found that many novice subjects had *pastiche* models of evaporation: they used locally coherent but globally inconsistent accounts. For example, a novice subject would give one kind of explanation for a towel drying in the sun and another for a puddle of water evaporating, failing to see any connection between these two phenomena. The existence of multiple models can make it difficult to decide how to partition the observations. A further difficulty with direct elicitation, as Morgan and others (1992) point out, is that questionnaires are vulnerable to flaws such as *illusory expertise* (restricting the expression of nonexpert beliefs) and *illusory discrimination* (suppressing the expression of inconsistencies in beliefs). Such effects can also occur using interview methods. Thus the knowledge revealed in an interview may be biased toward what the subject considers justifiable, respectable knowledge. Asked why paint dries more quickly on a wall than in a bucket, for example, a subject may invoke college science material about atomic binding. A final difficulty that may be particular to ecologically relevant domains is that there may be an *overcorrectness* or *illusory correctness* effect, in which people try to conform to what they believe to be the politically correct stance.

In an effort to mitigate these difficulties, in this research we explored a relatively novel method for eliciting mental models: we traced an exchange on our chosen topic of human population growth on several electronic forums. The method has several advantages: (1) respondents are self-selected to be interested in the material, increasing the likelihood that their responses reflect genuine beliefs; (2) the goal is to set forth their position so as to persuade someone roughly like themselves, rather than to impress an experimenter; (3) strings of replies and counterreplies sometimes occur, allowing, in effect, further probing without the need of further experimenter intervention.

This method has drawbacks as well: it lacks the systematic nature of standard sampling procedures; the respondents are not known to us, so their scientific and political background cannot be assessed; and there is no opportunity for further questioning. However, we suggest that this method can elicit the kinds of natural interactions indicative of mental models that occur outside the laboratory. Thus it may be a useful supplement to the current methods used.

To investigate models of human population growth, we sought to reach a variety of electronic forums, ranging in their likely opinions on human population control. As it happens, most of our respondents were concerned about human population and favored some kind of control. We turn now to the experiment and results.

Method

Our method was to note all replies to an initial pair of Internet messages—a query and a reply—that went out to several electronic forums. In electronic forums, once a comment is posted, any number of users can post replies. Thus we could survey a range of responses to the same initial posting. In order to stimulate interest, we decided to use a debate as the seed. The idea was to capitalize on the *flame* effect, in which people respond more frequently and forcefully in the context of an ongoing debate than they do to an individual statement. Another advantage of using a debate as seed is that it provides the respondents with both sides of the issue to react to, thus (we hoped) providing a broad arena of discourse.

The initial comments were (1) a query about overpopulation that hinted that it is not an important issue and (2) a reply that argued that population gain is indeed a problem and used a petri dish analogy. These messages went to seventeen usergroups: nine ecology-related groups, three religious groups, two science-education groups, and three others not easily categorizable.

The initial messages were as follows:

INITIAL MESSAGE (POPULATION QUERY)

From: User 1

Subject: Is there a problem with population size?

Message: I don't understand why people are so concerned with the size of the population. Don't we have the technology to make more food? Or at least use it better? These people and their "overpopulation" thing seem a little paranoid to me.

RESPONSE (PETRI DISH ANALOGY)
From: User 2
Subject: re: Is there a problem with population size?
Message: Okay . . . first of all . . . anyone who tells you that there ISN'T a problem with overpopulation should start paying attention to the world we ALL live in. There IS a problem with overpopulation and the sooner people wake up and realize it, the better. The idea that the problem is just about food is the wrong outlook. Think of the analogy of humans as organisms in a petri dish with enough food for all of us. If the bacteria keep multiplying they will use up all of their food. The dish (the earth) will become a barren waste. Then the bacteria (us) will die . . . no matter how far technology stretches the food supply.

Personally, I'd love to believe that science will solve humanity's problems. I just don't see how it's possible, though. All you're looking at is the short term and avoiding the inevitable.

After this pair of messages was posted to the usergroups, we collected all replies for a period of ten days, by the end of which the response rate had diminished to nearly nothing.

Results

There were a total of fifty responses from the seventeen electronic forums described above. Most of the responses maintained that population increase is a problem. Fewer than one in five of the respondents took the "not a problem" position. It is important to note that these figures should not be considered representative. Our collection of usergroups was biased toward people interested in ecology. A more fundamental problem in making inferences from frequency stems from the nature of Internet interactions. In contrast with what happens in an experiment, in an electronic forum an individual can base her decision about whether to reply partly on whether an adequate statement of her position has already been given by another user. Therefore, counts of the frequency of various responses are of dubious value.

With this in mind, we have categorized the responses but have made no systematic attempt to record response frequencies. Responses are given as bulleted points; they are averaged or in some cases altered syntactically in order to protect the privacy of the respondents. Occasional portions (enclosed in quotation marks) are directly quoted from one or more respondents. We first give responses arguing that human population is not a problem, then those arguing that it is a problem. Within this large division, we have subdivided the models into a provisional set of categories.

Responses Stating That Population Growth Is Not a Problem

REJECTION OF THE PETRI DISH ANALOGY. Some respondents disagreed with the petri dish analogy, either on the grounds that humans are different from bacteria because they can work to make more food or on the grounds that the food scarcity problem among humans is not one of amount but of distribution.

- The human population is not "mere consumers and multipliers"; humans are born not only "with mouths and stomachs but . . . with mouths, stomachs, and a pair of hands."
- It is not the amount of food but the distribution of the food that is important.

HUMAN POTENCY. Some felt that human persistence will always counter any potentially destructive situation.

- Humans will always be able to "overcome any problem . . . when people direct their energies in these directions."

HUMAN CULPABILITY. The reason people are hungry is that the food sent to help does not reach the hungry.

- Food "gets stolen, hoarded, or blocked so that it doesn't get to the intended targets. Again, *sin is the problem; NOT overpopulation.*"
- Governments interfere with Third World countries and disturb their cultures.

CHICKEN LITTLE

- "Chicken Little's crying about the sky falling doesn't do any good."

JUST LOCAL TROUBLES

- Famines, desertification, and other ecological problems are seen as "short-lived" and "localized."

POPULATION PROBLEMS RECONSTRUED

- Families should have more children to counteract the bad effects of immigrants on U.S. population.
- "Population control is a big push for the pro-choice movement."

APPEAL TO RELIGION. One form of resistance to the population control idea came from people who invoked religion.

- "Problems can only be solved by God."
- "Be fruitful and multiply, and fill the earth and subdue it and have domination over the fish of the sea, and over the birds of the air, and over the cattle, and over all the wild animals of the earth, and over every creeping thing that creeps upon the earth."
- "I feel sorry for these people . . . Mother Earth?" Don't they know God? Do they not think anyone is capable of wanting a large family?

Responses Stating That Population Growth Is a Problem

One group of responses used analogies—the petri dish and Easter Island—in arguing that population growth is a problem. Others used a variety of quantitative models in their discussions.

EXTENSIONS OF THE PETRI DISH ANALOGY. A few respondents addressed the petri dish analogy directly. The most elaborate response accepted the analogy and elaborated it into four stages: lag phase, logarithmic growth (log) phase, stationary phase, and death phase.

- In the lag phase, bacteria "acclimate to their new surroundings." This is followed by the log phase of "uncontrolled exponential growth" and then by the stationary phase due to "limiting factors" such as the lack of food. Lastly, the death phase takes place, in which the bacterial culture "becomes choked on its own toxins and lack of nutrients" and typically enters an exponential negative growth curve.
- Human population is currently in the log phase of exponential growth (see Figure 10.1). How soon we will enter the stationary phase is not clear because the carrying capacity of the earth is not known.

EASTER ISLAND ANALOGY. Some respondents offered the historical analogy of Easter Island, which is consistent with the petri dish analogy. As described by Diamond (1995) in *Discover* magazine, the history of Easter Island is one of an initial wealth of natural resources followed by rapid population growth, destruction of resources, and subsequent degradation of the ecosystem, cultural losses, and rapid decrease in population size.

Figure 10.1. Exponential Growth of the Human Population.

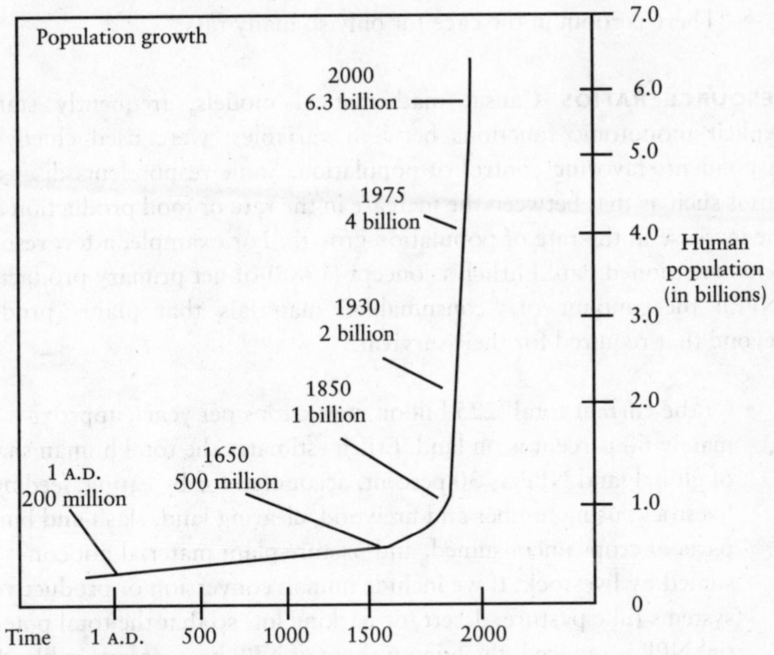

Population growth

2000
6.3 billion

1975
4 billion

1930
2 billion

1850
1 billion

1650
500 million

1 A.D.
200 million

Time 1 A.D. 500 1000 1500 2000

7.0 6.0 5.0 4.0 3.0 2.0 1.0 0

Human population (in billions)

Source: The Population Institute.

- "Put a few thousand people on a small island and see how long they last. . . . [This happened] on Easter Island, and the ecosystem was degraded so badly . . . that it could only support a handful of people."
- Population reaches its limit "when the use of resources in an ecosystem exceeds its carrying capacity and there is no way to recover or replace what was lost."

LIMITS. The concept of limits on the earth's resources—on land, water, biomaterial, and so on—was a central and commonly mentioned idea in these responses.

- "We do not live in an open system."
- "The earth has limited space and resources."
- "We live on a finite planet."
- "I suppose people can adjust to being crowded, but they can't

reduce their food requirements indefinitely, so there must be a limit somewhere."

- "There is room in the cage for only so many rats."

RESOURCE RATIOS. Causal mathematical models, frequently stating explicit monotonic functions between variables, were used chiefly by respondents favoring control of population. Some respondents discussed ratios such as that between the increase in the rate of food production and the increase in the rate of population growth. For example, a few respondents mentioned Paul Ehrlich's concept (1988) of net primary production (NPP): the amount of "consumable" materials that plants produce beyond that required for their survival.

- Of the current total (225 billion metric tons per year), approximately 60 percent is on land. Erlich estimates the total human share of global land NPP as 30 percent, accounted for by eating, feeding livestock, using lumber and firewood, clearing land, slash and burn, parts of crops unconsumed, and pasture plant material not consumed by livestock. If we include human conversion of productive systems (like pasture, desert, or parking lot) so that the total potential NPP is reduced, the human share of NPP becomes more like 40 percent of global land NPP.

Other respondents raised related issues:

- "Can technology increase rates of food production equal to the rate of population growth?"
- "The denser the population, the greater the damage to the environment."
- "Environmental degradation is a function of consumption, technology, and population."
- Currently, 1.8 acres per person are used for agriculture production in the United States. This will drop in the next few decades to only 1.2 acres per person, at present levels of population growth. The amount of land available for this use will then decrease to 0.6 acres per person.

COST AND AVAILABILITY OF OTHER RESOURCES. Certain aspects of population were referred to in terms of *price* or *cost* in relation to the availability of resources.

- "Any positive benefits produced by technical advances will be negated by the tremendous growth in the world's population."
- "It takes *land* to grow the lumber to build your house, . . . to dispose of your human waste products, . . . to produce the material and gas for your car."
- "Increasing food production comes with a price tag. More and more land must be committed to this endeavor."

LAGS. Some respondents commented on various kinds of fatal lags, in which a problem is always one step ahead of the solution.

- Human population growth is exponential. The time it takes to cope with current world population problems—inappropriate population density, chlorine air pollution, overfishing, aquifer and other groundwater contamination—will always be outpaced by additional strain.
- "Technology to grow . . . more food may become available, but the world's population will undoubtedly increase faster."
- "There's always a time lag between the need for new technology and its production."
- "Unfortunately, overpopulation is one of those things that by the time you can clearly see that it is a problem, it is too late."

STANDARD OF LIVING EQUILIBRATION. Some respondents factored in the idea that the current disparity between levels of consumption around the planet is unstable. They projected the effects of equalizing consumption in two ways:

1. *Downscaling calamity.* The United States decreases its consumption (and hence its standard of living) to the level of Third World countries.
   - At the U.S. level of consumption, it takes at least twenty acres to care for one person. But world population density is about ninety-seven people per acre. This leads to the conclusion that we could support all the earth's people *if* everyone had the same low standard of living that many people in Third World countries do.
   - "Since food resources are fixed and land area is fixed, increasing population will require reduction in food and land area per person."

2. *Upscaling calamity.* The entire world population increases its consumption to the level of the U.S. and western Europe.
   - The United States, with 5 percent of the world's population, exploits 20 percent of global resources.
   - I don't think it has been really shown that we could support the current world population (6 billion?) at a U.S. standard of living sustainably.

APOCALYPTIC ARGUMENTS. Some respondents argued for extreme and far-ranging negative effects from over-population.

- "Increased incidence of disease, starvation, and internecine conflict" will result.
- If our population were one-fourth what it is now, there would be no significant pollution, a great deal less crime and mental illness, and a great deal less "poverty."
- The effects of overpopulation are felt even in U.S. cities: for example, people commit more violent crimes, such as drive-by shootings.
- Disease, famine, and even wars are nature's way of controlling populations.

QUALITY OF LIFE. Some respondents' concerns went beyond simply sustaining human population and dealt with the issue of how we live.

- Whether or not food production can meet demand is simply outweighed by the loss of the natural heritage of the planet.
- "Crowded or not crowded? Which do you prefer?"
- "Where do you go to be alone?"

CONSIDERATION OF OTHER SPECIES. We had expected to find many mentions of species endangered due to human population pressure (such as the Sumatran tiger or the black rhino). However, only a few respondents mentioned the welfare of other animals.

CONTRIBUTORS TO NONCONCERN. Of those who agreed that human population is a problem, some devoted their responses to trying to figure out why this fact is not obvious to everyone. The following factors were proposed:

- American optimism. "Part of the 'American Spirit' is the idea that we can overcome any problem."

- Short attention span. The problem is people saying, "I worried about overpopulation already—I'm tired of that."
- Consumerism and corporate agendas. "Consume like there's no tomorrow." "Save the economy—buy . . ."
- Organized religion. "The pope and the fundamentalist religions aren't helping . . . they can't change fast, and the Bible says, 'Be fruitful and multiply.' " "It's easier to be reborn than to stop using two gas-guzzlers."

Discussion

Our study turned up more responses favoring population control than dismissing it. Further, in our admittedly biased view, the responses favoring population control were more cogent than those on the other side. Responses arguing that population increase is not a problem constitute important data because they might yield insight into sources of societal resistance to population control policies. The fact that our study turned up very few of these is probably due to problems in our sampling method. First, we had a disproportionate number of ecologically active usergroups in our sample. A wider range of opinion would have improved the study. A second issue is that the response rate appeared lower in the groups judged likely to oppose population control. It may be that the wording of our exchange was not inviting to those opposing population control, or that in the usergroups we reached, members opposing population control were less willing to enter this particular debate.

Change of Knowledge

Assuming that there is a problem with population growth, the question becomes whether and how it is possible to change mental models and belief systems. We will use the term *change of knowledge* to include shifts in how often a person uses one model compared to another. As discussed earlier, people often possess multiple mental models within the same domain, with various scopes and privileges. Rather than restricting ourselves to cases of classical conceptual change in which an old model or theory gives way entirely to a new, incommensurable model (for example Carey, 1985), we believe the notion of change of knowledge should be applied to cases in which the frequencies and contexts of use of various models change markedly. For example, consider a learner who initially relies chiefly on the model of *air as heaven's protectorate* (and hence not humanity's business) but who also knows the *air as a commons resource* model. If, after attending an ecology class, she shifts from using the scarce resource model in 5 percent of the possible contexts to using it in 30 percent of the possible contexts, we will consider this an instance of change of knowledge.

The sources of resistance to change of knowledge go beyond cognition, of course. As Peters and Slovic (1995) note, resistance to change can arise from interactions with affective variables, values, and issues of worldview, that is, generalized attitudes toward the world and society. An individual who feels that religion, morality, or even humanism stands against any efforts to curtail human reproduction will not be easy to persuade. But even at the level of simple mundane cognition there is resistance to change.

There is abundant evidence from educational research that change of knowledge is hard to achieve, even when nonaffective domains like heat and temperature are concerned (Brown, Bransford, Ferrara, and Campione, 1983; Chi, 1992). One reason is cognitive commitment to existing knowledge (Lesgold, 1984; Mayer, 1992). Another reason that change of knowledge is difficult is the *transfer problem.* Research on similarity-based transfer has shown that retrieval from long-term memory is typically highly conservative, in the sense that retrieval is responsive to overall overlap and is influenced strongly by concrete surface commonalities (Gentner, Rattermann, and Forbus, 1993; Clement, Mawby, and Giles, 1994; Holyoak and Koh, 1987; Keane, 1987, 1988; Ross, 1987, 1989; Seifert, McKoon, Abelson, and Ratcliff, 1986). People tend to be reminded of things that are strongly similar or strongly associated with their current representations, and these in turn are heavily influenced by their current context. One result of this pattern is the problem of *inert learning:* the failure to use new learning outside of the immediate context in which it has been learned. The classic example of this is the student who learns a new "correct" model in science class but then fails to apply it to real-life problems, reverting instead to older, incorrect mental models when outside the immediate learning context (Bransford, 1979; diSessa, 1982; Weisberg, DiCamillo, and Phillips, 1978). Thus a given individual may learn in ecology class the model that water is a scarce resource and apply the model well in the class context but fail to retrieve that model when back at work. In the familiar situations of the business day, the contextually supported remindings are of models of water that have been used before in these contexts, such as water as a spendable commodity. Even when it is easy to teach new models, further techniques may be needed to induce people to actually use them.

Analogy and Conceptual Change

Despite these reasons to be pessimistic about effecting change of knowledge, some techniques have promise. Research on conceptual change in science suggests that a major mechanism of change is analogy (Clement, 1983; Donnelly and McDaniel, 1993; Gentner, 1989). Historical retracing of scientists' journals (Gentner, 1982; Gentner, Brem, Ferguson, Wolff, Levidow, Markman, and Forbus, forthcoming; Nersessian, 1992; Thagard, 1992) reveals the frequent use of analogy in scientific discovery. Dunbar (1995) concluded on the basis of real-time studies of working microbiology laboratories that two major factors in promoting discovery are attention to inconsistencies and use of analogy. (A third factor is group dynamics.) We suggest that these two cognitive factors have quite different status. Detecting inconsistencies in the current model, or between the current model and the data, weakens commitment to the model and promotes willingness to consider alternatives. Analogy provides a set of possible alternatives.

An overview of this research suggests a rough methodology that maximizes the chance of achieving change of knowledge: (1) provide experiences that lead to detection of inconsistencies in current knowledge; (2) provide analogies designed to reveal the desired commonalities and differences; (3) provide extensive experience with the analogy or analogies; and (4) in difficult cases, provide multiple parallel analogies. To take these in turn, on the issue of inconsistency, there is considerable evidence that people are capable of holding two or more inconsistent models within the same domain, as the pastiche model phenomenon attests (Brewer, 1989; Brown and Burton, 1975; Collins and Gentner, 1987; diSessa, 1982). So long as each model is narrowly accessed in contexts specific to it, the inconsistencies may never come to the learner's attention. However, juxtaposing a model with another inconsistent model or with inconsistent data can promote conceptual change (Collins and Gentner, 1987; Dunbar, 1995; Thagard, 1992).

There is also evidence that analogies can be used to induce new models or in domains for which people already have mental models. One technique that has been used successfully for this purpose is that of *bridging analogies* (Clement, 1983, 1991, 1993). Learners are given a series of analogies, with the first comparison example being a close match to their existing model (and therefore easy to map). As the comparisons become progressively more distant, their common structure decreases. However, the progressive nature of the series helps the learner to preserve the intended system of commonalities and not to jump at a radically wrong interpretation. For example, students can readily picture bacteria proliferating beyond the resources of their petri dish, but applying this analogy to humans may seem a far stretch. By using intermediate analogs such as moose overpopulating their habitat and the Easter Island case, it may be possible to induce learners to apply such models to current human population.

The method of multiple parallel analogies has two further advantages. First, the use of multiple comparisons should promote attention to less obvious but important aspects of the domains. We have found that comparison between similar items promotes attention to common systems and also the detection of *alignable differences:* differences that occupy corresponding relational roles (Gentner and Markman, 1994; Markman and Gentner, 1993). The second advantage of using multiple parallel analogies is that it should provide a greater number of potential routes to memory retrieval (for example, Forbus, Gentner, and Law, 1995). We suggest that the use of bridging analogies—and multiple analogies in general—may make knowledge more accessible and mitigate somewhat the inert knowledge problem of isolated and inaccessible knowledge.

Conclusion

We began the chapter by noting that an understanding of human cognition has become at least as important to the survival of our species—and other species as well—as an understanding of comets or plate tectonics. Our welfare as a species is at least as likely to be determined by our own actions as by natural forces.

Mental models of population growth are of course only part of the story. There are also issues of worldview and attitude that go beyond specific mental models (see Chapter Eleven and Peters and Slovic, 1995). A case could even be made that we are evolutionarily programmed to increase in numbers and that the cultural mental models supporting this increase are after the fact. But even if this were true, change would remain possible, for evolutionary tendencies can be mitigated by human learning. And because any such learning must begin with the current system of beliefs, it is crucial to understand current models of human population growth. In view of the rapid expansion of human influence on our environment, such efforts to understand human cognition are an investment in survival.

REFERENCES

Adelson, B. "Problem Solving and the Development of Abstract Categories in Programming Languages." *Memory and Cognition,* 1981, *9,* 422–433.

Bassok, M. "Transfer of Domain-Specific Problem-Solving Procedures." *Journal of Experimental Psychology: Learning, Memory and Cognition,* 1990, *16,* 522–533.

Bazerman, M. H. *Judgment in Managerial Decision Making.* New York: Wiley, 1994.

Bostrom, A., Atman, C. J., Fischhoff, B., and Morgan, M. G. "Evaluating Risk Communications: Completing and Correcting Mental Models of Hazardous Processes. Part II." *Risk Analysis,* 1994, *14*(5), 789–798.

Bransford, J. D. *Human Cognition: Learning, Understanding, and Remembering.* Belmont, Calif.: Wadsworth, 1979.

Brewer, W. F. "The Activation and Acquisition of Knowledge." In S. Vosniadou and A. Ortony (eds.), *Similarity and Analogical Reasoning.* New York: Cambridge University Press, 1989.

Brown, A. L., Bransford, J. D., Ferrara, R. A., and Campione, J. C. "Learning, Remembering, and Understanding." In P. H. Mussen (ed.), *Handbook of Child Psychology,* Vol. 3: *Cognitive Development.* (4th ed.) New York: Wiley, 1983.

Brown, J. S., and Burton, R. R. "Multiple Representations of Knowledge for Tutorial Reasoning." In D. G. Bobrow and A. Collins (eds.), *Representation and Understanding: Studies in Cognitive Science.* Orlando, Fla.: Academic Press, 1975.

Burstein, M. H. "Analogical Learning with Multiple Models." In T. M. Mitchell, J. G. Carbonell, and R. S. Michalski (eds.), *Machine Learning: A Guide to Current Research.* Norwell, Mass.: Kluwer, 1986.

Burstein, M. H. "Combining Analogies in Mental Models." In D. H. Helman (ed.), *Analogical Reasoning: Perspectives of Artificial Intelligence, Cognitive Science, and Philosophy.* Dordrecht, Netherlands: Kluwer, 1988.

Byrne, R.M.J. "Suppressing Valid Inferences with Conditionals." *Cognition,* 1989, *31,* 61–83.

Byrne, R.M.J., and Johnson-Laird, P. N. "Spatial Reasoning." *Journal of Memory and Language,* 1989, *28*(5), 564–575.

Carey, S. *Conceptual Change in Childhood.* Cambridge, Mass.: MIT Press, 1985.

Chee, Y. S. "Applying Gentner's Theory of Analogy to the Teaching of Computer Programming." *International Journal of Man-Machine Studies,* 1993, *38,* 347–368.

Chi, M.T.H. "Conceptual Change Within and Across Ontological Categories: Examples from Learning and Discovery in Science." In R. Giere and H. Feigl (eds.), *Cognitive Models of Science: Minnesota Studies in the Philosophy of Science.* Minneapolis: University of Minnesota Press, 1992.

Chi, M.T.H., Feltovich, P. J., and Glaser, R. "Categorization and Representation of Physics Problems by Experts and Novices." *Cognitive Science,* 1981, *5,* 121–152.

Clement, C. A., Mawby, R., and Giles, D. E. "The Effects of Manifest Relational Similarity on Analog Retrieval." *Journal of Memory and Language,* 1994, *33,* 396–420.

Clement, J. "A Conceptual Model Discussed by Galileo and Used Intuitively by Physics Students." In D. Gentner and A. L. Stevens (eds.), *Mental Models.* Hillsdale, N.J.: Erlbaum, 1983.

Clement, J. "Nonformal Reasoning in Experts and in Science Students: The Use of Analogies, Extreme Cases, and Physical Intuition." In J. Voss, D. Perkins, and J. Siegal (eds.), *Informal Reasoning and Education.* Hillsdale, N.J.: Erlbaum, 1991.

Clement, J. "Using Analogies to Deal with Students' Preconceptions in Physics." *Journal of Research in Science Teaching,* 1993, *30*(10), 1241–1257.

Clement, J. "Imagistic Simulation and Physical Intuition in Expert Problem Solving." In *Proceedings of the Sixteenth Annual Meeting of the Cognitive Science Society.* Hillsdale, N.J.: Erlbaum, 1994.

Collins, A., and Gentner, D. "How People Construct Mental Models." In D. Holland and N. Quinn (eds.), *Cultural Models in Language and Thought.* New York: Cambridge University Press, 1987.

de Kleer, J., and Brown, J. S. "Assumptions and Ambiguities in Mechanistic Mental Models." In D. Gentner and A. L. Stevens (eds.), *Mental Models.* Hillsdale, N.J.: Erlbaum, 1983.

de Kleer, J., and Brown, J. S. "A Qualitative Physics Based on Confluences." *Artificial Intelligence,* 1984, *24,* 7–85.

Diamond, J. "Easter's End." *Discover,* Aug. 1995, pp. 63–69.

diSessa, A. A. "Unlearning Aristotelian Physics: A Study of Knowledge-Based Learning." *Cognitive Science,* 1982, *6,* 37–75.

Donnelly, C. M., and McDaniel, M. A. "Use of Analogy in Learning Scientific Concepts." *Journal of Experimental Psychology: Learning, Memory and Cognition,* 1993, *19*(4), 975–987.

Dunbar, K. "How Scientists Really Reason: Scientific Reasoning in Real-World Laboratories." In R. J. Sternberg and J. E. Davidson (eds.), *The Nature of Insight.* Cambridge, Mass.: MIT Press, 1995.

Ericksson, K. A., and Simon, H. A. *Protocol Analysis*. Cambridge, Mass.: MIT Press, 1984.

Erlich, P. "The Loss of Diversity: Causes and Consequences." In E. O. Wilson and F. M. Peter (eds.), *Biodiversity,* 1988, *21,* 23.

Forbus, K. D. "Qualitative Reasoning About Space and Motion." In D. Gentner and A. L. Stevens (eds.), *Mental Models*. Hillsdale, N.J.: Erlbaum, 1983.

Forbus, K. D. "Qualitative Process Theory." *Journal of Artificial Intelligence,* 1984, *24,* 85–168.

Forbus, K. D. "Qualitative Physics: Past, Present and Future." In D. S. Weld and J. de Kleer (eds.), *Readings in Qualitative Reasoning About Physical Systems*. San Mateo, Calif.: Morgan Kaufmann, 1990.

Forbus, K. D., and Gentner, D. "Learning Physical Domains: Toward a Theoretical Framework." In R. S. Michalski, J. G. Carbonell, and T. M. Mitchell (eds.), *Machine Learning: An Artificial Intelligence Approach*. Vol. 2. San Mateo, Calif.: Morgan Kaufmann, 1986.

Forbus, K. D., Gentner, D., and Law, K. "MAC/FAC: A Simulation of Similarity-Based Retrieval and Mapping." *Cognitive Science,* 1995, *19*(2), 141–205.

Gentner, D. *The Structure of Analogical Models in Science*. Technical Report No. 4451. Cambridge, Mass.: Bolt, Beranek and Newman, 1980.

Gentner, D. "Are Scientific Analogies Metaphors?" In D. S. Miall (ed.), *Metaphor: Problems and Perspectives*. Brighton, England: Harvester Press, 1982.

Gentner, D. "The Mechanisms of Analogical Learning." In S. Vosniadou and A. Ortony (eds.), *Similarity and Analogical Reasoning*. New York: Cambridge University Press, 1989.

Gentner, D., and Gentner, D. R. "Flowing Waters or Teeming Crowds: Mental Models of Electricity." In D. Gentner and A. L. Stevens (eds.), *Mental Models*. Hillsdale, N.J.: Erlbaum, 1983.

Gentner, D., and Markman, A. B. "Structural Alignment in Comparison: No Difference Without Similarity." *Psychological Science,* 1994, *5*(3), 152–158.

Gentner, D., Rattermann, M. J., and Forbus, K. D. "The Roles of Similarity in Transfer: Separating Retrievability and Inferential Soundness." *Cognitive Psychology,* 1993, *25,* 524–575.

Gentner, D., and Schumacher, R. M. "Use of Structure Mapping Theory for Complex Systems." *Proceedings of the 1986 IEEE International Conference on Systems, Man, and Cybernetics*. New York: Institute of Electrical and Electronics Engineers, 1986.

Gentner, D., and Stevens, A. L. (eds.). *Mental Models.* Hillsdale, N.J.: Erlbaum, 1983.

Gentner, D., Brem, S., Ferguson, R. W., Wolff, P., Levidow, B. B., Markman, A. B., and Forbus, K. D. "Analogical Reasoning and Conceptual Change: A Case Study of Johannes Kepler." *Journal of the Learning Sciences* (special issue on conceptual change), forthcoming.

Glenberg, A. M., and McDaniel, M. A. "Mental Models, Pictures and Text: Integration of Spatial and Verbal Information." *Memory and Cognition,* 1992, *20*(5), 458–460.

Glenberg, A. M., Meyer, M., and Lindem, K. "Mental Models Contribute to Foreground During Text Comprehension." *Journal of Memory and Language,* 1987, *26*(1), 69–83.

Halford, G. S. "Reflections on 25 Years of Piagetian Cognitive Developmental Psychology, 1963–1988." *Human Development,* 1989, *32,* 325–387.

Halford, G. S. *Children's Understanding: The Development of Mental Models.* Hillsdale, N.J.: Erlbaum, 1993.

Hayes, P. J. "Naive Physics I: Ontology for Liquids." In J. R. Hobbs and R. C. Moore (eds.), *Formal Theories of the Commonsense World.* Norwood, N.J.: Ablex, 1985.

Hegarty, M. "Mental Animation: Inferring Motion from Static Displays of Mechanical Systems." *Journal of Experimental Psychology: Learning, Memory and Cognition,* 1992, *18,* 1084–1102.

Hegarty, M., and Just, M. A. "Constructing Mental Models of Machines from Text and Diagrams." *Journal of Memory and Language,* 1993, *32,* 717–742.

Holyoak, K. J., and Koh, K. "Surface and Structural Similarity in Analogical Transfer." *Memory and Cognition,* 1987, *15,* 332–340.

Hutchins, E. "Understanding Micronesian Navigation." In D. Gentner and A. L. Stevens (eds.), *Mental Models.* Hillsdale, N.J.: Erlbaum, 1983.

Johnson-Laird, P. N. *Mental Models: Towards a Cognitive Science of Language, Inference, and Consciousness.* Cambridge, Mass.: Harvard University Press, 1983.

Johnson-Laird, P. N., and Bara, B. G. "Syllogistic Inference." *Cognition,* 1984, *16*(1), 1–61.

Johnson-Laird, P. N., and Byrne, R.M.J. *Deduction.* Hove, England: Erlbaum, 1991.

Johnson-Laird, P. N., Byrne, R.M.J., and Schaeken, W. "Propositional Reasoning by Model." *Psychological Review,* 1992, *99*(3), 418–439.

Johnson-Laird, P. N., Byrne, R.M.J., and Tabossi, P. "Reasoning by Model: The Case of Multiple Quantification." *Psychological Review,* 1989, *96*(4), 658–673.

Kahneman, D., Slovic, P., and Tversky, A. *Judgment Under Uncertainty: Heuristics and Biases.* New York: Cambridge University Press, 1982.

Keane, M. T. "On Drawing Analogies When Solving Problems: A Theory and Test of Solution Generation in an Analogical Problem-Solving Task." *British Journal of Psychology,* 1985, *76,* 449–458.

Keane, M. T. "On Retrieving Analogues When Solving Problems." *Quarterly Journal of Experimental Psychology,* 1987, *39A,* 29–41.

Keane, M. T. *Analogical Problem Solving.* New York: Wiley, 1988.

Kempton, W. "Two Theories of Home Heat Control." *Cognitive Science,* 1986, *10,* 75–90.

Kempton, W., Boster, J. S., and Hartley, J. *Environmental Values in American Culture.* Cambridge, Mass.: MIT Press, 1994.

Kieras, D. E., and Bovair, S. "The Role of a Mental Model in Learning to Operate a Device." *Cognitive Science,* 1984, *8,* 255–273.

Klahr, D., and Dunbar, K. "Dual-Space Search During Scientific Reasoning." *Cognitive Science,* 1988, *12,* 1–55.

Lesgold, A. M. "Acquiring Expertise." In J. R. Anderson and S. M. Kosslyn (eds.), *Tutorials in Learning and Memory.* New York: Freeman, 1984.

Mani, K., and Johnson-Laird, P. N. "The Mental Representation of Spatial Descriptions." *Memory and Cognition,* 1982, *10*(2), 181–187.

Markman, A. B., and Gentner, D. "Splitting the Differences: A Structural Alignment View of Similarity." *Journal of Memory and Language,* 1993, *32,* 517–535.

Mayer, R. E. *Thinking, Problem Solving, Cognition.* New York: Freeman, 1992.

McCloskey, M. "Intuitive Physics." *Scientific American,* 1983, *248*(4), 122–130.

McMichael, A. J. *Planetary Overload.* New York: Cambridge University Press, 1993.

McNamara, T. P. "Mental Representations of Spatial Relations." *Cognitive Psychology,* 1986, *18*(1), 87–121.

Miyake, N. "Constructive Interaction and the Iterative Process of Understanding." *Cognitive Psychology,* 1986, *10*(2), 151–177.

Morgan, M. G., and others. "Communicating Risk to the Public." *Environmental Science Technology,* 1992, *26*(11), 2048–2056.

Nersessian, N. J. "How Do Scientists Think? Capturing the Dynamics of Conceptual Change in Science." In R. N. Giere and H. Feigl (eds.), *Cognitive Models of Science: Minnesota Studies in the Philosophy of Science.* Minneapolis: University of Minnesota Press, 1992.

Nisbet, E. G. *Leaving Eden: To Protect and Manage the Earth.* New York: Cambridge University Press, 1991.

Norman, D. A. "Some Observations on Mental Models." In D. Gentner and A. L. Stevens (eds.), *Mental Models.* Hillsdale, N.J.: Erlbaum, 1983.

Norman, D. A. *The Psychology of Everyday Things.* New York: Basic Books, 1988.

Novick, L. R., and Holyoak, K. J. "Mathematical Problem Solving by Analogy." *Journal of Experimental Psychology: Learning, Memory, and Cognition,* 1991, *17*(3), 398–415.

Peters, E., and Slovic, P. *The Role of Affect and Worldviews as Orienting Dispositions in the Perception and Acceptance of Nuclear Power.* Decision Research Report No. 95–1. Eugene, Ore.: Decision Research, 1995.

Peters, R. L., and Lovejoy, T. E. "Terrestrial Fauna." In B. L. Turner and others (eds.), *The Earth as Transformed by Human Action: Global and Regional Changes in the Biosphere over the Past 300 Years.* New York: Cambridge University Press with Clark University, 1990.

Proffitt, D. R., Gilden, D. L., Kaiser, M. K., and Whelan, S. M. "The Effect of Configural Orientation on Perceived Trajectory in Apparent Motion." *Perception and Psychophysics,* 1988, *43,* 465–474.

Rips, L. J. "Mental Muddles." In H. Brand and R. M. Harnish (eds.), *The Representation of Knowledge and Belief.* Tucson: University of Arizona Press, 1986.

Ross, B. H. "This Is Like That: The Use of Earlier Problems and the Separation of Similarity Effects." *Journal of Experimental Psychology: Learning, Memory and Cognition,* 1987, *13*(4), 629–639.

Ross, B. H. "Distinguishing Types of Superficial Similarities: Different Effects on the Access and Use of Earlier Examples." *Journal of Experimental Psychology: Learning, Memory and Cognition,* 1989, *15*(3), 456–468.

Schumacher, R. M., and Gentner, D. "Transfer of Training as Analogical Mapping." *IEEE (Institute of Electrical and Electronics Engineers) Transactions of Systems, Man, and Cybernetics,* 1988a, *18*(4), 592–600.

Schumacher, R. M., and Gentner, D. "Remembering Causal Systems: Effects of Systematicity and Surface Similarity in Delayed Transfer." In *Proceedings of the Human Factors Society 32nd Annual Meeting.* Santa Monica, Calif.: Human Factors Society, 1988b.

Schwartz, D. L., and Black, J. B. "Analog Imagery in Mental Model Reasoning: Depictive Models." *Cognitive Psychology,* 1996, *30,* 154–219.

Seifert, C. M., McKoon, G., Abelson, R. P., and Ratcliff, R. "Memory Connection Between Thematically Similar Episodes." *Journal of Experimental Psychology: Learning, Memory and Cognition,* 1986, *12,* 220–231.

Socolow, R. H. (ed.). *Saving Energy in the Home: Princeton's Experiments at Twin Rivers.* New York: Ballinger, 1978.

Stevens, A., and Collins, A. "Multiple Conceptual Models of a Complex System." In R. Snow, P. Federico, and W. Montague (eds.), *Aptitude, Learning and Instruction: Cognitive Process Analysis.* Vol. 2. Hillsdale, N.J.: Erlbaum, 1980.

Thagard, P. *Conceptual Revolutions.* Princeton, N.J.: Princeton University Press, 1992.

Tversky, B. "Distortions in Memory for Visual Displays." In S. R. Ellis, M. Kaiser, and A. Grunewald (eds.), *Spatial Instruments and Spatial Displays.* Hillsdale, N.J.: Erlbaum, 1991.

Vosniadou, S., and Brewer, W. F. "Mental Models of the Earth: A Study of Conceptual Change in Childhood." *Cognitive Psychology,* 1992, *24*(4), 535–585.

Weisberg, R., DiCamillo, M., and Phillips, D. "Transferring Old Associations to New Situations: A Nonautomatic Process." *Journal of Verbal Learning and Verbal Behavior,* 1978, *17,* 219–228.

Williams, M. D., Hollan, J. D., and Stevens, A. L. "Human Reasoning About a Simple Physical System." In D. Gentner and A. L. Stevens (eds.), *Mental Models.* Hillsdale, N.J.: Erlbaum, 1983.

Wilson, E. O. *The Diversity of Life.* Cambridge, Mass.: Harvard University Press, 1992.

World Resources Institute. *World Resources 1992–93: A Guide to the Global Environment.* New York: Oxford University Press, 1992.

11

WHY IS THE NORTHERN ELITE MIND BIASED AGAINST COMMUNITY, THE ENVIRONMENT, AND A SUSTAINABLE FUTURE?

Thomas N. Gladwin, William E. Newburry, and Edward D. Reiskin

THE OPERATIONAL SPECIFICS of sustainable development (or sustainability) are likely to remain elusive and controversial for some time to come, but a consensus about the meaning of the concept is emerging at a high level of abstraction (see Daly, 1994; Hawken, 1993; Pezzey, 1992). Thousands of organizations worldwide have endorsed the most influential definition of the idea, stated by the World Commission on Environment and Development as "development which meets the needs of the present without compromising the ability of future generations to meet their own needs" (1987, p. 8). Sustainability can similarly be conceptualized as (1) improving the quality of life while living within the long-run carrying

The authors express their appreciation to the Energy Foundation (a joint initiative of the John D. and Catherine T. MacArthur Foundation, the Pew Charitable Trusts, and the Rockefeller Foundation), the Merck Family Fund, and the U.S. National Science Foundation (grant DMI-9421398) for their support of the Global Environment Program at New York University, which partially financed preparation of the paper on which this chapter is based. We also thank Elena Cabada for her able assistance. The viewpoints herein should be attributed only to the authors.

capacities of supporting biophysical and social systems (see Daily and Ehrlich, 1992; World Conservation Union, United Nations Environment Programme, and Worldwide Fund for Nature, 1991); (2) protecting, maintaining, and restoring the integrity, resilience, and productivity of life-support services provided by natural and social systems (see Daly, 1990; Ehrlich, 1994); (3) maintaining or increasing per capita stocks of all forms of productive ecological, material, human, and social capital (see Daly, 1994; Gladwin and Kennelly, (forthcoming); and (4) ensuring that current human activities do not shift costs or risks onto, or appropriate the property or resource rights of, other human interests, today or tomorrow, in the absence of appropriate compensation (see Jansson, Hammer, Folke, and Costanza, 1994). A content analysis of these and many other conceptions suggests an emerging consensus that sustainable development "is a process of widening or enlarging the range of human choice in an inclusive, connected, equitable, prudent, and secure manner" (Gladwin, Kennelly, and Krause, 1995, p. 878).

Are current patterns of human development on this planet sustainable by these definitions? According to many observers, the answer is a resounding no. Figure 11.1 charts many of the vital trends bearing upon the health or integrity of the planet's natural and social systems as monitored by the World Bank (1992), United Nations Development Programme (1995), Worldwatch Institute (Brown, Lenssen, and Kane, 1995), and World Resources Institute (1994). The data indicate a steady deterioration of the earth's physical condition in the form of declining renewable resources, altered biogeochemistry, and a threatened biological base. The trends also suggest a stagnant or falling quality of life for the human majority, attributable to swelling population, persistent deprivation, and exploding social disintegration. The gestalt painted by these trends is characterized by complex interconnection, exponential acceleration, grave consequence, and transformational urgency. It is also one of gross inequity, for it is the northern (Europe, North America, Japan) elites (about 15 percent of the world population) who are directly or indirectly responsible for the great bulk (an estimated 80 percent) of planetary resource consumption and toxic pollution while enjoying the proceeds of an escalating global redistribution of wealth from poor to rich (see Durning, 1992; Gore, 1992; Hawken, 1993; Korten, 1995; Lind, 1995).

The evidence is robust that northern elites are maintaining themselves only through the exhaustion and dispersion of a one-time inheritance of natural capital, including fossil fuels, high-grade mineral ores, rich topsoil, groundwater stored up during the Ice Age, and biodiversity (see Ehrlich, 1994) but doing little to ensure the availability of renewable

Figure 11.1. Signals of Human-Caused Unsustainability.

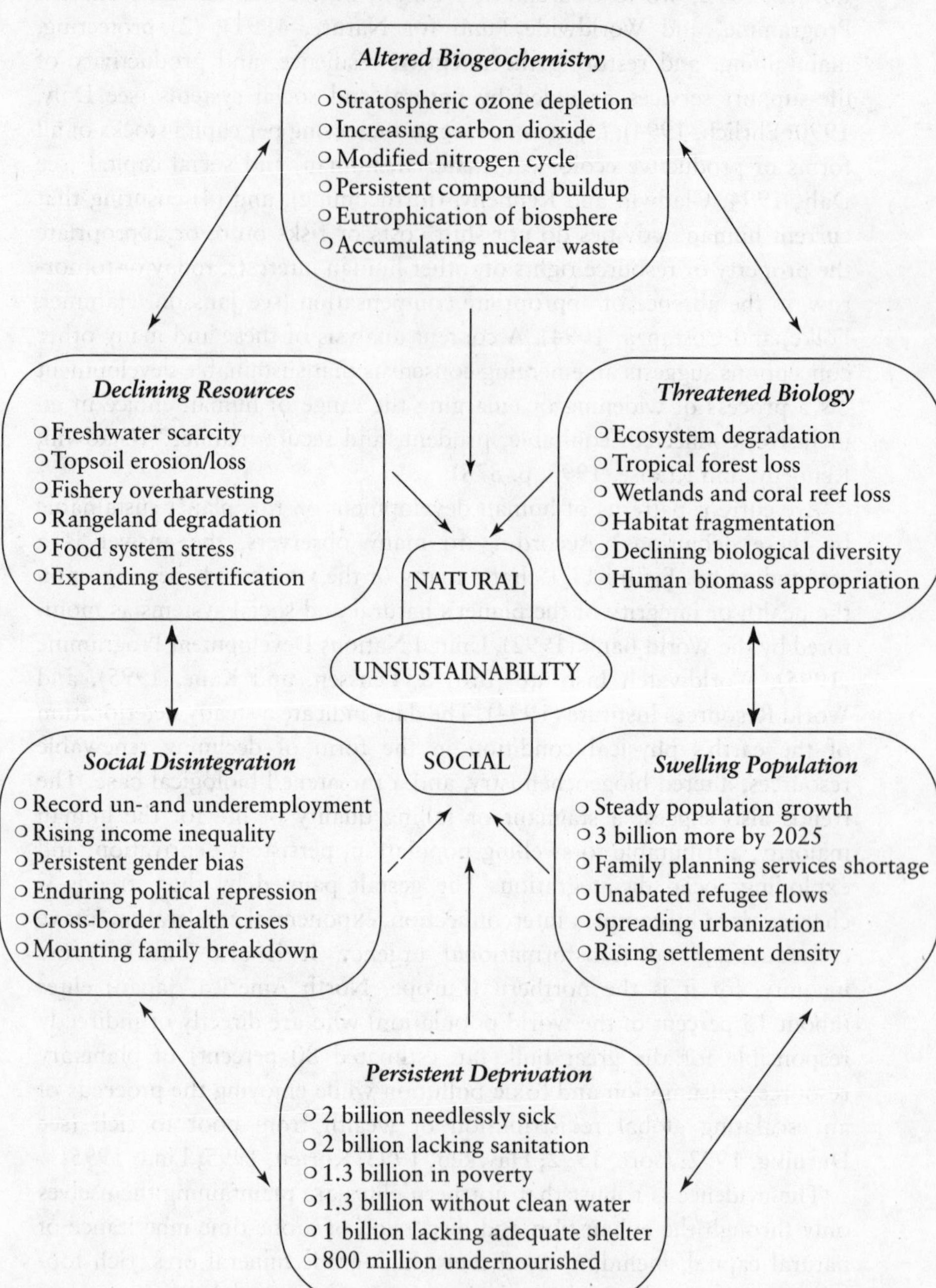
Altered Biogeochemistry
○ Stratospheric ozone depletion
○ Increasing carbon dioxide
○ Modified nitrogen cycle
○ Persistent compound buildup
○ Eutrophication of biosphere
○ Accumulating nuclear waste
Declining Resources
○ Freshwater scarcity
○ Topsoil erosion/loss
○ Fishery overharvesting
○ Rangeland degradation
○ Food system stress
○ Expanding desertification
Threatened Biology
○ Ecosystem degradation
○ Tropical forest loss
○ Wetlands and coral reef loss
○ Habitat fragmentation
○ Declining biological diversity
○ Human biomass appropriation
NATURAL
UNSUSTAINABILITY
SOCIAL
Social Disintegration
○ Record un- and underemployment
○ Rising income inequality
○ Persistent gender bias
○ Enduring political repression
○ Cross-border health crises
○ Mounting family breakdown
Swelling Population
○ Steady population growth
○ 3 billion more by 2025
○ Family planning services shortage
○ Unabated refugee flows
○ Spreading urbanization
○ Rising settlement density
Persistent Deprivation
○ 2 billion needlessly sick
○ 2 billion lacking sanitation
○ 1.3 billion in poverty
○ 1.3 billion without clean water
○ 1 billion lacking adequate shelter
○ 800 million undernourished

substitutes to replace this depleted inheritance. Despite some positive trends regarding reduction of pollution and increased energy efficiency (see Easterbrook, 1995), elites are still exceeding the carrying capacities of renewable resource systems and thus reducing the self-organizing capacities of the planet to support life in community. Growing resource scarcities, in turn, are setting in motion powerful forces of social decomposition and political upheaval that are unlikely to respect national borders (see Homer-Dixon, Boutwell, and Rathjens, 1993; Kennedy, 1993; Kaplan, 1994). Northern elites are thus seen as "gambling with survival" (World Conservation Union, United Nations Environment Programme, and Worldwide Fund for Nature, 1991, p. 4).

What could possibly explain this pervasive manifestation of collective human irrationality? While mainstream psychology, economics, and management have been virtually mute about the crisis of ecological and social unsustainability (for critiques see Daly and Cobb, 1994; Gladwin, Kennelly, and Krause, 1995; Kidner, 1994), an emerging band of "ecopsychologists" invoke the metaphor of psychopathology to explain the predicament of our world: Theodore Roszak traces the deepest root of "collusive madness in industrial society" to a "repression of the ecological unconscious" (1992, p. 320); Ken Wilber diagnoses the crisis as "a worldwide collective psychoneurosis—a denial, alienation, dissociation of the biosphere by the noosphere" (1995, p. 382); Thomas Berry believes that the human species has become "autistic" in relation to the earth (1988, p. 215); Chellis Glendinning blames unsustainability on an "original trauma," endured by technological people that took the form "of a systemic and systematic removal of our lives from the natural world" (1995, p. 51); and James Hillman suggests that we have become aesthetically or sensually numb and are collectively suffering from an "inability to let the world into one's perceptual field" (1995).

Though there certainly may be some truth in the above diagnoses, we contend that the only honest answer as to why northern elites have chosen to behave so unsustainably is not yet known. Dozens of possible and competing primary, predisposing, precipitating, and reinforcing causes have been delineated (for a long list of candidates, see Gladwin, Krause, and Kennelly, 1995). Given the embryonic state of thinking and research about sustainability, along with the paucity of attention by mainstream psychologists, among others, to matters of the public interest in general (see Smith, 1990) and to destructive patterns of people's relationship to the natural world in particular (see Stern, 1992; Stokols, 1995), the explanation of unsustainable human behavior and thinking is wide open for theorizing and empirical research. This potential exists, we believe, at all levels of analysis—individual, group, community, organization, culture, nation, and world.

Sustainability is inherently a matter of life or death, which raises the big questions: Who are we? Where do our loyalties lie? How should progress be measured? And the most fundamental question of human existence, posed by Socrates long ago: "How shall we live?" We contend that there is no more worthy an enterprise than improving the understanding of the human condition and prospect as it relates to sustainability. Moreover, given the destructive behaviors and consequences just reviewed, there is probably no challenge greater than that of transforming the ways human beings think and exist in the world.

We acknowledge the complex determination of human behavior as shaped by a not yet fully understood interaction of primitive beliefs, intelligence, consciousness, cognitive style, motivation, emotion, personality, values, ethics, and situation or context, but we will concentrate herein predominantly on how cognitive heuristics and mental assumptions shape unsustainable thought and behavior. Because we currently lack a single, comprehensive, and internally consistent viewpoint that accurately reflects what we know empirically about unsustainability, this chapter necessarily pursues an eclectic approach. The novel and consequential status of the topic demands that naive questions be asked, that conventional assumptions be challenged, and that uncharted avenues be proposed for exploration. The following integrative assembly of propositions about why the human (northern elite) mind is unsustainable, and how it might be made less so, is thus offered in the spirit of humility, creative imagination, and constructive provocation. We acknowledge that our arguments are at times strong and one-sided, but they are positioned as such to encourage discussion and debate. We here assume that scholars wish to contribute to "recreating a more humane and sustainable world" by concentrating on the "urgent issues of our time concerning survival and justice" (Smith, 1990, pp. 530, 535).

Origins of the Unsustainable Mind

Figure 11.2 overviews the conceptual framework employed here. It suggests that the alleged unsustainable mind of northern elites has four principal and interrelated origins: (1) a cognitively bounded *biological mind*, inherited from our ancient ancestors, which is maladapted to the modern challenges of systemic complexity; (2) an obsolete *worldview mind* guided by tacit and outmoded assumptions about how the world works, based on religious, philosophical, and early scientific traditions; (3) an addicted

Figure 11.2. Sources of Unsustainable Thinking.

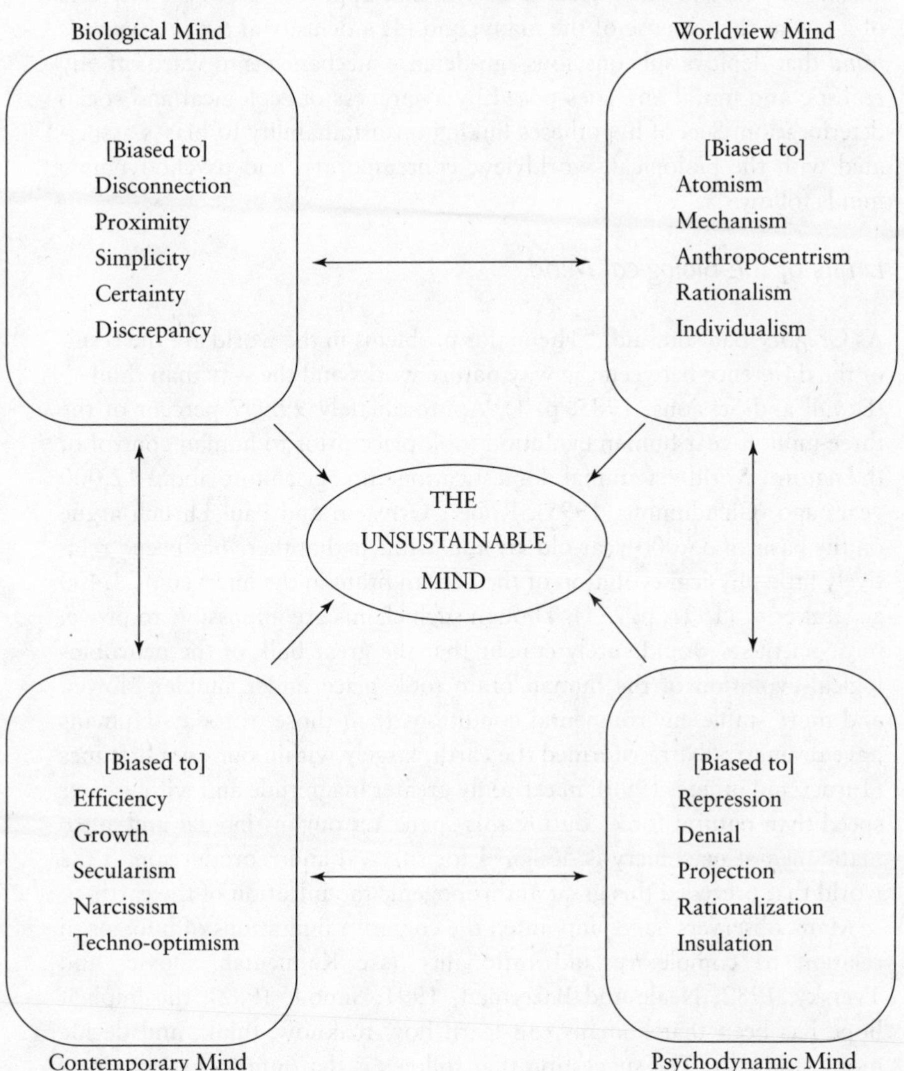

contemporary mind that has been powerfully programmed to believe in various myths and ideological doctrines that appear to serve the interests of a few at the expense of the many; and (4) a delusional *psychodynamic mind* that deploys subconscious ego-defense mechanisms to ward off any realistic and moral anxieties posed by awareness of ecological and social deterioration. Sets of hypotheses linking unsustainability to biases associated with the biological, worldview, contemporary, and psychodynamic minds follow.

Limits of the Biological Mind

As Gregory Bateson said, "The major problems in the world are the result of the difference between the way nature works and the way man thinks" (Devall and Sessions, 1985, p. 1). Approximately 99.997 percent of the three-million-year human evolution took place prior to human control of the natural world via animal domestication and agriculture about 12,000 years ago (Glendinning, 1995). Robert Ornstein and Paul Ehrlich argue on the basis of 35,000-year-old art and artifacts that there has been "relatively little physical evolution of the human brain in the intervening 1,400 generations" (1991, p. 271). Though such claims are impossible to prove, most scientists would surely concur that the great bulk of the neurobiological evolution of the human brain took place under simpler, slower, and more stable environmental conditions than those of today. Humans have dramatically transformed the earth, largely within our own lifetimes (Turner and others, 1990), in certainly greater magnitude and with greater speed than natural forces during this span. Yet our instinctual and automatic mental machinery is designed for survival and reproduction in the world that preceded this great anthropogenic modification of the earth.

Many observers have pinpointed the cognitive limitations of humans in relation to complexity and rationality (see Kahneman, Slovic, and Tversky, 1982; Neale and Bazerman, 1991; Simon, 1982); the implicit hope has been that humans can learn how to know, think, and decide more rationally. The suggestion that follows is that human brains are as biologically developed as currently possible and that further advances in the uniquely human neocortex will only occur over a long evolutionary period. By juxtaposing the mental requirements of comprehending and coping effectively with the "world problematique" and "resolutique" (King and Schneider, 1991) against the apparent capacities of the current human biological brain (here referred to as the *biomind*), we suggest the following five hypotheses:

HYPOTHESIS 1: THE BIOMIND IS ADAPTED FOR DISCONNECTION RATHER THAN INTERCONNECTION.

Problems such as poverty, gender bias, population growth, and environmental degradation are highly interdependent (see Dasgupta, 1995), often resulting in vicious downward spirals of ecological and economic decline (Durning, 1992). Comprehension of unsustainability thus necessitates systems thinking, emphasizing wholes over parts, relationships over things, process over structure, quality over quantity, inclusiveness over exclusiveness, and so on (see Senge, 1990). Humans, however, tend toward static, isolated, one-factor-at-a-time analysis rather than dynamic whole-systems appraisal. Feedback processes, side effects, and multiple interconnections are generally ignored or misperceived in the cognitive maps used to judge causal relationships (see Sterman, 1989). Virtually no feedback loops, for example, were found in the cognitive maps employed by political elites (Axelrod, 1976). People tend to think in single-strand causal series (Dörner, 1980), tend to assume that a single effect has a single cause (Plous, 1993), and generally ignore base rates and situational factors. People, in short, tend to be linear rather than systems thinkers.

HYPOTHESIS 2: THE BIOMIND IS ADAPTED FOR PROXIMITY RATHER THAN DISTANCE.

Many of the most challenging problems of unsustainability, such as climate change, stratospheric ozone depletion, tropical rain forest depletion, and oceanic overfishing, are global in connection and consequence. The problems are also transgenerational, with adverse and effectively irreversible changes extending over decades or centuries. Though cognition of sustainability necessitates distant horizons, humans tend to overemphasize proximity via excessive temporal, spatial, and specific discounting (see Loewenstein, 1988).

With typical discount rates, the future, faraway places, and phylogenetically far-removed species disappear quickly from decision salience. With proximity comes a propensity for immediacy, whereby humans tend to underestimate time delays or to ignore them altogether; they thus also tend to focus on the symptoms of any trouble when trying to determine a cause. This tendency probably originated from the fact that our ancestors' survival depended in large part on the ability to respond quickly to threats that were immediate, personal, and palpable (Ornstein and Ehrlich, 1991). People's propensity for contemporaneous interpretation and quick physiological response manifests itself today in an inability to appreciate that current problems are often derived from previous solutions. Instead of considering longer-term implications of systemic problems, people display a preference for easy or obvious quick fixes, which too often merely shift problems from one part of a system to another.

HYPOTHESIS 3: THE BIOMIND IS ADAPTED FOR SIMPLICITY RATHER THAN COMPLEXITY.

The intertwined ecological, economic, and social challenges of unsustainability are "fundamentally nonlinear in causation and discontinuous in both their spatial structure and temporal behavior" (Holling, 1994, p. 57). Complexity flows both from details (many variables) and from dynamism (subtle, diffuse, and multiple patterns of cause and effect) (see Costanza, Wainger, Folke, and Mäler, 1993; Forrester, 1971). Humans, however, tend toward simplicity in causal mapping, seeing snapshots rather than processes, and straight lines rather than circles of influence (Senge, 1990). Humans are generally insensitive to nonlinearity and negative correlations and tend to anticipate the future by linear extrapolation of the past (see Brehmer, 1980; Wagenaar and Sagaria, 1975). Solutions to higher order and several nonlinear differential equations appear to exceed human cognitive capabilities (see Simon, 1982). Normal heuristic cues to causality—such as temporal and spatial proximity of cause and effect, temporal precedence of cause, covariation, and similarity in cause and effect—lose their utility under high complexity (see Einhorn and Hogarth, 1986). As "dynamically deficient" (Sterman, 1989), human performance in complex dynamic environments is poor relative to normative standards and even simple decision rules (see Brehmer, 1992; Funke, 1991). Humans are furthermore seemingly unable to learn how to improve their performance as the feedback complexity within environments grows (Paich and Sterman, 1993). This bias to simplicity causes people to experience the world as small rather than big (Ornstein and Ehrlich, 1991), monological rather than dialogical or dialectical (Wilber, 1995), and empty rather than full (Goodland, 1992).

HYPOTHESIS 4: THE BIOMIND IS ADAPTED FOR CERTAINTY RATHER THAN UNCERTAINTY.

The most important challenges of unsustainability that lie ahead could be those that are still unknown and are likely to arise from discontinuities (passing over unknown thresholds of disruption or irreversibility) and synergisms (problem interaction producing multiplicative rather than additive effects) (see Dovers and Handmer, 1995). Though these problems are thus "not amenable to assumptions of constancy or stability of fundamental relationships" (Holling, 1994, p. 58), it appears that human perceptual systems are oriented toward order, maintenance, optimization, and predictable equilibrium states of adaptation to the external world.

People tend to ignore or underestimate large uncertainties or unknowns, to seek evidence consistent with current beliefs rather than to confront potential disconfirmation (Einhorn and Hogarth, 1978; Klayman and Ha, 1987), to procrastinate in making costly changes until convinced of the "facts," to generally deviate from the principles of the scientific method (Hogarth, 1987), and to prefer normal incremental "puzzle solving" over postnormal science (see Funtowicz and Ravetz, 1993). As a result, societies often display imprudent risk aversion and underinvest in precaution, preemptive safeguards, reversible actions, safety margins, and preparation for perpetual surprise (see Ludwig, Hilborn and Walters, 1993). Biases toward certainty may be closely tied to human propensities to cognitively process on the basis of "positive illusions" (Taylor and Brown, 1988) and "unrealistic optimism" in thinking about the future (see Tiger, 1979). These biases to certainty, constancy, and stability serve to impede adaptive learning, particularly double loop learning (see Davis and Hogarth, 1992), deemed essential for sustainability.

HYPOTHESIS 5: THE BIOMIND IS ADAPTED FOR DISCREPANCY RATHER THAN GRADUALITY.

The most critical threats to sustainability take the form of cumulative, slow, and gradual processes. Slowly developing and steadily compounding environmental catastrophes include time bombs such as tropical rain forest depletion, global warming, overpopulation, urbanization, and freshwater shortages. Human perception, however, tends to be sensitive only to rapidity, discontinuity, and discrepancy. Human nervous systems do not attend to slight or slowly presented differences and therefore experience great difficulty in discriminating between gradual changes and system states (see Bateson, 1979). Mental routines automatically amplify the new, unusual, sudden, and dramatic and tend to ignore the constant and familiar (see Ornstein and Ehrlich, 1991). Special attention is paid to vivid and colorful event-based beginnings and endings of processes, while the greater and duller interim changes are typically overlooked (see Tversky and Kahneman, 1974). People thus tend to react too quickly and excessively to sudden shifts, scarcities, or emergencies, but fail to engage or trigger flight or fight responses to often more threatening gradual yet exponential change. The possession of quick reflexes but not slow ones makes humans prone to the classic boiled frog syndrome.

Biomind Summary

In summary, minds that have evolved toward disconnection, proximity, simplicity, certainty, and discrepancy are unable, we submit, to comprehend the modern challenge of sustainability. This inability is due to the exclusion of systemic, nonlinear, large-scale, long-term, and slow-motion environmental processes from instinctual causal mapping and mental simulation. Moreover, perceptual and judgmental errors and biases that individually work against sustainability may get compounded and magnified as human minds interact. When combined with defensive routines, game playing, and herd instincts at the group level (see Argyris, 1985; Argyris and Schön, 1978; Janis, 1982) and social traps, prisoner's dilemmas, and tragedies of common property at the societal level (see Cross and Guyer, 1980; Fox, 1985; Hardin, 1982), the chances of achieving ecological and social sustainability decline markedly.

We are quite pessimistic about the chances of adequately and opportunely reducing the mismatch between the automatic programming of the "old" biological brain and the perceptual and decisional capabilities required for achieving ecological and social sustainability. We can certainly promote the development of "insight skills" (Davis and Hogarth, 1992), the use of "virtual worlds" (Schön, 1983), "reflective conversations with the situation" (Schön, 1992), and the advancement of systems thinking and dynamics (see Graham, Morecroft, Senge, and Sterman, 1994), but we cannot expect the pace of unconscious biological evolution to change much about our cognitive and neural machinery anytime soon.

We suggest that it is constructive to accept that humanity is collectively intellectually disabled, insufficiently programmed, and fundamentally bounded vis-à-vis the cognitive challenges posed by sustainable development. With biological evolution thus insufficient to ensure the survival of human civilization, people must instead rely on another type of evolutionary development in the form of cultural or "symbolic DNA." Cultural modifications transmitted by teaching and learning must advance rapidly and appropriately to counteract, override, and subdue the unsustainable influences of the old biological brain on human behavior. The only practical hope of attaining sustainability, in other words, resides in consciously modifying culturally inherited worldviews, reversing pathogenic contemporary social programming, and reducing human reliance on psychodynamic defense mechanisms, to which we now turn.

Reliance on Outdated Worldviews

Worldviews refer to "the constellations of beliefs, values, and concepts that give shape and meaning to the world a person experiences and acts within" (Norton, 1991, p. 75). They rarely take the form of highly developed systematic philosophies, typically remaining sets of incomplete and fragmented background assumptions that tend to organize language, thought, perceptions, and actions. Palmer suggests that, "what we face in the West today is not an ecological crisis, nor a crisis of economics, nor a crisis of structure. It is a crisis of the mind. A crisis of the stories we tell ourselves, of the position we wish to give ourselves in the creation, and of the purpose that we give to our existence" (Palmer, 1992, p. 178). These presuppositions and convictions may lie beneath hermetic levels of reasoning, for people are typically hard pressed to articulate or defend them. Even though the central axioms of a worldview are often tacit, hidden, and unjustified, they powerfully serve to channel attention, filter information, categorize experience, anchor interpretation, orient learning, establish moods, secrete norms, and legitimate narratives, ideologies, and power structures.

A wide-ranging body of research and commentary asserts that modern Western industrial societies remain entrapped in a dominant Cartesian-Newtonian mechanistic worldview as defined hereafter. The embedded beliefs were engendered by the scientific revolution of the sixteenth and seventeenth centuries, in combination with influences of the eighteenth century Age of Enlightenment and older biases toward human domination over the earth and separation from the biotic community embodied in Old Testament–based Judeo-Christian tradition and Greek philosophy. The acquired epistemological, ontological, and methodological assumptions still profoundly undergird theories of modern conventional management (see Gladwin, Kennelly, and Krause, 1995), economics (see Daly and Cobb, 1994), and psychology (see Kidner, 1994). The problem, however, is that these inherited presumptions and modes of thought are no longer relevant (Bateson, 1979). We thus confront a "crisis of perception," derived "from the fact that we are trying to apply the concepts of an outdated worldview . . . to a reality that can no longer be understood in terms of these concepts" (Capra, 1982, pp. 15–16).

We suggest that these intellectually inherited and largely subconscious assumptions about how the world works profoundly bias current modes of knowing and information processing against environmental sustainability. The mechanistic, worldview-shaped mind (the *viewmind*) is likely to experience great difficulties in seeing, interpreting, and responding sustainably for the following closely interconnected reasons.

HYPOTHESIS 6: THE VIEWMIND CONCEIVES REALITY ACCORDING TO ATOMISM RATHER THAN HOLISM.

Newtonian science, building upon Greek and Roman cosmologies, brought us the assumptions that matter and nature are made up of atomic or (discrete and separable) individual parts moved by external forces, that the whole is equal to the sum of its parts, that knowledge of parts and wholes is context independent, and that change occurs by the rearrangement of parts (see Merchant, 1992). With atomistic materialism came elementalism and reductionism—that is, the point of view that complex phenomena are best understood when broken down into their most fundamental or primitive parts. The accompanying Cartesian dualism of mind and matter served to drastically separate "subject and object, culture and nature, thoughts and feelings, values and facts, spirit and matter, human and nonhuman" (Wilber, 1995, p. 4).

Sustainability entails irreducibles not subject to analytic decomposition. It ultimately requires a reconciliation of mind and nature, that is, some transcendent unity of "subjective freedom with objective union" (Wilber, 1995, p. 483). Nearly all environmentalists reject atomism and dualism in favor of holism, because an embrace of sustainability requires a comprehensive, integrative view of co-evolving ecological, economic, and social systems. Holistic metaphysics assumes that everything is related to everything else, that the whole is greater than the sum of its parts, that parts are not interchangeable or exchangeable, that knowledge is context dependent, and that process takes primacy over parts (see Merchant, 1992). Pluralistic and systemic study of connections, rather than reductionism, is needed to regain a sense of the whole and the proper human role within it.

HYPOTHESIS 7: THE VIEWMIND CONCEIVES REALITY ACCORDING TO MECHANISM RATHER THAN ORGANICISM.

With atomism came the philosophical doctrine maintaining that all phenomena of the universe, including life, regardless of complexity, can be ultimately understood in a mechanical framework, that is, can be explained in terms of physics and chemistry. With Newtonian physics, nature could be reduced to basic building blocks linked by mechanisms of interaction. Reality came to be conceptualized as a clocklike machine, made up of atomic parts and operating according to laws and rules in an ordered sequence. This mechanical structure of reality assumed the earth to be dead and inert, thus legitimating human manipulation and control over it.

The mechanical conception replaced the Renaissance worldview of nature as a living organism, to which the challenge of sustainability calls for a return. Nature, in this view, is a set of related processes rather than a collection of parts (see Norton, 1991). In the cosmos of the Renaissance world, "the image of the earth as a living organism and nurturing mother served as a cultural constraint restricting the actions of human beings. . . . As long as the earth was conceptualized as alive and sensitive, it could be considered a breach of human ethical behavior to carry out destructive acts against it" (Merchant, 1992, p. 43).

HYPOTHESIS 8: THE VIEWMIND CONCEIVES REALITY ACCORDING TO ANTHROPOCENTRISM RATHER THAN BIOCENTRISM.

The Old Testament, Greek intellectual traditions, and Enlightenment philosophy all placed humans at the center of the cosmos, at the top of some hierarchy of evolution. Nonhuman nature was made for humans; all value in nonhuman nature was only instrumental. Similarly, combined with traditional patriarchy, reality came to be viewed in terms of power-based vertical-hierarchical modes of organization. Hierarchy, anthropocentrism, and mechanism combined to sanction domination of both nature and women. With the rise of Newtonian science, nature came to be viewed as a gigantic storehouse and mechanical system to be manipulated and exploited. This worldview espoused the rise of "mechanistic quantitative consciousness," with dominion over nature to be achieved through science (see Merchant, 1992).

Sustainability proponents call for a worldview that acknowledges and reveres the intrinsic value of nature and that does not presume human dominance. Humans must adopt a "land ethic" that "changes the role of Homo Sapiens from conqueror of the land community to plain member and citizen of it. It implies respect for his fellow members, and also respect for the community itself" (Leopold, 1949, pp. 224–225). Hierarchy and patriarchy are to be renounced in favor of pluralistic, egalitarian unity in diversity. The proper role of humans is to live humbly and harmoniously with, and act as stewards of, nonhuman nature.

HYPOTHESIS 9: THE VIEWMIND CONCEIVES REALITY ACCORDING TO RATIONALISM RATHER THAN INTUITIONISM.

The Enlightenment produced the doctrine that knowledge comes wholly from pure reason, independent of the senses. The scientific method became the predominant approach to knowledge, with truth arising from rational thinking. Galileo, Bacon, Descartes, and Newton had earlier postulated that the language of nature and truth lay in mathematics and that merely subjective contemplation had no relevance in the realm of science. The modern mind is still haunted by the belief that the only meaningful concepts are those capable of mathematical elucidation. The obsession with quantifiable properties predisposes humans to subdue their natural, qualitative, ethical, and emotional senses along with their relevant experiences and memories (Laing, 1982). This rationalism supports the doctrine of objectivism, that is, that facts should be separate from values and that truth is a function of objective reality, uncolored by interpretative bias or prejudice. True science is thus value free, and facts derived from such science have no moral significance in and of themselves.

Such scientific rationalism cannot cope with many dimensions of sustainability, particularly those of a moral or aesthetic character that cannot be deduced empirically. Creative and synthetic intuition, along with other nonrational processes, are thus needed to complement pure reason in the search for the social conventions and ethical structures by which to live. The sustainability movement thus rejects objectivism and positivism as the only sources of wisdom. Truth and value are deeply intertwined; all human experience is value-laden; not all of sustainability can be observable; and issues of sustainability demand deep internal interpretation and social reconstruction.

HYPOTHESIS 10: THE VIEWMIND CONCEIVES REALITY ACCORDING TO INDIVIDUALISM RATHER THAN COMMUNITARIANISM.

Assumptions engendered by the scientific revolution profoundly shaped social, economic, and political philosophies—such as those promulgated by John Locke, John Stuart Mill, Thomas Hobbes, Adam Smith, and Herbert Spencer—that continue to influence the "socially dominant language" of Homo Oeconomicus today (see Oelschlaeger, 1994). Atomism, rationalism, economic liberalism, and social Darwinism all promoted the idea that "rational egoism, or selfishness" is not only "an objectively valid approach to ethical action," but also "the only rational approach to human action in general" (Hargrove, 1989, p. 209).

These philosophers of the Age of Enlightenment expanded the rationalistic Cartesian-Newtonian paradigm of critical reasoning to a teleological conception of liberalism and individualism. Locke posited an atomistic view of society with the ideals of individualism, property rights, free markets, and representative government. This "organic" right to movement and self-determinism served to provide the basis for the traditional American view of property owners' independence from societal restraints.

The primary reality in the world came to be seen as "autonomous individual subjects existing independently of body, society and nature and freely pursuing their ends in fierce isolation" (Engel, 1992, p. 69). Modern proponents of sustainability lament the destruction of community, civil society, participation, and spirituality attributable to such utilitarian and expressive individualism. They call instead for a shift from private happiness to public citizenship, that is, to "person-in-community" (Daly and Cobb, 1994) and renewed "habits of the heart" (Bellah and others, 1985), to countervail the destructive forces of individualism.

Worldview Summary

In summary, though surely not all northern elites are enmeshed in this old, mechanistic worldview, we submit that the thinking of those in power is still predominantly atomistic-dualistic, mechanistic, anthropocentric, rationalistic, and individualistic. To the extent that this assertion is true, these elites operate in fragmented, disengaged, alienated, and disenchanted worlds—worlds of "totalitarian" objectification and subjugated subjectivity (see Habermas, 1990). The abiotic and mechanistic worldview severs and represses people's connections with nature, both externally and internally. These elites suffer, in short, from what Georg Hegel called "a vanity of understanding" or what Charles Taylor has described as "a monster of arrested development" (see Wilber, 1995, for critiques of the Enlightenment by these theorists). The mechanistic worldview, in sum, fails the tests of sustainability (that is, inclusiveness, connectivity, equity, prudence, and security) on all counts. One would hope that the modern worldview is becoming more unified. Czech playwright turned statesman Václav Havel, however, recently observed that "the abyss between the rational and the spiritual, the external and the internal, the objective and the subjective, the technical and the moral, the universal and the unique, constantly grows deeper" (1995, p. 48).

Pathogenic Contemporary Mental Programming

"The aims of productivity, profitability, efficiency, limitless growth, limitless mechanization, and automation can enrich and empower the few (for a while), but they will sooner or later ruin us all" (Berry, 1993, p. 103). A wide variety of contemporary basic assumptions have mutated from, or been appended to, the historic mechanical worldview surveyed previously in this chapter. They work the same way as the ancient ones in influencing thoughts, attitudes, and behaviors. They tend, however, to be more consciously recognized, yet are rarely debated or questioned in mainstream public discourse. These modern rules of the game are deeply imbedded in current institutions, public policies, norms, values, ideas, and techniques and are buttressed by a triad of contemporary moral philosophies, intellectual theories, and vested interests of political elites (see Korten, 1995; Viederman, 1994). They represent the world according to Wall Street, Madison Avenue, Hollywood, the U.S. Congress, the World Bank, and academic societies. This socially legitimated and institutionalized conventional wisdom has been dubbed technocentrism, cornucopianism, expansionism, growthmania, or cowboy economics, and broadly explored in economics (Daly, 1994; Turner, 1993), sociology (Catton and Dunlap, 1980; Redclift and Benton, 1994), philosophy (Naess and Rothenberg, 1989; Oelschlaeger, 1994), political science (Milbrath, 1989; Eckersley, 1992), and psychology (Buss and Craik, 1983; Wilber, 1995).

We suggest five hypotheses below by which the contemporary mind *(contempmind)* is being subjected to mental programming that many observers believe is biased against sustainability. A number of the charges were foreseen by the foundational figures of social science (for example, James, Jung, Freud, Weber, Durkheim, Veblen, Heidegger, Huxley, Mumford, Nietzsche, Kierkegaard, and Marcuse). The modern crisis of unsustainability can thus be viewed as a culmination of the crises of value, personal meaning, community, social allegiance, and purpose of life that intellectuals have been lamenting throughout the century. One critic has gone so far as to say that the conventional wisdom of northern elites "may itself be the single greatest barrier we face to progress toward sustainability" (Korten, 1995, p. 14).

HYPOTHESIS 11: THE CONTEMPMIND IS PROGRAMMED TO FAVOR MARKET EFFICIENCY RATHER THAN SOCIAL JUSTICE.

Modern economic rationalists, market liberalists, and most corporate executives subscribe to the theory that free markets, unrestrained by government interference, automatically work to meet human needs, preserve individual liberty, assure the interests of future generations, and produce the most efficient and socially optimal allocation of resources. Government intervention, conversely, assaults liberty, impedes innovation, and reduces efficiency. In the extreme, it is assumed that a capitalist economy is a self-sufficient social system.

Free markets may be efficient tools for resource allocation, but they are limited in their capacities for sensing justice because of the aggregated nature of welfare measurements and the difficulty of pricing equity. Similarly, unregulated markets possess no mechanisms for assessing sustainable aggregate scale (physical volume of energy and matter throughput flowing from and back into the environment) (see Daly and Cobb, 1994). To the extent that economic markets are freed from constraints of justice, scale, government regulation, or a vigilant civil society to protect the public interest, and absent a minimum of responsibility, foresight, and deferral of gratification (see Friedman, 1962), unfettered markets may in actuality lead to advancement of individualistic goals at the expense of social goals; externalization of costs onto the powerless and future generations; promotion of unsustainable consumption; and concentration of wealth at the expense of income equality (see Korten, 1995 for a review of these alleged effects of free-market economics).

The burgeoning trend toward globalization is a major manifestation of market efficiency supported by the principle of comparative advantage. Conventional wisdom contends that "economic globalization . . . spurs competition, increases economic efficiency, creates jobs, lowers consumer prices, increases consumer choice, increases economic growth, and is generally beneficial to almost everyone" (Korten, 1995, p. 70). Additionally, arguments can be made that large, global firms are more visible to the public eye and, accordingly, are subject to a greater public reaction when they commit acts against nature (see Hamilton, 1995). Though the benefits of globalization just listed are recognized, from the viewpoint of sustainability, a chorus of critics increasingly claims that globalization poses threats to economic security, ecological and sociological integrity, and democracy (see Barnet and Cavanagh, 1994; Daly and Cobb, 1994; Hawken, 1993; Kennedy, 1993; Korten, 1995; Lang and Hines, 1993). It is seen, for example, as distancing consumers from the negative impacts of their consumption, reducing the accountability of firms to workers and communities, and shifting power away from democratic institutions into the hands of the corporate elite.

The logic of market efficiency alone is most unlikely to deliver sustainability. A sustainable society does not abandon markets but places their allocative efficiency roles within a framework of public accountability and social justice. A sustainable society also does not abandon globalization. Rather, it calls for a balance between local control of capital, awakened civil society, and local self-reliance, on one hand, with external trade that consists of balanced and mutually beneficial exchanges of goods and services whose prices reflect the social and ecological truth, on the other.

HYPOTHESIS 12: THE CONTEMPMIND IS PROGRAMMED TO FAVOR QUANTITATIVE GROWTH RATHER THAN QUALITATIVE DEVELOPMENT.

Conventional wisdom holds that perpetual economic growth is possible, normal, and essential. There are no limits to material expansion, as human-made capital can be infinitely substituted for natural resources. Therefore, sustained economic growth, as measured by gross domestic product or gross national product, is the answer to all social problems, and it will provide the financial resources needed for environmental protection. While this notion is expounded by many economists, politicians, and business school professors, mounting evidence indicates that growth has not improved the collective quality of life but has instead perpetuated poverty, deepened economic and social disparities, exhausted a one-time inheritance of natural capital, reduced the welfare of future generations, legitimized the concentration of power, and redistributed wealth from the human majority to a privileged minority (Daly and Cobb, 1994; Korten, 1995).

Northern elites' pursuit of growth has led to a preoccupation with consumption, material comfort, bodily well-being, luxury, and spending and acquisition to fill the "empty self" (Cushman, 1990). According to *Business Week,* the average American is exposed to about 3,000 commercial advertisements each day (cited in Kanner and Gomes, 1995, p. 23). If one conservatively estimates one second of cognitive embrace per ad, this subjection amounts to fifty minutes of mental programming per day equating happiness with consumption. Only a hermit could conceivably escape this commercialization and commoditization of reality; virtually all of modern American experience now has a commercial sponsor.

Proponents of sustainable development assert that the human economy is a subsystem of a finite, nongrowing, and materially closed ecosystem and thus cannot grow forever. Sustainability calls for qualitative improvement rather than quantitative expansion. It means scaling back, spending less, and saving more. It requires a cultivation of the deeper, nonmaterial sources of fulfillment that are the main psychological sources of true happiness, such as family and social relations, leisure, and meaningful work. Those who live a materially simpler life report higher life satisfaction and greater concern for ecological well-being and social justice (see Elgin, 1993).

HYPOTHESIS 13: THE CONTEMPMIND IS PROGRAMMED TO FAVOR SECULARISM RATHER THAN SPIRITUALISM.

The gradual decline or decay of religion among America's elites has been charted as creating "a skeptical, iconoclastic state of mind" (Lasch,

1995, p. 215) or secular culture of critical discourse (Gouldner, 1979). Philip Rieff (1990) contends that the former religious worldview has been replaced by a therapeutic one that is intellectually and morally bankrupt. This postmodern critical sensibility excommunicates the world of the spirit, absolutizes earthly man, instrumentally rationalizes all of life, and clings to the belief that fates can be mastered through science. Such secularization is believed to have led to moral anarchy, moral relativism, and cultural nihilism. With the dimming of spiritual life, society has become demoralized and self-restraint has evaporated. Many see the crisis of global unsustainability as fundamentally a moral problem because it requires an attitude shift away from morally corrosive values, and also a religious problem in that it demands a reawakening to arouse compassion and inspire motivation. Sustainable development therefore necessitates a confluence of scientific awareness with life- and world-affirming moral and religious values (Rockefeller, 1992).

Calls for a spiritual or moral reformation in support of sustainability take diverse forms, both within and outside of the institutional religions, yet share a common ethical core embracing self-restraint and sacred connectedness with the natural order. Christian philosopher Albert Schweitzer, for example, defined a moral person as one who "accepts as being good: to preserve life, to promote life, to raise to its highest values life which is capable of development; and as being evil: to destroy life, to injure life, to repress life which is capable of development. This is the absolute fundamental principle of the moral. A man is ethical only when life, as such, is sacred to him" (1933, pp. 158–160). Similarly, nature philosopher Aldo Leopold set forth that "all ethics so far evolved rest upon a single premise: that the individual is a member of a community of interdependent parts . . . [and that] a thing is right when it tends to preserve the integrity, stability and beauty of the biotic community. It is wrong when it tends otherwise" (1949, pp. 237–239).

HYPOTHESIS 14: THE CONTEMPMIND IS PROGRAMMED TO FAVOR NARCISSISM RATHER THAN ALTRUISM.

Materialism and secularism are closely connected with the emergence of a "culture of narcissism" (Lasch, 1978) among northern elites. The narcissism syndrome is characterized by an inflated, grandiose, entitled, and masterful self-image, or "false self," that masks deep-seated but unacknowledged feelings of worthlessness and emptiness (Cushman, 1990). It is marked by profound egoism, hyperindividualism, self-assertion, and private ethics of psychotherapeutic growth and self-actualization. All of the major forces in modern psychology—the psychoanalytic, the behavioral, and the humanistic—appear to have supported this basic self-centeredness (Smith, 1990). The resulting selfishness and personal isolation are biased against altruistic feelings and action, and engender a lost sense of community and civic obligation (see Bellah and others, 1985). Rights have thus become more important than responsibilities, and civic engagement and social capital have experienced a precipitous decline (see Putnam, 1996). Sustainability seeks to reverse this trend for the sake of the common good.

Along with personal narcissism, America's professional and managerial elites are seen to be collectively disengaging from the common life. The growing secession of the elites manifests profound shifts in U.S. society: from the ideal of a classless society to a two-class society, from a pluralistic democracy to an oligarchy of professionals, from republicanism back to a form of feudalism (see Lasch, 1995; Lind, 1995). Elite disengagement is viewed as dangerous, for as the rich secure the private services that the public at large cannot afford, they then refuse to make sacrifices for the declining public services they no longer need, setting in motion a self-fulfilling vicious cycle of deprivation and insecurity for the working and underclasses. Sustainability, conversely, requires a sense of place, a rich civic life accessible to all, an ethic of civil responsibility, and genuine participation in economic and political decisions.

HYPOTHESIS 15: THE CONTEMPMIND IS PROGRAMMED TO FAVOR TECHNO-OPTIMISM RATHER THAN TECHNO-SKEPTICISM.

Paul Hawken has concluded that "in America we have been surfeited with cornucopian fantasies of technological prowess wherein human ingenuity bypasses natural limits and creates unimagined abundance. Optimism easily intertwines with the belief that nanotechnology, biotechnology, computers, and technologies yet to be developed will eliminate hunger, disease, and want" (in Prugh, 1995, p. xi). The techno-entrancement of northern elites holds that the planet can be managed and mastered through human knowledge, skills, and tools. Proponents of sustainability, however, remind us that today's problems are mainly the result of yesterday's technological solutions, that natural and manufactured capital are generally complements rather than substitutes, and that technologies are never neutral and sometimes hurtful. Social critics go even further, claiming that a technology-dominated society suffers more than it gains in terms of human survival and satisfaction (see Mander, 1991; Sale, 1995).

Sustainability does not abandon technology but urges prudence and greater reliance on organic, small, community-based, peaceful, renewable, and democratically controlled technological development and application.

Special emphasis is placed on technologies that increase resource productivity rather than rates of material throughput. Unbridled technology does not offer all the answers to a sustainable planet. As the conservative U.S. National Academy of Sciences and the Royal Society of London have warned: "If current predictions of population growth prove accurate and patterns of human activity on the planet remain unchanged, science and technology may not be able to prevent either irreversible degradation of the environment or continued poverty for much of the world" (1992, p. 1).

Mental Programming Summary

In summary, minds that are socially, politically, and commercially programmed to believe in and pursue the dictates of market efficiency, quantitative growth and consumption, relativistic secularism, exaggerated narcissism, and technological mastery are unlikely, we submit, to be sustainable. Most of these assumptions or myths of modern living are in conflict with real social and economic needs, with fairness and justice, with moral and spiritual wisdom, and with common sense. They separate the head from the heart and do nothing for the passionate side of life. The circumstances under which they arose have disappeared, causing them to become increasingly implausible and risky. As with the older assumptions of the mechanistic worldview, these contemporary appendages appear to fail all the conservative litmus tests of contributing positively to sustainable development.

The danger of these contemporary assumptions is that our minds may have become so thoroughly controlled by "imagesmiths, propagandists, mythmakers, gossips, and newsmen" that we have lost the capacity to "question the authorities, to be critical of our institutions, to talk back to advertisers and propagandists, and to say no to the seductions of the image merchants" (Keen, 1995, p. 29). The resultant silence within ourselves fosters ever-expanding efforts at mind control.

Unconscious Deployment of Ego-Defense Mechanisms

If the biases engendered by the biological, worldview, and contemporary minds have not served to completely deflect all attention from, or eliminate all worries about, threats of ecological and social unsustainability, then a variety of defense mechanisms may come into use to handle any residual anxiety. Anxiety, according to David H. Barlow, can be characterized as a "diffuse cognitive-affective structure" whose "essence is arousal-driven apprehension" (1988, p. 235). Freudian and other psychodynamic theories suggest that dangers in the external world leading to realistic anxiety, along with dangers to conscience resulting in moral anxiety, produce intrapsychic conflict—conflicting motives, drives, impulses, and feelings held within various components of the mind. A group of mental processes, called ego-defense mechanisms, operate outside of and beyond our immediate awareness and supposedly enable the mind to reach compromise solutions to conflicts that it is unable to resolve (see Laughlin, 1979). These relatively involuntary and unconscious defenses ward off unacceptable or intolerant mental content and thereby reduce the psychic and physiological wear and tear of stress. Dozens of ego-defense mechanisms have been hypothesized and vary according to the character of the threat with which they deal, the cognitive complexity they embody, and the extent of reality distortion they induce. They rarely function independently, typically acting in concert and reinforcing one another.

We acknowledge that academic psychology retains a mistrust of the unconscious in general and of defense mechanisms in particular. In the midst of a currently fashionable and savage wave of Freud-bashing, an intellectual war is being fought "over our culture's image of the human soul. Are we to see humans as having depth—as complex psychological organisms who generate layers of meaning which lie beneath the surface of human understanding? Or are we to take ourselves as transparent to ourselves" (Lear, 1995, p. 24)? We are unable here to settle the debate over the very existence of unconscious meanings and motivation. We instead simply defer to one of America's preeminent psychiatrists, George E. Vaillant of Harvard, who claims that "the study of the ego's mechanisms of defense is a fit subject for serious social scientists" (1993, p. 14), for research suggests that they can be reliably identified, have predictive validity, and operate independently of social class or environment. Even if all cognitive regulatory mechanisms come to be fully explained by biological or neurological psychiatry in the future, unscientific psychodynamic analysis of how humans distort inner and outer reality still constitutes a useful interpretive system (Rycroft, 1995).

Defense mechanisms probably originated "to enhance social cooperation, to enable us to avoid unmanageable pain, and simply to help us sift through the barrage of stimuli bombarding our senses. Ultimately, they probably came about to keep our attention free from the terrifying fact that we are frail and vulnerable beings and that—somehow, someday—each of us will die" (Glendinning, 1990, p. 121). By easing the pain of mental anguish, and therefore contributing to emotional well-being, it is likely that "the muting of awareness to avoid anxiety has been largely helpful, even necessary, in the development of our species and of civilization" (Goleman, 1985, p. 245). The ingenious self-deceptions provided by the "wisdom of the ego" are thus generally healthy and adaptive (Vaillant, 1993). We suggest, however, that exaggerated and persistent dependence on ego-defense mechanisms to avoid ecological and social anxiety is bound to lead to maladaptive means of dealing with the world. This reliance is likely to be especially counterproductive if it creates gaping holes in our attention, pushes the challenge of unsustainability completely out of our conscious awareness, and forever insulates us from the "vital lies" at the heart of our global problematique. Five hypotheses linking psychodynamic (hence our use of the term *psychomind*) defense mechanisms to unsustainable thinking are offered for consideration here.

HYPOTHESIS 16: THE PSYCHOMIND PROTECTS THE SELF FROM ANXIETY VIA REPRESSION RATHER THAN REMEMBRANCE.

The "pivotal psychological reality" of unsustainability is that "until the late twentieth century, every generation throughout history lived with the tacit certainty that there would be generations to follow. That certainty is now lost to us" (Macy, 1995, p. 241). Confronted with "apprehensions of collective suffering" and "so vast and final a loss," we tend to repress our terror, rage, guilt, sorrow, and "pain for the world" (Macy, 1995, p. 242). Repression, as perhaps the most significant, distorting, and precursory of all defense mechanisms, involves "the automatic, effortless, and involuntary assignment or relegation of consciously repugnant or intolerable ideas, impulses, and feelings to the unconscious" (Laughlin, 1979, p. 359). Primary repression serves to curb painful ideas or feelings before they have attained consciousness, while secondary repression works to exclude from awareness what was once experienced at a conscious level: "One forgets, and then forgets one has forgotten" (Goleman, 1985, p. 119). Repression serves to hide information regarding potential threats to our livelihoods and the ways we view the world. With diminished attention or blank minds, we fall victim to forces of sociological and political propaganda. And because what is repressed from conscious memory is not deactivated, but remains unconsciously active, emotionally charged, and potent, it tends to manifest itself in disguised symbolic form as generalized anxiety disorders.

HYPOTHESIS 17: THE PSYCHOMIND PROTECTS THE SELF FROM ANXIETY VIA DENIAL RATHER THAN AVOWAL.

Whereas repression serves to keep certain unpleasant meanings away from conscious awareness, denial works to ignore or "literally obliterate" external reality (Vaillant, 1993, p. 43). The basic formula is that "there is no pain, no anticipation of pain, no danger, no conflict" (Haan, 1974, p. 152). Troubling facts and feelings are blanked from awareness via avoided associations, numbness, flattened responses, dimming of attention, daze, constricted thought, memory failure, disavowal, and blocking through fantasy. In the form of dissociation, painful ideas and affects are replaced with pleasant ones; as distortion, external reality is transformed to conform to our wishes. Denial, as "the psychological analogue of the endorphin attentional tune-out" (Goleman, 1985, p. 43), serves to diminish reality testing, to foment hostility toward messengers who suggest the need for change, and to block us from honestly confronting (that is, feeling, thinking, absorbing, owning) the real pain of the world. We instead fall prey to, even thrive on, purveyors of environmental optimism and business as usual (see Bailey, 1993; Easterbrook, 1995).

HYPOTHESIS 18: THE PSYCHOMIND PROTECTS THE SELF FROM ANXIETY VIA PROJECTION RATHER THAN INTERNALIZATION.

A common response to evidence of ecological or social harm is to deny any role in producing it and to subconsciously externalize our unacceptable, anxiety-provoking feelings onto the shoulders of others. Such projection represents "a process by which an objectionable, internal tendency is unrealistically attributed to another person or persons in the environment instead of being recognized as a part of one's self" (Haan, 1974, p. 152). Feelings are distanced, relationships distorted, reality exaggerated, and responsibility for facets of our own self-image (our "shadows," in Jungian terms) imputed to others, thus creating images of external threats or enemies. Projectional tendencies during times of psychic angst produce the "snake oil of scapegoating," with the poor, minorities, or recent immigrants, for example, being blamed for problems of unemployment and social breakdown. People become vulnerable to sloganeering, hate mongering, conspiracy theories, nativism, racism, xenophobia, demagogic politicians, and radio talk-show hosts. When projection is employed for psychic avoidance and enemy creation, "truth is the first sacrifice" (Keen, 1986, p. 19).

HYPOTHESIS 19: THE PSYCHOMIND PROTECTS THE SELF FROM ANXIETY VIA RATIONALIZATION RATHER THAN ACCURATENESS.

When confronted with unacceptable impulses, needs, feelings, behaviors, and motives, people also often resort to rationalization, defined as offering "apparently plausible causal context to explain behavior and/or intention, which allows impulse sub rosa gratification to escape attention, but omits crucial aspects of situation, or is otherwise inexact" (Haan, 1974, p. 150). With rationalization, true, unworthy, and unconscious motives remain hidden, while reasonable, safe, and creditable (yet counterfeit) explanations are employed to account for one's practices or beliefs. It allows one to hide the truth, to evade personal responsibility, and to adopt a false "assurance about the safety and morality of one's actions" (Glendinning, 1990, p. 131).

Closely allied with rationalization, the defense mechanism of intellectualization entails the excessive use of "pseudo-intellectuality" to avoid affective expressions or experiences and thus defends against anxiety attributable to unacceptable emotional conflicts or complexes. Problems are analyzed in remote and jargon-filled terms, while affective or practical considerations are effectively neglected or excluded. Stress is often placed on irrelevant details and pedantic precision at the expense of perceiving the whole. Problems of global warming or biodiversity loss dealt with in this manner thus lose their emotional significance, their sensationalism, and their capacity to induce human problem-solving responses. In the form of extreme isolation or total affect divorcement, humans become morally sterile technocrats lacking aesthetic or spiritual sensitivity, capacities for caring or compassion, and a sense of wonder for the created world (see Orr, 1994).

HYPOTHESIS 20: THE PSYCHOMIND PROTECTS THE SELF FROM ANXIETY VIA INSULATION RATHER THAN SENSITIZATION.

The net result of using many of the defense mechanisms reviewed above is a dulled human response to the world—that is, reduced ego involvement via protective insulation, withdrawal, apathy, and passivity. Psychic retreat from external reality can take many forms: dimming of awareness via selective perceptual attention; disengagement from contacts, relationships, social situations, and painful conflicts; learned helplessness produced by exposure to noxious, unpleasant, inescapable situations that result in apathy and constricted affect; personal disconnection, by which we admit there are problems but come to believe that they will not happen to us; psychic erasure, often motivated by guilt, which abolishes or annuls the painful thoughts or acts; and regression or ego retreat toward more protected, dependent, or simpler mental or behavioral levels. The combined impact of emotional insulation is *psychic numbing*, a term coined by Robert Lifton (1981) in his noted study of Hiroshima survivors. People seem to anesthetize themselves, becoming unable "to let themselves feel the fear, anger, and rebelliousness that fully grasping the human predicament . . . might bring them; [they] avoid acquiring information that would make vague fears specific enough to require decisive action . . . and contrive to ignore the implications of the information they allow to get through" (Goleman, quoting Lester Grinspoon, 1985, p. 19).

Psychomind Summary

In summary, to the extent that we attempt to cope with the anxieties of ecological and social unsustainability by means of repressing, denying, projecting, rationalizing, and insulating defense mechanisms, we run great risks of failing to see things as they are. Exaggerated or excessive use of ego and perceptual defense mechanisms distorts reality, provides false senses of security, blocks personal growth, fosters faulty learning, inhibits action, depletes adaptive resources, and leads to irrational behavior.

Reliance on ego-defense mechanisms is addictive; favored defenses become habitual mental routines and, over time, humans tend to acquire thick "character armor" and "neurotic styles" to ward off anxieties. Moreover, individual reliance on self-deception becomes magnified in group situations, compounding through interaction into diversionary schemes such as illusions of invulnerability and unanimity, suppressed personal doubts, mindguards, rationalizations, ethical blinders, and stereotypes (see Goleman, 1985; Janis, 1982). The divorce of thinking from feeling, along with the mixing of self-deception and free will engendered by the defense mechanisms, allows humans to do evil while believing they are doing good.

Though the defensive urge to avoid anxiety through self-deceptions and shared illusions is an ancient malady, the modern challenges of securing curative insight, of surfacing dark meanings and irrational motivations, of achieving comprehension undistorted by deceptions, and of mobilizing psychic resources to deal with the actual sources rather than the symptoms of anxiety, loom larger than ever. With entire societies growing resentful, alienated, cynical, insecure, anxious, and gloomy about prosperity (see Dionne, 1991), rising angst is probably increasing human resort to defense mechanisms that are ever more distortive of reality. The palliatives may appear in the short run to promote comfort and survival, "but in the long run they work against them, actually bringing us closer to death" (Glendinning, 1990, p. 132). But how much honest or blatant confrontation with painful reality can humans endure while remaining sane? As Henrik Ibsen once noted: "Deprive the average man of his vital lie, and you've robbed him of happiness as well" (in Goleman, 1985, p. 246). Most importantly, how do we confront and change what we cannot see?

Toward Sustainable Minds: The Journey Ahead

Figure 11.3 sets forth our utopian vision of the sustainable mind of the future: a biological mind capable of systems thinking in all its regards; a worldview mind that honors the entire web of life and makes humans stewards of its continuity; a contemporary mind providing a genuine sense of personal meaning, purpose in living, and community; and a psychodynamic mind willing to accept more of reality and to reduce the real sources of anxiety rather than fleeing from them.

We have been quite somber regarding the possibilities of change, particularly in regard to speeding up the evolution of the biological brain and in confronting the things that we do not see. Based upon some "biology of hope" (Tiger, 1979), however, we are in agreement with Herman E. Daly and John B. Cobb that "human beings still have the possibility of choosing a livable future for themselves and their descendants. Humanity is not simply trapped in a dark fate. People can be *attracted* by new ways of ordering their lives, as well as *driven* by the recognition of what will happen if they do not change. . . . Nevertheless, the obstacles are enormous. Century-old habits of mind do not give way readily, especially when they are established in all the places of prestige and high leverage" (1994, pp. 362–363).

Moving toward a psychology of sustainable thinking represents a long and difficult, yet exciting and rewarding, journey of intellectual discovery. The ultimate destination of a life-sustaining earth and the requisite human behavior is uncertain, shrouded in a deep fog of abstractions. One must be willing to collaborate with a diverse crew of fellow travelers—biologists, economists, chemists, poets, philosophers, and so on—who talk and think in ways very foreign to the disciplines of psychology and organizational behavior. Scholars will be forced to mix descriptive and normative content; to contend with irreducible uncertainties, massive complexities, and perpetual surprise; to practice second-order or postnormal science; to accept that their work will be subversive to mainstream theories; and to acknowledge that the transition from a paradigm in crisis to a new progressive one will rely on "a reconstruction of the field from new fundamentals" (Kuhn, 1970, p. 85). The journey is scheduled to last a lifetime and may be fraught with considerable personal danger, ranging from dizziness over the profundity of life, to mental anguish from constant exposure to cries of suffering, to publication rejections or denials of promotion decided by powerful colleagues who refuse to accept or make the same mental journey. While risky, it represents a tremendous opportunity for enrichment, inner renewal, and achievement of genuine meaning.

Figure 11.3. Moving Toward Sustainable Thinking.

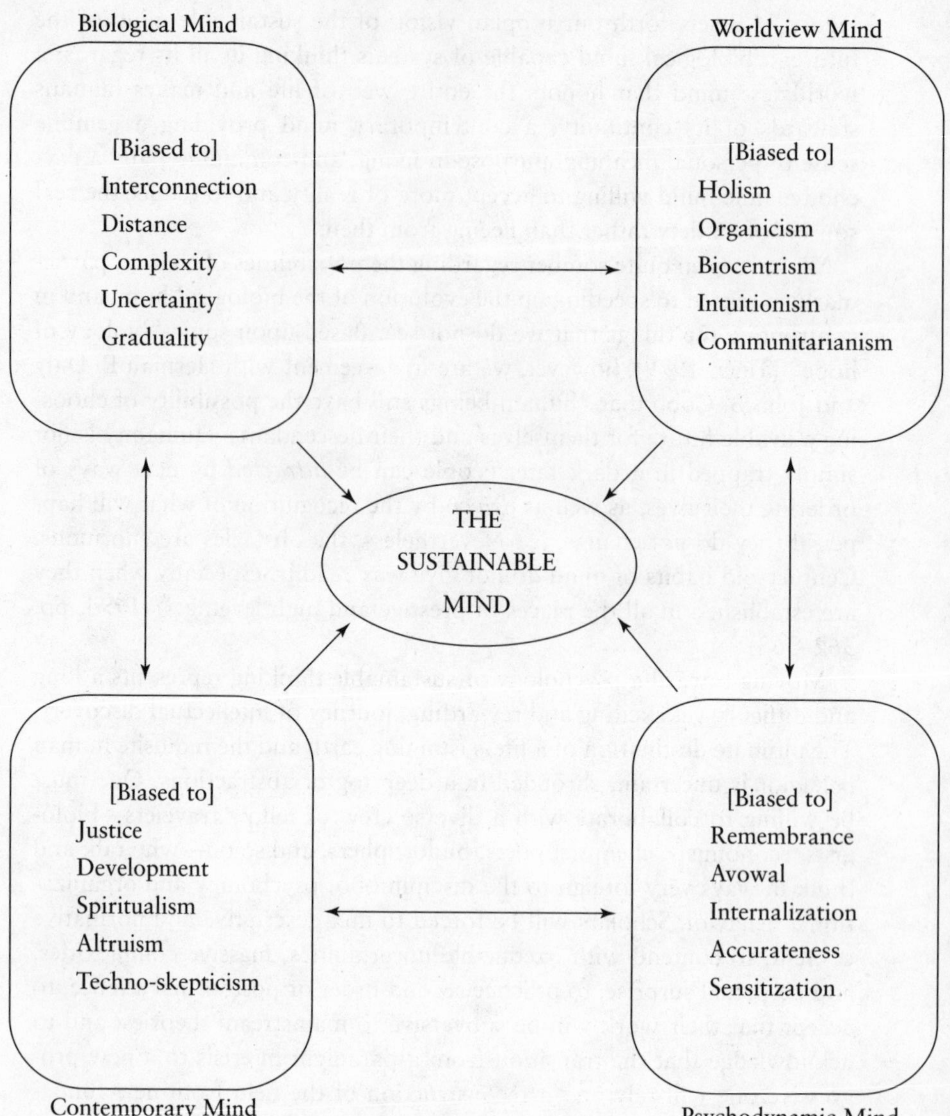

What could be nobler than helping to nourish and perpetuate "the historical fulfillment of the whole community of life on Earth" (Engel, 1990, pp. 10–11)?

According to the World Bank, "the achievement of sustained and equitable development remains the greatest challenge facing the human race" (1992, p. 1). Yet liberating ourselves from the myriad sources of unsustainable thinking—which serve to separate the human from nature, the individual from extended community, and truth from morality—will be extraordinarily difficult and painful, requiring an enormous effort in all segments of society.

The Sustainable Mind Research Agenda

If psychologists and management scientists are "to help make the Earth a secure and hospitable home for present and future generations" (The Earth Pledge of the June 1992 United Nations Conference on Environment and Development), they must discover answers to many questions, as follow.

What Are the Most Important Determinants of Unsustainable and Sustainable Thinking?

How much can we attribute to the biological and cognitive versus the social and cultural? What relative weight should be given to (1) incapacities for complex systems thinking; (2) false worlds of inherited representation that cut us off from the full web of life; (3) cultural myths propagated by contemporary prophets of illusion; and (4) psychic numbing or dormitive framing engendered by ego-defense mechanisms? Are psychologists willing to overcome their traditional theoretical egocentricity, patriarchal assumptions, biospheric denial, and skepticism of psychodynamic concepts so as to explore the full gamut of possible causation?

Is Sustainable Thought a Multidimensional Rather than a Unidimensional Construct?

Are different components (that is, cognitively related processes versus socially fostered and constituted ones) influenced by different determinants? Do they vary in intensity at any given point in time or change at different rates over time? How should we mix quantitative distinctions (for example, higher or lower systems thinking capacity) with qualitative ones (for example, better or worse assumptions about how the natural world functions)? How do we mix the objective with the subjective? Can we arrive at an understanding of sustainable thinking via traditional, hypothetico-deductive, experimental methodology, or does the topic require new methods of understanding or phenomenology?

How Do the Biomind, Viewmind, Contempmind, and Psychomind Interact?

How do the cognitive heuristics and psychodynamic regulatory mechanisms interact? How do historically inherited and contemporaneously constructed presuppositions or premises of thought interact? How do cognitive operations shape social construction, and vice versa? Are the biases of the different minds causally connected—for example, biological predilections toward simplicity and disconnection favoring atomistic and mechanistic worldviews? What are the metapatterns that connect all the minds?

How Do Unsustainable and Sustainable Cognition Interact with Concomitant Emotion and Behavior?

How does thinking sustainably relate to feeling sustainably and behaving sustainably? Are these cognitive, affective, and behavioral components of a complete notion of human sustainability likely to vary in amount or intensity, follow different time courses, lead or lag each other, and thus combine to produce many varieties of the phenomenon? Can we think and feel our way into sustainable behavior, or will we need to act our way into sustainable cognition and emotion? How can sustainable cognition, emotion, and behavior be measured?

How Universal Versus Contextual Are Sustainable Cognition and Behavior?

What role might national culture play? For example, are variations in the use of time and space, relative levels of collectivism, uncertainty avoidance, power distance, masculinity, and so on relevant? Why is sustainable thinking apparently quite advanced in nations such as The Netherlands, Germany, Denmark, and Sweden? Why do innovations in sustainable living in the U.S. tend to emerge first on the West Coast? How does sustainable psychology vary according to level of industrialization, type of political system, rates of social and physical mobility, settlement densities, levels of urbanization, and exposure to advertising?

What Explains Individual Level Variation in Sustainable Thinking, Feeling, and Behavior?

Are females likely to be more sustainable in their psychology than males? Similarly, are generalists more likely than specialists to think sustainably? How are different types of intelligence and levels of scientific literacy related to the construct? What role might variations in personality traits play—for example, perseverance, risk taking, tolerance of ambiguity, locus of control, openness to experience, and so on? Are those who spend most of their time in built or urban environments likely to be less sustainable than those who spend more of their time in closer and broader contact with nonhuman nature? Are right-brained thinkers likely to be more sustainable than those who are left-brained?

Can the Implied Components of Sustainable Thinking Be Developed in Current and Future Human Beings?

How does one speed up the conscious evolution of postconventional morality, emotional intelligence, future time perspective, worldcentric consciousness, prosocial orientation, dialogical and dialectical reasoning, relational total-field imaging, integral-aperspectival processing, and so on? At what stage of life are the various components of sustainable thinking acquired, and what are the potential side effects of acquiring such cognitive capacity? What roles can parents, schools, television, cyberspace, and religious institutions play in shaping deeper awareness, wider vision, and higher embrace?

What Therapies Are Indicated for Unsustainable Patterns of Thinking?

Do healing of the self and healing of the planet go together? Can we devise and propagate a beneficial social virus to induce sustainable psychology? Are advances in relevant psychopharmacology and neuropsychiatry on the horizon? Who shall be our doctor? How does one put an entire popular culture onto a therapeutic couch? Does everyone first have to suffer with our world and work through environmental despair? What experiential, imaginal, consciousness-altering and -opening experiences make sense for reconnecting humans with the earth? Should advertising be restricted or banned? Can we and are we willing to take conscious command of our mental evolution?

Given the Urgency of Needed Transformation, How Fast Can Human Minds and Behaviors Be Effectively Changed?

Are we truly willing to know more, see more, and feel more? Is human inventiveness now overwhelming human adaptiveness? How do we overcome the incredible apathy and lack of attention by academics to ecological and social unsustainability? Given that there has not been much moral or spiritual progress over the last few millennia, what could bring it about in a hurry? Is a deep crisis needed to induce massive second-order learning? Should we give up on adults and place our emphasis on developing a new generation of worldcentric systems-thinking children? Is the time to get the world on a sustainable path rapidly running out?

Does the Ultimate Resolution of Unsustainability via Unification of Mind and Nature Depend on a Transcendence into the Transpersonal or Spiritual Realm?

Does sustainability require the integration of Plato's the true, the good, and the beautiful, or Kant's pure reason, practical reason, and aesthetic judgment? Can we get to a sustainable psychology without a communion of the self with some higher spiritual being or force? Do we need to reconnect spirit and nature, so as to endow nonhuman nature with inherent sacred significance? Is mainstream Western psychology willing to pursue these realms of spiritual renewal, faith with life, normative rightness, subjective truthfulness, and higher states of consciousness? Do we all need a new going within ourselves in order to then go beyond?

> I call heaven and earth to witness against you this day: I have put before you life and death, blessing and curse. Therefore choose life, if you and your offspring would live [Deuteronomy 30:19].

REFERENCES

Argyris, C. *Strategy, Change, and Defensive Routines.* Boston: Pitman, 1985.

Argyris, C., and Schön, D. *Organizational Learning: A Theory of Action Approach.* Reading, Mass.: Addison-Wesley, 1978.

Axelrod, R. *The Structure of Decision: The Cognitive Maps of Political Elites.* Princeton, N.J.: Princeton University Press, 1976.

Bailey, R. *Eco-Scam: The False Prophets of Ecological Apocalypse.* New York: St. Martin's Press, 1993.

Barlow, D. H. *Anxiety and its Disorders: The Natural Treatment of Anxiety and Panic.* New York: Guilford Press, 1988.

Barnet, R. J., and Cavanagh, J. *Global Dreams: Imperial Corporations and the New World Order.* New York: Simon & Schuster, 1994.

Bateson, G. *Mind and Nature: A Necessary Unity.* New York: Dutton, 1979.

Bellah, R. N., and others. *Habits of the Heart.* Berkeley: University of California Press, 1985.

Berry, T. *The Dream of the Earth.* San Francisco: Sierra Club Books, 1988.

Berry, W. "Decolonizing Rural America." *Audubon,* 1993, *95*(2), 100–105.

Brehmer, B. "In One Word: Not from Experience." *Acta Psychologica,* 1980, *45,* 223–241.

Brehmer, B. "Dynamic Decision Making: Human Control of Complex Systems." *Acta Psychologica,* 1992, *81,* 211–241.

Brown, L. R., Lenssen, N., and Kane, H. *Vital Signs 1995: The Trends That Are Shaping Our Future.* New York: Norton, 1995.

Buss, D. M., and Craik, K. H. "Contemporary Worldviews: Personal and Policy Implications." *Journal of Applied Social Psychology,* 1983, *13,* 280–295.

Capra, F. *The Turning Point: Science, Society and the Rising Culture.* New York: Bantam Books, 1982.

Catton, W. R., and Dunlap, R. E. "A New Ecological Paradigm for Post-Exuberant Sociology." *American Behavioral Scientist,* 1980, *20*(1), 15–47.

Costanza, R., Wainger, L., Folke, C., and Mäler, K. G. "Modeling Complex Ecological-Economic Systems." *Bioscience,* 1993, *43*(8), 545–555.

Cross, J. G., and Guyer, M. J. *Social Traps.* Ann Arbor: University of Michigan Press, 1980.

Cushman, P. "Why the Self Is Empty: Toward a Historically Situated Psychology." *American Psychologist,* 1990, *45,* 599–611.

Daily, G. C., and Ehrlich, P. R. "Population, Sustainability, and Earth's Carrying Capacity." *Bioscience,* 1992, *42,* 761–771.

Daly, H. E. "Toward Some Operational Principles of Sustainable Development." *Ecological Economics,* 1990, *2*(1), 1–6.

Daly, H. E. "Operationalizing Sustainable Development by Investing in Natural Capital." In A. Jansson, M. Hammer, C. Folke, and R. Costanza (eds.), *Investing in Natural Capital: The Ecological Economics Approach to Sustainability.* Washington, D.C.: Island Press, 1994.

Daly, H. E., and Cobb, J. B. *For the Common Good: Redirecting the Economy Toward Community, the Environment, and a Sustainable Future.* Boston: Beacon Press, 1994.

Dasgupta, P. S. "Population, Poverty and the Local Environment." *Scientific American,* 1995, *272*(2), 40–45.

Davis, H., and Hogarth, R. *Rethinking Management Education: A View from Chicago.* Selected Paper 72. Chicago: Graduate School of Business, University of Chicago, 1992.

Devall, B., and Sessions, G. *Deep Ecology: Living as If Nature Mattered.* Salt Lake City: Gibbs Smith, 1985.

Dionne, E. J., Jr. *Why Americans Hate Politics.* New York: Simon & Schuster, 1991.

Dörner, D. "On the Difficulties People Have in Dealing with Complexity." *Simulations and Games,* 1980, *11*(1), 87–106.

Dovers, S. R., and Handmer, J. W. "Ignorance, the Precautionary Principle, and Sustainability." *Ambio,* 1995, *24*(2), 92–97.

Durning, A. T. *How Much Is Enough?* London: Earthscan Publications, 1992.

Easterbrook, G. *A Moment on the Earth: The Coming Age of Environmental Optimism.* New York: Viking Penguin, 1995.

Eckersley, R. *Environmentalism and Political Theory: Toward an Ecocentric Approach.* London: UCL Press, 1992.

Ehrlich, P. "Ecological Economics and the Carrying Capacity of Earth." In A. Jansson, M. Hammer, C. Folke, and R. Costanza (eds.), *Investing in Natural Capital: The Ecological Economics Approach to Sustainability.* Washington, D.C.: Island Press, 1994.

Einhorn, H., and Hogarth, R. "Confidence in Judgment: Persistence of the Illusion of Validity." *Psychological Review*, 1978, *85,* 395–476.

Einhorn, H., and Hogarth, R. "Judging Probable Cause." *Psychological Bulletin,* 1986, *99,* 3–19.

Elgin, D. *Voluntary Simplicity.* New York: Quill, 1993.

Engel, J. R. "Introduction: The Ethics of Sustainable Development." In J. R. Engel and J. G. Engel (eds.), *Ethics of Environment and Development: Global Challenge and International Response.* London: Belhaven Press, 1990.

Engel, J. R. "Liberal Democracy and the Fate of the Earth." In S. C. Rockefeller and J. C. Elder (eds.), *Spirit and Nature.* Boston: Beacon Press, 1992.

Forrester, J. W. "Counterintuitive Behavior of Social Systems." *Technology Review,* 1971, *73*(3), 52–68.

Fox, D. R. "Psychology, Ideology, Utopia, and the Commons." *American Psychologist,* 1985, *40,* 48–58.

Friedman, M. *Capitalism and Freedom.* Chicago: University of Chicago Press, 1962.

Funke, J. "Solving Complex Problems: Exploration and Control of Complex Systems." In R. Sternberg, and P. Frensch (eds.), *Complex Problem Solving: Principles and Mechanisms.* Hillsdale, N.J.: Erlbaum, 1991.

Funtowicz, S. O., and Ravetz, J. R. "Science for the Post-Normal Age." *Science,* 1993, *25*(7), 739–755.

Gladwin, T. N., and Kennelly, J. J. *Business, Nature and Society: Toward Sustainable Enterprise.* Burr Ridge, Ill.: Irwin, forthcoming.

Gladwin, T. N., Kennelly, J. J., and Krause, T. S. "Shifting Paradigms for Sustainable Development: Implications for Management Theory and Research." *Academy of Management Review,* 1995, *20*(4), 874–907.

Gladwin, T. N., Krause, T., and Kennelly, T. S. "Beyond Eco-Efficiency: Towards Socially Sustainable Business." *Sustainable Development,* 1995, *30*(1), 35–43.

Glendinning, C. *When Technology Wounds: The Human Consequence of Progress.* New York: Morrow, 1990.

Glendinning, C. "Technology, Trauma, and the Wild." In T. Roszak, M. E. Gomes, and A. D. Kanner (eds.), *Ecopsychology: Restoring the Earth, Healing the Mind.* San Francisco: Sierra Club Books, 1995.

Goleman, D. *Vital Lies, Simple Truths: The Psychology of Self Deception.* New York: Simon & Schuster, 1985.

Goodland, R. "The Case That the World Has Reached Limits." In R. Goodland, H. E. Daly, and S. E. Serafy (eds.), *Population, Technology and Lifestyle: The Transition to Sustainability.* Washington, D.C.: Island Press, 1992.

Gore, A. *Earth in Balance: Ecology and the Human Spirit.* Boston: Houghton Mifflin, 1992.

Gouldner, A. *The Future of Intellectuals and the Rise of the New Class.* New York: Seabury Press, 1979.

Graham, A. K., Morecroft, J. D., Senge, P. M., and Sterman, J. D. "Model Supported Case Studies for Management Education." *European Journal of Operational Research,* 1992, *59*(1), 151–166.

Haan, N. "The Implications of Family Ego Patterns for Adolescent Members." Unpublished doctoral dissertation, California School for Professional Psychology, 1974.

Habermas, J. *The Philosophical Discourse of Modernity.* (F. Lawrence, trans.) Cambridge, Mass.: MIT Press, 1990.

Hamilton, J. T. "Pollution as News: Media and Stock Market Reaction to the Toxic Release Inventory data." *Journal of Environmental Economics and Management,* 1995, *28*(1), 98–113.

Hardin, R. *Collective Action.* Baltimore: Johns Hopkins University Press, 1982.

Hargrove, E. C. *Foundations of Environmental Ethics.* Englewood Cliffs, N.J.: Prentice Hall, 1989.

Havel, V. "The Need for Transcendence in the Postmodern World." *The Futurist,* 1995, *30*(4), 46–49.

Hawken, P. *The Ecology of Commerce: A Declaration of Sustainability.* New York: HarperCollins, 1993.

Hillman, J. "A Psyche the Size of the Earth: A Psychological Foreword." In T. Roszak, M. E. Gomes, and A. D. Kanner (eds.), *Ecopsychology: Restoring the Earth, Healing the Mind.* San Francisco: Sierra Club Books, 1995.

Hogarth, R. *Judgment and Choice.* (2nd ed.) New York: Wiley, 1987.

Holling, C. S. "New Science and New Investments for a Sustainable Biosphere." In A. Jansson, M. Hammer, C. Folke, and R. Costanza (eds.), *Investing in Natural Capital: The Ecological Economics Approach to Sustainability.* Washington, D.C.: Island Press, 1994.

Homer-Dixon, T. F., Boutwell, J. H., and Rathjens, G. W. "Environmental Change and Violent Conflict." *Scientific American,* 1993, *268,* 16–23.

Janis, I. L. *Groupthink: Psychological Studies of Policy Decisions and Fiascoes.* (2nd ed.) Boston: Houghton Mifflin, 1982.

Jansson, A., Hammer, M., Folke, C., and Costanza, R. (eds.). *Investing in Natural Capital: The Ecological Economics Approach to Sustainability.* Washington, D.C.: Island Press, 1994.

Kahneman, D., Slovic, P., and Tversky, A. *Judgment Under Uncertainty: Heuristics and Biases.* New York: Cambridge University Press, 1982.

Kanner, A. D., and Gomes, M. E. "The All-Consuming Self." *Adbusters,* Summer 1995, pp. 20–28.

Kaplan, R. D. "The Coming Anarchy." *The Atlantic Monthly,* 1994, *273*(2), 43–76.

Keen, S. *Faces of the Enemy: Reflections of the Hostile Imagination.* San Francisco: Harper San Francisco, 1986.

Keen, S. "The Silence Within." *Adbusters,* 1995, *4*(1), 29.

Kennedy, P. *Preparing for the Twenty-First Century.* New York: Random House, 1993.

Kidner, D. W. "Why Psychology Is Mute About the Environmental Crisis." *Environmental Ethics,* 1994, *16*(4), 359–376.

King, A., and Schneider, B. *The First Global Revolution.* London: Simon & Schuster, 1991.

Klayman, J., and Ha, Y. "Confirmation, Disconfirmation, and Information in Hypothesis Testing." *Psychological Review,* 1987, *94,* 211–228.

Korten, D. C. *When Corporations Rule the World.* San Francisco: Berrett-Koehler, 1995.

Kuhn, T. S. *The Structure of Scientific Revolutions.* (2nd ed.) Chicago: University of Chicago Press, 1970.

Laing, R. D. *The Voice of Experience.* New York: Pantheon, 1982.

Lang, T., and Hines, C. *The New Protectionism: Protecting the Future Against Free Trade.* London: Earthscan, 1993.

Lasch, C. *The Culture of Narcissism: American Life in an Age of Diminishing Expectations.* New York: Norton, 1978.

Lasch, C. *The Revolt of the Elites and the Betrayal of Democracy.* New York: Norton, 1995.

Laughlin, H. P. *The Ego and Its Defenses.* (2nd ed.) New York: Jason Aronson, 1979.

Lear, J. "The Shrink Is In." *The New Republic,* 1995, *213*(26), 18–25.

Leopold, A. *A Sand County Almanac.* New York: Oxford University Press, 1949.

Lifton, R. "In a Dark Time." In R. Adams and S. Cullen (eds.), *The Final Epidemic: Physicians and Scientists on Nuclear War.* Chicago: Education Foundation for Nuclear Science, 1981.

Lind, M. *The Next American Nation: The New Nationalism and the Fourth American Revolution.* New York: Free Press, 1995.

Loewenstein, G. "Frames of Mind in Intertemporal Choice." *Management Science,* 1988, *34,* 200–214.

Ludwig, D., Hilborn, R., and Walters, C. "Uncertainty, Resource Exploitation, and Conservation: Lessons from History." *Science,* 1993, *260,* 17, 36.

Macy, J. "Working Through Environmental Despair." In T. Roszak, M. E. Gomes, and A. D. Kanner (eds.), *Ecopsychology: Restoring the Earth, Healing the Mind.* San Francisco: Sierra Club Books, 1995.

Mander, J. *In the Absence of the Sacred.* San Francisco: Sierra Club Books, 1991.

Merchant, C. *Radical Ecology: The Search for a Livable World.* New York: Routledge, 1992.

Milbrath, L. W. *Envisioning a Sustainable Society.* Albany: State University of New York Press, 1989.

Naess, A., and Rothenberg, D. *Ecology, Community and Lifestyle.* New York: Cambridge University Press, 1989.

Neale, M. H., and Bazerman, M. H. *Cognition and Rationality in Negotiation.* New York: Free Press, 1991.

Norton, B. G. *Toward Unity Among Environmentalists.* New York: Oxford University Press, 1991.

Oelschlaeger, M. *Caring for Creation: An Ecumenical Approach to the Environmental Crisis.* New Haven, Conn.: Yale University Press, 1994.

Ornstein, R., and Ehrlich, P. *New World New Mind.* London: Paladin, 1991.

Orr, D. W. *Earth in Mind: On Education, Environment, and the Human Prospect.* Washington, D.C.: Island Press, 1994.

Paich, M., and Sterman, J. "Boom, Bust, and Failures to Learn in Experimental Markets." *Management Science,* 1993, *39*(12), 1439–1458.

Palmer, M. *Dancing to Armageddon.* London: Aquarium Press, 1992.

Pezzey, J. "Sustainability: An Interdisciplinary Guide." *Environmental Values,* 1992, *1,* 321–362.

Plous, S. *The Psychology of Judgment and Decision Making.* New York: McGraw-Hill, 1993.

Prugh, T. *Natural Capital and Human Economic Survival.* Solomons, Md.: International Society for Ecological Economics, 1995.

Putnam, R. D. "The Strange Disappearance of Civic America." *The American Prospect,* Winter 1996, pp. 34–49.

Redclift, M., and Benton, T. (eds.). *Social Theory and the Global Environment.* New York: Routledge, 1994.

Rieff, P. *The Feeling Intellect: Selected Writings.* (J. Imber, ed.) Chicago: University of Chicago Press, 1990.

Rockefeller, S. C. "Faith and Community in an Ecological Age." In S. C. Rockefeller and J. C. Elder (eds.), *Spirit and Nature: Why the Environment Is a Religious Issue.* Boston: Beacon Press, 1992.

Roszak, T. *The Voice of the Earth.* New York: Simon & Schuster, 1992.

Rycroft, C. *A Critical Dictionary of Psychoanalysis.* New York: Penguin Books, 1995.

Sale, K. *Rebels Against the Future: The Luddites and Their War on the Industrial Revolution.* Reading, Mass.: Addison-Wesley, 1995.

Schön, D. *The Reflective Practitioner.* New York: Basic Books, 1983.

Schön, D. "The Theory of Inquiry: Dewey's Legacy to Education." *Curriculum Inquiry,* 1992, *22*(2), 119–139.

Schweitzer, A. *Out of My Life and Thought: An Autobiography.* (C. T. Campion, trans.) New York: Holt, 1933.

Senge, P. M. *The Fifth Discipline: The Art and Practice of the Learning Organization.* New York: Doubleday, 1990.

Simon, H. A. *Models of Bounded Rationality.* Cambridge, Mass.: MIT Press, 1982.

Smith, M. B. "Psychology in the Public Interest: What Have We Done? What Can We Do?" *American Psychologist,* 1990, *45*(4), 530–536.

Sterman, J. "Misperceptions of Feedback in Dynamic Decision Making." *Organizational Behavior and Human Decision Processes,* 1989, *43*(3), 301–335.

Stern, P. C. "Psychological Dimensions of Global Environmental Change." *Annual Review of Psychology,* 1992, *43,* 269–302.

Stokols, D. "The Paradox of Environmental Psychology." *American Psychologist,* 1995, *50*(10), 821–837.

Taylor, S. E., and Brown, J. D. "Illusion and Well-Being: A Social Psychological Perspective." *Psychological Bulletin,* 1988, *103,* 193–210.

Tiger, L. *Optimism: The Biology of Hope.* New York: Simon & Schuster, 1979.

Turner, B. L., II, and others (eds.). *The Earth as Transformed by Human Action and Regional Changes in the Biosphere over the Past 300 Years.* New York: Cambridge University Press, 1990.

Turner, R. K. (ed.). *Sustainable Environmental Economics and Management: Principles and Practice.* London: Belhaven Press, 1993.

Tversky, A., and Kahneman, D. "Availability: A Heuristic for Judging Frequency and Probability." *Cognitive Psychology,* 1974, *5,* 207–232.

United Nations Development Programme. *Human Development Report 1995.* New York: UNDP, 1995.

U.S. National Academy of Sciences and Royal Society of London. *Population Growth, Resource Consumption, and a Sustainable World.* Washington, D.C.: National Academy of Sciences, 1992.

Vaillant, G. E. *The Wisdom of the Ego.* Cambridge, Mass.: Harvard University Press, 1993.

Viederman, S. "The Economics of Sustainability: Challenges." Paper presented at the workshop on the Economics of Sustainability, Fundacao Joaquim Nabuco, Recife, Brazil, 1994.

Wagenaar, W., and Sagaria, S. "Misperception of Exponential Growth." *Perception and Psychophysics,* 1975, *18,* 416–422.

Wilber, K. *Sex, Ecology, Spirituality: The Spirit of Evolution.* Boston: Shambhala, 1995.

World Bank. *World Development Report 1992: Development and the Environment.* New York: Oxford University Press, 1992.

World Commission on Environment and Development. *Our Common Future.* New York: Oxford University Press, 1987.

World Conservation Union, United Nations Environment Programme, and Worldwide Fund for Nature. *Caring for the Earth: A Strategy for Sustainable Living.* Gland, Switzerland: IUCN, UNEP, and WWF, 1991.

World Resources Institute. *World Resources 1994–95: A Guide to the Global Environment.* New York: Oxford University Press, 1994.

PART FOUR

ASSESSMENT OF RISK AND THE ENVIRONMENT

12

TRUST, EMOTION, SEX, POLITICS, AND SCIENCE

Surveying the Risk-Assessment Battlefield

Paul Slovic

THE PRACTICE OF RISK assessment has steadily increased in prominence during the past several decades as risk managers in government and industry have sought to develop more effective ways to meet public demands for a safer and healthier environment. Dozens of scientific disciplines have been mobilized to provide technical information about risk, and billions of dollars have been expended to create this information and distill it in the context of risk assessments.

Ironically, as our society and other industrialized nations have expended this great effort to make life safer and healthier, many in the public have become more, rather than less, concerned about risk. These individuals see themselves as exposed to more serious risks than were faced by people in the past, and they believe that this situation is getting worse rather than better. Nuclear and chemical technologies (except for

Preparation of this chapter was supported by the Alfred P. Sloan Foundation, the Electric Power Research Institute, and the National Science Foundation under grants 91–10592 and SBR 94–122754. Portions of the text appeared in H. Kunreuther and P. Slovic, "Science, Values, and Risk," *The Annals of the American Academy of Political and Social Science*, 1996, *545*, 116–125.

medicines) have been stigmatized by being perceived as entailing unnaturally great risks (Gregory, Flynn, and Slovic, 1995). As a result, it has been difficult, if not impossible, to find host sites for disposal of high-level or low-level radioactive wastes, or for incinerators, landfills, and other chemical facilities.

Public perceptions of risk have been found to determine the priorities and legislative agendas of regulatory bodies such as the Environmental Protection Agency (EPA), much to the distress of agency technical experts who argue that other hazards deserve higher priority. The bulk of the EPA's budget in recent years has gone to hazardous waste primarily because the public believes that the cleanup of Superfund sites is the most serious environmental threat that the country faces. Hazards such as indoor air pollution are considered more serious health risks by experts but are not perceived that way by the public (Environmental Protection Agency, 1987).

Great disparities in monetary expenditures designed to prolong life, as shown in Table 12.1, may also be traced to public perceptions of risk. As noteworthy as the large sums of money devoted to protection from radiation and chemical toxins are the relatively small sums expended to reduce mundane hazards such as automobile accidents. Other studies have shown that serious risks from national disasters such as floods, hurricanes, and earthquakes generate relatively little public concern and demand for protection (Palm, 1995; Kunreuther, forthcoming).

Such discrepancies are seen as irrational by many harsh critics of public perceptions. These critics draw a sharp dichotomy between the experts and the public. Experts are seen as purveying risk assessments, characterized as objective, analytic, wise, and rational—based upon the *real risks*. In contrast, the public is seen to rely upon *perceptions of risk* that are subjective, often hypothetical, emotional, foolish, and irrational (see for example DuPont, 1980, or Covello, Flamm, Rodricks, and Tardiff, 1983). Weiner (1993, p. 495) defends the dichotomy, arguing that "This separation of reality and perception is pervasive in a technically sophisticated society, and serves to achieve a necessary emotional distance."

In sum, polarized views, controversy, and overt conflict have become pervasive within risk assessment and risk management. A desperate search for salvation through risk-communication efforts began in the mid-1980s. Yet despite some localized successes, this effort has not stemmed the major conflicts or reduced much of the dissatisfaction with risk management. This dissatisfaction can be traced, in part, to a failure to appreciate the complex and socially determined nature of the concept *risk*. In the remainder of this chapter, I shall describe several streams of research that

Table 12.1. Cost of a Year of Life Saved by Various Interventions.

Flu shots	$500
Water chlorination	$4,000
Pneumonia vaccination	$12,000
Breast cancer screening	$17,000
All medical interventions	$19,000
Construction safety rules	$38,000
All transportation interventions	$56,000
Highway improvement	$60,000
Home radon control	$141,000
Asbestos controls	$1.9 million
All toxin controls	$2.8 million
Arsenic emission controls	$6.0 million
Radiation controls	$10.0 million

Source: Adapted from Tengs and others, 1995.

demonstrate this complexity and point toward the need for new definitions of risk and new approaches to risk management.

Need for a New Perspective

New perspectives and new approaches are needed to manage risks effectively in our society. Social science research has provided some valuable insights into the nature of the problem that, without indicating a clear solution, do point to some promising prescriptive actions.

For example, early studies of risk perception demonstrated that the public's concerns could not simply be blamed on ignorance or irrationality. Instead, research has shown that many of the public's reactions to risk (including reactions that may underlie the data in Table 12.1) can be attributed to a sensitivity to technical, social, and psychological qualities of hazards that are not well modeled in technical risk assessments (qualities such as uncertainty in risk assessments, perceived inequity in the distribution of risks and benefits, and aversion to being exposed to risks that are involuntary, not under one's control, or dreaded). The important role of social values in risk perception and risk acceptance has thus become apparent (Slovic, 1987).

More recently, another important aspect of the risk-perception problem has come to be recognized. This is the role of trust. In recent years numerous articles and surveys have pointed out the importance of trust in risk management and documented the extreme distrust we now have in many of the individuals, industries, and institutions responsible for risk management (Slovic, 1993). This pervasive distrust has also been shown to be strongly linked to the perception that risks are unacceptably high and to political activism to reduce those risks.

A third insight pertains to the very nature of the concept *risk*. Current approaches to risk assessment and risk management are based upon the traditional view of risk as some objective function of probability (uncertainty) and adverse consequences. I shall argue for a conception of risk that is starkly different from this traditional view. This new approach highlights the subjective and value-laden nature of risk and conceptualizes risk as a game in which the rules must be socially negotiated within the context of a specific problem.

Risk Assessment's Subjective and Value-Laden Nature

Attempts to manage risk must confront the question: What is risk? The dominant conception sees risk as "the chance of injury, damage, or loss" (*Webster's New Twentieth Century Dictionary*, 2nd ed.). The probabilities and consequences of adverse events are assumed to be produced by physical and natural processes in ways that can be objectively quantified by risk assessment. Much social science analysis rejects this notion, arguing instead that risk is inherently subjective (Funtowicz and Ravetz, 1992; Krimsky and Golding, 1992; Otway, 1992; Pidgeon and others, 1992; Slovic, 1992; Wynne, 1992). In this view, risk does not exist "out there," independent of our minds and cultures, waiting to be measured. Instead, human beings have invented the concept *risk* to help them understand and cope with the dangers and uncertainties of life. Although these dangers are real, there is no such thing as "real risk" or "objective risk." The nuclear engineer's probabilistic risk estimate for a nuclear accident or the toxicologist's quantitative estimate of a chemical's carcinogenic risk are both based on theoretical models, whose structure is subjective and assumption-laden and whose inputs are dependent on judgment. As we shall see, nonscientists have their own models, assumptions, and subjective assessment techniques (intuitive risk assessments), which are sometimes very different from the scientists' models.

One way in which subjectivity permeates risk assessments is in the dependence of such assessments on judgments at every stage of the

Table 12.2. Some Ways of Expressing Mortality Risks.

- Deaths per million people in the population
- Deaths per million people within *x* miles of the source of exposure
- Deaths per unit of concentration
- Deaths per facility
- Deaths per ton of toxic air released
- Deaths per ton of toxic air absorbed by people
- Deaths per ton of chemical produced
- Deaths per million dollars of product produced
- Loss of life expectancy associated with exposure to the hazard

process, from the initial structuring of a risk problem to deciding which endpoints or consequences to include in the analysis, identifying and estimating exposures, choosing dose-response relationships, and so on.

For example, even the apparently simple task of choosing a risk measure for a well-defined endpoint such as human fatalities is surprisingly complex and judgmental. Table 12.2 shows a few of the many different ways that fatality risks can be measured. How should we decide which measure to use when planning a risk assessment, recognizing that the choice is likely to make a big difference in how the risk is perceived and evaluated?

An example taken from Wilson and Crouch (1983) demonstrates how the choice of one measure or another can make a technology look either more or less risky. For example, between 1950 and 1970, coal mines became much less risky in terms of deaths from accidents per ton of coal, but they became marginally riskier in terms of deaths from accidents per employee. Which measure one thinks more appropriate for decision making depends on one's point of view. From a national point of view, given that a certain amount of coal has to be obtained, deaths per million tons of coal is the more appropriate measure of risk, whereas from a labor leader's point of view, deaths per thousand persons employed may be more relevant.

Each way of summarizing deaths embodies its own set of values (National Research Council, 1989). For example, "reduction in life expectancy" treats deaths of young people as more important than deaths of older people, who have less life expectancy to lose. Simply counting fatalities treats deaths of the old and young as equivalent; it also treats as equivalent deaths that come immediately after mishaps and deaths that follow painful and debilitating disease or long periods during which many who will not suffer disease live in daily fear of that outcome. Using number of deaths as the summary indicator of risk implies that it is as important to prevent deaths of people who engage in an activity by choice and deaths of those who have been benefiting from a risky activity or technology as to protect those who get no benefit from it. One can easily imagine a range of arguments to justify different kinds of unequal weightings for different kinds of deaths, but to arrive at any selection requires a value judgment concerning which deaths one considers most undesirable. To treat the deaths as equal also involves a value judgment.

Framing the Risk Information

After negotiating a risk analysis through all the subjective steps of defining the problem and its options, selecting and measuring risks in terms of particular outcomes, determining the people at risk and their exposure parameters, and so on, one comes to the presentation of this information to the decision maker, often referred to as *framing*. This process of presentation is also rife with subjectivity.

Numerous research studies have demonstrated that different (but logically equivalent) ways of presenting the same risk information can lead to different evaluations and decisions. One dramatic example of this comes from a study by McNeil, Pauker, Sox, and Tversky (1982), who asked people to imagine that they had lung cancer and had to choose between two therapies, surgery or radiation. The two therapies were described in some detail. Then one group of subjects was presented with the cumulative probabilities of surviving for varying lengths of time after the treatment. A second group of subjects received the same cumulative probabilities framed in terms of dying rather than surviving (for example, instead of being told that 68 percent of those having surgery will have survived after one year, they were told that 32 percent will have died). Framing the statistics in terms of dying changed the percentage of subjects choosing radiation therapy over surgery from 44 percent to 18 percent. The effect was as strong for physicians as for laypersons.

Equally striking changes in preference result from framing the information about consequences in terms of either lives saved or lives lost (Tversky and Kahneman, 1981) or from describing an improvement in a river's water quality as a *restoration* of lost quality or an *improvement* from the current level (Gregory, Lichtenstein, and MacGregor, 1993).

We now know that every form of presenting risk information is a frame that has a strong influence on the decision maker. Moreover, when we contemplate the equivalency of lives saved versus lives lost, mortality rates versus survival rates, restoring lost water quality versus improving water quality, and so forth, we see that there are often no "right frames" or "wrong frames"—just "different frames."

Multidimensionality of Risk

As noted, research has also shown that the public has a broad conception of risk, qualitative and complex, that incorporates considerations such as uncertainty, dread, catastrophic potential, controllability, equity, and risk to future generations into the risk equation. In contrast, experts' perceptions of risk are not closely related to these dimensions or the characteristics that underlie them. Instead, studies show that experts tend to see riskiness as synonymous with expected mortality, consistent with the dictionary definition already given and consistent with the ways that risks tend to be characterized in risk assessments (see, for example, Cohen, 1985). As a result of these different perspectives, many conflicts over "risk" may result from experts' and laypeople's having different definitions of the concept. In this light, it is not surprising that expert recitations of "risk statistics" often do little to change people's attitudes and perceptions.

Legitimate, value-laden issues underlie the multiple dimensions of public risk perceptions, and these values need to be considered in risk-policy decisions. For example, is risk from cancer (a dread disease) worse than risk from auto accidents (not dreaded)? Is a risk imposed on a child more serious than a known risk accepted voluntarily by an adult? Are the deaths of fifty passengers in separate automobile accidents equivalent to the deaths of fifty passengers in one airplane crash? Is the risk from a polluted Superfund site worse if the site is located in a neighborhood that has a number of other hazardous facilities nearby? The difficult questions multiply when outcomes other than human health and safety are considered.

The Risk Game

There are clearly multiple conceptions of risk (Shrader-Frechette, 1991). Dean and Thompson (1995) note that the traditional view of risk characterized by the event probabilities and consequences treats the many subjective and contextual factors described above as secondary or accidental dimensions of risk, just as coloration might be thought of as a secondary or accidental dimension of an eye. Accidental dimensions might be extremely influential in the formation of attitudes toward risk, just as having blue or brown coloration may be influential in forming attitudes toward eyes. Furthermore, it may be that all risks possess some accidental dimensions, just as all organs of sight are in some way colored. Nevertheless, accidental dimensions do not serve as criteria for determining whether someone is or is not at risk, just as coloration is irrelevant to whether something is or is not an eye.

I believe that the multidimensional, subjective, value-laden, frame-sensitive nature of risky decisions, as described above, supports the very different view that Dean and Thompson call "the contextualist conception." This conception places probabilities and consequences on the list of relevant risk attributes along with voluntariness, equity, and other important contextual parameters. In the contextualist view, the concept of risk is more like the concept of a game than the concept of the eye. Games have time limits, rules of play, opponents, criteria for winning or losing, and so on, but none of these attributes is essential to the concept of a game, nor is any of them characteristic of all games. Similarly, a contextualist view of risk assumes that risks are characterized by some combination of attributes such as voluntariness, probability, intentionality, and equity, but that no one of these attributes is essential. The bottom line is that, just as there is no universal set of rules for games, there is no universal set of characteristics for describing risk. The characterization must depend on which risk game is being played.

Sex, Politics, and Emotion in Risk Judgments

Given the complex and subjective nature of risk, it should not surprise us that many interesting and provocative things occur when people judge risks. Recent studies have shown that factors such as gender, race, political worldviews, affiliation, emotional affect, and trust are strongly correlated with risk judgments. Equally important is that these factors influence the judgments of experts as well as judgments of laypersons.

Sex

Sex is strongly related to risk judgments and attitudes. Several dozen studies have documented the finding that men tend to judge risks as smaller and less problematic than do women (Brody, 1984; Carney, 1971; DeJoy, 1992; Gutteling and Wiegman, 1993; Gwartney-Gibbs and Lach, 1991; Pillisuk and Acredolo, 1988; Sjöberg and Drottz-Sjöberg, 1993; Slovic, Flynn, Mertz, and Mullican, 1993; Slovic and others, 1989; Spigner,

Hawkins, and Loren, 1993; Steger and Witte, 1989; Stern, Dietz, and Kalof, 1993).

A number of hypotheses have been put forward to explain sex differences in risk perception. One approach has been to focus on biological and social factors. For example, women have been characterized as more concerned about human health and safety because they give birth and are socialized to nurture and maintain life (Steger and Witte, 1989). They have been characterized as physically more vulnerable to violence, including rape, and this may sensitize them to other risks (Baumer, 1978; Riger, Gordon, and LeBailly, 1978). The combination of biology and social experience has been put forward as the source of a "different voice" that is distinct to women (Gilligan, 1982; Merchant, 1980).

A lack of knowledge and familiarity with science and technology has also been suggested as a basis for these differences, particularly with regard to nuclear and chemical hazards. Women are discouraged from studying science and there are relatively few women scientists and engineers (Alpen, 1993). However, Barke, Jenkins-Smith, and Slovic (1995) have found that female physical scientists judge risks from nuclear technologies to be higher than do male physical scientists. Similar results with scientists were obtained by Malmfors and others (1996), who found that female members of the British Toxicological Society were far more likely than male toxicologists to judge societal risks as high (see Figure 12.1). Certainly the female scientists in the studies by Barke and others and Malmfors and others cannot be accused of lacking knowledge and technological literacy. Something else must be going on.

Hints about the origin of these sex differences come from a study by Flynn, Slovic, and Mertz (1994) in which 1,512 Americans were asked, for each of twenty-five hazard items, to indicate whether the hazard posed (1) little or no risk, (2) slight risk, (3) moderate risk, or (4) high risk to society. Figure 12.2 shows the difference in the percentage of males and females who rated a hazard as a "high risk." All differences are to the right of the 0 percent mark, indicating that the percentage of "high risk" responses was greater for women on every item. A similar graph (Figure 12.3) shows that the percentage of "high risk" responses was greater among people of color than among white respondents for every item studied.

Perhaps the most striking result from this study is shown in Figure 12.4, which presents the mean risk ratings separately for white males, white females, nonwhite males, and nonwhite females. Across the twenty-five hazards, white males produced risk-perception ratings that were consistently much lower than the means of the other three groups.

When the data underlying Figure 12.4 were examined more closely,

Figure 12.1. Perceived Health Risk to the Average Exposed British Citizen as Judged by Members of the British Toxicological Society.

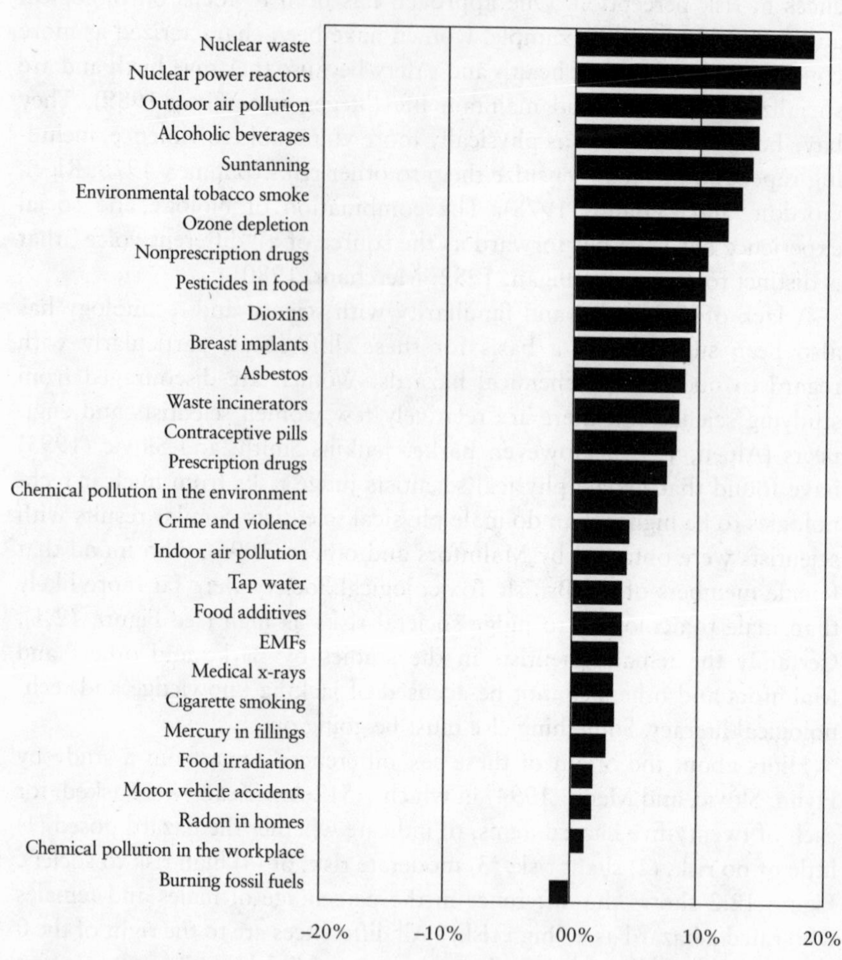

Note: Percentage difference is percentage female "moderate" and "high risk" responses minus percentage male "moderate" and "high risk" responses. N = 92 females and 208 males.

Source: Malmfors and others, 1996.

Figure 12.2. Perceived Health Risks to American Public by Gender: Difference Between Males and Females.

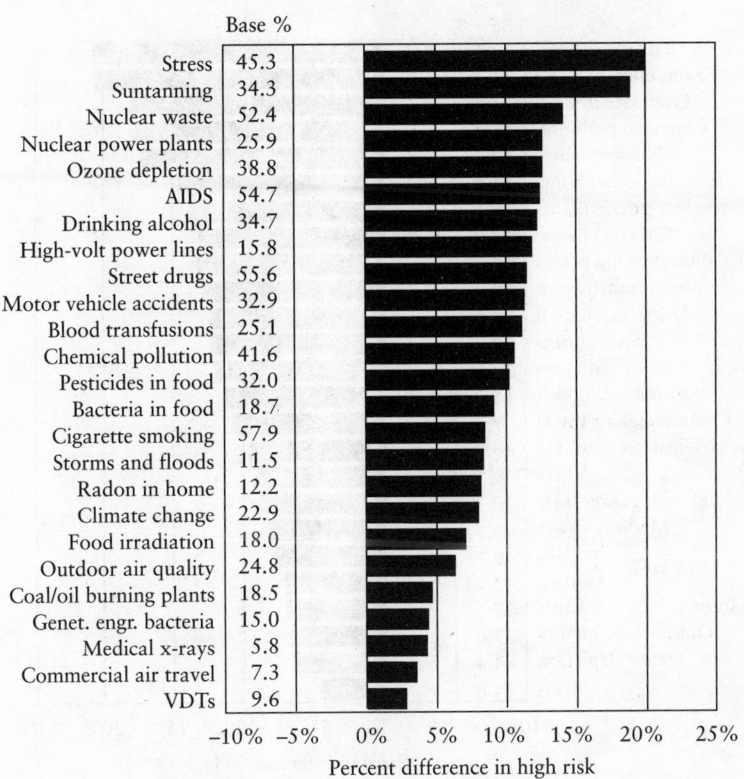

Note: Base percentage equals male "high risk" response. Percentage difference is female "high risk" response minus male "high risk" response.
Source: Flynn, Slovic, and Mertz, 1994.

Flynn, Slovic, and Mertz observed that not all white males perceived risks as low. The "white-male effect" appeared to be caused by about 30 percent of the white-male sample who judged risks to be extremely low. The remaining white males were not much different from the other subgroups with regard to perceived risk.

What differentiated these white males who were most responsible for the effect from the rest of the sample, including other white males who judged risks as relatively high? When compared to the remainder of the sample, the group of white males with the lowest risk-perception scores were better educated (42.7 percent college or postgraduate degree versus

Figure 12.3. Perceived Health Risks to American Public by Race: Difference Between Whites and Nonwhites.

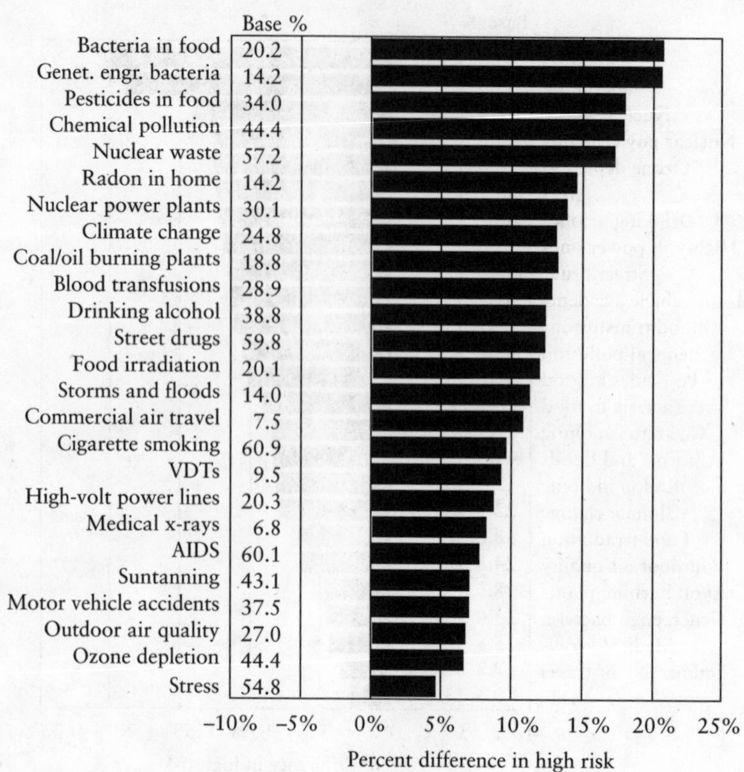

Note: Base percentage equals white "high risk" response. Percentage difference is nonwhite "high risk" response minus white "high risk" response.
Source: Flynn, Slovic, and Mertz, 1994.

26.3 percent in the other group), had higher household incomes (32.1 percent above $50,000 versus 21.0 percent), and were politically more conservative (48.0 percent conservative versus 33.2 percent). Although perceived risk was inversely related to income and educational level, controlling for these differences statistically did not reduce much of the white-male effect on risk perception. Figure 12.5 shows, for example, that white males exhibited far lower perceived risk at each of three levels of income and educational status.

Particularly noteworthy is the finding that the low risk–perception subgroup of white males also held very different attitudes than the other respondents. Specifically, they were *more likely* than the others to

Figure 12.4. Mean Risk-Perception Ratings by Race and Gender.

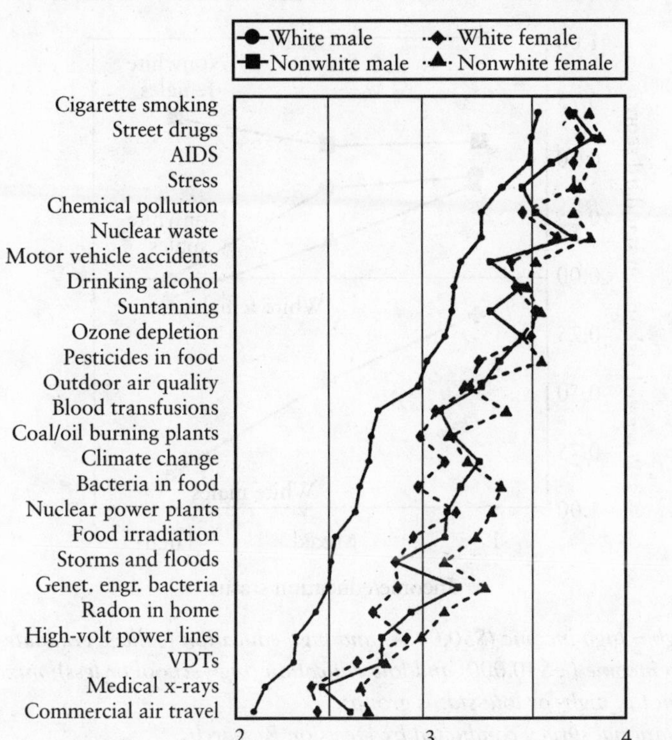

Source: Flynn, Slovic, and Mertz, 1994.

- Agree that future generations can take care of themselves when facing risks imposed upon them from today's technologies (64.2 percent versus 46.9 percent).
- Agree that if a risk is very small it is okay for society to impose that risk on individuals without their consent (31.7 percent versus 20.8 percent).
- Agree that science can settle differences of opinion about the risks of nuclear power (61.8 percent versus 50.4 percent).
- Agree that government and industry can be trusted with making the proper decisions to manage the risks from technology (48.0 percent versus 31.1 percent).
- Agree that we can trust the experts and engineers who build, operate, and regulate nuclear power plants (62.6 percent versus 39.7 percent).

Figure 12.5. Risk-Perception Index by Race, Gender, Income, and Education.

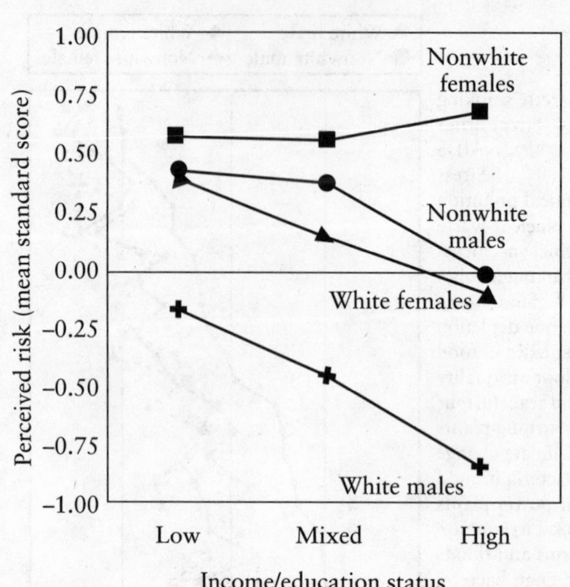

Note: High = high income ($50,000+) and high education (college graduate+); low = low income (< $30,000) and low education (high school or less); mixed = all those not in high- or low-status groups.
Source: National survey conducted by Decision Research.

- Agree that we have gone too far in pushing equal rights in this country (42.7 percent versus 30.9 percent).
- Agree with the use of capital punishment (88.2 percent versus 70.5 percent).
- Disagree that technological development is destroying nature (56.9 percent versus 32.8 percent).
- Disagree that they have very little control over risks to their health (73.6 percent versus 63.1 percent).
- Disagree that the world needs a more equal distribution of wealth (42.7 percent versus 31.3 percent).
- Disagree that local residents should have the authority to close a nuclear power plant if they think it is not run properly (50.4 percent versus 25.1 percent).
- Disagree that the public should vote to decide on issues such as nuclear power (28.5 percent versus 16.7 percent).

In sum, the subgroup of white males who perceive risks to be quite low can be characterized by trust in institutions and authorities and by anti-egalitarian attitudes, including a disinclination toward giving decision-making power to citizens in areas of risk management.

The results of this study raise new questions. What does it mean for the explanations of gender differences when we see that the sizable differences between white males and white females do not exist for nonwhite males and nonwhite females? Why do a substantial percentage of white males see the world as so much less risky than everyone else sees it?

Obviously, the salience of biology is reduced by these data on risk perception and race. Biological factors should apply to nonwhite men and women as well as to white people. The present data thus move us away from biology and toward sociopolitical explanations. Perhaps white males see less risk in the world because they create, manage, control, and benefit from many of the major technologies and activities. Perhaps women and nonwhite men see the world as more dangerous because in many ways they are more vulnerable, because they benefit less from many of its technologies and institutions, and because they have less power and control over what happens in their communities and their lives. Although the survey conducted by Flynn, Slovic, and Mertz was not designed to test these alternative explanations, the race and gender differences in perceptions and attitudes point toward the role of power, status, alienation, trust, perceived government responsiveness, and other sociopolitical factors in determining perception and acceptance of risk.

Inasmuch as these sociopolitical factors shape public perception of risks, we can see why traditional attempts to make people see the world as white males do by showing them statistics and risk assessments are unlikely to succeed. The problem of risk conflict and controversy goes beyond science. It is deeply rooted in the social and political fabric of our society.

Risk Perception and Worldviews

The influence of social, psychological, and political factors can also be seen in studies examining the impact of worldviews on risk judgments.

Worldviews are general social, cultural, and political attitudes that appear to have an influence over people's judgments about complex issues (Buss, Craik, and Dake, 1986; Dake, 1991; Jasper, 1990). Dake (1991) has conceptualized worldviews as "orienting dispositions" because of their role in guiding people's responses. Some of the worldviews identified to date are listed below, along with representative attitude statements:

- Fatalism: "I feel I have very little control over risks to my health."
- Hierarchy: "Decisions about health risks should be left to the experts."
- Individualism: "In a fair system, people with more ability should earn more."
- Egalitarianism: "If people were treated more equally, we would have fewer problems."
- Technological enthusiasm: "A high-technology society is important for improving our health and social well-being."

People differ from one another in these views. Fatalists tend to think that what happens in life is preordained and one cannot change that. Hierarchists like a society organized so that commands flow down from authorities and obedience flows up the hierarchy. Egalitarians prefer a world in which power and wealth are more evenly distributed. Individualists like to do their own thing, unhindered by government or any other kind of constraints.

Dake (1991, 1992), Jenkins-Smith (1993), and others have measured worldviews with survey techniques and found them to be strongly linked to public perceptions of risk. My colleagues and I have obtained similar results. Peters and Slovic (1996), using the same national survey data analyzed for race and gender effects by Flynn, Slovic, and Mertz (1994), found particularly strong correlations between worldviews and attitudes toward nuclear power. Egalitarians tended to be strongly antinuclear; persons endorsing fatalist, hierarchist, and individualistic views tended to be pronuclear. Tables 12.3 and 12.4 illustrate these findings for one individualism item (Table 12.3) and one egalitarian item (Table 12.4). When scales measuring the various worldviews were combined into a regression equation, they exhibited considerable ability to predict perceptions of risk from nuclear power and attitudes toward accepting a new nuclear power plant in one's community (see Figure 12.6).

Risk Perception and Affect

The studies described in the preceding section illustrate the role of worldviews as orienting mechanisms. Research suggests that affect is also an orienting mechanism that directs fundamental psychological processes such as attention, memory, and information processing. Zajonc (1980), for example, argued that affective reactions to stimuli are often the very first reactions, occurring without extensive perceptual and cognitive encoding and subsequently guiding information processing and judgment.

Table 12.3. Individualism Worldview Associated with Support for New Nuclear Power Plants.

Individualism worldview: in a fair system people with more ability should earn more	*Build new nuclear power plants*[a] *(% agree)*
Strongly disagree	37.5
Disagree	37.7
Agree	47.2
Strongly agree	53.4

Note: N = 1,512

[a]*The precise statement was, "If your community was faced with a potential shortage of electricity, do you agree or disagree that a new nuclear power plant should be built to supply that electricity?"*

According to Zajonc, all perceptions may contain some affect. "We do not just see 'a house': We see a *handsome* house, an *ugly* house, or a *pretentious* house" (p. 154). He later adds, "We sometimes delude ourselves that we proceed in a rational manner and weigh all the pros and cons of the various alternatives. But this is probably seldom the actual case. Quite often 'I decided in favor of X' is no more than 'I liked X'. . . . We buy the cars we 'like,' choose the jobs and houses we find 'attractive,' and then justify these choices by various reasons" (p. 155).

Table 12.4. Egalitarian Worldview Inversely Associated with Support for New Nuclear Power Plants.

Egalitarian worldview: what this world needs is a more equal distribution of wealth	*Build new nuclear Power Plants*[a] *(% agree)*
Strongly disagree	73.9
Disagree	53.7
Agree	43.8
Strongly agree	33.8

Note: N = 1,512.

[a]*The precise statement was, "If your community was faced with a potential shortage of electricity, do you agree or disagree that a new nuclear power plant should be built to supply that electricity?"*

Figure 12.6. Relationship Between Actual Nuclear Support and Predictions of Nuclear Support Based on Fatalism, Hierarchism, Individualism, and Egalitarian Worldviews.

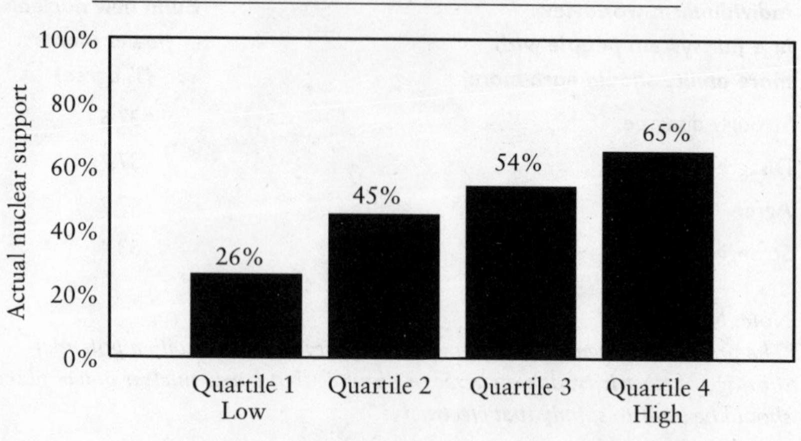

Note: Actual nuclear support was based on the percentage agreeing that if their community was faced with a potential shortage of electricity, a new nuclear power plant should be built to supply that electricity.

If Zajonc is correct regarding the primacy and automaticity of affect, then affective reactions may also serve as orienting dispositions. Affect and worldviews may thus be functionally similar in that both may help us navigate quickly and efficiently through a complex, uncertain, and sometimes dangerous world. This view is schematized in Figure 12.7, which indicates that people's perceptions of risk and acceptance of risk and their trust in risk management are based on knowledge and experience. But the model in this figure also assumes that knowledge, experience, and ultimately our risk evaluations are themselves colored by two overarching phenomena—worldviews and affect.

One demonstration of the influence of affect on risk perception comes from a study by Johnson and Tversky (1983). They found that reading about a tragic death increased people's frequency estimates for many other causes of death. Johnson and Tversky interpreted this as an indication that the negative affect generated by the tragic story influenced all the subsequent estimates, regardless of the similarity between the tragic event and other fatal events.

Support for the conception of affect as an orienting mechanism also comes from a study by Alhakami and Slovic (1994). They observed that,

Figure 12.7. Worldviews and Affect as Orienting Dispositions.

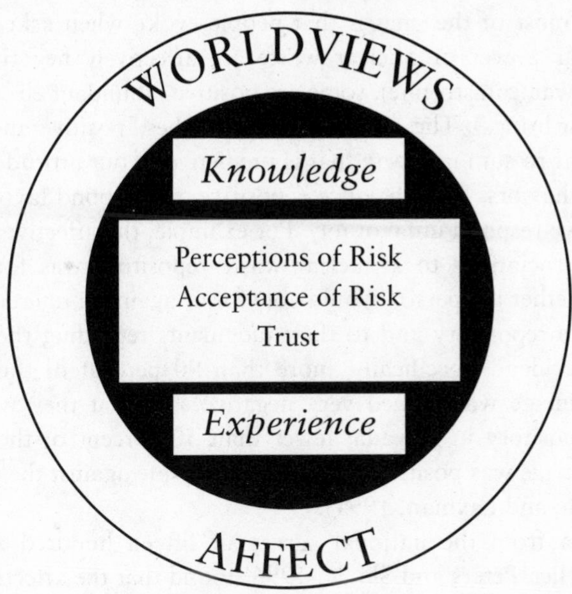

whereas the risks and benefits to society from various activities and technologies (such as nuclear power and commercial aviation) tend to be *positively* associated in the world, they are *inversely* correlated in people's minds (higher perceived benefit is associated with lower perceived risk; lower perceived benefit is associated with higher perceived risk). This inverse relationship had been observed previously in numerous studies of risk perception (for example, Fischhoff and others, 1978; Slovic, Kraus, Lappe, and Major, 1991). Alhakami and Slovic found that this inverse relationship was linked to people's reliance on general affective evaluations when making risk/benefit judgments. When the affective evaluation was favorable (as with automobiles, for example), the activity or technology being judged was seen as having high benefit and low risk; when the evaluation was unfavorable (as with pesticides), risks tended to be seen as high and benefits as low. It thus appears that the affective response is primary, and the risk and benefit judgments are derived (at least partly) from it.

Slovic, Flynn, and Layman (1991) and Slovic and others (1991) studied the relationship between affect and perceived risk for hazards related to nuclear power. For example, Slovic, Flynn, and Layman, asked respondents, "What is the first thought or image that comes to mind when you hear the phrase 'nuclear waste repository?'" After providing up to three associations to the repository stimulus, each respondent rated the affective quality of these associations on a 5-point scale, ranging from extremely negative to extremely positive.

Although most of the images that people evoke when asked to think about nuclear power or nuclear waste are affectively negative (death, destruction, war, catastrophe), some are positive (abundant electricity and the benefits it brings). The affective values of these positive and negative images appear to sum in a way that is predictive of our attitudes, perceptions, and behaviors. If the balance is positive, we respond favorably; if it is negative, we respond unfavorably. For example, the affective quality of a person's associations to a nuclear waste repository was found to be related to whether the person would vote for or against a referendum on a nuclear waste repository and to their judgments regarding the risk of a repository accident. Specifically, more than 90 percent of those people whose first image was judged very negative said that they would vote against a repository in Nevada; fewer than 50 percent of those people whose first image was positive said they would vote against the repository (Slovic, Flynn, and Layman, 1991).

Using data from the national survey of fifteen hundred Americans described earlier, Peters and Slovic (1996) found that the affective ratings of associations to the stimulus "nuclear power" were highly predictive of responses to the question, "If your community was faced with a shortage of electricity, do you agree or disagree that a new nuclear power plant should be built to supply that electricity?" Among the 25 percent of respondents with the most positive associations to nuclear power, 69 percent agreed to building a new plant. Among the 25 percent of respondents with the most negative associations, only 13 percent agreed. A comparison of these percentages with those in the extreme quartiles of Figure 12.6 (65 percent and 26 percent, respectively) shows that affect was even more powerful as a predictor of nuclear power support than the combined worldviews. When affect plus the various worldviews were combined into one prediction equation, the ability to predict support for nuclear power was even stronger (see Figure 12.8).

Worldviews, Affect, and Toxicology

Affect and worldviews seem to influence the risk-related judgments of scientists as well as laypersons. Evidence for this comes from studies of "intuitive toxicology" that Torbjörn Malmfors, Nancy Neil, Iain Purchase, and I have been conducting in the United States, Canada, and the United Kingdom during the past eight years. These studies have surveyed both toxicologists and laypersons about a wide range of concepts relating to

Figure 12.8. Relationship Between Predictions of Nuclear Support Based on Affect and Worldviews and Actual Nuclear Support.

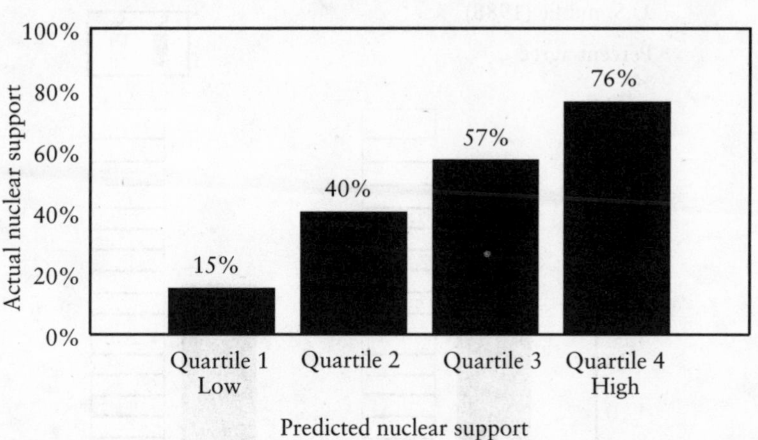

Note: Actual nuclear support was based on the percentage agreeing that if their community were faced with a potential shortage of electricity, a new nuclear power plant should be built to supply that electricity.
Source: Peters and Slovic, 1996, p. 1449.

risks from chemicals. We have examined judgments about the effects of chemical concentration, dose, and exposure on risk. We have also questioned our respondents about the value of animal studies for predicting the effects of chemicals on humans. Before showing how worldviews and affect enter into toxicologists' judgments, a brief description of some basic results will be presented.

Consider two survey items that we have studied repeatedly. One is statement S_1: "Would you agree or disagree that the way an animal reacts to a chemical is a reliable predictor of how a human would react to it?" The second statement, S_2, is a little more specific: "If a scientific study produces evidence that a chemical causes cancer in animals, then we can be reasonably sure that the chemical will cause cancer in humans."

When members of the American and Canadian public responded to these items, they showed moderate agreement with S_1; about half the people agreed and half disagreed that animal tests were reliable predictors of human reactions to chemicals. However, in response to S_2, which stated that the animal study found evidence of cancer, there was a jump in agreement to about 70 percent among both men and women respondents (see Figure 12.9). The important point about the pattern of response is that agreement was higher on the second item.

Figure 12.9. Public's Agreement with Two Statements Regarding Extrapolation of Chemical Effects on Animals to Effects on Humans.

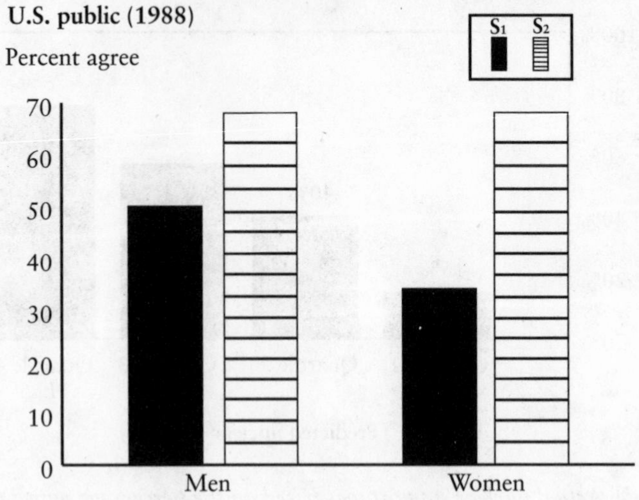

Source: Data from Kraus, Malmfors, and Slovic, 1992.

What happens if toxicologists are asked about these two statements? Figure 12.10 shows that toxicologists in the United States and in the United Kingdom responded similarly to the public on the first statement but differently on the second. They exhibited the same rather middling level of agreement with the general statement about animal studies as predictors of human health effects. (This is actually a very surprising result, given the heavy reliance on animal studies in toxicology.)

However, when these studies were said to find evidence of carcinogenicity in animals, then the toxicologists were less likely to agree that the results could be extrapolated to humans. Thus the same findings that lead toxicologists to be less willing to generalize to humans lead the public to see the chemical as more dangerous for humans. (This pattern of results suggests that animal studies may be scaring the public without informing science.)

Figure 12.11 presents the responses for S_1 and S_2 among men and women toxicologists in the United Kingdom (208 men and 92 women). Here we see another interesting finding. The men agree less on the second statement than on the first, but the women agree more, just like the general public. Women toxicologists are more willing than men to say that one can generalize to humans from the positive carcinogenicity findings in animals.

Figure 12.10. Public's and Toxicologists' Agreement with the Two Statements.

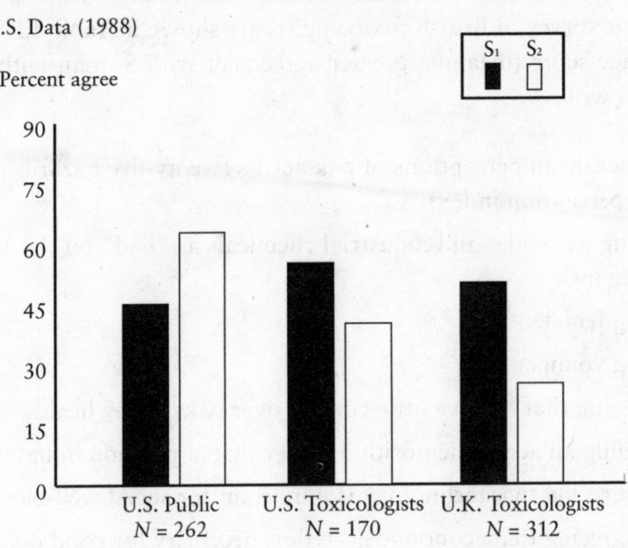

Figure 12.11. Agreement of U.K. Toxicologists with the Two Statements, by Sex.

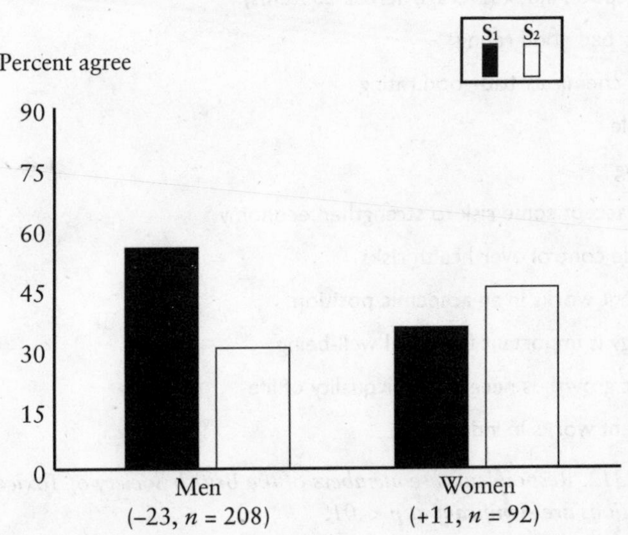

We created a change score between statements S_1 and S_2, with each individual getting a score of increasing agreement, decreasing agreement, or no change. Selected correlations between this change score and other items in the survey of British toxicologists are shown in Table 12.5. A positive change score (meaning greater agreement with S_2 than with S_1) was associated with

- Higher mean perceptions of risk across twenty-five hazards (the risk-perception index)
- Rating pesticides and industrial chemicals as "bad" on the affective rating task
- Being female
- Being younger
- Agreeing that "I have little control over risks to my health"
- Holding an academic position rather than a position in industry
- Disagreeing that technology is important for social well-being
- Disagreeing that economic growth is necessary for good quality of life.

Table 12.5. Correlations with the $S_1 - S_2$ Change Score.

• Belief that there is a threshold dose for nongenotoxic carcinogens	–.33
• Risk perception index (average across 25 items)	.26
• Pesticides: bad-good rating	–.26
• Industrial chemicals: bad-good rating	–.25
• Sex: female	.25
• Age: young	–.23
• Agree to accept some risk to strengthen economy	–.23
• I have little control over health risks	.22
• Respondent works in an academic position	.19
• Technology is important for social well-being	–.17
• Economic growth is necessary for quality of life	–.17
• Respondent works in industry	–.16

Note: N = 312. Respondents are members of the British Society of Toxicology. All correlations are significant at $p < .01$.

These studies of intuitive toxicology have yielded a number of intriguing findings. One is the low percentage of agreement that animal studies can predict human health effects. Another is that toxicologists show even less confidence in studies that find cancer in animals resulting from chemical exposure. The public has high confidence in animal studies that find cancer. Disagreements among toxicologists are systematically linked to gender, affiliation (academic versus other), worldviews, and affect. Thus affective and sociopolitical factors appear to influence scientists' risk evaluations in much the same way as they influence the public's perceptions.[1]

Trust

The research described so far has painted a portrait of risk perception influenced by the interplay of psychological, social, and political factors. Members of the public and experts can disagree about risk because they define risk differently, have different worldviews, different affective experiences and reactions, or different social status. Another reason why the public often rejects scientists' risk assessments is lack of trust. Trust in risk management, like risk perception, has been found to correlate with gender, race, worldviews, and affect.

Social relationships of all types, including risk management, rely heavily on trust. Indeed, much of the contentiousness that has been observed in the risk-management arena has been attributed to a climate of distrust that exists between the public, industry, and risk-management professionals (Slovic, 1993; Slovic, Flynn, and Layman, 1991). The limited effectiveness of risk-communication efforts can be attributed to the lack of trust. If you trust the risk manager, communication is relatively easy. If trust is lacking, no form or process of communication will be satisfactory (Fessenden-Raden, Fitchen, and Heath, 1987).

How Trust Is Created and Destroyed

One of the most fundamental qualities of trust has been known for ages. Trust is fragile. It is typically created rather slowly, but it can be destroyed in an instant—by a single mishap or mistake. Thus, once trust is lost, it may take a long time to rebuild it to its former state. In some instances, lost trust may never be regained. Abraham Lincoln understood this quality. In a letter to Alexander McClure, he observed: "If you *once* forfeit the confidence of your fellow citizens, you can *never* regain their respect and esteem" (emphasis added).

The fact that trust is easier to destroy than to create reflects certain fundamental mechanisms of human psychology called here the *asymmetry principle*. When it comes to winning trust, the playing field is not level. It is tilted toward distrust, for each of the following reasons:

1. Negative (trust-destroying) events are more visible or noticeable than positive (trust-building) events. Negative events often take the form of specific, well-defined incidents such as accidents, lies, discoveries of errors, or other mismanagement. Positive events, although sometimes visible, more often are fuzzy or indistinct. For example, how many positive events are represented by the safe operation of a nuclear power plant for one day? Is this one event? dozens of events? hundreds? There is no precise answer. When events are invisible or poorly defined, they carry little or no weight in shaping our attitudes and opinions.

2. When events are well defined and do come to our attention, negative (trust-destroying) events carry much greater weight than positive events. This second psychological tendency is illustrated by a study in which 103 college students rated the impact on trust of forty-five hypothetical news events pertaining to the management of a large nuclear power plant in their community (Slovic, 1993). Some of these events were designed to be trust increasing, such as the following:

- There have been no reported safety problems at the plant during the past year.
- There is careful selection and training of employees at the plant.
- Plant managers live nearby the plant.
- The county medical examiner reports that the health of people living near the plant is *better* than the average for the region.

Other events were designed to be trust decreasing, such as the following:

- A potential safety problem was found to have been covered up by plant officials.
- Plant safety inspections are delayed in order to meet the electricity production quota for the month.
- A nuclear power plant in another state has a serious accident.
- The county medical examiner reports that the health of people living near the plant is *worse* than the average for the region.

The respondents were asked to indicate, for each event, whether their trust in the management of the plant would be increased or decreased upon learning of that event. After doing this, they rated how strongly their trust would be affected by the event on a scale ranging from 1 (very small impact on trust) to 7 (very powerful impact on trust).

The percentages of category 7 ratings, shown in Figure 12.12, demonstrate that negative events are seen as far more likely to have a powerful effect on trust than are positive events. The data shown in Table 12.6 are typical. The negative event, reporting plant neighbors' health as *worse* than average, was rated 6 or 7 on the impact scale by 50.0 percent of the respondents. A matched event, reporting neighbors' health to be *better* than average, was rated 6 or 7 by only 18.3 percent of the respondents.

There was only one event perceived to have any substantial impact on increasing trust. This event was stated as follows:

- "An advisory board of local citizens and environmentalists is established to monitor the plant and is given legal authority to shut the plant down if they believe it to be unsafe."

This strong delegation of authority to the local public was rated 6 or 7 on the impact scale by 38.4 percent of the respondents. Although this was a far stronger showing than for any other positive event, it would have been a rather average performance in the distribution of impacts for negative events.

The importance of an event is at least in part related to its frequency (or

Table 12.6. Judged Impact of Trust-Increasing Event and a Similar Trust-Decreasing Event.

	IMPACT ON TRUST						
	Very Small					***Very Powerful***	
	1	**2**	**3**	**4**	**5**	**6**	**7**
Trust-increasing event							
The county medical examiner reports that the health of people living near the plant is *better* than average.	21.5	14.0	10.8	18.3	17.2	16.1	2.2
Trust-decreasing event							
The county medical examiner reports that the health of people living near the plant is *worse* than average.	3.0	8.0	2.0	16.0	21.0	26.0	24.0

Note: Numbers indicate the percentage of respondents in each impact rating.

Source: Slovic, 1993.

Figure 12.12. Differential Impact of Trust-Increasing and Trust-Decreasing Events.

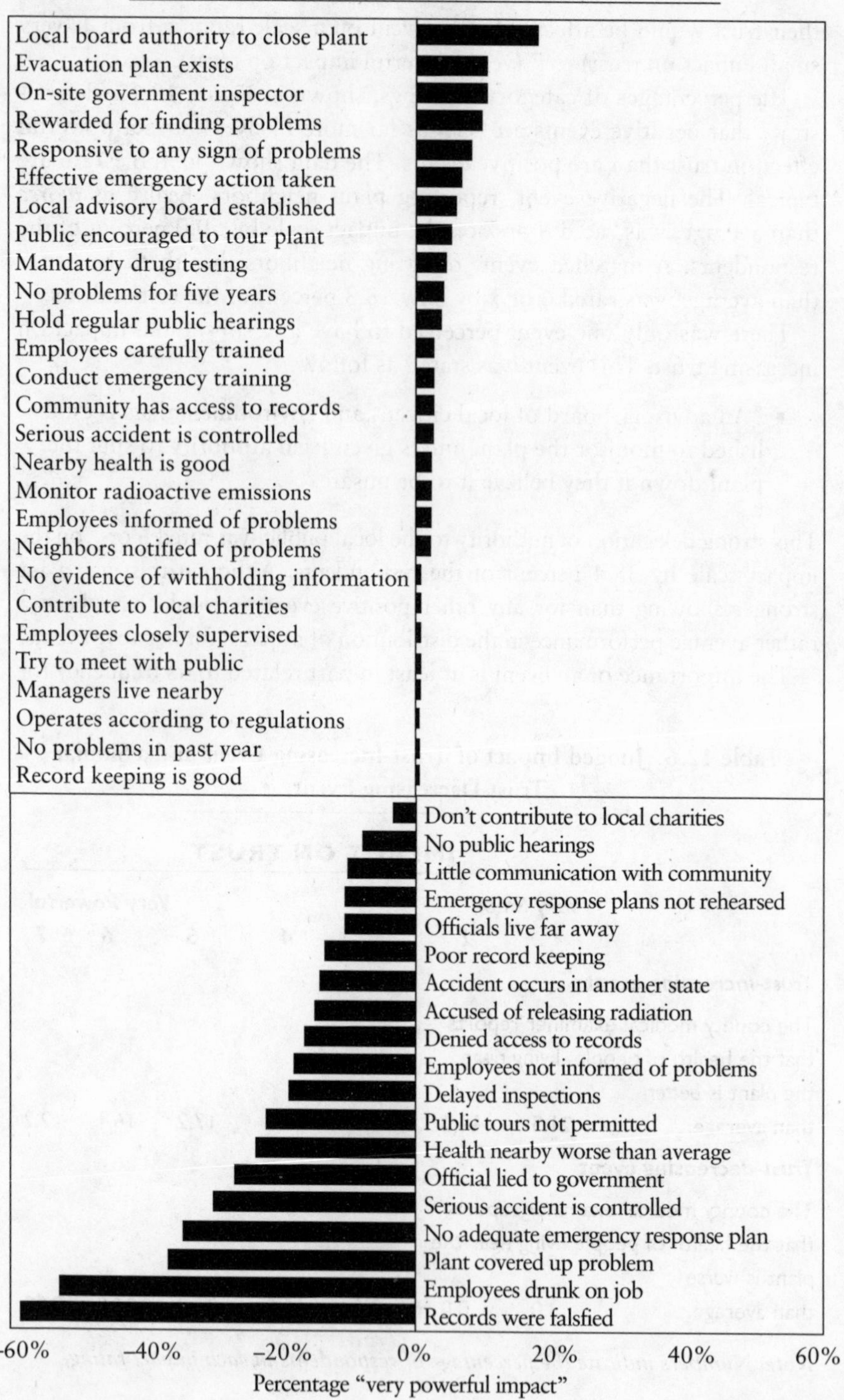

Source: Slovic, 1993.

stronger showing than for any other positive event, it would have been a rather average performance in the distribution of impacts for negative events.

The importance of an event is at least in part related to its frequency (or rarity). An accident in a nuclear plant is more informative with regard to risk than is a day (or even a large number of days) without an accident. Thus, in systems where we are concerned about low-probability/high-consequence events, adverse events will increase our perceptions of risk to a much greater degree than favorable events will decrease them.

3. Adding fuel to the fire of asymmetry is yet another idiosyncrasy of human psychology—sources of bad (trust-destroying) news tend to be seen as more credible than sources of good news. The findings reported for extrapolating chemical effects on animals to effects on humans illustrate this point. In general, confidence in the validity of animal studies is not particularly high. However, when told that a study has found that a chemical is carcinogenic in animals, members of the public express considerable confidence in the validity of this study for predicting health effects in humans.

4. Another important psychological tendency is that distrust, once initiated, tends to reinforce and perpetuate distrust. This occurs in two ways. First, distrust tends to inhibit the kinds of personal contacts and experiences that are necessary to overcome distrust. By avoiding others whose motives or actions we distrust, we never get to see that these people are competent, well meaning, and trustworthy. Second, initial trust or distrust colors our interpretation of events, thus reinforcing our prior beliefs. Persons who trusted the nuclear power industry saw the events at Three Mile Island as demonstrating the soundness of the "defense in depth" principle, noting that the multiple safety systems shut the plant down and contained most of its radiation. Persons who distrusted nuclear power prior to the accident took an entirely different message from the same events, perceiving that those in charge did not understand what was wrong or how to fix it and that catastrophe was averted only by sheer luck.

"The System Destroys Trust"

Thus far we have been discussing the psychological tendencies that creat and reinforce distrust in situations of risk. Appreciation of those psycho logical principles leads us toward a new perspective on risk perceptio trust, and conflict. Conflicts and controversies surrounding risk manag ment are not due to public irrationality or ignorance but, instead, can seen as expected side effects of these psychological tendencies, interac with a highly participatory democratic system of government and amp by certain powerful technological and social changes in society

technological change has enabled the electronic and print media to inform us of news from all over the world—often right as it happens. Moreover, just as individuals give greater weight and attention to negative events, so do the news media. Much of what the media reports is bad (trust-destroying) news (Koren and Klein, 1991; Lichtenberg and MacLean, 1992).

The second important change, a social phenomenon, is the rise of powerful special interest groups, well funded (by a fearful public) and sophisticated in using their own experts and the media to communicate their concerns and their distrust to the public in order to influence risk policy debates and decisions ("How a PR Firm . . . ," 1989). The social problem is compounded by the fact that we tend to manage our risks within an adversarial legal system that pits expert against expert, contradicting each other's risk assessments and further destroying the public trust.

The young science of risk assessment is too fragile, too indirect, to prevail in such a hostile atmosphere. Scientific analysis of risks cannot allay our fears of low-probability catastrophes or delayed cancers unless we trust the system. In the absence of trust, science (and risk assessment) can only feed public concerns by uncovering more bad news. A single study demonstrating an association between exposure to chemicals or radiation and some adverse health effect cannot easily be offset by numerous studies failing to find such an association. Thus, for example, the more studies that are conducted looking for effects of electric and magnetic fields or other difficult-to-evaluate hazards, the more likely it is that these studies will increase public concerns, even if the majority of these studies fail to find any association with ill health (MacGregor, Slovic, and Morgan, 1994; Morgan and others, 1985). In short, because evidence for lack of risk often carries little weight, risk-assessment studies tend to increase perceived risk.

Conclusion

There has been no shortage of high-level attention given to the risk conflicts described and the question, Where do we go from here?

Technical Solutions

One prominent proposal by Justice Stephen Breyer (1993) attempts to break what he sees as a vicious circle of public perception, congressional overreaction, and conservative regulation that leads to obsessive and costly preoccupation with reducing negligible risks as well as to inconsistent standards among health and safety programs. Breyer sees public mispercep-

tions of risk and low levels of mathematical understanding at the core of excessive regulatory response. His proposed solution is to create a small centralized administrative group charged with creating uniformity and rationality in highly technical areas of risk management. This group would be staffed by civil servants with experience in health and environmental agencies, Congress, and the Office of Management and Budget. A parallel is drawn between this group and the prestigious Conseil d'Etat in France.

Similar frustration with the costs of meeting public demands led the 104th Congress to introduce numerous bills designed to require all major new regulations to be justified by extensive risk assessments. Proponents of this legislation argue that such measures are necessary to ensure that regulations are based upon "sound science" and effectively reduce significant risks at reasonable costs.

The language of this proposed legislation reflects the traditional narrow view of risk and risk assessment based "only on the best reasonably available scientific data and scientific understanding." Agencies are further directed to develop a systematic program for external peer review using "expert bodies" or "other devices comprised of participants selected on the basis of their expertise relevant to the sciences involved." (U.S. Senate, 1995, pp. 57–58). Public participation in this process is advocated, but no mechanisms for this are specified.

The proposals by Breyer and the 104th Congress are typical in their call for more and better technical analysis and expert oversight to rationalize risk management. There is no doubt that technical analysis is vital for making risk decisions better informed, more consistent, and more accountable. However, value conflicts and pervasive distrust in risk management cannot easily be reduced by technical analysis. Trying to address risk controversies primarily with more science is, in fact, likely to exacerbate conflict.

Process-Oriented Solutions

A major objective of this chapter has been to demonstrate the complexity of risk and its assessment. To summarize the earlier discussions, danger is real, but risk is socially constructed. Risk assessment is inherently subjective and represents a blending of science and judgment with important psychological, social, cultural, and political factors. Finally, our social and democratic institutions, remarkable as they are in many respects, breed distrust in the risk arena.

Whoever controls the definition of risk controls the rational solution to the problem at hand. If you define risk one way, then one option will rise to the top as the most cost-effective or the safest or the best. If you define it another way, perhaps incorporating qualitative characteristics and other contextual factors, you will likely get a different ordering of your action solutions (Fischhoff, Watson, and Hope, 1984). Defining risk is thus an exercise in power.

Scientific literacy and public education are important, but they are not central to risk controversies. The public is not irrational. The public is influenced by emotion and affect in a way that is both simple and sophisticated. So are scientists. The public is influenced by worldviews, ideologies, and values; so are scientists, particularly when they are working at the limits of their expertise.

The limitations of risk science, the importance and difficulty of maintaining trust, and the subjective and contextual nature of the risk game point to the need for a new approach—one that focuses upon introducing more public participation into both risk assessment and risk decision making in order to make the decision process more democratic, improve the relevance and quality of technical analysis, and increase the legitimacy and public acceptance of the resulting decisions. Work by scholars and practitioners in Europe and North America has begun to lay the foundations for improved methods of public participation within deliberative decision processes that include negotiation, mediation, oversight committees, and other forms of public involvement (English, 1992; Kunreuther, Fitzgerald, and Aarts, 1993; National Research Council, 1996; Renn, Webler, and Johnson, 1991; Renn, Webler, and Wiedemann, 1995).

Recognizing interested and affected citizens as legitimate partners in the exercise of risk assessment is no short-term panacea for the problems of risk management. But serious attention to participation and process issues may, in the long run, lead to more satisfying and successful ways to manage risk.

NOTE

1. Although we have focused only on the relationship between toxicologists' affective reactions to chemicals and their responses to S_1 and S_2, there were many other links between affect and attitudes in the survey. For example, the very simple bad-good rating of pesticides correlated significantly (r = .20) with agreement that there is a threshold dose for nongenotoxic carcinogens. The same rating correlated .27 with the belief that synergistic effects of chemicals cause animal studies of single chemicals to underestimate risk to humans.

REFERENCES

Alhakami, A. S., and Slovic, P. "A Psychological Study of the Inverse Relationship Between Perceived Risk and Perceived Benefit." *Risk Analysis,* 1994, *14*(6), 1085–1096.

Alpen, J. "Science Education: The Pipeline Is Leaking Women All the Way Along." *Science,* 1993, *260,* 409–411.

Barke, R., Jenkins-Smith, H., and Slovic, P. *Risk Perceptions of Men and Women Scientists.* Report No. 95–6. Eugene, Ore.: Decision Research, 1995.

Baumer, T. L. "Research on Fear of Crime in the United States." *Victimology,* 1978, *3,* 254–264.

Breyer, S. *Breaking the Vicious Circle: Toward Effective Risk Regulation.* Cambridge, Mass.: Harvard University Press, 1993.

Brody, C. J. "Differences by Sex in Support for Nuclear Power." *Social Forces,* 1984, *63,* 209–228.

Buss, D. M., Craik, K. H., and Dake, K. M. "Contemporary Worldviews and Perception of the Technological System." In V. T. Covello, J. Menkes, and J. Mumpower (eds.), *Risk Evaluation and Management.* New York: Plenum, 1986.

Carney, R. E. "Attitudes Toward Risk." In R. E. Carney (ed.), *Risk Taking Behavior: Concepts, Methods, and Applications to Smoking and Drug Abuse.* Springfield, Ill.: Thomas, 1971.

Cohen, B. L. "Criteria for Technology Acceptability." *Risk Analysis,* 1985, *5,* 1–2.

Covello, V. T., Flamm, W. G., Rodricks, J. V., and Tardiff, R. G. *The Analysis of Actual Versus Perceived Risks.* New York: Plenum, 1983.

Dake, K. "Orienting Dispositions in the Perception of Risk: An Analysis of Contemporary Worldviews and Cultural Biases." *Journal of Cross-Cultural Psychology,* 1991, *22,* 61–82.

Dake, K. "Myths of Nature: Culture and the Social Construction of Risk." *Journal of Social Issues,* 1992, *48,* 21–37.

Dean, W. R., and Thompson, P. B. *The Varieties of Risk.* Environmental Risk Management Working Paper ERC 95–3. Edmonton: University of Alberta, 1995.

DeJoy, D. "An Examination of Gender Differences in Traffic Accident Risk Perception." *Accident Analysis and Prevention,* 1992.

DuPont, R. L. *Nuclear Phobia—Phobic Thinking About Nuclear Power.* Washington, D.C.: Media Institute, 1980.

English, M. R. *Siting Low-Level Radioactive Waste Disposal Facilities.* New York: Quorum, 1992.

Environmental Protection Agency. *Unfinished Business: A Comparative Assessment of Environmental Problems.* Washington, D.C.: Environmental Protection Agency, 1987.

Fessenden-Raden, J., Fitchen, J. M., and Heath, J. S. "Providing Risk Information in Communities: Factors Influencing What Is Heard and Accepted." *Science Technology and Human Values,* 1987, *12,* 94–101.

Fischhoff, B., Watson, S., and Hope, C. "Defining Risk." *Policy Sciences,* 1984, *17,* 123–139.

Fischhoff, B., and others. "How Safe Is Safe Enough? A Psychometric Study of Attitudes Towards Technological Risks and Benefits." *Policy Sciences,* 1978, *9,* 127–152.

Flynn, J., Slovic, P., and Mertz, C. K. "Gender, Race, and Perception of Environmental Health Risks." *Risk Analysis,* 1994, *14*(6), 1101–1108.

Funtowicz, S. O., and Ravetz, J. R. "Three Types of Risk Assessment and the Emergence of Post-Normal Science." In S. Krimsky and D. Golding (eds.), *Social Theories of Risk.* Westport, Conn.: Praeger, 1992.

Gilligan, C. *In a Different Voice: Psychological Theory and Women's Development.* Cambridge, Mass.: Harvard University Press, 1982.

Gregory, R., Flynn, J., and Slovic, P. "Technological Stigma." *American Scientist,* 1995, *83,* 220–223.

Gregory, R., Lichtenstein, S., and MacGregor, D. G. "The Role of Past States in Determining Reference Points for Policy Decisions." *Organizational Behavior and Human Decision Processes,* 1993, *55,* 195–206.

Gutteling, J. M., and Wiegman, O. "Gender-Specific Reactions to Environmental Hazards in the Netherlands." *Sex Roles,* 1993, *28,* 433–447.

Gwartney-Gibbs, P. A., and Lach, D. H. "Sex Differences in Attitudes Toward Nuclear War." *Journal of Peace Research,* 1991, *28,* 161–174.

"How a PR Firm Executed the Alar Scare." *Wall Street Journal,* Oct. 3, 1989, pp. A1–A3.

Jasper, J. M. *Nuclear Politics: Energy and the State in the United States, Sweden, and France.* Princeton, N.J.: Princeton University Press, 1990.

Jenkins-Smith, H. C. *Nuclear Imagery and Regional Stigma: Testing Hypotheses of Image Acquisition and Valuation Regarding Nevada.* Technical report. Albuquerque: University of New Mexico, Institute for Public Policy, 1993.

Johnson, E. J., and Tversky, A. "Affect, Generalization, and the Perception of Risk." *Journal of Personality and Social Psychology,* 1983, *45,* 20–31.

Koren, G., and Klein, N. "Bias Against Negative Studies in Newspaper Reports of Medical Research." *Journal of the American Medical Association,* 1991, *266,* 1824–1826.

Kraus, N., Malmfors, T., and Slovic, P. "Intuitive Toxicology: Expert and Lay Judgments of Chemical Risks." *Risk Analysis,* 1992, *12,* 215–232.

Krimsky, S., and Golding, D. *Social Theories of Risk.* Westport, Conn.: Praeger-Greenwood, 1992.

Kunreuther, H. "Mitigating Disaster Losses Through Insurance." *Journal of Risk and Uncertainty,* forthcoming.

Kunreuther, H., Fitzgerald, K., and Aarts, T. D. "Siting Noxious Facilities: A Test of the Facility Siting Credo." *Risk Analysis,* 1993, *13,* 301–318.

Lichtenberg, J., and MacLean, D. "Is Good News No News?" *Geneva Papers on Risk and Insurance,* 1992, *17,* 362–365.

MacGregor, D., Slovic, P., and Morgan, M. G. "Perception of Risks from Electromagnetic Fields: A Psychometric Evaluation of a Risk-Communication Approach." *Risk Analysis,* 1994, *14*(5), 815–828.

Malmfors, T., and others. *Evaluating Chemical Risks: Results of a Survey of the British Toxicological Society.* Report No. 96–1. Eugene, Ore.: Decision Research, 1996.

McNeil, B. J., Pauker, S. G., Sox, H. C., Jr., and Tversky, A. "On the Elicitation of Preferences for Alternative Therapies." *New England Journal of Medicine,* 1982, *306,* 1259–1262.

Merchant, C. *The Death of Nature: Women, Ecology, and the Scientific Revolution.* New York: HarperCollins, 1980.

Morgan, M. G., and others. "Powerline Frequency Electric and Magnetic Fields: A Pilot Study of Risk Perception." *Risk Analysis,* 1985, *5,* 139–149.

National Research Council. *Improving Risk Communication.* Washington, D.C.: National Academy Press, 1989.

National Research Council. *Understanding Risk: Informing Decisions in a Democratic Society.* Washington, D.C.: National Academy Press, 1996.

Otway, H. "Public Wisdom, Expert Fallibility: Toward a Contextual Theory of Risk." In S. Krimsky and D. Golding (eds.), *Social Theories of Risk.* Westport, Conn.: Praeger, 1992.

Palm, R. I. *Natural Hazards: An Integrative Framework for Research and Planning.* Baltimore: Johns Hopkins University Press, 1995.

Peters, E., and Slovic, P. "The Role of Affect and Worldviews as Orienting Dispositions in the Perception and Acceptance of Nuclear Power." *Journal of Applied Social Psychology,* 1996, *26*(16), 1427–1453.

Pidgeon, N., and others. "Risk Perception." In Royal Society Study Group (ed.), *Risk: Analysis, Perception and Management.* London: Royal Society, 1992.

Pillisuk, M., and Acredolo, C. "Fear of Technological Hazards: One Concern or Many?" *Social Behavior,* 1988, *3,* 17–24.

Renn, O., Webler, T., and Johnson, B. "Citizen Participation for Hazard Management." *Risk—Issues in Health and Safety,* 1991, *3,* 12–22.

Renn, O., Webler, T., and Wiedemann, P. *Fairness and Competence in Citizen Participation.* Dordrecht, The Netherlands: Kluwer, 1995.

Riger, S., Gordon, M. T., and LeBailly, M. R. (1978). "Women's Fear of Crime: From Blaming to Restricting the Victim." *Victimology,* 1978, *3,* 274–284.

Shrader-Frechette, K. S. *Risk and Rationality.* Berkeley: University of California Press, 1991.

Sjöberg, L., and Drottz-Sjöberg, B. M. *Attitudes Toward Nuclear Waste.* Rhizikon Research Report No. 12. Stockholm, Sweden: Stockholm School of Economics, Center for Risk Research, Aug. 1993.

Slovic, P. "Perception of Risk." *Science,* 1987, *236,* 280–285.

Slovic, P. "Perception of Risk: Reflections on the Psychometric Paradigm." In S. Krimsky and D. Golding (eds.), *Social Theories of Risk.* New York: Praeger, 1992.

Slovic, P. "Perceived Risk, Trust, and Democracy: A Systems Perspective." *Risk Analysis,* 1993, *13,* 675–682.

Slovic, P., Flynn, J., and Layman, M. "Perceived Risk, Trust, and the Politics of Nuclear Waste." *Science,* 1991, *254,* 1603–1607.

Slovic, P., Flynn, J., Mertz, C. K., and Mullican, L. *Health Risk Perception in Canada.* Report No. 93-EHD-170. Ottawa: Department of National Health and Welfare, 1993.

Slovic, P., Kraus, N., Lappe, H., and Major, M. "Risk Perception of Prescription Drugs: Report on a Survey in Canada." *Canadian Journal of Public Health,* 1991, *82,* S15–S20.

Slovic, P., and others. "Risk Perception of Prescription Drugs: Report on a Survey in Sweden." *Pharmaceutical Medicine,* 1989, *4,* 43–65.

Slovic, P., and others. "Perceived Risk, Stigma, and Potential Economic Impacts of a High-Level Nuclear Waste Repository in Nevada." *Risk Analysis,* 1991, *11,* 683–696.

Spigner, C., Hawkins, W., and Loren, W. "Gender Differences in Perceptions of Risk Associated with Alcohol and Drug Use Among College Students." *Women and Health,* 1993, *20,* 87–97.

Steger, M. A., and Witte, S. L. "Gender Differences in Environmental Orientations: A Comparison of Publics and Activists in Canada and the U.S." *Western Political Quarterly,* 1989, *42,* 627–649.

Stern, P. C., Dietz, T., and Kalof, L. "Value Orientations, Gender, and Environmental Concerns." *Environment and Behavior,* 1993, *25,* 322–348.

Tengs, T. D., and others. "Five Hundred Life-Saving Interventions and Their Cost Effectiveness." *Risk Analysis,* 1995, *15,* 369–390.

Tversky, A., and Kahneman, D. "The Framing of Decisions and the Psychology of Choice." *Science,* 1981, *211,* 453–458.

U.S. Senate. *The Comprehensive Regulatory Reform Act of 1995* (Dole/Johnson discussion draft to S. 343), 1995.

Weiner, R. F. "Comment on Sheila Jasanoff's Guest Editorial." *Risk Analysis,* 1993, *13,* 495–496.

Wilson, R., and Crouch, E. *Risk/Benefit Analysis.* New York: Ballinger, 1982.

Wynne, B. "Risk and Social Learning: Reification to Engagement." In S. Krimsky and D. Golding (eds.), *Social Theories of Risk.* Westport, Conn.: Praeger, 1992.

Zajonc, R. B. "Feeling and Thinking: Preferences Need No Inferences." *American Psychologist,* 1980, *35,* 151–175.

13

PERCEPTION AND EXPECTATION OF CLIMATE CHANGE

Precondition for Economic and Technological Adaptation

Elke U. Weber

CLIMATE CHANGE, STRATOSPHERIC ozone depletion, and the loss of biodiversity are the three most significant environmental changes currently occurring on a global scale (National Research Council, 1992, pp. 18–21). Macroeconomic impact models of environmental change crucially depend on a realistic set of assumptions about human adaptation to such change. These assumptions should incorporate knowledge about human capabilities and limitations in attention, perception, memory, and information processing. A comprehensive summary of the current state of knowledge and future research directions on these issues was provided by the Committee on the Human Dimensions of Global Change, commissioned by the National Research Council. Its report divides human

This research was supported by grant SES-9109942 from the National Science Foundation, Program on Human Dimensions of Global Environmental Change. I am grateful to Steve Sonka for his input during the planning and execution stages of the project, to the editors of this volume, Hadi Dowlatabadi, Baruch Fischhoff, Granger Morgan, and other members of the Climate Assessment Group in the Department of Engineering and Public Policy at Carnegie-Mellon University, and to Ilana Ritov for providing useful comments on an earlier version of this chapter.

response to global changes into a hierarchical set of seven interacting systems, with the most fundamental system being "individual perception, judgment, and action" (National Research Council, 1992, p. 5). The study reported in this chapter is intended to contribute to our understanding of the human response to one important class of environmental change, namely climate change and the possibility of global warming. As agriculture is one area of the economy that will be affected by climate change in a direct and major fashion, the perceptions, judgments, and actions of farmers are a crucial component in the determination of the immediate and ultimate consequences of climate change and are the topic of this chapter.

Growing concern about greenhouse gases and their effect on the global climate over the last decade has resulted in analyses of the impact of climate change in a variety of areas, including agricultural production and food security. In a review of such studies, Sonka (1991) noted several methodological weaknesses. One weakness is the assumption of an instantaneous change in climate rather than a gradual warming trend over a number of decades. Another is that climate is the only factor assumed to change from current conditions, despite the likelihood that a changed climate some twenty to fifty years into the future will face a world greatly different from today's. Global population growth and technological change are only two factors that, in addition to climate change, will significantly affect food security.

Global change in agricultural production will come about as the sum of gradual adjustments made by individual farmers as they perceive gradual local changes in weather and climate. Yet few agricultural impact assessments consider adaptation to a changing climate as a dynamic process. One exception is the work of Kaiser and others (1991), which simulates individual farm decisions over a series of years. Agricultural production is affected by climate change through changes in annual production decisions. The simulation assumes, however, that decisions are made with perfect accuracy in expectations of the altered climate. Absence of a better alternative (such as a more realistic set of assumptions about the nature and quality of decision makers' climate expectations) is a likely explanation for this clearly unrealistic assumption (Bullard, 1990).

In summary, one may question the answers provided by previous agricultural impact assessments because these models have tended to (1) assume an instantaneous change in climate, (2) focus exclusively on physical and biological processes, (3) assume perfect accuracy in expectations about climate changes, and (4) ignore the adaptations that individuals and society can and will implement over time as climate changes (Ausubel, 1983; Bartlett, 1980;

Glantz, Robinson, and Krentz, 1985). The goal of this chapter is to provide information that will help modelers to make more realistic assumptions on all four issues, but in particular on issues 3 and 4.

Detection of Climate Change

Changes and trends in local weather and climate patterns are not easily detected. A lot of scientific uncertainty surrounds the nature and magnitude of climate change (Begley, 1993; National Research Council, 1979, 1982, 1992; Smith, 1995; Trefil, 1990). The Intergovernmental Panel on Climate Change (IPCC), established by the World Meteorological Organization and the United Nations Environmental Program in 1988, reported in 1990 that the size of global increases in surface air temperature was "broadly consistent with predictions of climate [change], but also of the same magnitude as natural climate variability," with an "unequivocal detection of the enhanced greenhouse effect from observations not likely for a decade or more" (Houghton, Jenkins, and Ephraums, 1990, p. 2). General circulation models, the complex computer simulation models used to predict the effect of greenhouse gases on local and global climate, are highly sensitive not only to assumptions about future levels of greenhouse gases but also to design features such as the density of the grid imposed on the earth's surface (Dickinson, 1986; Trefil, 1990). Thus IPCC's 1990 estimate of climate change by the year 2030 for central North America forecasts warming between two and four degrees in winter and two to three degrees in summer, and precipitation increases from 0 percent to 15 percent in winter and decreases of 5 percent to 10 percent in summer. Its best-case scenario, however, reduces these numbers by 30 percent, and the worst-case scenario increases them by 50 percent.

Given the scientific uncertainty surrounding climate change and the gradual nature of any change, in conjunction with the importance of detecting such change at the local level in order to develop adaptive responses, it is imperative to obtain answers to the following questions: Can individuals detect gradual changes in local temperature and precipitation against a background of large variability? What factors will facilitate or delay the perception or detection of such changes?

Role of Expectations

Presumably, the expectation of climate change plays a large role in both the detection of and adaptation to climate change. The literature on covariation assessment documents the impact of prior theories and expectations. Chapman and Chapman (1967) showed that the expectation of a relationship between two variables prompted by semantic associations is sufficient for people to perceive and report covariation even in sets of data where no covariation exists. Nisbett and Ross (1980) summarized a long string of studies showing that people will under- or overestimate actual statistical relationships depending on their prior expectations, a phenomenon that is mediated by people's tendency to focus on observations that conform to their beliefs (Mynatt, Doherty, and Tweney, 1977; Wason, 1960). While the strength of the objective evidence of covariation clearly plays some role in its detection (Wright and Murphy, 1984), the evidence is overwhelming that covariation detection is dominated by prior expectations. Alloy and Tabachnik (1984) showed that, as a mechanism in addition to confirmatory information search, people with and without expectations also differ in the amount of information they seek out. In particular, they seek out less situational information if they hold strong preconceptions about a given relationship. Finally, Bower and Masling (1978) showed that people's ability to encode and subsequently retrieve correlated information is greatly enhanced when those correlations can be explained on the basis of prior expectations.

An interesting historical example of how climate expectations can affect the detection and acknowledgment of objective weather patterns is provided by Kupperman (1982). English settlers who arrived in North America in the early colonial period operated under the assumption that climate is a function of latitude. Newfoundland, which is south of London, was thus expected to have a moderate climate, and Virginia was expected to have the climate of southern Spain. Despite high death rates due to weather that was consistently much colder than expected, the resulting failure of settlements, and pressure from investors disappointed by the colonies' inability to produce the rich commodities associated with hot climates, colonists clung persistently to their expectations about local climate based on latitude. Reluctant to accept the different climatic conditions as a new fact in need of explanation, they instead generated ever more complex rationalizations and alternative explanations for these persistent deviations from their expectations. Samuel de Champlain, for example, took a single mild winter in 1610 as an indication that his mild climate expectations were justified after all, and suggested that the severe winters he had experienced during each of the six preceding years must have been what would nowadays be called statistical outliers.

Role of Experience

Given the large random fluctuations of climate variables over time, more experience with the natural variability in the level of these variables can be predicted to make it more difficult to believe that local patterns are evidence of long-term trends (von Furstenberg, 1990). Extended practice of an occupation (for example, farming) that focuses attention on weather and climate year after year may therefore make it more difficult to detect small climate trends embedded in random variability. A young farmer may, for example, see a succession of five or six hotter or drier years as evidence of a warming trend, whereas an older farmer may recall that similar runs occurred in the 1950s and 1960s but did not result in any permanent changes.

The importance of climate factors and climate change in agriculture and the importance of agriculture for the national economy and food security make farmers' expectations, perceptions, and adaptive responses to climate change an important topic of study. For this reason, the present study investigates the relationship between these variables in a convenience sample of Illinois cash-crop farmers.

Field Study

The present study addresses several questions.

Experimental Questions and Predictions

What proportion of farmers believe in climate change, and what is the nature and magnitude of temperature and precipitation changes they expect to see over the next twenty to thirty years? What causes farmers to believe in climate change? Does the expectation of climate change affect farmers' interpretations of current weather patterns? Do expectations or perceptions or both affect their adaptive responses? In what ways are farmers already responding to present or anticipated climate change? What are the consequences of their expectations for the success of their farm operations?

Participants and Instruments

Forty-eight farms were selected from a pool of participants in the Illinois Farm Business Farm Management (FBFM) association, a voluntary record-keeping cooperative. To keep the sample homogeneous on external variables, participation was restricted to farms that produced cash crops, were family operations, and had one primary and full-time owner and decision maker.

Use of FBFM participants provided access to detailed farm-level annual financial and production records for the seven years between 1985 and

1992. Survey responses could thus be linked to actual farm performance. Average farm size was 740 acres and ranged from 263 to 1,608 acres; approximately half of most farms' acreage was devoted to corn, the other half to soya bean production. Respondents were all male, had an average of 26.5 years of experience as the primary farm decision maker (with a range from four to sixty years), and fewer than half had attended college.

Individual structured interviews were conducted shortly before spring planting in 1993. They lasted between two and two and a half hours and involved 154 numerical, multiple-choice, and open-ended answers. Farmers provided information about their production and pricing decisions and other farm practices, and in particular about the following set of annual decisions: (1) what varieties of corn to plant, (2) when to start planting, (3) what tillage practice to use, (4) whether to buy, replace, or rent new equipment, (5) whether to purchase crop insurance and how much, and (6) how to price the crop. For each of these decisions, farmers reported what and how much information (past and present) they considered, from what sources they received this information, by what decision rule or process they arrived at their decisions, and what factors contributed to perceived decision difficulty. Details about this portion of the study can be found in Weber and Sonka (1994). Their main results, namely the identification of a set of management traits and the relationship of these traits to farm success, are summarized in the next section, as reference will be made to the management trait and farm success variables later on. I will then return to the topic of this chapter, namely farmers' beliefs and expectations about climate change and their current and anticipated responses to perceived or expected change.

Summary of Results of Weber and Sonka (1994)

Farmers' answers to questions asked about the seven annual decisions, their responses to other questions about production and pricing practices (the number of varieties of corn planted each year, acres allocated to experimentation, ownership and use of a personal computer), the keeping of climate records, the purchase of crop or hail insurance or both, the use of forward contracts or the futures market or both, the use of a regular before- or after-harvest pricing strategy either of their own design or provided by an expert, and their age, years of experience as primary farm decision maker, and education level were used as input variables into a principal components factor analysis that identified an underlying structure of seven management traits. Descriptive labels for these traits and the

Table 13.1. Management Traits and Contributing Variables with Factor Loading.

Trait	*Factor Loading*	*Contributing Variables*
Pricing sophistication	+.94	Prices production before harvest
	+.94	Uses forward contracts
	+.72	Uses pricing strategy of own design
Practical experience	–.60	Does not experience goal conflict
	+.79	Is older
	+.82	Primary farm decision maker longer
	–.60	Has less education
Active experimentation	+.57	Plants more varieties of corn
	+.53	Uses more acreage to experiment
	+.84	Owns personal computer (PC)
	+.87	Uses PC for farm business
Belief in collective wisdom	+.90	Other farmers provide information
	+.81	Does what other farmers do
Micromanaging	+.54	Uses short-term weather forecasts
	+.77	Time pressure makes decisions difficult
	+.60	Keeps weather and climate records
	–.57	No regular after-harvest pricing strategy
Systematic analysis	+.81	Uses market and price information
	+.50	Gets information from cooperative extension service
	+.57	Decides by objectively weighing options
	+.50	Conflicting information makes decisions difficult
Macromanaging	+.88	Farm magazines as source of information
	–.53	Professional consultant information not used
	–.51	No weather and climate records kept

list of contributing variables that had factor loadings greater than the absolute value of .50 for each trait are shown in Table 13.1.

Table 13.2 shows the distribution of the seven management traits in the sample of farmers. Trait strength for each farmer was classified as strongly negative ($t_i \le -1$), moderately negative ($-1 < t_i \le 0$), moderately positive ($0 < t_i < 1$), or strongly positive ($t_i \ge 1$), based on its estimated factor score. Table 13.2 shows that the distribution of some traits is skewed. Although the majority of farmers (74 percent) had positive scores on pricing sophistication, for example, the majority also had negative scores on active experimentation (63 percent).

Weber and Sonka (1994) argued that farm success can be described and quantified in different ways; they used five different proxies for it. The first one, net farm income standardized by the number of crop acres, is a measure of a farm's operational efficiency. The second and third, average prices received for either corn or soya beans received in a given year (in dollars per bushel), are measures of a farmer's pricing success. The last two, average crop yields for either corn or soya beans achieved in a given year (in bushels per acre), are measures of a farmer's production success. These measures were available for the seven years between 1985 and 1992.

To examine the relationship between the seven management traits on farm success, Weber and Sonka (1994) conducted a repeated measures analysis that included the five success measures for each of the seven years as dependent variables, the management traits as independent variables, and a variety of other variables that can be expected to affect the different

Table 13.2. Distribution of Management Traits Among Farmers.

	TRAIT DIRECTION AND STRENGTH			
Trait	***Strongly Negative***	***Moderately Negative***	***Moderately Positive***	***Strongly Positive***
Pricing sophistication	17	9	72	2
Practical experience	21	21	44	14
Active experimentation	12	51	21	16
Belief in collective wisdom	12	45	27	17
Micromanaging	13	45	25	17
Systematic analysis	16	37	21	26
Macromanaging	10	45	40	5

measures of farm success as covariates. These covariates were total crop acreage, total capital investment, total months of labor, soil quality, and the percentage of acreage in either corn, soya beans, or a government program. The most interesting result is that different management traits were associated with different dimensions of farm success. Micromanaging had a negative effect on prices but a positive effect on yields. Pricing sophistication had a positive effect on operational efficiency but no effect on prices or yields. Finally, active experimentation and systematic analysis had a positive effect on prices, in particular during the severe drought year of 1988.

Expectations of Climate Change

A large section of the survey evolved around farmers' attitudes and opinions about climate change. As shown in Table 13.3, responses to an open-ended request to describe the climate they were expecting in east-central Illinois in twenty to thirty years (which were subsequently content-coded) indicate that 53 percent of farmers did not expect any significant change in the climate; the other 47 percent expect the climate to be either warmer and drier (42 percent) or more variable (5 percent).

Farmers also rated their beliefs in the greenhouse effect, ozone depletion, and global warming on a scale from 1 (no belief) to 10 (very strong belief), with the opportunity to express no opinion. Only two farmers took advantage of the no-opinion option, and only for the greenhouse effect question. Mean belief ratings were 3.4 for the greenhouse effect, 4.8 for ozone depletion, and 3.7 for global warming, each with a range from 1 to 9. Belief in global warming had a correlation of .46 with belief in ozone depletion and of .78 with belief in the greenhouse effect. As the terms *global warming* and *greenhouse effect* refer to the same phenomenon (that the addition of carbon dioxide and other greenhouse gases to

Table 13.3. Expectations About Climate over the Next Twenty to Thirty Years.

Opinion	***% of Respondents Holding Opinion***
No or very little change	53
Warmer	19
Drier	2
Warmer and drier	21
More variable	5

the earth's atmosphere will cause the temperature of the earth to rise), the correlation of .78 between belief in global warming and belief in the greenhouse effect was appropriate and warranted. The depletion of the ozone layer that protects the earth from harmful ultraviolet rays, however, is a different phenomenon with a different set of causes (mostly the release of chlorofluorocarbon [CFC] gases used in air conditioners and industrial applications). Though CFCs alone cause warming, their ozone destruction can cause cooling, and these two effects tend to balance each other. That there was a significant and sizable correlation of .46 between farmers' belief in ozone depletion and in global warming can either be seen as an indication of a general disposition to believe or not believe in global environmental change or as an additional indication that the general population as well as media accounts in the United States tend to conflate these two issues (Bostrom, Morgan, Fischhoff, and Read, 1994; Read and others, 1994).

When belief ratings in global warming from 1 to 3 were coded as disbelief, 49 percent of the farmers fell into this category, broadly consistent with responses on the open-ended question about expectation of local climate in twenty to thirty years, where 53 percent indicated that they were not expecting any significant change from today. These two measures of belief were highly correlated with each other ($r = .92$, across respondents). None of the demographic variables (age, level of education) or length of farming experience were reliable predictors of whether farmers did or did not believe in global warming.

Two follow-ups to the open-ended question about local long-term climate expectations asked farmers for the change in average temperature and average annual rainfall they expect to see over the next twenty to thirty years. They were told to respond with zero if they expected no change, a negative number if they expected a decrease, and a positive number if they expected an increase. The two numerical change estimates were significantly different for those who indicated little or no belief in climate change (ratings of 1–3 on the belief scale) and those who indicated moderate or strong belief in climate change (ratings > 3): mean expected changes in temperature for the two groups were 0.8 and 2.5 degrees, and mean expected changes in rainfall were 1.0 and 3.7 inches, respectively ($F(1, 40) = 4.17$ and 4.23, $p < .05$).

Table 13.4 provides farmers' responses to a series of questions about the nature of the changes in temperature and precipitation that they would need to see in order to believe in the reality of global warming. Overall, farmers were looking for year-round temperature increases between two and five degrees and changes in rainfall between two and five inches over a period of at least ten years, with more variability in the direction of changes in precipitation than in temperature. It is encouraging to note that these changes given as requirements for a belief in global warming are well within the range of temperature and precipitation changes predicted by the IPCC that were described in the introduction.

Sources of Climate Change Expectations

Farmers were asked for the sources of their beliefs in global warming and climate change. They were given a list of five sources and asked to indicate which had influenced their opinion and to rank order those that had done so. The five source categories were popular media, agricultural newspapers, own experience, other farmers, and a catchall category, "other." Most farmers checked off either one or two of these categories as having had an influence on their opinion, with responses relatively evenly distributed across the first four categories. When the frequency with which different sources were acknowledged was cross-classified by whether farmers did or did not believe in global warming, there was a significant association between the two variables (chi-squared (4) = 9.10, $p < .05$). Farmers who believed in global warming were less likely to include popular media and more likely to include agricultural newspapers among their sources. They also listed more sources of influence than those who did not believe in global warming ($t(46) = 2.31$, $p < .05$).

Accuracy of Weather Memories

Prior to being asked about their beliefs regarding climate change, farmers were asked a series of questions about their memories of weather events in recent years. In particular, they were asked to indicate on a sheet of graph paper what they remembered about the total rainfall during the months of April and July over the previous seven years. The amount of rainfall during April and July is a crucial determinant of the quality and quantity of corn and soya bean crops and thus a salient variable in farmers' minds. The true values of total rainfall for east-central Illinois and their means between 1985 and 1991 are shown as solid lines in Figures 13.1 and 13.2 for April and July, respectively. Mean remembered values are indicated by the dashed lines, showing that, overall, farmers systematically misremembered April rainfalls as greater than they actually were and July rainfalls as smaller than the true amounts. It should be noted that this is the pattern of changes predicted by climate change models (see IPCC predictions in the introduction).

Table 13.4. Temperature and Precipitation Changes Required for Farmers to Believe in Global Warming.

Pattern of Change	***% of Responses***
Required temperature change pattern	
Warmer in summer	5
Warmer in winter	7
Warmer year-round	88
Over what number of years	
Five or less	27
Five to ten	36
Ten or more	36
Change in number of degrees	
Less than two	18
Two to five	70
More than five	12
Season of required rainfall changes	
In summer	5
In spring	2
All year	93
Required pattern of rainfall changes	
More variable	14
More	17
Less	43
Unsure or no opinion	26
Over what number of years	
Less than three	0
Three to five	27
Five to ten	60
More than ten	13
Change in number of inches	
Less than two	20
Two to five	60
More than five	20

Figure 13.1. True and Remembered Rainfall in East-Central Illinois During April, 1985 to 1991.

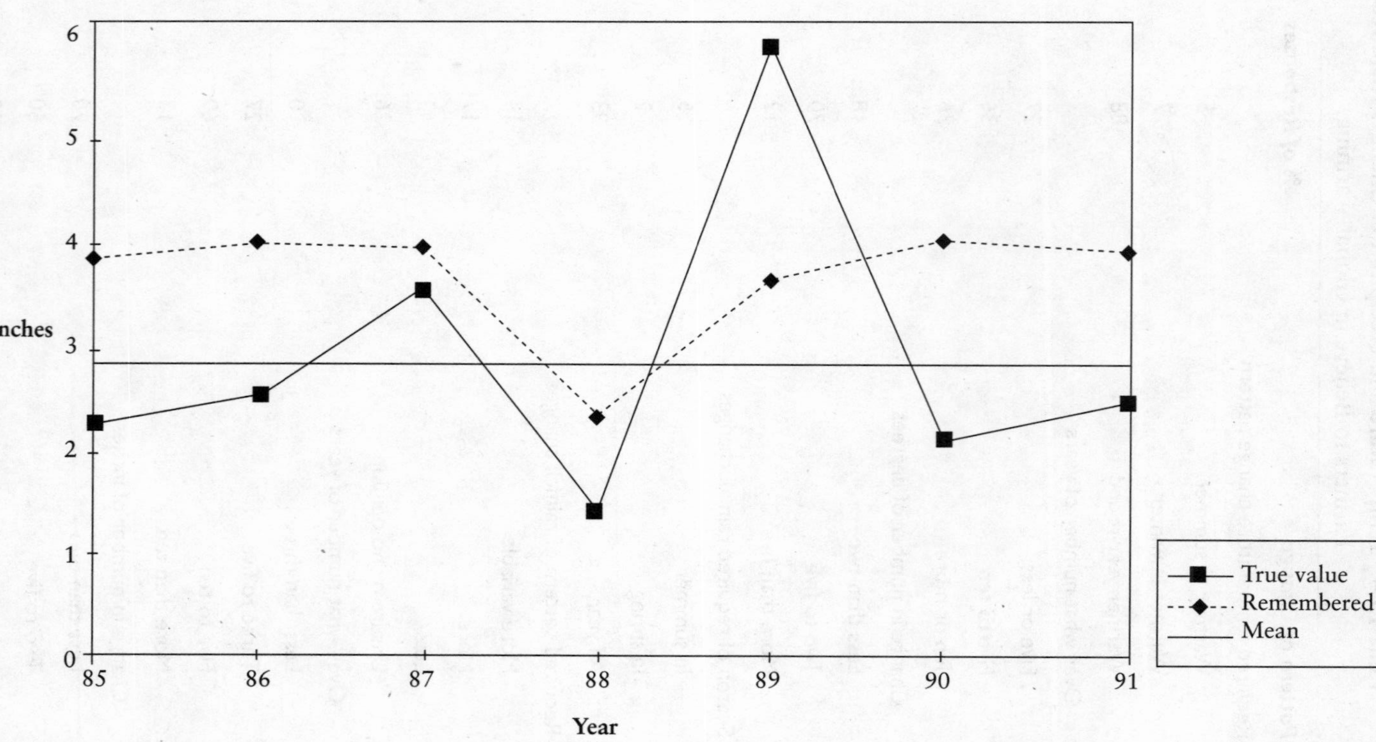

Figure 13.2. True and Remembered Rainfall in East-Central Illinois During July, 1985 to 1991.

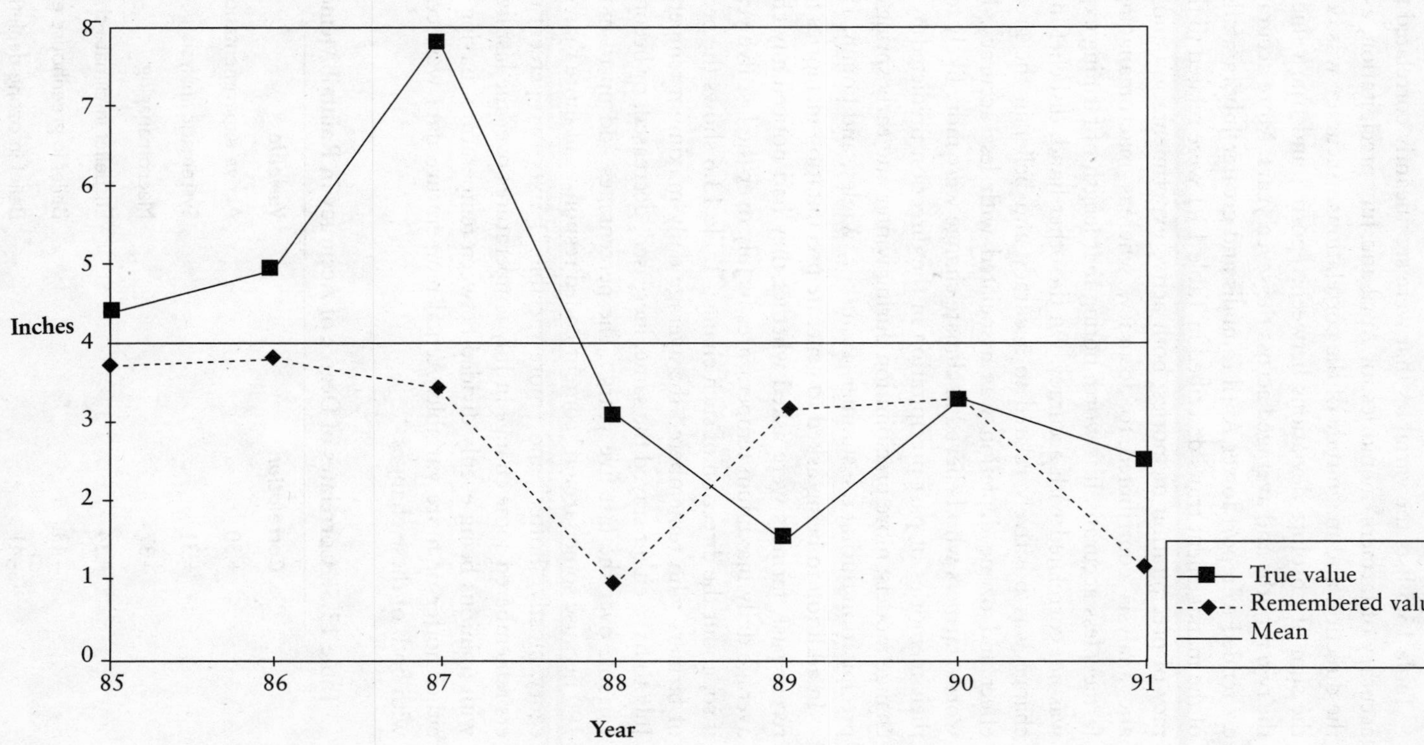

Table 13.5 lists the variables that were significantly correlated with the accuracy of farmers' memories for April and July precipitation, as well as the direction and magnitude of the correlations. Accuracy was defined as the sum of absolute deviations between reported and true values across the two months and averaged across the seven years. More accurate farmers tended to report lower April rainfalls and greater July rainfalls. Three of the management traits described in Table 13.1 were related to the accuracy of precipitation memories; both active experimentation and systematic analysis contributed to accuracy, whereas macromanaging made farmers less accurate. It is worth noting that length of farming experience was *not* correlated with accuracy. On the other hand, disbelief in climate change was positively related to accuracy and belief in the greenhouse effect and ozone depletion was associated with less accuracy. In other words, farmers who believed in climate change were more likely to distort their memories of past precipitation in the direction predicted by climate change models: more precipitation during winter and early spring and less precipitation during the summer (Palutikof, Wigley, and Lough, 1984).

In addition to being asked to generate precipitation memories from the recent past, farmers were asked whether they had noticed any change in average daily maximum temperatures in July over the last five years and, if so, about the direction of such change. Table 13.6 shows the percentage of farmers who remembered the average daily maximum temperature in July to have either stayed the same, increased, decreased, or become more variable over the last five years. (The percentages add up to more than 100 because some farmers' content-coded responses fit more than one category, mostly "hotter" and "more variable.") Sixty-two percent of farmers remembered some change in July temperatures over the last five years, with opinions being evenly divided between temperatures having become either hotter or more variable. Actual temperature data were consistent with both of these changes.

Table 13.5. Correlates of Degree of Accuracy in Rainfall Memories.

Correlation	*Variable*
+.30	Active experimentation
+.31	Systematic analysis
–.37	Macromanaging
+.34	Disbelief in climate change
–.43	Belief in greenhouse effect
–.41	Belief in ozone depletion

Table 13.6. Respondents Remembering Specified Change in Average Daily Maximum July Temperature over Last Five Years.

	RESPONDENTS (%)		
Remembered Change	***All Farmers***	***Disbelievers***	***Believers***
Same	42	52	27
Hotter[a]	30	16	54
Colder	2	0	2
More variable[a]	30	40	17

[a]*Remembered change corresponds to actual change.*

Table 13.6 also shows the distribution of temperature change memories as a function of whether farmers did or did not believe in global warming. There was a significant association between belief in global warming and prediction of July temperature changes (chi-squared (3) = 6.21, $p < .05$). Fifty-four percent of the believers but only 16 percent of the disbelievers in global warming remembered a short-run increase in July temperature.

Effects of Farming Experience

Consistent with theoretical predictions, farmers with more farming experience, who consequently had more experience with random (or nonrandom but cyclical) fluctuations of temperature and precipitation, were less likely to believe in the existence of possible contributors to climate change (that is, the greenhouse effect or ozone depletion) and were also less likely to remember July temperatures over the last five years as evidence of a warming trend. Yet, although the direction of these correlations was in the predicted direction, none of them reached statistical significance. Predictions about the negative effect of experience on farmers' perceptions of a warming trend thus received much weaker empirical support than the theoretical predictions about the facilitating effect of prior expectations.

Behavioral Adaptations Designed to Reduce Climate Risk

Pilot interviews with several farmers resulted in the identification of two classes of behavior that allow for the reduction of the downside potential associated with the possibility of a global and local warming trend. One class of risk-reduction behaviors consists of production practices. Farmers were asked in the survey whether they thought that changing climate patterns would eventually force them to change any of their farming practices. Fifty-two percent of respondents replied in the affirmative and were asked to list those practices and the nature of the change. The most commonly mentioned changes in production practices are shown in Table 13.7. It is interesting to note that a more conventional risk-reduction method, the purchase of crop insurance (or more of it), was listed by only 5 percent of respondents, whereas changes in tilling practice and associated changes in the use of pesticides were mentioned by 72 percent and the use of different (more drought-resistant) varieties of corn by 50 percent. (The percentages again add to more than 100 because farmers were allowed to give more than one response alternative, if so desired.)

The other class of risk-reduction behaviors involves financial responses and concerns the way in which farmers insure and price their crops. Farmers can price a crop before it is harvested and lock into a particular known price either by selling it by a forward contract to a local grain elevator or by hedging against price fluctuations with futures contracts. Alternatively they can assume the price risk themselves and sell the crop

Table 13.7. Anticipated Behavioral Adaptations to Climate Change and Their Determinants.

Adaptation	*Percentage of Responses*
Change in production practice	
Change in tilling practice or pesticide	72
Use of different crops or varieties	50
More irrigation	10
Earlier planting	14
Change in pricing practice	
Greater use of futures market	32
More crop insurance	5
Determinant for change in current pricing strategy	
Supply and demand factors	63
Weather in general and drought in particular	30
Tax reasons	14
Failure of current strategy	12
Cash-flow problems	12

after harvest in the spot market, selling it either all at once or stockpiling it to wait for better prices in the future.

An early part of our questionnaire ascertained to what extent farmers currently used these different pricing mechanisms (16 percent used the futures market and 32 percent used forward contracts), whether they had regular before- or after-harvest pricing strategies as opposed to deciding yearly on an ad hoc basis (25 percent had a regular before-harvest and 21 percent a regular after-harvest pricing strategy), and whether and to what extent they used crop and hail insurance (47 percent used crop insurance and 86 percent used hail insurance; of those who purchased insurance, crop insurers covered an average of 34 percent of their crops and hail insurers an average of 78 percent of their crops).

Anticipated changes in pricing practices most commonly mentioned as responses to possible changes in climate are also listed in Table 13.7. It is obvious that the percentage of farmers anticipating some pricing adaptation is much smaller than the percentage anticipating some production adaptation. Of those who did mention some pricing adaptation, the vast majority expected to make greater use of the futures market.

To understand the causal underpinnings of farmers' pricing strategies, the interviewer asked under what circumstances the farmers would change their current pricing strategies. Their responses, also in Table 13.7, show that although weather circumstances in general and drought in particular were mentioned only 30 percent of the time in a direct fashion, supply and demand factors (which are, of course, very sensitive to weather and drought conditions) were mentioned 63 percent of the time.

In addition to information about anticipated changes in production or financial practices, farmers also provided information about recent or currently ongoing changes in either the decisions or problems they were grappling with, as well as in the solutions to such problems or decisions. Interviews took place shortly before spring planting, and farmers were asked for the three most important decisions related to spring planting that they were currently facing. Their open-ended responses were subsequently content-coded, and three response categories emerged. As shown in Table 13.8, the largest percentage of farmers brought up issues related to climate or physical conditions for all three decisions. When asked how (if at all) these decisions or problems had changed over the last two to five years, about 60 percent of respondents indicated for each of the three decisions that they had not changed. Of the remaining 40 percent, however, the vast majority indicated that the changes were related to new circumstances, which mostly referred to less predictable weather. Last, farmers were asked how (if at all) the solutions to these problems or the way they dealt with these decisions had changed. As also shown in Table 13.8, more than half of the farmers indicated no change. For the remaining farmers, the largest categories of change in their solutions involved changes in farming practice (about 25 percent across the three decisions), followed by changes in information use (about 11 percent).

In summary, Tables 13.7 and 13.8 provide several interesting observations. Fully half of the respondents listed decisions related to climate conditions as foremost in their minds in their current spring planting, and 20 percent reported that the nature of the decisions had changed due to new circumstances. Thus the hypothetical question about anticipated adaptations to possible climate change was not necessarily hypothetical for a good subset of farmers. More importantly, comparison of Tables 13.7 and 13.8 shows that the frequency with which farmers listed particular types of changes as anticipated adaptations was very similar to the frequency with which they mentioned certain issues as important in their current

Table 13.8. Current Changes in Production Practices.

Decision Category and Change	*% of Responses*
Important decisions related to current spring planning	
Related to climate or physical conditions	50
Related to product (fertilizer) or process (tillage) selection	24
Related to pricing or other financial issues	12
Change in decisions or problems over last 2–5 years	
No change in problem	63
Change related to new circumstances	20
Change related to more information	9
Change related to new technology	5
Other change	2
Change in solution to problems over last 2–5 years	
No change	57
Change in farming practice	22
Change in information use	10
Change in equipment	5
Change in product	4
Other change	2

farming practice. Just as pricing decisions were not mentioned very frequently as current concerns (Table 13.8), changes in pricing practices were mentioned far less frequently than other possible future adaptations (Table 13.7).

Relationship Between Beliefs and Behavior

Table 13.9 shows that there were significant correlations between farmers' belief that global warming was a reality and a variety of reported and observed behaviors. Though there was no relationship between beliefs about climate change and keeping weather and climate records (which were kept by only 28 percent of our respondents), farmers who believed in global warming judged long-term climate forecasts (four to six months into the future) to be more important in their spring planting decisions and were more likely to report using both long-term and medium-term (two- to four-week) weather forecasts on a couple of different occasions during the interview. They also were more likely to report changes in their production methods over the last few years, primarily changes in tillage practice and use of chemicals, as well as changes in crops and varieties of seeds. Finally, climate change expectations were associated with some financial decisions. The more strongly farmers believed in the reality of global warming, the more likely they were to insure their crops against hail and crop failure, hedge against price fluctuations with futures contracts, and have a regular before-harvest pricing strategy using forward contracts and the futures market.

Though the correlations between belief in global warming and the five measures of farming success across the seven years of records were mostly positive, they were not significant. An *F*-test of the effect of belief in global warming in a repeated measures ANOVA was also not significant, and analysis of the farming success variables as a time series over the seven years also revealed no significant differences in slope as a function of belief in global warming.

Two additional regularities in farmers' adaptations and responses to the prospect of climate change are worth noting. First, correlations between production adaptations to possible climate change (for example, shifting to crops that use less water) and pricing adaptations (for example, using futures contracts more extensively) were mostly negative across farmers ($r = -.44$, on average). Secondly, there were also significant negative correlations between farmers' likelihood of engaging in risk-reduction behaviors that require some personal initiative (mostly production changes, such as

Table 13.9. Correlates to Belief in Global Warming.

Correlation	*Variable*
.52	Long-term climate forecasts being judged more important
.35	Greater use of medium- and long-term climate forecasts
.33	Climate forecasts used more
.59	Changes in tillage method over last few years
.41	Changes in types of crop
.47	Changes in varieties of seed corn
.40	Greater percentage of crops insured against crop failure
.32	Greater percentage of crops insured against hail
.33	Greater percentage of crops priced by futures
.30	Regular before-harvest pricing strategy

planting more varieties of corn or allocating more acres to experimentation with new varieties, but also some pricing changes, such as developing a different before-harvest strategy) and their support of government interventions designed to reduce carbon dioxide emissions. In particular, farmers were asked to express their support (on a scale from 1 to 10, with the option of expressing no opinion) for three government initiatives: promotion of ethanol, higher gasoline taxes, and restriction of fossil fuel usage. Mean support of these initiatives was 7.3, 3.4, and 4.5, respectively, but more importantly, the less likely farmers were to engage in risk-reduction behavior requiring some personal initiative, the stronger was their support for these government interventions ($r = -.41$, on average).

These results suggest that the farmers in our sample fell into three approximately equal-sized groups with respect to their proactive or reactive responses to climate change. Group one was inclined to support government initiatives to reduce the threat of global warming but less likely to modify either their production or their pricing practices. Groups two and three were less likely to support government intervention but favored personal initiative. Group two was more likely to apply its personal initiative to adaptations and modifications of production practices, whereas group three was more likely to translate its concern and initiative into adaptations and modifications of financial practices.

In order to determine whether the management traits described in Table 13.1 predicted farmers' choice of adaptation response, I correlated indicator variables denoting membership in group one, two, or three with farmers' scores on the seven management traits. Only some of the correlations reached statistical significance (which should be considered in light of the relatively small sample for the purposes of testing for individual differences), but membership in group one (defined by a mean expression of support for the three government policies of 6 or greater) showed the largest positive correlations with belief in collective wisdom ($r = .23$) and macromanaging ($r = .19$). Membership in group two had its highest positive correlation with active experimentation ($r = .26$) and micromanaging ($r = .20$), and membership in group three was correlated with pricing sophistication ($r = .21$) and systematic analysis ($r = .18$). There was no significant association between the type of adaptation response (membership in the three groups) and belief versus disbelief in global warming (chi-squared (2) = 2.37, $p > .10$).

Conclusion

The field study described in this chapter surveyed the beliefs and expectations of a subset of the general population in the United States that can be expected to be closely interested in local and global weather and climate: Illinois cash-crop farmers. It related those beliefs to farmers' perceptions and recollections of weather patterns in the recent past and to their adaptations at the farm level to current and expected local climate change. In this sample of individuals, slightly less than half believed that the climate of east-central Illinois would undergo any noticeable change over the next twenty to thirty years. For those who did, expectations of the nature and magnitude of change were quite close to those of professional organizations such as the IPCC and well within the range of several "most likely" scenarios provided for the American Midwest.

While there was strong support for the hypothesized effect of prior expectations in facilitating the detection of small climate trends, there was little evidence for a negative effect of prior experience with natural weather and climate variability on the detection of small trends.

Expectations of Climate Change: Antecedents and Consequences

Belief in global warming was not associated with age, experience, or level of education, nor with any of the seven management traits. Those who believed in global warming were more likely, however, to mention agricultural newspapers and less likely to mention popular media (daily newspapers, newsmagazines, radio, or television) as having influenced their belief and mentioned a larger number of sources of influence. A range of production and financial practices with the capacity to reduce the negative consequences of climate risk showed significant correlations with farmers' strength of belief in climate change, which is at least consistent with the belief as a causal agent for adaptive responses.

Belief in Global Warming and Farm Success

None of the measures and analyses of farm success over the previous seven years showed a significant effect on farmers' current belief in global warming, even though the vast majority of correlations were nonsignificantly positive. The positive relationship between belief in global warming and farm success may be partially mediated by the fact that the last two correlates of such a belief listed in Table 13.9 are contributing variables to two of the measures of farm success as shown in Table 13.1. In particular, pricing a greater percentage of crops by use of the futures market was found to contribute to operational efficiency, and having a regular pricing strategy was found to contribute to better prices. Though it seems reasonable to assume that these pricing practices causally contribute to farm success, the causal relationship between a belief in climate change and the production and pricing practices found to be associated with such a belief is less obvious and awaits further study.

As the point in time at which farmers started to believe in climate change was not determined in this study—it may have been relatively recent—it is perhaps not surprising that the observed effects of a belief in climate change on the success of the farming operations measured up to seven years into the past were positive but not significant. Even if current adaptations have positive effects on profitability, prices, or yields in the long run, farmers' beliefs and associated adaptations may not extend that far into the past.

Belief in Global Warming and Accuracy of Memories of Past Climate Patterns

The expectation of climate change made it more likely that a small local warming trend was interpreted and remembered as such. Maximum daily July temperatures over the previous five years had been both hotter on average and more variable; however, as shown in Table 13.6, believers in global warming overwhelmingly remembered the former and disbelievers mostly the latter. The expectation of climate change also made farmers less accurate with respect to remembered levels of precipitation over the previous seven years, biasing their memory in the direction predicted by global warming models.

Previous work on the potential value of externally provided weather and climate forecasts for decisions whose outcomes are affected by climate variables has investigated the accuracy levels necessary for short-term weather forecasts (Baquet, Halter, and Conklin, 1976; Lave, 1963) and longer-term climate forecasts (Winkler, Murphy, and Katz, 1983; Brown, Katz, and Murphy, 1986) to have economic value. These studies generally evaluate the value of climate information under the assumption of rational profit maximization and unlimited processing capacity. An exception is a study by Changnon, Sonka, and Hofing (1988), which investigated the value of climate predictions for the seed corn production sector by looking at the allocation decisions of actual seed corn producers in the Midwestern United States made either with or without the benefit of climate predictions. Allocation decisions were entered into an economic model that simulated the stochastic nature of summer growing conditions in the region and calculated the financial outcome of the allocation decision. The analysis documented that predictions of even low accuracy could have potentially large economic value if available with sufficient lead time. This suggests that, given the base rate assigned to the reality of climate change over the next few decades, an expectation of climate change may have economic value even if it is associated with some schema-consistent distortions of climate memories that may possibly reduce the accuracy of internally generated predictions and forecasts.

Individual Differences in Method of Adaptation

The study demonstrated the existence of individual differences in the way Illinois cash-crop farmers reacted and adapted to the possibility of global warming. Related to other differences in management practices, one group of farmers strongly supported government interventions designed to reduce the possibility of climate change but were less likely to modify any of their farm practices, whereas two other groups were less supportive of government interventions but more likely to take personal steps to reduce the downside potential of climate change, with one group relying mainly on production adaptations and the other relying mainly on financial adaptations. Although the current study did not provide any information about the relative success of these different adaptation strategies, it is useful to know that farmers do not automatically employ the full range of adaptive responses, even if they believe in the need for adaptation and change. Instead, individual differences and management style factors seem to predispose them toward certain classes of responses. Engagement in one class of adaptation and risk reduction seems to limit farmers' awareness of other, potentially complementary, risk-reduction mechanisms. This suggests the importance of external aids in the generation of adaptive responses (for example, brochures or checklists) that provide farmers with a full complement of interventions that have the capacity to hedge climate risk.

Summary of Research and Policy Implications

The results and implications of this field study can be summarized as follows.

First, no clear mechanism or set of determinants for a belief in global warming was identified. As such a belief seems to help in the detection and amplification of existing warming trends, it is unfortunate that no more is known about how to foster such a belief. The present study showed, however, that farmers who expressed belief in a warming trend tended to cite more sources as having influenced their opinion than those who did not. Even though this relationship may not be causal, it suggests that up-to-date information about current and projected climate trends ought to be distributed through a wide variety of sources (for example, agricultural newspapers and cooperative extension services). Future research ought to address the following two sets of questions: (1) How general is the relationship between number of influential information sources and belief in global warming? Does it translate to beliefs in other categories of uncertain environmental changes or in other phenomena? (2) Is the relationship indeed causal (in the sense that increased exposure to [confirming] information sources would increase belief in the phenomenon), or is it the result of an individual difference on a third variable that is responsible for both a greater willingness to believe in environmental change and to expose oneself to more sources of information?

Second, and partly as a consequence of the first point, research funds should be allocated to assess the effectiveness of different types of adaptive responses and the determinants of individual differences between farmers in their beliefs and expectations about climate change as well as in their adaptation strategies.

Finally, as argued in the last section, farmers and other individuals faced with potentially consequential environmental change should be provided with external guidance about the full range of adaptive risk-reduction responses available to them. That the present study found that farmers were limiting themselves to one of three classes of risk-reduction methods has important policy implications. It exemplifies a shortcoming in the problem-solving process that has also been identified in other problem domains: once a solution to a problem has been identified, people tend to stop the search process and, as a result, may fail to generate alternative or additional solutions. Berman and others (1991), for example, found that radiologists often halt their search for abnormalities in radiographs after finding one lesion, leaving additional lesions undetected. A single solution seems to provide sufficient assurance that a problem has been dealt with, and the resulting peace of mind seems to prevent the generation of additional solutions or adaptations. I hope the results of the present study will serve as a reminder to both researchers and policymakers that complex problems tend to have a variety of causes and call for a range of solutions that involve different aspects of the problem. A single cause or solution often needs to be studied in isolation, and it is easy to forget but important to remember that an effective response to a complex problem at either the research or the policy level will involve a concerted effort to integrate insights and proven interventions from a wide range of different perspectives.

REFERENCES

Alloy, L. B., and Tabachnik, N. "Assessment of Covariation by Humans and Animals: The Joint Influence of Prior Expectations and Current Situational Information." *Psychological Review,* 1984, *91,* 112–149.

Ausubel, J. E. (1983). "Can We Assess the Impacts of Climatic Change?" *Climatic Change,* 1983, *5,* 7.

Baquet, A. E., Halter, A. N., and Conklin, F. S. "The Value of Frost Forecasting: A Bayesian Appraisal." *American Journal of Agricultural Economics,* 1976, *58,* 511–520.

Bartlett, P. F. "Adaptive Strategies in Peasant Agricultural Production." *Annual Review of Anthropology,* 1980, *9,* 545–573.

Begley, S. "Is the Ozone Hole in our Heads?" *Newsweek,* Oct. 11, 1993, p. 71.

Berman, K. S., and others. "Time Course of Satisfaction of Search." *Investigative Radiology,* 1991, *26,* 640–648.

Bostrom, A., Morgan, M. G., Fischhoff, B., and Read, D. "What Do People Know About Global Climate Change? 1. Mental Models." *Risk Analysis,* 1994, *14,* 959–970.

Bower, G. H., and Masling, M. *Causal Explanations as Mediators for Remembering Correlations.* Unpublished manuscript, 1978.

Brown, B. G., Katz, R. W., and Murphy, A. H. "On the Economic Value of Seasonal Precipitation Forecasts: The Fallowing/Planting Problem." *Bulletin of the American Meteorological Society,* 1986, *67,* 833–841.

Bullard, J. "Rethinking Rational Expectation." In G. M. von Furstenberg (ed.), *Acting Under Uncertainty: Multidisciplinary Conceptions.* Norwell, Mass.: Kluwer, 1990.

Changnon, S. A., Sonka, S. T., and Hofing, S. L. "Assessing Climate Information Use in Agribusiness: Part I, Actual and Potential Use and Impediments to Usage." *Journal of Climate,* 1988, *1,* 389–398.

Chapman, L. J., and Chapman, J. "Genesis of Popular but Erroneous Psychodiagnostic Observations." *Journal of Abnormal Psychology,* 1967, 72, 271–280.

Dickinson, R. E. "How Will Climate Change: The Climate System and Modeling of Future Climate." In *Scope 29, The Greenhouse Effect, Climatic Change and Ecosystems.* New York: Wiley, 1986.

Glantz, M. G., Robinson, J., and Krentz, M. E. "Recent Assessments." In R. W. Kates, J. H. Ausubel, and M. Berberian (eds.), *Scope 27, Climate Impact Assessment.* New York: Wiley, 1985.

Houghton, J. T., Jenkins, G. J., and Ephraums, J. J. (eds.). *Climate Change: The IPCC Scientific Assessment.* New York: Cambridge University Press, 1990.

Kaiser, H. M., and others. "A Multi-Disciplinary Protocol for Studying the Agronomic and Economic Impacts of Gradual Climate Warming." *American Journal of Agricultural Economics,* 1991, *57,* 117–131.

Kupperman, K. O. "The Puzzle of the American Climate in the Early Colonial Period." *American Historical Review,* 1982, *87,* 1262–1289.

Lave, L. B. "The Value of Better Weather Information to the Raisin Industry." *Econometrica,* 1963, *31,* 151–164.

Mynatt, C. R., Doherty, M. E., and Tweney, R. D. "Confirmation Bias in a Simulated Research Environment: An Experimental Study of Scientific Inference." *Quarterly Journal of Experimental Psychology,* 1977, 29, 85–95.

National Research Council. *Carbon Dioxide and Climate: A Scientific Assessment.* Washington, D.C.: National Academy of Sciences, 1979.

National Research Council. *Carbon Dioxide and Climate: A Second Assessment.* Washington, D.C.: National Academy of Sciences, 1982.

National Research Council. *Global Environmental Change: Understanding the Human Dimensions.* Washington, D.C.: National Academy of Sciences, 1992.

Nisbett, R. E., and Ross, L. *Human Inference: Strategies and Shortcomings of Social Judgment.* Englewood Cliffs, N.J.: Prentice Hall, 1980.

Palutikof, J. P., Wigley, T.M.L., and Lough, J. M. *Seasonal Climate Scenarios for Europe and North America in a High-CO_2 Warmer World.* Technical Report TRO12. Washington, D.C.: U.S. Department of Energy, Carbon Dioxide Research Division, 1984.

Read, D., and others. "What Do People Know About Global Climate Change? Part 2. Survey Studies of Educated Lay People." *Risk Analysis,* 1994, *14,* 971–982.

Smith, E. T. "Global Warming: The Debate Heats Up." *Business Week,* Feb. 27, 1995, pp. 19–20.

Sonka, S. T. "Evaluating Socio-Economic Assessments of the Effect of Climate Change on Agriculture." In T. J. Matthews (ed.), *Global Change: Economic Issues in Agriculture, Forestry, and Natural Resources.* Washington, D.C.: World Resources Institute, 1991.

Trefil, J. "Modeling Earth's Future Climate Requires Both Science and Guesswork." *Smithsonian,* Dec. 1990, pp. 29–37.

von Furstenberg, G. M. "Neither Gullible Nor Unteachable Be: Signal Extraction and the Optimal Speed of Learning from Uncertain News." In G. M. von Furstenberg (ed.), *Acting Under Uncertainty: Multidisciplinary Conceptions.* Norwell, Mass.: Kluwer, 1990.

Wason, P. C. "On the Failure to Eliminate Hypotheses in a Conceptual Task." *Quarterly Journal of Experimental Psychology,* 1960, *12,* 129–140.

Weber, E. U., and Sonka, S. "Production and Pricing Decisions in Cash-Crop Farming: Effects of Decision Traits and Climate Change Expectations." In B. H. Jacobsen, D. E. Pedersen, J. Christensen, and S. Rasmussen (eds.), *Farmers' Decision Making: A Descriptive Approach.* Copenhagen: Institute for Agricultural Economics, 1994.

Winkler, R. L., Murphy, A. H., and Katz, R. W. "The Value of Climatic Information: A Decision-Analytic Approach." *Journal of Climatology,* 1983, *3,* 187–197.

Wright, J. C., and Murphy, G. L. "The Utility of Theories in Intuitive Statistics: The Robustness of Theory-Based Judgments." *Journal of Experimental Psychology: General,* 1984, *113,* 301–322.

14

RANKING RISKS

Baruch Fischhoff

BY PROVIDING MATERIAL resources, the natural environment is essential to our physical well-being, as a source of food, energy, and raw materials. By its very existence, it is essential to our spiritual well-being, as a place to escape our mundane lives and as an object of contemplation. The environment also provides threats to our survival, including floods, storms, diseases, and natural toxins such as radon. Moreover, the natural environment itself is often at risk, imperiling its ability to provide its benefits. These risks include direct assaults, such as habitat destruction and chemical spills, which we might stop if they were taken seriously. These risks also include less direct results of human activity, such as reductions in genetic diversity and in the buffers against the emergence of new diseases.

These environmental risks are many and varied. Moreover, they are but a subset of the risks that we all face, taking their place alongside the possibilities of crime, injury, shame, and economic calamity, among others. How we manage these risks will determine, in part, the quality of our physical and spiritual lives. Yet they are so numerous that we can barely attend to them all, much less control them. If we misallocate our

The research reported here was supported by the Office of Science and Technology Policy, the National Science Foundation, and the Environmental Protection Agency. Its exposition benefited from several anonymous reviews. All are gratefully acknowledged, as are the authors whose presentations prompted the concluding sections of this chapter. The views expressed are my own.

resources, we may worry too much or too little about specific environmental risks or about the environment as a whole. This chapter considers the problems of setting risk priorities.

In an ideal world, we would, on some regular basis, review our priorities systematically. That review would begin by listing all the risks we face, ordered according to the threat each poses. It would continue by listing each option for controlling each risk, characterized by some estimate of its effectiveness and cost. The review would conclude by identifying the "best buys" in risk reduction, the strategies that achieve the greatest reductions at the least cost. Those costs might be measured in dollars, time, effort, nagging, or whatever other resources we have to invest in risk management. As a by-product, this analytical process would leave a list of residual risks, which we cannot reduce at any reasonable price but which continue to be matters of concern.

In reality, though, such systematic reviews of risk are as rare as systematic reviews of how we spend our time, money, or emotions. One obvious constraint on any of these activities is lack of time to perform them. However, even with all the time in the world, there would still be daunting obstacles. Risks are so many and diverse that it is hard to compile either the list of threats or the set of possible control strategies. We seldom have ready access to credible estimates of the sizes of the risks, the chances for control, or the costs of amelioration. Often, the ranking scientific experts know little more.

If we had those figures, we would then have to face difficult trade-offs. Many of these involve wrenching choices between "your money or your life." More precisely, they ask about our willingness to sacrifice concrete dollars in return for changes in the probability of injury or death. For example, will we pay more for environmentally sound products or zoning laws? Will we buy cars with additional safety features? Will we purchase cheaper products from countries with lax standards for pollution or civil rights? Even if we knew how to make the trade-offs posed by specific risk-control options, we would still have to prioritize the different risks competing for the same limited resources. For example, do we invest our research dollars in attempts to reduce the risks of injury, heart disease, cancer, or species extinction? Do we invest our nagging budget in warning teens about sex, drugs, beer, mixed drinks, AIDS, or driving (not to mention skipping school, cheating, and getting assignments in late)?

These are not only intellectual challenges. They confront us with difficult ethical, social, and emotional choices. What we do about risks defines us as individuals and as citizens, showing what we value and what we accept as our personal responsibility. Any risk that we neglect can come back to haunt us. Any risk that we face (or explicitly ignore) can raise uncomfortable concerns. Any risk that we place on our own agenda may be taken off the plates of others, including those who create and benefit from it. These choices shape our world, as well as that of people elsewhere on the planet and in future generations—not to mention their effects on the natural environment, which might be seen as having rights independent of our interests.

The next section of this chapter offers an account of how individuals might respond to these challenges, whether considering risks under their personal control or ones that they hope to influence through social and political processes. The two sections following that consider the role of government in helping citizens to manage risks, first in principle and then in the practical context of recent public experiments in risk ranking. Next is a general procedure for risk ranking and for exploiting the lists of risks that it could reduce. The chapter concludes by asking what our science can offer to this challenge, as well as what grappling with it can contribute to our science.

A Descriptive Account

Faced with such complex problems, we usually just muddle along. At any time, we have in place a set of risk-reducing practices that have somehow evolved. Some of these practices we adopt deliberately (such as voluntary recycling, vegetarian diets, contributing to environmental causes). Others are imposed upon us (automatic seat belts, mandated recycling, using electricity produced under strict pollution controls). Still others are copied from friends with little attention to risk (smoking, littering) or are of uncertain origin (triple checking the stove before leaving the house, leaving lights on when leaving the room).

Every once in a while, something happens that calls our habits into question. It may make us wonder whether we are needlessly investing in risk control or recklessly leaving ourselves exposed. In many lives, these occasions may come with unnerving frequency. Every Thursday's *New England Journal of Medicine* brings revisions in estimates of some risk's size or some control strategy's effectiveness. Many Tuesdays' *Science Times* bring coverage of more slowly breaking revisions. Most weeks, some television newsmagazine features a health risk or quack cure or environmental blight. Almost every night, local news broadcasts present threats to personal safety from crime, fire, or traffic. Over time, these reports filter into everyday conversation, reaching those who are not news junkies or direct observers. News about risks also arises sporadically in our personal lives through, for example, injuries to friends, reports of radon or asbestos in schools, scares over emerging diseases, or plans to site nuisances in our neighborhoods (ranging from hazardous waste facilities to halfway houses).

On the positive side, these confrontations offer chances to rethink our priorities. They may force us to think in some depth about unpleasant topics that we might otherwise ignore. They may facilitate collective action or changes in long-standing behaviors. Over time, reviewing the treatment of individual risks should bring our overall priorities in line.

However, having our agenda set in this way has its limitations. One such limit is that the nomination process may have little to do with the magnitude of the risks involved, the usefulness of any new information, or the opportunities to take action. It is often hard to tell whether a featured risk is worth worrying about. It is rare to find a concise summary of a risk's magnitude or the quality of the underlying science (Funtowicz and Ravetz, 1990; Morgan and Henrion, 1991). As a result, citizens must divine the size and certainty of the risk from indirect cues. One common, reasonable, but imperfect inference is that if seemingly responsible people raise a risk issue, then it must be important and they must know something about it. A complementary assumption is that important risks will get reported expeditiously because it must be someone's job to identify them and alert us. However, scientists can seize center stage with studies that are important to them personally but that add little to our overall understanding; news media often retell familiar stories while neglecting more serious risks; issues may be ignored just because their stories are hard to tell.

Once an issue attracts attention, group processes can take on lives of their own, generating further cues as to the magnitude of the risk. For example, if institutions are perceived as responding callously, citizens may conclude, "if they're so high-handed, they must be hiding something." A forceful public may be construed as strident or hysterical, leading technical experts to discount its concerns. A debate conducted in terms of risk may really be about not losing to the villains or the jerks on the other side (Glickman and Gough, 1990; Krimsky and Plough, 1988; National Research Council, 1989; Vaughan, 1993). Whether inadvertent or deliberate, poor communication can aggravate whatever "natural" misunderstandings people have about risks (Fischhoff, Bostrom, and Quadrel, 1993; Laughery, 1993; Leventhal and Cameron, 1987; Reason, 1990).

Moreover, even the best reporting leaves open the question of how important each risk is and how much its control is worth (Fischhoff, 1994; Lowrance, 1976). Better communication will sometimes reveal dominating alternatives and clear-cut "best buys" in risk reduction. At other times, though, it will just paint a starker picture of a difficult reality. Coping with that reality requires not only processing a lot of information but also seeing it from a variety of perspectives. It means avoiding the risk of framing, whereby, in circumstances offering limited opportunities for reflection, people's preferences prove sensitive to formally irrelevant aspects of how trade-offs are described (Bazerman and Neale, 1992, Dawes, 1988; Kahneman and Tversky, 1984; Thaler, 1991).

As a result of these complexities, it is hard to know what risks one should worry about, much less what worries are appropriate for other people. Indeed, a common source of potentially avoidable social conflict is naive misinterpretations of others' risk priorities. It is all too easy to fault others for worrying about different things than we do, without recognizing the possibilities of their having different values or different perceptions of the scientific evidence. Such superficial analyses of others' risk priorities can lead us to be unduly critical of them and insufficiently critical of ourselves (Fischhoff, 1989). Doing so may protect us from facing anew difficult value conflicts that we have somehow resolved. It may absolve us from recognizing the high-handed behavior of the experts we trust, which undermines the credibility of the evidence that they would like to alarm or reassure others. A more deliberate process is needed to reveal and reconcile alternative views of risk.

Possible Roles for Government

Government has some natural advantages in facing these tasks. It has far greater resources than individuals for assembling evidence and analyzing it from diverse perspectives. However, government faces the same obstacles as do individuals. It too must compile a comprehensive list of risks, including those that are, for whatever reason, commonly ignored. It must summarize the scientific evidence, with adequate representation of uncertainties. For the sake of comparisons, it must render those risks into some common units (Hornstein, 1992).

Yet even with unlimited budgets government analysts could not solve the risk-ranking problem unambiguously. Each step of the process involves value judgments. It is a question of ethics, not science, to decide which risks can even be considered, how risk is to be measured, how the different dimensions of risk should be weighted, and how uncertainty should be treated (Crouch and Wilson, 1981; Fischhoff, Watson, and Hope, 1984). The rankings of risks, and of risk-reduction strategies, will depend on how these issues are resolved. As a result, there will be differences in whose welfare is protected and whose risk-producing activities are restrained. The open nature of government analyses could make these choices relatively transparent. Unfortunately, government analysts often lack the explicit legal mandate needed to make hard choices. Even where there is statutory guidance, it may lack credibility. For example, it is one thing to require cost-benefit analyses when evaluating programs affecting health and safety. It may be quite another thing to make people comfortable with value-of-a-life calculations.

Under these circumstances, government analysts can address value issues in several ways. One general strategy is to make as few assumptions as possible, reporting the results in something approaching raw form, assembling the data without digesting them. Their work product might include weakly comparable estimates, expressed in different measures of risk and accompanied by frank discussions of the data's sources, assumptions, and limitations. Any integration would be done by the consumers of the reports, who would be left to complete the analyses on their own.

A second strategy is to integrate the evidence in several different ways, each reflecting an alternative set of values. Doing so would not prejudge which values are appropriate (among those that are considered). Rather, the analysts would run the numbers under these different assumptions. Relieved of this computational load, citizens could locate themselves in the "space" created by the alternative value systems. For example, Lave and Dowlatabadi (1993) show how people with different social philosophies might interpret the uncertain evidence about global climate change.

A third strategy is to elicit values from citizens, then derive the rankings analytically implied by them. Its success depends on these citizens' ability to express their values in the abstract form required by analytical models. That means grappling with difficult ethical questions, using unfamiliar formats, and producing public statements of value. It requires the analysts to carry the citizens along, so that they will see the rankings as expressing the values that they have provided. The snap judgments elicited by typical survey research procedures are ill-suited to eliciting meaningful values on such complex issues. Jenni, Merkhofer, and Williams (1995) offer an unusually candid account of the obstacles facing attempts to elicit citizens' values in a case study of setting priorities for cleaning up defense nuclear sites.

Finally, one could allow citizen panels to determine the rankings with technical staff at their service, explicating the risk data and perhaps suggesting alternative perspectives. The credibility of a citizen panel would depend on the populations whose values it represents. If a panel could not converge on a single ranking, it could at least show the array (or disarray) of lay opinion.

Experiments in Ranking

The choice of approach depends, obviously, on the particulars of the situation. For example, the late Office of Technology Assessment (OTA)(1995) adopted the first approach in its study of risks to students in school. It performed the arduous chore of identifying and assembling data from diverse sources. However, it left it for others to conduct the protracted interactions with citizens needed to impose some socially acceptable order among the risks.

In contrast, the Environmental Protection Agency (EPA) (1987, 1990) has conducted several internal ranking exercises as a way of articulating its own priorities. However, participants were restricted to its own staff and advisory committees. Citizens were consulted only through the indirect and imprecise medium of public opinion surveys. The EPA concluded that these surveys showed marked discrepancies between the agency's rankings and those of the public. If real and not just methodological artifacts, these discrepancies could reflect differences in perceptions of either scientific or value issues. The sources of such disagreements are, however, notoriously difficult to decode (Fischhoff, 1989). Surveys typically offer respondents little time to think, opportunity to express complicated thoughts, or chance to clarify ambiguous questions.

The EPA has attempted to bridge this gap through direct interaction with citizens (Environmental Protection Agency, 1993; Resources for the Future, 1993). Specifically, it has promoted state and local risk-ranking exercises. In them, diverse panels of citizens develop rankings of risk over a period of time and with considerable staff support. These protracted interactions allow participants to mull the complicated issues, clarify apparent differences, recruit needed information, and negotiate compromises (if they are to be found). Several dozen such exercises are in varying stages of planning and completion, producing consensus documents from surprisingly diverse audiences. Their very existence shows a perhaps surprising willingness to seek understanding and compromise.

One critical ingredient in this success has apparently been allowing each panel to structure the work as it wishes (such as deciding which nonenvironmental risks to include in their set). The price for conferring such freedom is that there is no common format for the different ranking exercises, no explicit role for analytical procedures, and no systematic way to uncover the values underlying the rankings. As a result, it is difficult to generalize results and explicate their rationale. Nonparticipants may have difficulty accepting rankings expressing such unspecified values. Government analysts lack the explicit guidance needed to translate the rankings into regulations. There is no clear way to integrate the results of different ranking exercises. The next section presents one possible way of overcoming these limitations.

One Way to Rank Risks

A successful risk-ranking method faces many simultaneous demands. It must reflect the underlying science faithfully, capture the critical dimensions of that science, present the information comprehensibly, secure the input of citizens' values, reach a stable conclusion, and convey it credibly to the broad public.

Recently, my colleagues and I proposed a risk-ranking method that, we hope, represents a reasonable compromise among these demands (Morgan, Fischhoff, Lave, and Fischbeck, 1996). It is not perfect or completely specified. However, it identifies the critical design issues that any deliberate ranking process would face and offers an initial approach to them. That is, it provides a task analysis for those who would rank risks, along with one possible response to it. It hopes to capitalize on the successful social process and thoughtful treatment of risk assessment in EPA's risk-ranking process, while strengthening its decision analytical core. It was initially produced in response to a request from the Office of Science and Technology Policy for a method that federal agencies could use to prioritize risks within programs, across programs, and across agencies (Davies, 1996).

Legislation introduced into the 104th Congress (and its immediate predecessors) calls for a dramatic expansion in the use of risk comparisons (for example, HR9). Whatever form these proposals eventually take, they need to address the issues raised here. Our procedure involves six steps. They require the expertise of technically qualified experts working to the specification of citizens panels, whom they will help to select and instruct.

Step One: Define and Categorize the Risks

The universe of relevant risks first must be identified and then must be sorted into a modest number (less than thirty) of roughly comparable risk categories. Those categories should be simple, well defined, exhaustive, mutually exclusive, and sufficiently homogenous that each can be considered in the same evaluative light. A rough screening for order of magnitude is needed to avoid creating a few categories lumping extremely large risks, which would merely postpone the hard work of ranking the contents of those large categories.

One natural categorization is according to existing regulatory programs. However, such programs may reflect the chaotic bureaucratic and political processes that prompt the need for systematic prioritization in the first place. Categorization might also reflect the *source* of the risk (for example, power plants), the *agent* of risk (such as ozone), or the *failure mode* (low-level wind shear, for instance). Thus, for example, the Federal Aviation Administration might decide to categorize risks by source and failure mode. Its sources might be civilian and commercial aircraft, and its failure modes might include icing problems, wind shear, engine fires, loss of communication, and others. If so, then one category of risks to be ranked by the FAA might be wind shear accidents involving commercial aircraft.

Step Two: Identify the Relevant Attributes of Risk

Risk is a complex concept. Expected numbers of deaths and injuries are clearly important, but a variety of other considerations or attributes may also matter. To the extent possible, these attributes should be comprehensive (to ensure that nothing important has been left out), nonredundant (to avoid double counting), preferentially independent (to allow simpler evaluation procedures), measurable (to allow explicit and consistent estimates), and minimal in number (to reduce complexity). Because some of these criteria may conflict (such as comprehensiveness and using minimal numbers of attributes), the process of choosing attributes will have to involve compromises.

The compromise that we proposed characterizes each risk according to the three dimensions of risk that have emerged in psychometric studies of perceived risk (Fischhoff and others, 1978; Slovic, 1987; Slovic, Fischhoff, and Lichtenstein, 1979): number of people affected, knowledge, and dread. These studies have found that ratings on a wide variety of attributes can be summarized effectively by these three dimensions. For any given hazard, people's judgments about attributes that load heavily on one of these dimensions show high interattribute correlations. In contrast, attributes that load primarily on different dimensions display low interattribute correlations. Thus, as long as the attributes used in the ranking process include an attribute or two representing each dimension, the results of a ranking process should not depend very much on which specific attributes are used. Because these studies focused on risks to humans as a result of environmental and other changes, ecological impact was added as a fourth dimension.

We propose that rankers select two marker attributes for each dimension from the set of highly correlated possibilities. For example, dread could be measured by individual controllability, catastrophic potential, and outcome equity (among other possibilities). This procedure will allow rankers to choose marker attributes that they find meaningful while ensuring that the rankings produced by groups using different markers will be similar (because of the correlations among alternative markers and the coverage of the four dimensions). Our full proposal offers operationalizations of four to six possible markers for each dimension, as displayed in Table 14.1.

Step Three: Describe the Risks

Once the categories and attributes are set, technical staff would summarize the scientific evidence for each. In a standard format, that summary would include a qualitative description of the risk, a quantitative evaluation of the risk in terms of each chosen attribute, and a brief description

Table 14.1. A Possible Quantitative Summary of Risks.

Number of People Affected	***Degree of Environmental Impact***	***Knowledge***	***Dread***
Annual expected number of fatalities: 0 – 450 – 600 (10% chance of zero)	Area affected by ecosystem stress or change: 50 km^2	Degree to which impacts are delayed: 1–10 years	Catastrophic potential: 1000 times expected annual fatalities
Annual expected number of person-years lost: 0 – 9,000 – 18,000 (10% chance of zero)	Magnitude of environmental impact: modest (15% chance of large)	Quality of scientific understanding: medium	Outcome equity: medium (ratio = 6)

Source: Morgan and others, 1992.

of the state of scientific understanding (expressing uncertainty, broadly defined). Table 14.1 shows a possible format for the quantitative summary. In order to accommodate rankers with diverse educational background, the narrative summaries should be no more technical than, say, *Popular Science*. In order to facilitate making comparisons, the summary forms should be small enough to be easily handled and sorted. For example, one might use a legal-sized sheet of paper, turned sideways and folded in half, with the tabular summary of Table 14.1 appearing on the cover page under a brief description of the risk and followed by the narrative. Technical staff would be available to provide whatever additional details and explication are needed.

Step Four: Select the Groups of Rankers

The rankers should represent those citizens whose values are to be captured. In our work example, focused on establishing priorities for federal agencies, we proposed four independent groups: one with federal agency risk personnel, one with state and local risk managers, and two with laypeople. Each group would reflect the diversity of its underlying population. Group members' opinions would be interpreted as the conclusions that similar citizens would reach were they to invest similar effort in these topics. Membership would be limited to between ten and fifteen to allow for active participation by all. Groups would manage their own affairs, with staff support. Each would select its own chair and vice chair, who would receive suitable training in the procedure and in group process. Multiple groups are used to increase confidence that the results are robust and not just the product of particular group dynamics. Constituting groups with similar levels of technical expertise (about risks and about regulation) is intended to promote interaction among equals.

Step Five: Perform the Rankings

We propose a series of four meetings, during which each group would seek a consensual ranking. Before beginning this process in earnest, members would individually evaluate the risks using a simplified multiattribute weighting approach. Toward the end of a group's sessions, members would review its tentative conclusions in the light of their personal initial rankings. This form of triangulation is intended to protect individuals against framing effects by asking them to reconcile two potentially different ways of looking at the problem. It is intended to protect groups against dominating personalities or collective myopia by giving equal standing to each member's initial position. The protracted deliberative process itself is intended to reduce the risks of the framing effects that have been so amply demonstrated in the much more casual questioning of experiments and surveys (Fischhoff, 1991).

Upon completing its work, each group would select representatives to an intergroup synthesis meeting. This meeting would seek the maximum consensus possible within the constraints the constituent groups set for their representatives. The final agreement would be ratified by the four groups and announced with suitable fanfare.

In all these deliberations, the emphasis is on sorting the risk categories into a few broad classes, paying particular attention to identifying those risks that deserve the highest and lowest ranks. The groups should not expend energy on the meaningless task of precisely ordering risk categories whose ranks broadly overlap. The greatest benefit of the whole exercise is likely to come from identifying risks with clear ranks, especially ones that are not commensurate with the resources invested in their management.

Step Six: Provide a Reasonably Rich Description

The same summary ranking can mean quite different things if it reflects a strong consensus or a weak plurality of views. It can motivate different actions if residual disagreements reflect conflicting values or alternative interpretations of uncertain scientific evidence. As a result, an appropriate summary is needed to capture these sources of disagreement as well as any problematic procedural issues. Although a clear consensus may be needed to break political deadlocks, clearly characterized disagreements can still focus future research and debate.

Our full proposal considers various other issues, such as how to balance the confidentiality needed for frank discussions with the openness needed for credibility with nonparticipants (as well as for compliance with open-meeting laws). It also identifies unresolved issues, and highlights the need to evaluate procedures before implementation.

What Can One Do with a Risk Ranking?

In a sense, risk ranking can do little more than satisfy curiosity. A list of risks carries no necessary implications for action. Big risks might be neglected if nothing could be done about them. Small risks might be reduced if that could be done cheaply. Ultimately, one wants to rank not risks but actions, in order to identify the best buys in risk reduction.

Public risk-ranking processes have typically stopped short of recommending actions. In part, this is because those conducting the processes lacked the authority to go further. For example, the OTA was not asked to determine what to do about risks to students in school; the EPA's voluntary consensus-building exercises might have collapsed had the agency attempted to take the big next step of ranking actions.

In principle, this is a disappointing conclusion to such ambitious efforts. In practice, though, consensual risk rankings can make a difference even without resolving either the political problems of securing a mandate for action or the full intellectual problems of moving from risks to actions. Some action implications may emerge without the complete treatment. For example, if a risk is clearly small, cheap ways to control it should not be forgone; however, neither should they be sought too actively. If a risk is clearly large, it deserves attention unless there is some immutable reason why it cannot be reduced. At times, there will be a simple risk-action connection, so that consensus on the former will carry to the latter. If several small risks obviously have a common treatment, they could be grouped (and moved up the list). One implicit promise of risk ranking is to transfer resources from overmanaged risks to undertreated ones. At times, though, it may become apparent that there is no way to effect that transfer. For example, different agencies or industries with no legal connection between them may be involved. Reducing the regulatory burden on one industry may work its way through the economy to the benefit of all. However, those diffuse benefits may hold little appeal for individuals whose protection from that industry are reduced. They may be downright offended if risk prioritization is justified by false claims of fungibility. Why compare risks if nothing can be done about reordering priorities among them? Meaningless risk comparisons are widely held to be a source of public anger at risk managers (Covello, Sandman, and Slovic, 1988; Fischhoff and others, 1981; Roth and others, 1990). However, anger may be needed to create a mandate for change. An agency frustrated with its enabling legislation might even take the calculated gamble of inviting public anger, hoping that the resulting furor will position it better for the long run.

The danger with provoking anger is that the resulting turmoil might throw out the good with the bad. Times of change are often times for mischief, with those closest to the seats of power attempting to settle private accounts under the banner of public reform. Our proposal is intended to promote the possibility of orderly change by increasing confidence that it can be done in an open, regulated, and scientifically credible way. Its underlying article of faith is that a well-managed, mutually respectful process will reveal some significant areas of agreement, even among diverse individuals. The result will be fewer but better-focused conflicts than would arise without such an opportunity.

The Work Cut Out for Us (All?)

Alan Baddeley (1979) distinguishes between *applied basic* and *basic applied* psychology. The former refers to using basic results from psychology in the solution of applied problems. The latter refers to conducting the basic science needed to address issues arising from applied problems. The former is needed for psychology to fulfill its promise of improving the lot of the society that supports it. The latter is needed for psychology to flourish as a science energized, rather than drained, by its confrontations with the real world (Fischhoff, 1996).

The risk-ranking scheme that we have proposed might be seen as a task analysis, identifying the work that needs to be done to solve the complex problem of reaching consensus. In some cases that work can simply apply existing methods. Other cases seem to require the imaginative extension of existing results. In still other cases, people need to improvise until basic research issues have been addressed. Our task analysis shows risk ranking to be a complex social institution requiring contributions of behavioral, social, and natural scientists. A successful ranking exercise would allow individuals to understand complex trade-offs and articulate their preferences among them; it would allow groups to establish the mutually respectful relations needed to identify common ground and residual differences; it would allow the summarization of scientific evidence about risk in an accurate and useful form (National Research Council, 1996).

This is a tall order, requiring many skills and much work. Our initial work focused, naturally, on applying the basic research in which we have been schooled or had a hand in creating. We have also identified basic research issues where the applied problem demands progress. The next section describes some of the basic applied research on our current agenda. Readers may form their own judgments about the advisability of this investment.

Some Risk-Ranking Challenges We Hope to Address

In this and other policy-related research, we have adopted parallel applied basic and basic applied research programs. The former is primarily the responsibility of faculty, with technical support from graduate students; the roles are reversed in the latter research program. This division of labor exploits faculty members' broader experience with applications and wider web of personal contacts with practitioners. It also takes advantage of their greater professional security, allowing them to spend time on these more prosaic (although still intellectually challenging) methodological tasks. It allows graduate students to assume ownership of the sort of basic research problems that might establish their professional identity, while still assuming a greater risk than with a conventional disciplinary problem. The topics that follow are representative of those arising from this kind of confrontation. (They are, in effect, dissertations in progress that may be completed by the time this book is released; the intent here is not to steal their thunder but to show how they arise from the use of the methods described in this chapter.)

The Transition from Ranking Risks to Ranking Options

Several things can be done with a ranked list of risks, but typically such a list is a prelude to ranking options—that is, to identifying the best strategies for managing the risks. As noted, large risks might prompt no action if they bring large benefits and there are no inexpensive options for risk reduction. A general understanding of the relationship between these two processes would allow one to know how advised risk ranking is and how much effort should be invested in it. It might allow one to structure risk rankings in more advantageous ways (such as through the choice of risk categories). It might reveal something about the reality facing people who are attempting to cope with their everyday world of risks (Fischer and others, 1991).

Systemic Versus Systematic Ranking

Systematically ranking a large set of risks means giving each a relatively small amount of attention, its proportionate share of the effort invested in the whole risk-ranking exercise. Looking at many risks at once may effect some intellectual economies of scale, insofar as the same issues arise with many risks, and people think more effectively when focused on the overall topic. However, dividing attention over many risks may lead to understanding none of them very well, even with multiple sessions and technical support. A polar alternative strategy is to focus on individual risks, one at a time, within some common framework. That attention would allow a thorough understanding of each risk, and result in its being placed more appropriately in the overall risk ranking. Although that ranking is admittedly imperfect, improving the placement of individual risks in it should bring it gradually into line. The general theoretical question is how quickly that reordering will occur compared to the reordering achieved by looking at the whole set simultaneously (but with much less attention to each member). The answer to that question will likely depend on issues such as how chaotic the original list was and how risks are nominated for individual detailed attention (for example, as the result of new research or investigative reporting).

Objective Standards for Reactive Measurement

A pragmatic reason for measuring risk priorities with surveys rather than citizen commissions is cost. Advocates of risk-ranking exercises must believe that the precision of this measurement procedure justifies its added expense. Doing it once right may be cost effective, even at a great cost. A more philosophical reason is that surveys are a nonreactive form of measurement, in contrast with protracted group processes that necessarily change participants. In situations where current beliefs are too superficial to be useful for policymaking, reactive measurement is essential. For it to have credibility, a philosophy of science is needed, specifying which reactions are desired, as is a methodology for assessing how well those reactions have been achieved (Fischhoff, forthcoming). It would also be nice to have better-developed analyses of the trade-off between cost and precision.

Convergence of Holistic and Multi-Attribute Ratings

As a protection against overpowering group processes and against the power of issue framing, our proposal would have participants perform simple multi-attribute evaluations early in the procedure. These lightly informed judgments would be compared with the holistic ranking judgments produced later in the process. This is an imperfect comparison, insofar as the latter judgments benefit from participants having had much greater exposure to information about the risks and to potentially relevant views of other panelists. Still, the opportunity for triangulation provides a way for participants to reflect on the process that they have undergone. Little, though, is known about how, and how appropriately, values evolve through such deliberative processes. In a study involving the evaluation of alternative energy strategies, Keeney, von Winterfeldt, and Eppel (1990) found that holistic and decomposed judgments initially diverged but eventually converged to the satisfaction of participants. If constructed values are important, this particular contrast might be a good place to start their exploration (Payne, Bettman, and Johnson, 1992).

The Normative Status of Risk Dimensions

Many descriptive studies have found that the risk dimensions appearing in Table 14.1 do a good job of predicting summary judgments of diverse hazards (Slovic, 1987). Those dimensions are invoked in our proposal as a way to provide a common representation of the universes of hazards deemed relevant in different risk-ranking exercises. But this presumes that people want to be guided by their intuitive judgments (as captured in the risk dimensions). Determining the legitimacy of this presumption will require both normative analysis to clarify the meaning of such preferences (beyond what people can quickly intuit), and descriptive research to allow people to reflect on the contrast between actual and desired judgments.

The issue of preferences among preferences emerges at several points in the next section as well when it considers issues in risk ranking that other researchers might find worth addressing. Although they are a portion of the research needed for successful risk ranking, these projects are far from all of it. The following section is a request for additional help from the authors of the other chapters in this book. Although none of the conference papers on which these chapters are based were written with risk ranking in mind, each has something to offer on the topic; each also comes up somewhat short. It is not hard to show, for each chapter, where the underlying basic research could be applied to risk ranking and how it could be extended by grappling with the special problems of this task. Of course, it is presumptuous to evaluate other authors' ability to help solve a problem whose existence they may not even recognize and perhaps even worse to try to set others' research agendas; I apologize for it but hope that such speaking out of turn will provide insight into what happens when people look at others' research for potential solutions to their environmental problems.

Some Risk-Ranking Challenges That Others Might Address

Table 14.2 presents a telegraphic summary of some basic applied and applied basic research issues that might be faced by the confrontation between risk ranking and the lines of work presented by each chapter in this collection.

Table 14.2. Possible Contributions of Psychological Research to Risk Ranking and Vice Versa.

Author(s)	***Applied Basic Research Opportunities***	***Basic Applied Research Opportunities***
Tenbrunsel, Wade-Benzoni, Messick, and Bazerman	Identifying the cognitive component in adherence to standards	Understanding anti-standard pressure leading to risk ranking; situating individual judgment in social and political processes
Arkes and Hutzel	Characterizing options in common terms	Identifying the preferences revealed in risk ranks
Thompson and Gonzalez	Creating the conditions for agreement	Testing theories of agreement in light of the success of ranking exercises
Knetsch	Understanding ordering principles	Determining normatively and descriptively appropriate tasks
Ritov and Kahneman	Determining the conditions for faithful value elicitation	Examining how general attitudes evolve into stable, specific values
Eagly and Kulesa	Characterizing the kinds of values elicited by ranking exercises	Understanding how dual processes merge over time
Gladwin, Newburry, and Reiskin	Ensuring that diverse values are allowed expression	Charting the course of specific (such as communitarian) values
Slovic	Focusing initial discussions on salient issues	Examining the normative status of risk dimensions
Loewenstein and Frederick	Clarifying adaptation processes, prior to evaluating future states	Analyzing the normative status of experienced utility
Atran and Medin; Gentner and Whitley	Conveying risk levels	Contrasting alternative representational schemes
Weber	Summarizing pertinent scientific estimates of risk	Bridging risk ranking and option ranking

Tenbrunsel, Wade-Benzoni, Messick, and Bazerman

Tenbrunsel, Wade-Benzoni, Messick, and Bazerman note the pitfalls of undue reliance on rigid standards. The EPA's risk-ranking exercises reflect just such an awareness of the limits to standards. Indeed, the EPA's prioritization efforts over the past decade represent one agency's determined attempts to overturn the standard-enforcement mentality forced on it by its enabling legislation. Its experiences provide a case study in the difficulty of securing the flexibility needed by a government agency recognized as being essential to sensible regulation. A fully developed version of Tenbrunsel's account might provide a diagnostic guide to residual standard-based thinking, as well as some cognitively informed ways to circumvent it. Conversely, confrontation with the EPA's experience might enrich the Tenbrunsel account. For example, it might be instructive to examine the people and circumstances leading to the legislation mandating the EPA's historic reliance on standards. To what extent does it reflect explicit public pressure for that specific regulatory mechanism, politicians' propensity for simplistic solutions, or the prerogatives of bureaucracy? Indeed, despite the ease with which we can criticize a generalized public, it is unclear whether any of the EPA's standards have any direct tie to citizens' explicit desires. Perhaps we understand the limits of standards but do not know how to run a government without them. Although inefficient, the limits would reflect an administrative failure rather than an intellectual one.

Arkes and Hutzel

Arkes and Hutzel's studies show a fundamental conflict between values that arises often in choices with environmental consequences. A risk-ranking procedure that fails to recognize this conflict could produce unstable and superficial solutions. Detailed work is needed to present these concerns cogently to risk rankers and to clarify how they map onto the dimensional representation shown in Table 14.1). Conversely, the thirty-odd completed risk-ranking reports show how some groups of citizens have resolved various versions of these value conflicts. It might be productive to study the trade-offs revealed in these rankings in light of the circumstances—protracted deliberations among diverse citizens with ready access to scientific information—that accompanied their creation.

Thompson and Gonzalez

Thompson and Gonzalez describe the conditions under which negotiations are most likely to reach a satisfactory resolution. They seem in many ways to be the conditions approximated by the EPA (1993) in its guidelines for the conduct of risk-ranking exercises. This large-scale social experiment should benefit from the more systematic application of the research results that Thompson summarizes. Conversely, it provides a field test of the generalizability of that research, with thirty to fifty more successful and less successful replicates of the same basic group process (Chociolko, 1996). The exercises vary in theoretically interesting ways in terms of both dependent variables (such as degree of consensus achieved) and independent ones (such as group composition and moderator training). Moreover, the reports and processes are well documented, thanks to the EPA's creation of two regional Centers for Comparative Risk Analysis.

Knetsch

Knetsch demonstrates the conceptual and measurement problems that plague attempts to reduce complex consequences to unitary indicators. Monetization—valuing goods by their market value—is infeasible for environmental goods, which are often not traded in any marketplace. The contingent valuation method tries to circumvent this limitation by asking people how they would behave were there a market for, say, good visibility or an endangered species (Mitchell and Carson, 1989; Pommerehne, Kopp, and Schwarz, forthcoming). As Knetsch notes, this enterprise faces fundamental conceptual limitations. Although risk ranking avoids monetization, it still requires reducing diverse options to the single metric of risk as defined by Fischhoff, Watson, and Hope (1984). Applying Knetsch's analysis to risk ranking might be informative for both. For example, it might force sharper thinking on the choice of reference point when evaluating risk levels.

Ritov and Kahneman

Ritov and Kahneman describe further flaws in contingent valuation conventions, which require individuals to respond to complex, novel questions while deprived of necessary time and context. Not surprisingly, people's responses often fail simple tests of extensionality. That is, people respond differently to formally equivalent versions of the same question. Ritov and Kahneman's perspective suggests the need for the sort of intensive, protracted, interactive elicitation procedure offered by risk-ranking exercises (whether the EPA's or ours). It might also provide guidance for the detailed design of such processes. Doing so would require stretching Kahneman and Ritov's perspective to prescribe the conditions under which stable, specific values toward the environment can emerge from attitudes expressing a general appreciation (Fischhoff, 1991).

Eagly and Kulesa

Eagly and Kulesa offer those chapters in the science of attitudes most relevant to understanding how people view their environment. Their exposition is couched in terms of dual-process theories. In this view, attitudes exist at both a specific level, approaching the explicit valuations resource economists would like to obtain in contingent valuation studies, and a general level akin to the vague expressions of support that they are likely to get (according to Kahneman, Knetsch, and Ritov). More detailed application of attitude research might help to characterize the conditions created, and needed, by various risk-ranking procedures if they are to achieve their goals. Experience with risk ranking might clarify how the two levels of attitude evolve and merge over time in such intense yet controlled environments. This might be done by studying the case record of completed exercises, or instrumenting future ones (to track the changes in general and specific values).

Gladwin, Newburry, and Reiskin

Gladwin, Newburry, and Reiskin cast a wide net, demonstrating the diversity of values that might arise in risk ranking if participants deem them relevant. Their tenfold lists might serve as the basis for auditing exercises in terms of the freedom of expression they allow. That is, which of the many potential values ever arose in the discussion, and when did they hold sway? For example, one might chart the role of communitarian values over the life span of a risk-ranking panel as participants realize it is a consensus-driven process charged with identifying a broad community's risk priorities. Conducting such studies would require operationalizing the values in the authors' lists, which might, in turn, help to refine this basic science.

Slovic

Slovic provides direct evidence for a critical subset of the values in Gladwin, Newburry, and Reiskin's lists, as represented in a diverse set of experimental and survey research. These results can provide an initial focus for risk rankings, increasing the chances that the deliberations begin with issues that occupy people. Indeed, earlier studies in Slovic and others' research program underlie the dimensional approach that we have proposed for spanning the space of potential concerns (Table 14.1). A potential extension of this research is to examine the normative status of these concerns. That is, are the issues that intuitively capture people's attention ones that they want to form the basis of their decisions? Such normative analysis can also structure group deliberations, helping participants clarify what they want to worry about when they think about risks.

Loewenstein and Frederick

Loewenstein and Frederick suggest that there are significant limitations to people's ability to anticipate their own future values. The most notable of these is a tendency to underestimate one's ability to adapt to changing circumstances, which raises the question of the normative status of intuitive preferences. If people want their evaluations to reflect how they will actually experience future environmental states, then they cannot rely on superficial elicitation. They need help to understand their own adaptation processes, the sort of help that a risk-ranking exercise might provide. But that understanding may also lead them to reject experienced utility as the normative standard for evaluating future risk levels. People may decide to resist their own ability to adjust. That is, they may realize that they can accommodate to a gradually worsening environment, but refuse to accept that diminished version of their future selves. Such preferences among preferences are a worthy topic of research.

Atran and Medin; Gentner and Whitley

Authors Atran and Medin and also Gentner and Whitley examine a necessary precursor to evaluating risks: understanding them. Drawing on appropriate chapters in cognitive psychology and anthropology, they demonstrate methods that might be used in risk-ranking exercises to ensure that participants know what they are talking about. Their approaches are similar in spirit to the mental models approach we have used to explain various environmental risks (Fischhoff and others, 1993; Morgan and others, 1992) and plan to employ in our proposed procedure. On practical grounds, one should use the method best suited for conveying the meaning of particular risks. That might mean any of these approaches, or others (Kempton, Boster, and Hartley, 1995; Rouse and Morris, 1986). On theoretical grounds, it would be interesting to know more about the cognitive reality of these alternative representation languages for audiences of varying sophistication.

Weber

Weber's analysis of the possible impacts of climate change on agricultural practices shows how natural science research can be applied to clarifying the meaning of risks. The detailed character of her work makes the case for the sort of extended deliberation that risk ranking allows (while making the case against the brief reflection in survey-like elicitations). Her decision theoretic formulation provides a disciplined way to identify the most relevant information, and the precision with which it must be known. This focus is in keeping with the quantitative summary proposed in our method and its explicit representation of uncertainty. However, Weber's work highlights an inherent limitation of risk ranking: its lack of the explicit connection to action that is essential to conducting value-of-information analysis. Some of the research needed to bridge this gap is described earlier.

Creating a Sustainable Psychology of the Environment

The chapters in this volume connect some of the most relevant areas in psychology to some of the most significant general problems in environmental management. The preceding section speculates on how these areas might contribute to (and benefit from) application to risk ranking, a specific problem that is currently a focus of environmental policymaking. The section before that discussed our profession's own current attempts to identify and address some of these basic applied research topics. Risk ranking is a mission we accepted but that the other authors presumably never even contemplated. They might legitimately prefer wrestling with other applications, or none at all. How all of us position ourselves with respect to current policy debates is a critical strategic choice for our future contributions to the environment and to psychology. To a first approximation, one might identify three general strategies, each with upside and downside risks.

Invite Them In

The simplest strategy for addressing policymakers is just to make our conventional research accessible to them. That would mean providing expositions that eliminate jargon, suggest possible applications, and admit to limitations. Although this may seem a weak response to major social problems, it avoids overselling our wares or presuming to understand the intricacies of complex environmental problems. It reduces our risk of making poorly informed statements about substantive issues and undermining our credibility in the eyes of the very practitioners we hope to help. It makes the important statement that human behavior is subject to systematic research, a great deal of which already exists. For many natural scientists, human behavior seems bewildering and refractory, encouraging heavy-handed attempts to manipulate the public (Fischhoff, 1990). If we write honestly and clearly, we can convey a balanced view of laypeople's strengths and weaknesses—and even some recognition that technical experts are laypeople outside of their narrow domains of expertise. But by lingering at the margins of environmental management, we risk being ignored by those setting policy, for whom our truths are neither self-evident nor immediately applicable. We risk smugly reassuring ourselves that we deserve more attention than we are getting while ignoring the unique features of environmental problems that keep our work from being applied.

Solve Their Problem

If the action will not come to us, then we might go to it. The approach my colleagues and I have taken to risk ranking reflects this strategy. Its benefits include having some chance of getting a hearing, insofar as people with a real problem may listen to anyone who might help them solve it. Of course, if we develop personal ties with the problem holders it may be harder for us to ignore the messier parts of environmental problems that our conventional methods cannot address. But commitment to problems (rather than to our discipline) should increase credibility with those who cannot retreat to the lab, and increase our chances of identifying worthwhile basic applied research problems. One risk of attempting to help solve problems is wasting our time on ones whose formulation makes them intractable. For example, Tenbrunsel and others might argue that any attempt to improve standard setting is doomed to failure because all decisions should be made on a case-by-case basis. If a regulatory setting does not allow such flexibility, we might as well sit things out (although I [Fischhoff, 1983, 1984, 1994] offer other ways to think about standard settings). As noted, decision theory argues for ranking options rather than risks (except in some yet-to-be-specified circumstances). As a result, any romance with risk ranking may prove ill-conceived. Another risk with problem solving is losing the discipline that comes with disciplinary peer review. As the only psychologist involved with an environmental problem, one may be tempted to generalize existing research results beyond what is warranted and to be insufficiently critical of the new research one has created for practical purposes. Finally, one may never make it back to the basic science, either because the real-world problems prove too difficult to domesticate for conventional research or because the problems prove so interesting that the slow progress of basic research becomes unsatisfying (Fischhoff, 1996).

Take Them On

These risks arise in part because environmental problems are often framed in ways conceptually discontinuous with our conventional formulations. In some cases, the problems may be dominated by other disciplines that have excluded us. In other cases, the political process may have distorted problems into forms that make little sense from any disciplinary perspective. One way to resist sinking into such mire is to challenge the existing formulation and propose an alternate, more tractable one. Knetsch, Kahneman, and Ritov have done so with contingent valuation (see also Fischhoff, 1996; Fischhoff and Furby, 1988; Driver, Peterson, and Gregory, 1988). Their proposal may provide a way of liberating the evaluation of environmental goods from the survey-research mold into which it has been pressed. In a similar spirit, we have challenged conventional notions of cost-benefit analysis, acceptable risk, and standard setting (Fischhoff, 1977, 1983, 1984, 1994; Fischhoff and Cox, 1985; Fischhoff and others, 1981). In addition to preserving our own intellectual integrity, this strategy has some small chance of redirecting the overall debate. One obvious risk is that we could be ignored, the result of our being so far off the conventional path that practitioners cannot even absorb our critique. A complementary risk is that we could be vilified for cutting so close that we pose an unacceptable threat. Those daring to challenge contingent valuation have experienced both fates (Fischhoff and Furby, 1988; Kahneman and Knetsch, 1992). The political and economic stakes riding on environmental research often produce responses of unaccustomed intensity. Whether one wants to risk that kind of treatment is a personal and intellectual question.

For many investigators involved with it, contingent valuation is the *E. coli* of environmental research. It turns one's stomach to see that method used as an indicator of the public's environmental values, accurate to two or three significant figures. Nonetheless, so much attention has come to be focused on contingent valuation that studying it might provide an effective forum for airing a variety of scientific issues. As with *E. coli* research, there will be occasional irritating lapses in which the ecological realism of the biological model will be forgotten. However, if we can overcome our revulsion at seeing contingent markets treated as real markets, and perhaps revel in articulating the differences, then there may be some theoretical and practical value in staying this course.

Still, the cartel of resource economists and sociologists controlling contingent valuation is so powerful that interested psychologists might have little effect on the practice of this craft. If so, we would do well to focus on the basic research issues arising from this strange confrontation with complex environmental issues. Knetsch, Kahneman, and Ritov and also Loewenstein and Frederick have all shown how doing so can raise worthy questions about the nature of our values. Pursuing them can enrich psychology, regardless of the fate of contingent valuation.

Risk ranking might provide a more welcoming venue for focusing our efforts on a practical problem of environmental policymaking. The task is at least as complicated as contingent valuation (involving group processes as well as individual ones). Psychologists were invited, rather than excluded, early in the political and institutional process. Moreover, people and their psychologies lie at the center of risk ranking. That is quite unlike contingent valuation, which, like other survey research techniques, hopes to replace actual people with scientifically derived representations of their views. As long as the public makes itself heard, and does so in an unruly fashion, there should be roles for psychologists to help make the policymaking system work. In that sense, we may need the public more than it needs us.

REFERENCES

Baddeley, A. "Applied Cognitive and Cognitive Applied Research." In L. G. Nilsson (ed.), *Perspectives on Memory Research*. Hillsdale, N.J.: Erlbaum, 1979.

Bazerman, M. H., and Neale, M. A. *Negotiating Rationally.* New York: Free Press, 1992.

Chociolko, C. "Ranking Risks: An American Experiment." Unpublished doctoral dissertation, Queens University, Kingston, Ontario, 1996.

Covello, V. T., Sandman, P. M., and Slovic, P. *Risk Communication, Risk Statistics, and Risk Comparisons: A Manual for Plant Managers.* Washington, D.C.: Chemical Manufacturers Association, 1988.

Crouch, E.A.C., and Wilson, R. *Risk/Benefit Analysis.* New York: Ballinger, 1981.

Davies, J. C. (ed.). *Comparing Environmental Risks.* Washington, D.C.: Resources for the Future, 1996.

Dawes, R. M. *Rational Choice in an Uncertain World.* Orlando, Fla.: Harcourt Brace, 1988.

Driver, B., Peterson, G., and Gregory, R. (eds.). *Evaluating Amenity Resources.* New York: Venture, 1988.

Environmental Protection Agency. *Unfinished Business: A Comparative Assessment.* Washington, D.C.: Environmental Protection Agency, 1987.

Environmental Protection Agency. *Reducing Risk: Setting Priorities and Strategies.* Washington, D.C.: Environmental Protection Agency, 1990.

Environmental Protection Agency. *A Guidebook to Comparing Risks and Setting Environmental Priorities.* Washington, D.C.: Environmental Protection Agency, 1993.

Fischer, G. W., and others. "What Risks Are People Concerned About?" *Risk Analysis,* 1991, *11,* 303–314.

Fischhoff, B. "Cost-Benefit Analysis and the Art of Motorcycle Maintenance." *Policy Sciences,* 1977, *8,* 177–202.

Fischhoff, B. "Acceptable Risk: The Case of Nuclear Power." *Journal of Policy Analysis and Management,* 1983, *2,* 559–575.

Fischhoff, B. "Setting Standards: A Systematic Approach to Managing Public Health and Safety Risks." *Management Science,* 1984, *30,* 823–843.

Fischhoff, B. "Risk: A Guide to Controversy." Appendix to National Research Council, *Improving Risk Communications.* Washington, D.C.: National Academy Press, 1989.

Fischhoff, B. "Psychology and Public Policy: Tool or Tool Maker?" *American Psychologist,* 1990, *45,* 57–63.

Fischhoff, B. "Value Elicitation: Is There Anything in There?" *American Psychologist,* 1991, *46,* 835–847.

Fischhoff, B. "Acceptable Risk: A Conceptual Proposal." *Risk: Health, Safety & Environment,* 1994, *1,* 1–28.

Fischhoff, B. "The Real World: What Good Is It?" *Organizational Behavior and Human Decision Processes,* 1996, *65,* 232–248.

Fischhoff, B. "What Do Psychologists Want? Contingent Valuation as a Special Case of Asking Questions." In W. Pommerehne, N. Schwarz, and R. Kopp (eds.), *Determining the Value of Nonmarketed Goods.* New York: Plenum, forthcoming.

Fischhoff, B., Bostrom, A., and Quadrel, M. J. "Risk Perception and Communication." *Annual Review of Public Health,* 1993, *14,* 183–203.

Fischhoff, B., and Cox, L. A., Jr. "Conceptual Framework for Regulatory Benefit Assessment." In J. D. Bentkover, V. T. Covello, and J. Mumpower (eds.), *Benefits Assessment: The State of the Art*. Dordrecht, The Netherlands: D. Reidel, 1985.

Fischhoff, B., and Furby, L. "Measuring Values: A Conceptual Framework for Interpreting Transactions." *Journal of Risk and Uncertainty,* 1988, *1,* 147–184.

Fischhoff, B., Watson, S., and Hope, C. "Defining Risk." *Policy Sciences,* 1984, *17,* 123–139.

Fischhoff, B., and others. "How Safe Is Safe Enough? A Psychometric Study of Attitudes Towards Technological Risks and Benefits." *Policy Sciences,* 1978, *8,* 127–152.

Fischhoff, B., and others. *Acceptable Risk*. New York: Cambridge University Press, 1981.

Fischhoff, B., and others. "Embedding Effects: Stimulus Representation and Response Mode." *Journal of Risk and Uncertainty,* 1993, *6,* 211–234.

Funtowicz, S.O., and Ravetz, J. R. *Uncertainty and Quality in Science for Policy.* London: Kluwer, 1990.

Glickman, T. S., and Gough, M. (eds.). *Readings in Risk*. Washington, D.C.: Resources for the Future, 1990.

Hornstein, D. T. "Reclaiming Environmental Law: A Normative Critique of Comparative Risk Analysis." *Columbia Law Review,* 1992, *92,* 562–633.

Jenni, K. E., Merkhofer, M. W., and Williams, C. "The Rise and Fall of a Risk-Based Priority System: Lessons from DOE's Environmental Restoration Priority System." *Risk Analysis,* 1995, *15,* 397–410.

Kahneman, D., and Knetsch, J. L. "Valuing Public Goods: The Purchase of Moral Satisfaction." *Journal of Environmental Economics and Management,* 1992, 22, 57–70.

Kahneman, D., and Tversky, A. "Choices, Values, and Frames." *American Psychologist,* 1984, *39,* 341–350.

Keeney, R. L., von Winterfeldt, D., and Eppel, T. "Eliciting Public Values for Complex Policy Decisions." *Management Science,* 1990, *36,* 1011–1030.

Kempton, W., Boster, J. S., and Hartley, J. *Environmental Values in American Culture*. Cambridge, Mass.: MIT Press, 1995.

Krimsky, S., and Plough, A. *Environmental Hazards: Communicating Risks as a Social Process*. Westport, Conn.: Auburn House, 1988.

Laughery, K. R. "Everybody Knows—Or Do They?" *Ergonomics in Design,* July 1993, pp. 8–13.

Lave, L. B., and Dowlatabadi, H. "Climate Change Policy: The Effects of Personal Beliefs and Scientific Uncertainty." *Environmental Science and Technology,* 1993, *27,* 1962–1972.

Leventhal, H., and Cameron, L. "Behavioral Theories and the Problem of Compliance." *Patient Education and Counseling,* 1987, *10,* 117–138.

Lowrance, W. W. *Of Acceptable Risk: Science and the Determination of Safety.* Los Altos, Calif.: Kaufman, 1976.

Mitchell, R. C., and Carson, R. T. *Using Surveys to Value Public Goods: The Contingent Valuation Method.* Washington, D.C.: Resources for the Future, 1989.

Morgan, M. G., Fischhoff, B., Lave, L., and Fischbeck, P. "A Proposal for Ranking Risk Within Federal Agencies." In J. C. Davies (ed.), *Comparing Environmental Risks.* Washington, D.C.: Resources for the Future, 1996.

Morgan, M. G., and Henrion, M. *Uncertainty.* New York: Cambridge University Press, 1991.

Morgan, M. G., and others. "Communicating Risk to the Public." *Environmental Science and Technology,* 1992, *26,* 2048–2056.

National Research Council. *Improving Risk Communication.* Washington, D.C.: National Research Council, 1989.

National Research Council. *Understanding Risk: Informing Decisions in a Democratic Society.* Washington, D.C.: National Research Council, 1996.

Office of Technology Assessment. *Risks to Children in Schools.* Washington, D.C.: Office of Technology Assessment, 1995.

Payne, J. W., Bettman, J. R., and Johnson, E. J. "Behavioral Decision Research: A Constructive Processing Approach." *Annual Review of Psychology,* 1992, *43,* 87–131.

Pommerehne, W., Kopp, R., and Schwarz, N. (eds.). *Determining the Value of Nonmarketed Goods.* New York: Plenum, forthcoming.

Reason, J. *Human Error.* New York: Cambridge University Press, 1990.

Resources for the Future. *Setting National Environmental Priorities.* Washington, D.C.: Resources for the Future, 1993.

Roth, E., and others. "What Do We Know About Making Risk Comparisons?" *Risk Analysis,* 1990, *10,* 375–387.

Rouse, W. B., and Morris, N. M. "On Looking into the Black Box: Prospects and Limits in the Search for Mental Models." *Psychological Bulletin,* 1986, *100,* 349–363.

Slovic, P. "Perceptions of Risk." *Science,* 1987, *236,* 280–285.

Slovic, P., Fischhoff, B., and Lichtenstein, S. "Rating the Risks." *Environment,* 1979, *21*(4), 14–20, 36–39.

Thaler, R. H. *Quasi-Rational Economics.* New York: Russell Sage Foundation, 1991.

Vaughan, E. "Individual and Cultural Differences in Adaptation to Environmental Risks." *American Psychologist,* 1993, *48,* 673–680.

NAME INDEX

A

B

C

F

G

H

N

SUBJECT INDEX

A

B

N

O

S

W

Y